THE
ST. MARY'S CO
ST. MARY'S CITY, MARYLAND 2068

T3-BNU-385

WOMEN'S EQUALITY, DEMOGRAPHY AND PUBLIC POLICIES

Also by Alena Heitlinger

REPRODUCTION, MEDICINE AND THE
  SOCIALIST STATE

WOMEN AND STATE SOCIALISM: Sex Inequality
  in the Soviet Union and Czechoslovakia

Women's Equality, Demography and Public Policies

A Comparative Perspective

Alena Heitlinger
Professor of Sociology
Trent University, Canada

St. Martin's Press

© Alena Heitlinger 1993

All rights reserved. No reproduction, copy or transmission of
this publication may be made without written permission.

No paragraph of this publication may be reproduced, copied or
transmitted save with written permission or in accordance with
the provisions of the Copyright, Designs and Patents Act 1988,
or under the terms of any licence permitting limited copying
issued by the Copyright Licensing Agency, 90 Tottenham Court
Road, London W1P 9HE.

Any person who does any unauthorised act in relation to this
publication may be liable to criminal prosecution and civil
claims for damages.

First published in Great Britain 1993 by
THE MACMILLAN PRESS LTD
Houndmills, Basingstoke, Hampshire RG21 2XS
and London
Companies and representatives
throughout the world

A catalogue record for this book is available
from the British Library.

ISBN 0–333–51578–1

Printed in Great Britain by
Antony Rowe Ltd
Chippenham, Wiltshire

First published in the United States of America 1993 by
Scholarly and Reference Division,
ST. MARTIN'S PRESS, INC.,
175 Fifth Avenue,
New York, N.Y. 10010

ISBN 0–312–09638–0

Library of Congress Cataloging-in-Publication Data
Heitlinger, Alena.
Women's equality, demography, and public policies : a comparative
perspective / Alena Heitlinger.
p.   cm.
Includes bibliographical references (p.   ) and index.
ISBN 0–312–09638–0
1. Women—Government policy.   2. Women's rights.   I. Title.
HQ1236.H4   1993
305.42—dc20
                                                      93–12
                                                      CIP

For David

Contents

Acknowledgements

I would like to thank the Social Sciences and Humanities Research Council of Canada (SSHRC) and Trent University for their generous support of this study. SSHRC financial support facilitated data collection during 1988–91 in Canada, Great Britain, Australia and continental Europe. Partial release from teaching supported by both the SSHRC and Trent University enabled me to engage in more sustained analysis and writing than would have been possible with a full teaching load.

I would also like to gratefully acknowledge the support of friends and colleagues who discussed the project with me in the initial stages of its formulation, suggested additional references and colleagues to consult, facilitated the various interviews conducted with officials in relevant government departments, women's bureaux, voluntary agencies, trade unions and research institutes, or commented on earlier drafts of several chapters of the book. I want to thank in particular Georgina Ashworth, Diana Leonard Baker, Bronwen Cohen, Freda Hawkins, Heather Joshi, Jane Lewis, Peter Moss, Ann Oakley and Malcolm Wicks in Great Britain; Katharine Betts, W. D. Borrie, Bettina Cass, Robert W. Connell, Eva Cox, Lynne Davis, Lincoln H. Day, Meredith Edwards, Lois Foster, Renate Howe, Marian Sawer, Jocelyn Scutt, Sheila Shaver, Peter Whiteford and Christabel Young in Australia; Maureen Baker, Roderic Beaujot, Monica Boyd, Thelma McCormack, Maureen O'Neil, Anatole Romaniuc, Anthony Richmond and Peta Tancred in Canada.

Special thanks are due to my husband, David Morrison, who gave me encouragement, support and critical comments throughout the writing of this book and shared family responsibilities despite his busy schedule. Finally, it must be noted that I alone am responsible for any errors or deficiencies in this study.

Abbreviations

AAA	Affirmative Action Agency (Australia)
ACT	Australian Capital Territory
ACTU	Australian Council of Trade Unions
AECE	Association for Early Childhood Education (Canada)
AIRC	Australian Industrial Relations Commission
ALP	Australian Labor Party
ANU	Australian National University
APIC	Australian Population and Immigration Council
CACSW	Candian Advisory Council on the Status of Women
CAP	Canada Assistance Plan
CAI	Confederation of Australian Industry
CBI	Confederation of British Industry
CIA	Chemical Industries Association (Great Britain)
CCED	Child Care Expense Deduction (Canada)
CDCAA	Canadian Day Care Advocacy Association
CEDAW	Convention on the Elimination of All Forms of Discrimination Against Women (United Nations)
COFACE	Confédération des Organisations Familiales de la Communauté Européenne/Confederation of Family Organisations in the European Community
CPAG	Child Poverty Action Group (Great Britain)
CUPW	Canadian Union of Postal Workers
CREW	Centre for Research on European Women
DEET	Department of Employment, Education and Training (Australia)
DES	Department of Education and Science (Great Britain)
DGV	Directorate General for Employment, Social Affairs and Education (European Community)
DHSS	Department of Health and Social Security (Great Britain)
DILGEA	Department of Immigration, Local Government and Ethnic Affairs (Australia)
DSR	Dependent Spouse Rebate (Australia)
EC	European Community
ECJ	European Court of Justice (European Community)

EEC	European Economic Community
EEOC	Equal Employment Opportunities Commission (United States)
EOC	Equal Opportunities Commission (Great Britain)
FIS	family income supplement (Great Britain)
FMCs	First Ministers' Conferences (Canada)
GLC	Great London Council
ILO	International Labour Organisation
ICCC	Interim Committee for the Children's Commission (Australia)
IWY	International Women's Year (United Nations)
LEAF	Women's Legal Education and Action Fund (Canada)
NAC	National Action Committee (Canada)
Nairobi FLS	Nairobi Forward-looking Strategies (United Nations)
NDP	New Democratic Party (Canada)
NWAC	National Women's Advisory Council (Australia)
NOW	National Organization of Women (United States)
NWCC	National Women's Consultative Council (Australia)
OECD	Organisation for Economic Co-operation and Development
OSHA	Occupational Safety and Health Act (United States)
OSW	Office of the Status of Women (Australia)
PM&C	Department of Prime Minister and Cabinet (Australia)
RCSW	Royal Commission on the Status of Women (Canada)
REAL Women	Realistic, Equal, Active, for Life Women (Canada)
SUBs	Supplementary Unemployment Benefits Plans (Canada)
SWC	Social Welfare Commission (Australia)
SWC	Status of Women Canada
TFR	total fertility rate
TUC	Trade Union Congress (Great Britain)
UI	Unemployment Insurance (Canada)
UISP	universal income security program (Canada)
UN	United Nations
WAB	Women's Affairs Branch (Australia)
WBP	Women's Budget Program (Australia)
WBS	Women's Budget Statement (Australia)
WDOs	women's desk officers (Australia)
WEL	Women's Electoral Lobby (Australia)
WHO	World Health Organization
WNC	Women's National Commission (Great Britain)

WPRWE   Working Party on the Role of Women in the
             Economy (OECD)
WWWW   Women Who Want to be Women (Australia)

1 Women's Equality, Childbearing and the State: An Overview

INTRODUCTION

The main purpose of this study is to explore the compatibility between pronatalism and women's equality in Canada, Great Britain, Australia and to a more limited extent, the United States. Rather than assuming (as so many demographers, feminists, sociologists and policy-makers have done) that promoting women's equality and elevating birth rates is incompatible, this study is designed to examine the propositions that there is no inherently antagonistic relationship of this sort and that there may be mutually compatible pronatal and gender equality policies.

Pronatal policies have been classified according to a threefold distinction between (1) coercive policies limiting access to abortion and/or contraception, (2) 'facilitative' measures associated with 'social protection of motherhood' and (3) 'positive' pronatalist fiscal incentives. Since coercive pronatalist policies infringe upon individual reproductive rights, they cannot be seen in any way as being compatible with the goals of gender equality. As such, coercive pronatalist policies have been excluded from this study. The 'facilitative' policies that are included have been classified according to (a) whether the measures are based on or reinforce traditional sex roles, (b) whether they promote more egalitarian sex roles while retaining some emphasis on sex differences and the special needs of women, or (c) whether they can be described as androgynous or gender-neutral.

I have used the criterion of women's paid employment as an operationalisation of the concepts of traditional and egalitarian sex roles. This corresponds to the new, primarily labour market approach to women's equality, which has been described as state feminist. State feminism is typically characterised by broad bans on sex discrimination, positive action, strong emphasis on the need to built up monitoring systems, and a favourable attitude to active state intervention both in the labour market (for example encouraging or mandating employment equity

1

and/or equal pay for work of equal value) and in working life in general (for example promoting integration of work and family responsibilities, childcare, flexible working hours).

Since so many gender equality and pronatal measures supporting families with children are simultaneously components of social welfare policies, the study also addresses a variety of social welfare issues. These include child poverty, problems of lone parents (a growing proportion of families with dependent children), social provision for maternity and the care of young children, and the horizontal and vertical equity considerations arising out of the various forms of fiscal assistance for families with children. An adequate analysis of the prospects for pronatalist policies also requires a consideration of the costs and benefits of fertility-related measures *vis-à-vis*, or jointly with, immigration-related measures. In fact, both Canada and Australia have in recent years increased immigration levels at least in part as a response to low fertility and population ageing. The study therefore also includes a range of immigration issues.

WOMEN'S EQUALITY AND PRONATALISM

The last two decades were quite remarkable for women, both with respect to changes in their patterns of work and childbearing, and with respect to feminism emerging as an important social and political force. In several countries feminist movements have looked to the state as the major agency capable of redressing a whole range of grievances and inequities. The state has responded favourably in several countries, among them Canada and Australia. In a span of less than two decades, women's equality moved from being a radical demand of feminists and socialists to a legitimate issue on the economic and social policy agendas of various levels of the state, including major international organisations, private business corporations, and trade unions. Using the machinery of the state as a means to transform the situation of women raises important questions about the nature of the state and its national, subnational and international dimensions; the role of public policies in effecting social change; the nature of male dominance; the institutionalisation of social movements; and the changing meanings of women's equality.

Chapter 2 explores the ways in which the traditional liberal notions of non-discrimination, equal rights, equal treatment and formal equality of opportunity have given way to a much broader definition of equality of opportunity which recognises systemic and indirect discrimination, has a favourable attitude to state intervention, advocates 'compensatory' affirmative action, and is not always based on a comparison with men. The concept of affirmative action often encompasses not only measures directly related to the removal of discriminatory employment practices, but also efforts to facilitate women's access to the labour market. Such policies typically take the form of pre-employment and re-entry training programmes to improve employment-related skills of women; pregnancy, maternity and parental leaves; flexible part-time work; childcare services; and social security and taxation measures that discourage women's dependent status.

The central argument of this study is that, in so far as these broadly conceived equal opportunity policies attempt to reconcile family responsibilities with occupational aspirations, they can provide a new, quite powerful justification for policies which in other contexts may be called pronatal. For the most part, pronatalist intent is non-existent, but the potential for pronatalist outcome is significant.[1]

Broad affirmative action policies and programmes are of particular importance to women who have postponed their childbearing. The longer women do so, the more likely they are to be well educated and committed both to long-term continuous participation in the labour force and to sex equality. With the postponement of first births from the early to mid-20s (or even later), women increasingly are in the paid labour force when they are making decisions (often in conjuction with their spouses) as to whether and when to have their first or subsequent child. Their decision is likely to be constrained by the opportunity costs of having children, and by the poor availability of dependable, inexpensive childcare (Presser, 1986). Thus, health, family, taxation, social security and labour market policies that do not address the critical interaction between family and employment are unlikely to succeed in stimulating a higher birth rate. Needless to say, making the role of a mother (or a parent) more compatible with that of a wage-earner closely corresponds to the goals of women's equality, as viewed both from the traditional socialist perspective and from the liberal state feminist framework.

State feminism does not attempt equality in the socialist sense of equality of outcome. It accepts the fact that the promotion of equality of opportunity in a competitive society inevitably produces highly unequal results for both women and men. The main goals of state feminism are to redress past gender inequalities; ensure that women have equal access with men to the competitive spheres of politics and work; reward female-dominated occupations with better working conditions, higher pay and greater upward mobility; encourage the sharing of work and family responsibilities between the sexes; and eliminate or at least reduce violence against women. The ultimate outcome of state feminism would be a 'gender-blind' society in which class differences are the main, if not the only, source of social inequality.

As a labour market policy, positive (affirmative) action clearly rests upon a concept of work that is centred on *paid* work in the competitive market place, thus devaluing women's traditional unpaid work in the home and its associated values of nurturing, caring and altruism. The evident danger of masculine assimilation, and the desire to preserve at least some of the traditional women's values and lifestyles, have led many anti-feminists to oppose gender equality, and some feminists to question whether the drive for equality in a patriarchal world should be an important strategic goal.

While acknowledging these drawbacks, Chapters 2 and 3 suggest that state feminism offers an important strategic tool with which it is possible to challenge the existing legitimacy (and in some cases even structures) of male power, values and corporate practices that discriminate against women. The comparative experiences of Canada, Australia and Great Britain indicate that state feminism works best in countries with flexible political structures that are open to interest politics, and with innovative liberal feminist movements which are able and willing to engage in pragmatic reformist politics. The development of strong networks and coalitions to press women's demands both outside and inside the government and the judiciary appear to be far more important than the simple creation of an administrative agency (or a set of agencies) designed to promote women's equality and monitor sex discrimination. While the British Equal Opportunities Commission is an administrative body with wide-ranging powers, it is politically isolated and institutionally quite powerless. When success is measured in terms of bureaucratic innovation and policy outcomes, women's policy machineries in Canada and Australia have served women much better than their counterparts in Great Britain.

INTERNATIONAL ORGANISATIONS AND INSTRUMENTS

Behind most of the national and subnational policies promoting women's equality and providing maternity protection and childcare lies much work done by international organisations, such as the United Nations (UN), the International Labour Organisation (ILO), the World Health Organization (WHO), the Organisation for Economic Co-operation and Development (OECD), the European Economic Community (EEC) and the Council of Europe. The ILO, the OECD, and the EEC are mainly concerned with employment matters, and their respective policies on women reflect this emphasis. The concern of the UN and the Council of Europe are much broader, and as such are applicable to all aspects of life: civil, economic, political, scientific, cultural, and demographic.

As we shall see in Chapter 3, all of the international organisations under review support the notions of equal rights, equal treatment, broadly conceived equality of opportunity, maternity protection, equal sharing with men of domestic and employment roles, and various forms of affirmative action. They differ mainly with respect to the procedures they use for encouraging the adoption of their respective provisions into national legislation, and the extent to which they endorse sex differences and the special treatment or protection of women. The European Community permits no special provisions for women unless these cover the actual pregnancy, childbirth and postpartum, while WHO, ILO and the Council of Europe have been long-standing supporters of both equality and special protective measures.

CHILDBEARING, WORKPLACE HAZARDS AND WOMEN'S EQUALITY

The problem of how to develop social structures that encourage the equality of women without ignoring the fact that they bear and raise children has been historically posed as a debate about equal or special treatment of women workers. Like other questions of gender equality, the question of protection of women as a special group versus equality without special treatment for women workers was put on the political agenda by the growing entry of women into paid employment. As we shall see in Chapter 7, conflicts between equal employment opportunity and protective legislation are easier to solve when the latter aims to protect women as a 'weaker sex' or as persons who bear primary responsibility for domestic work than when the concerns are reproductive and foetal health.

MOTHERHOOD AND EMPLOYMENT

The significant increase in women's labour force participation through-out the developed world has been attributed to a combination of supply factors ('pushes') and demand factors ('pulls'). The 'pushes' include: the marked increase in women's educational attainment, average age at marriage and first birth; new, highly effective means of contraception; liberal abortion legislation making it easier to terminate an unwanted pregnancy; low fertility and compressed period of childbearing; high divorce rates; proliferation of domestic labour-saving devices; declining capacity of a single income to support a family; the high social and financial costs of having children; a shift in preferences away from familialism towards consumerism; and the growth of feminism as an ideology encouraging female economic independence and equality. Women increasingly think of themselves as individuals who have the same liberty as men to realise their own potential in non-family activities, rather than as individuals who gain their major source of identity and meaning from belonging to an interdependent family unit (Jones *et al.*, 1990).

The main 'pull' factors facilitating women's labour force participation have been deindustrialisation and the expansion of the public sector. As Armstong and Armstong (1987: 215) put it,

> relatively few jobs, if any, have been created on farms and in forests, mines, fisheries and factories – traditionally male areas of employment – and relatively many have been created in stores, offices, restaurants, schools, and hospitals – traditionally more female areas. Women were hired because they were cheap and available, and because they had the appropriate skills, training, and attitudes to do the work.

The increase in women's labour force participation is particularly striking in Canada and Australia. Between 1950 and 1982, Canadian women increased their share of the labour force by 20 per cent, from 21 to 41 per cent. Female share of the labour force in Australia increased by 15 per cent during this period, from 22 to 37 per cent. Because of a higher starting point, the increase was less marked in Great Britain, where the share of the labour force increased from 31 per cent in 1950 to 39 per cent in 1982 (OECD, 1985: 14).

With the exception of World War II, each succeeding generation of women has been more likely to work for pay than the one before it. When opinion polls in Canada asked in 1960 whether married women with young children should engage in paid work outside the home, an overwhelming 95 per cent of women and men aged 21–29 answered 'No'. The answers of the same age group in subsequent years show a fascinating progression: in 1970, 82 per cent were still opposed; in 1975, 68 per cent said no; and by 1982, only 49 per cent said no (National Council of Welfare, 1990: 49). While there is still a significant proportion of mothers who prefer full-time maternal care of young children, more and more young women believe that it is normal for mothers to have paid jobs. Similar trends have characterised Australia and to a lesser extent Great Britain (Cass and Radi, 1981; Martin and Roberts, 1984). The majority of Australian women of childbearing age now take a paid job, and the two-income family has become the norm. Work patterns of younger women are therefore quite different from older women, but they have not become like men's. Wives/mothers are less likely than husbands/fathers to hold jobs that interfere with their domestic responsibilities. Moreover, women typically work in jobs in secondary, unsheltered labour markets.

Because of women's domestic responsibilities and the way women's jobs have been organised – on a part-time or limited contract basis, and on the assumption that the job-holder can be easily replaced – women's work lives are more individualised, that is, more varied, fluid and idiosyncratic, than those of men. In general, men are life-long, full-time paid workers. They are rarely found in unpaid work or part-time work, and experience far fewer departures and re-entries into the labour force than women. If men leave the labour force, it is usually because of their own ill health or injury, loss of a job, retirement, or to pursue retraining and education. Virtually no men leave paid work for family reasons, while the 'kiddy dip' in women's labour force participation is found in all Western industrial countries. The shape of the 'kiddy-dip' varies from one country to another, however; it is deeper and longer lasting in Britain than in Canada and Australia, or for that matter any other OECD country except Japan (Joshi, 1989, 1991; Jones *et al.*, 1990; Young, 1990a).

As Cohen and Clarke (1986: 3) argue, childbearing has

a major and permanent effect on the pattern of women's employment. This effect is both prospective and retrospective, that is, it affects both the kinds of training and occupations open to women when they first enter the labour market, in anticipation of future childbearing, and the employment opportunities open to them when they return to the labour market after having a child.

The prospect of motherhood tends to inhibit women's acquisition of earning assets, like education, before they ever have children. Potential motherhood and earnings interruption may also affect the choice of occupation and women's access to on-the-job training. Actual motherhood either keeps women out of paid jobs altogether, or reduces the hours during which they are able to work. Women therefore pay a high personal price for bearing and raising the next generation. Those facing the greatest loss of earnings on motherhood – highly educated women with good career prospects – tend to defer childbearing, sometimes indefinitely.

Ni Bhrolchain (1986a, b) argues that a prospect of employment has a positive effect on fertility, because the attraction of future work leads to closer spacing of births. In contrast, current employment has a negative effect on fertility, because employed women tend to defer childbearing so that they can continue to work. During the 1950s and early 1960s, fertility in Great Britain was rising and a buoyant labour market encouraged optimism about the ease of re-entry into the labour force. During the economic downturn in the 1970s, the balance shifted to a greater attraction of current work. Deteriorating employment prospects, increased divorce rates and the declining capacity of the male wage to support a family both increased the importance of the women's wage and eroded women's earlier confidence about the ease of re-entering the labour market. Because the post-war trends in Canadian and Australian fertility and employment of married women have been so similar, Ni Bhrolchain's interpretation of the relation between women's work and their fertility in post-war Britain can be also applied to the Canadian and Australian experiences.

Where the expectation of two incomes is firmly established, withdrawal of the wife from the workforce for childbearing and child rearing brings severe economic disadvantage, which is neither offset by the tax rebate for a dependent spouse and children nor by family allowances – an issue discussed in Chapter 10. Since current market forces and modern urban life work against childbearing, specific policies that can assist women (and men) with better integration of the productive and reproductive aspects of their lives are assuming special importance. More effective implementation of legislation that prohibits discrimination against women in hiring, pay and promotion is bound to improve women's capacity to earn a decent living and become financially independent. Men might be more interested in childcare if their wives could earn as much (or more) than they, and if working shorter hours were not as much penalised as it is now. With widely available parental leaves and high-quality childcare, women could avoid taking long breaks from paid employment, and thus lower the current high opportunity cost of having children. Unless the mother's salary is relatively high, or childcare services are heavily subsidised, her paid work will hardly be financially rewarding. Australian data reviewed in Chapter 9 suggest that the cost of state subsidies for childcare could be more than offset by the greater tax revenue obtained from the income of the additional women workers. Thus the measures required to give women as much personal financial security as men may not be all that costly.

POLICY RESPONSE TO DEMOGRAPHIC TRENDS

Total fertility rate (TFR) in Canada, Australia, France, the United States and the United Kingdom is around 1.7–1.8 per women, higher than the rates of 1.3 to 1.4 found in Italy, West Germany and Austria. Despite the similarity in fertility, the first five countries exhibit considerable differences in the extent to which there is official concern about population. According to Teitelbaum (1990: 19),

> the concern is highest in France, which was the first country to experience fertility decline, beginning during the middle of the eighteenth century. The political and economic power of France declined over the same period, reaching a traumatic outcome in the Franco-Prussian War. These concerns have continued to this day; in fact there is no competitor for France among western countries in terms of concern about low fertility.

'Populationism' and a public concern over low fertility hardly exist at all in the United States or Great Britain. In both countries, changes in the birth rate, family size and population levels are of concern only to demographers and social planners, who tend to regard fertility trends as one of the 'given' parameters within which they operate. For example, number of annual births is relevant to the estimates of future demand for health and social services and income support programmes. Since demographic trends are not regarded as important indicators of national well-being, they are generally ignored by politicians. Programmes that provide education, social services and family benefits generally respond to changes in the birth rate, but they are not seen as appropriate vehicles for influencing the birth rate (Adams and Winston, 1980: 254).

The only exceptions in Great Britain were the inter-war period, World War II and its immediate aftermath, when there was considerable despondency and alarm over the low birth rate, both past and future as anticipated by demographers. Population fall and ageing acted as a backdrop of all proclamations and speculations about women, work, the family and the nation throughout the war, and contributed to the establishment of the Royal Commission on Population in 1944. However, the Commission did not report until 1949, and the papers of its supporting committees – Statistics, Economics, Biological and Medical – were not ready until 1950. By that time, the post-war baby boom made some of their premises and demographic data out of date. The concern over the low birth rate was also an important, though by no means a decisive, force behind the movement for family allowances which were introduced towards the end of World War II (Macnicol, 1980).

According to Riley (1983: 151, 152), the British pronatalist thinking

> generated a great deal of language about 'the mother', not all which was decisively conservative, and much of which believed itself to be progressive . . . for a brief period it sounded as if it spoke to the same needs for the 'protection of motherhood' about which various women's organisations had been agitating for decades. But the sources of pronatalist anxiety were different, and transient. The temporary coincidence of verbal object – the mother – in the diction of population policies, of social democratic 'progressiveness', and of women's labour organisations brought about an emphasis on the mother as a real worker in the home, equal or indeed greater in 'value' than the waged woman worker. In all this, the mother who did go out to work, and who consequently had special needs, became an impossibility, regarded by no-one.

Riley (1983: 154) goes on to argue that the post-war metaphor of the mother as a worker confirmed the most conservative understandings of gender, the family and work. It also firmly established the ideology of 'mothercare' (discussed in Chapter 9) and the idea that women's lives are stratified into a series of lifecycle stages: a spell of paid work before marriage and the birth of the first child, followed by full-time motherhood, then perhaps re-entry into the labour market once the last child starts attending school or leaves home. But this presumption of neatly autonomous strata overlooked the real drifts of the labour market. With the arrival of the post-war welfare state and the baby boom, British public opinion and policy-making returned to its traditional indifference to demographic questions. Fertility, desirable family size, or whether or not parents should seek to have a third or fourth child are generally regarded as questions of private domain rather than public policy.

The only demographic issue which has entered the British policy agenda in recent years has been a shortfall of skilled young males. A consequence of low fertility and the levelling out of the baby boom since the early 1970s, the projected shortage of school leavers has been referred to as 'the demographic time-bomb'. Experts are predicting a 23 per cent drop in school leavers during the 1990s and a decline by 1.2 million of young (that is, those aged 16–24) recruits to the labour market. These demographic and labour market trends are expected to result in women taking no fewer than 80 per cent of new jobs from 1995 onwards (ILO, 1988: 265; Oakley and Rudd, 1988). A high proportion of these labour market recruits will inevitably be mothers, many with pre-school children – hence the sudden interest in long-term maternity leaves (usually described as 'career breaks' schemes) and childcare.

Canada and Australia have exhibited more concern over demographic questions than Great Britain. The small size and low density of the Australian and Canadian populations, their historic links with Europe, especially Great Britain and (in the case of Quebec) France, and their large land mass and abundant natural resources have tended to produce a climate of opinion in favour of population growth, with immigration as the primary instrument of achieving it. During the 1980s, both Canada and Australia have increased immigration intakes at least in part as a response to low fertility and population ageing.

Demographic ageing, the increase in both the absolute numbers of aged persons (particularly in the oldest age groups) and the aged as a percentage of the population, is regarded as an unfavourable trend. Population ageing has generated a host of fears: of labour shortages and wage inflation; of labour market rigidities and lower economic growth; of weakened national defences, shortages of intellect and declines in national 'vigour' and dynamism; and of rural depopulation (Day, 1988a, b). Since social programmes are financed largely from taxes and social security contributions paid by the working population (pay-as-you-go system), the prospect of a decline in the number of working-age people, coupled with a significant rise in the proportion of the elderly, has raised fears that the fiscal burden may increase steeply and that the financing of social programmes may be jeopardised (OECD, 1988).

Canadians over the age of 65 receive government payments which are almost three times as large as those directed at children (Bégin, 1987: 216). In Australia, public expenditures by Commonwealth and State governments is on average twice as much for every older person as for every younger person. Assuming a continuation of current funding arrangements, between 1981 and 2001 population ageing is projected to increase government outlays on the aged by 131 per cent. The comparative decline in the numbers of children in the future is not expected to yield sufficient savings on government expenditure to cover the additional public costs of population ageing (Kendig and McCallum, 1986: xi). Accordingly, processes which may slow or reverse the rise in the proportions of older people in the population (namely increased fertility and immigration) are seen as advantageous (Rowland, 1986). Pronatalist policies attempting to increase fertility or slow its decline are discussed in Chapter 5; evaluation of immigration as a substitute for pronatalism and higher birth rates is undertaken in Chapter 6.

While the changes that can be anticipated in a near stationary population with an older population age structure are bound to require some adjustments, these adjustments may be less serious and less insoluble than is frequently suggested. Moreover, the ageing changes are not occurring suddenly, thus enabling those in the enlarged ageing cohort ample time to take care of their economic and non-economic needs without undue reliance on others. Many of the required adjustments in institutions and lifestyles (for example fewer age-based restrictions and greater flexibility in retirement, labour force participation and pay; better public transportation; shift of emphasis from hospital- to community-based healthcare) are also of use to others, and can be justified on universal grounds of justice, equity and human welfare (Day, 1988b). Both Australia and the English-speaking provinces in Canada have stopped short of seriously considering, let alone adopting, an explicit pronatalist policy. In contrast, the provincial government of Quebec, faced with one of the lowest fertility rates in the world and a prospect of decline of Quebec's population share within Canada, has adopted several pronatalist initiatives. These are reviewed in Chapters 9 and 10.

Thus, demographic policies tend to develop in response to specific national and international perceptions of demographic problems, priorities and issues. Few international organisations link demographic and equal opportunity policy considerations. 'Family friendly' reorganisation of employment and childcare is typically advocated as a measure of equal opportunity rather than pronatalism. Within the European Community, France has been the only country that has pressed, unsuccessfully, for some kind of pronatalist fertility policy at the international level (*CREW Reports*, vol. 4, nos. 3 and 4, April and May, 1984).

COMPARING SUBNATIONAL, NATIONAL AND SUPRANATIONAL LEVELS OF THE STATE

Canada, Australia, Great Britain and the United States share a number of common features. They are stable, prosperous, highly industrialised, modern 'Western' states, with common intellectual and political traditions and, with the exception of Quebec, a shared language. Although the legal and political institutions in the four countries are not identical, they work within the same liberal democratic framework. Extensive reliance on means-tested benefits targeted to the poor is another common feature of Anglo-American democracies. While Canada and Great Britain developed some noteworthy universal income security programs, such as family allowances and old age security, and an important universal health service, these provisions have been rather modest by international standards. Because the universal social measures in the four countries have been so minimal, they have not eliminated the need for extensive means-tested assistance targeted at the most needy. Thus a 'liberal' rather than a 'social democratic' model of the welfare state prevails in Anglo-Saxon societies (Esping-Andersen, 1989).

Great Britain and the United States are often regarded as the 'senior partners' of the Anglo-American democracies, and as

the major reference points – often polar reference points – for interpreting the social and political characteristics of the 'junior partners': Australia, Canada, and New Zealand. If the nineteenth century was Britain's, then the twentieth has been America's. Britain symbolizes the past, America the future, and when the United States replaced Britain as the West's great power, the magnet of British influence in the Commonwealth countries weakened and the pull of the United States became more powerful. Although this transformation was most clearly evident in the Canadian case, it was also evident in Australia and New Zealand. (Nevitte and Gibbins, 1990: 166–7)

The ways in which the 'pull' of the United States has influenced British, Canadian and Australian feminist movements, anti-discrimination and equal opportunity legislation, and in the case of Australia, pre-school education, is addressed in Chapters 2, 4 and 9. Chapters 7 and 8 examine the American-specific controversies surrounding the equal treatment/special treatment of women. Because the American political culture puts such a strong emphasis on privacy, self-sufficiency and a weak welfare state, state provisions for maternity are considerably worse in the US than in the other three countries under review. Thus like other advanced industrial societies, the Anglo-American democracies exhibit both similarities and differences.

Unlike the Canadian, Australian and American federations, Great Britain is essentially an unitary state,[2] with a political culture that favours government secrecy and bureaucratic neutrality. Legal advocacy on behalf of oppressed groups is also highly restricted, because the courts define themselves more as defenders of the state than as defenders of individual rights. Because of its unwritten constitution, Great Britain has no distinct concepts and rules that the courts can use to interpret (rather than simply apply) the law. Class action suits used to aid reform movements in the United States, or the various constitutional challenges under the Canadian Charter of Rights and Freedoms, are virtually unknown in Great Britain. The development of women's coalitions and networks across a broad spectrum of issues and ideological orientations, and lobbying of the national government, are much less in evidence in Great Britain than in Canada, Australia or the United States. In turn, these systemic constraints have inhibited the development of an effective women's policy machinery capable of translating specific women's demands into policies and monitoring all government policies (not just those specifically designed for women) for gender impact.

Because the British political system is so inhospitable to interest-group politics, women's groups have had to choose between political isolation or working through existing male-dominated representational structures, namely the established political parties and the trade unions. Neither has embraced women's issues with great enthusiasm, although the feminist presence in the trade unions and the Labour Party has grown visibly during the last two decades (Coote and Campbell, 1987; Rowbotham, 1989). Integration of the direct democracy of women's groups with the representative democracy of government has been more successful at the local level of government – an issue explored in Chapter 4. However, the unitary central government exerts much greater control over local authorities than is possible in the more decentralised federal Canada and Australia. The subnational provincial and state levels of government in Canada and Australia can impose their own taxes on earnings, car registration, consumption, and so on. In Canada, provinces act increasingly like nation-states (Cameron, 1981: xiii). Their fiscal and political independence gives them much more power to pursue their own policies. Moreover, at any given time at least one (and frequently more) of the subnational governments are run by political parties which are in opposition to the governing party at the national level. This form of political pluralism can give some oppositional ideologies and movements (such as feminism) much greater legitimacy than is possible in unitary states such as Great Britain, where feminism has been marginalised as an oppositional ideology promoted by the 'loony Left'.

This situation began to change, however, when Great Britain joined the European Community (EC) in the early 1970s and ceased to be a purely unitary state. In a strict legal sense, member states of the EC remain sovereign states, but in practical terms, they have given up a good deal of their freedom to act independently. For example, the European Court of Justice, which interprets community law, has ruled that community law takes precedence over national law. Moreover, some EEC treaty articles and legislation give individuals rights which they can enforce in their own national courts. Treaty of Rome Article 119 grants women equal pay for work of equal value. This right may be invoked by individuals in national courts, not only against public authorities but in all collective agreements and contracts. Women in Great Britain have been able to take advantage of this provision, despite the strong resistance from the British government.

The British government withstood more successfully EC initiatives on parental leave and leave for family reasons (explored in Chapter 8) and on the social charter covering workers' rights. However, the government was forced to replace the existing unequal, gender-specific retirement age with a more flexible system. It also had to compromise on EC rules on pay during pregnancy. Rather than mounting a legal challenge in the European Court against the EC's authority to legislate improved conditions for pregnant women, the British government agreed to a compromise. The European Commission's original proposal guaranteed pregnant women fourteen weeks on full pay. Great Britain, which has the worst provision for pregnant women in the European Community, eventually agreed to the fourteen-week period but at lower rates than those suggested by the Commission (Palmer, 1991). While the British are wedded to the Community less than the other member states, it would be economically and politically impossible for them to withdraw now. Judging from the evidence to date, the emerging federal European structure is good news for British women. It will give them another lever with which they can extract from their national state more favourable treatment.

There are increasing similarities between the 'creeping federalism' in Europe and the current 'executive federalism' in Canada. Indeed, if Quebec premier Robert Bourassa had his way, the political structure of Canada would be based on the European Community model. It would consist of two sovereign states, Quebec and Canada, which would share a common market and a common supranational parliament. Canada is one of the most decentralised federations in the world, despite the centralist design of its original constitution. The major factor which has checked the centralising tendency found in most of the other federations, and which may lead to the break-up of Canada, is its asymmetrical linguistic duality. The Francophone minority (in national terms) comprises a majority in only one constituent unit of the federation – the province of Quebec. An increasing number of Francophones in Quebec see themselves as Quebecois, as a majority in their own territory, rather than as French Canadians with a special minority status. Because of the uneven cultural and linguistic duality, the Canadian federation has an element of asymmetry not found to the same degree in any other federation.

As Breton (1988: 577–8) put it,

> Canada is a *plural* or segmented *society* divided along linguistic lines into two parallel institutional systems. To a large extent, the material well-being of English- and French-speaking Canadians depends on the opportunities and services provided by their linguistic sub-societies . . . members of each collectivity have an interest in the vitality and growth of their own subeconomies; in the cultural character of their own subsociety; and in the public status in relation to the other. They compare their societal condition with that of the other; they constantly 'watch' how well the other group is doing in different areas compared to their own.

The competition between these parallel institutional subsystems, and the diffusion of policy-making authority at the national level, has provided Canadian advocacy groups with more strategic opportunities to press their demands than is possible in more centralised and unitary states. When progress is blocked at one level of government, it is often possible to continue at another.

Canada was the first federation to combine a federal constitution with a Westminster model of parliament. The same design was followed later by Australia, Germany and several newer Commonwealth federations in Asia and Africa. The fusion of parliamentary and federal forms of government has created the conditions for intergovernmental coordination (and conflict) in the form of 'executive federalism'. Despite the well-entrenched British parliamentary tradition, Canada added in 1982 a Charter of Rights and Freedoms to its constitution. The Charter guarantees individual legal, civil, equality and mobility rights, as well as collective rights with respect to aboriginal people and official language minorities (for example Anglophones in Quebec, Francophones in the rest of Canada). Since the promulgation of the Charter, courts have assumed an expanded role in defining the contours of public policy, thus providing organised interests with yet another venue in which they can press their demands. For example, a successful court challenge under the equality provision of the Charter led to the extension of maternity leave provisions to fathers – an issue addressed in Chapter 8. The adoption of the Charter of Rights and Freedoms in 1982 and the free trade agreement with the United States in 1988 have accelerated the trend towards the Americanisation of the Canadian economy, media, mass culture and policy-making.

Australia has no entrenched bill of rights, despite a number of attempts by the Labor government since 1973 to introduce such a constitutional amendment. On each occasion, the federal government was rebuffed by the Senate and by the general public through referenda. The main reason for the failure seems to have been the fear that a constitutional bill of rights would further centralise an already heavily centralised federation (Institute of Intergovernmental Relations, 1991: 24). What Australia has and Canada lacks is a powerful national trade union movement.

Unlike most European social democratic movements, which have assumed that market-generated inequalities can be alleviated only by state redistribution via taxation and cash transfers, the Australian labour movement believed early on in its history that the state could be brought to bear directly on the wage mechanism. If it were possible to achieve full employment and a 'living' wage, then subsequent welfare redistribution would become unnecessary, or only a subsidiary objective of public policy. Thus from before the turn of the century, the main goal of the Australian trade union movement and its political embodiment, the Australian Labor Party (ALP), was the creation of a 'wage-earner' welfare state (Castles, 1985).

Not surprisingly, one of the earliest accomplishments of the ALP was in the area of wage policy. Adopted as a historic class compromise, the ALP established a quasi-judicial system that since the turn of the century has set most wages and working conditions and adjudicated industrial disputes at both state and federal level. The benefits to workers were obvious: assurance of fair treatment and a decent living wage. To satisfy business interests, the wage-setting tribunals were combined with a system of tariffs and import restrictions, explicitly established to shut out external competition, enable domestic manufacturers to make profits while paying the wages decreed by the tribunals, and maintain full employment. Without the protectionist trade policies, unemployment would have been much higher.

The wage-setting tribunals have set wages and work conditions with reference to domestic economic and political conditions, especially the cost of living, thus assuming an important role in defining the contours of public policy. In 1907 Judge Higgins ruled that a basic (that is, minimum) wage be based on the family needs of a man, his dependent wife and up to three children. This judgment was to influence negatively applications for equal pay for the next sixty years until the 1967 National Wage Case, which replaced the concept of basic wage with that of a total wage. Since women were deemed not to have dependants, female basic wages were based on lower rates than male basic wages. The total wage concept granted the same increase to women and men, thus opening the case for equal pay.

Hearings on the application for equal pay for work of equal value were concluded at the end of November 1972. After the election of the Whitlam Labor Government a week later, the case was reopened and the new government intervened in support of equal pay. The positive decision was made on 15 December, to be phased in over two and a half years. Unpaid maternity leave for up to 52 weeks was granted in 1979; in 1990 this was followed by parental leave. However, other women's policies, namely anti-discrimination, equal opportunity and affirmative action, were passed by parliaments (at both the federal and the state levels) rather than by the wage-fixing tribunals. The legislation is discussed in Chapter 2; the maternity and parental leave 'test cases' are reviewed in Chapter 8.

Another early accomplishment of the ALP was in the field of social welfare. The Invalid and Old Age Pensions Act was passed in 1909, while maternity allowance, a lump-sum payment made upon the birth of a child, was adopted in 1912. The ALP resisted contributory schemes and insisted on welfare provisions as a social right. However, welfare schemes were limited to instances falling outside the wage-safety net (Levi and Singleton, 1991). Rather than following the examples of British and Canadian social insurance programmes for income maintenance developed in the aftermath of World War II, Australia retained its earlier emphasis on means-tested programmes for non-workers. The selectivist ethos in welfare provision persists to this day. The only universal income security benefit, family allowances, became subject to an income test in December 1986. Since full employment ended in the early 1970s, rising levels of unemployment (reaching close to 10 percent during recessions in 1983 and 1992) and marital dissolution have led to more poverty, which the 'wage-earner' welfare state is ill equipped to address (Mishra, 1990: 84). The 'rediscovery' of poverty in the 1960s and the subsequent restructuring of family benefits is discussed in Chapter 10.

In 1983, the ALP was elected on a platform of prices and income accord with the trade union movement. With the Accord the trade unions agreed to forego inflationary wage increases and industrial action in return for economic growth, employment security and improvements in the social wage. One of the social wage demands successfully pursued under the Accord by the Australian Council of Trade Unions (ACTU) has been more government-subsidised childcare. Since 1983 the Hawke government has provided an extra 60 000 places. In the 1990 election, the ALP government committed itself to providing an extra 108 000 places over the next five years. As we shall see in Chapter 10, the ACTU also pushed for the work-based childcare programme, which the Hawke government adopted in 1988.

When the Accord was first signed, the ACTU also agreed to a tripartite management of the economy by the government, unions and business. Since the Accord was key to ALP victories in three subsequent elections (in 1984, 1987 and 1990), the path of social contract and tripartism has been quite successful in electoral terms. This is in contrast to Great Britain, where a similar social contract in the 1970s ended in a dismal failure, ushering in more than a decade of dominance of the Conservative Party and Thatcherism.

Tripartism hardly exists at all in Canada. There is a long history of markedly adversarial labour relations; the organisation of both labour and business interests is fragmented at the national level; Canada lacks the strong centralised state tradition with which these structures have been associated; and organised labour remains highly sceptical of the benefits of tripartism. The only sectoral area in which tripartite structures are somewhat more fully developed is that of occupational health and safety, which is under provincial jurisdiction (Tuohy, 1990). The implications of the tripartite structures for reproductive health in Quebec and Ontario are explored in Chapter 7.

Public advocacy groups that seek a consultative role in the policy-making process can be only rarely integrated into party and bureaucratic politics. As we shall see in Chapter 4, this has happened to different degrees in Canada and Australia. Since the 1970s, the Canadian and Australian feminist movements have been remarkably successful in imprinting some of their demands upon their respective national and subnational governments. Chapter 4 explores why the pattern of inter-action between promotional women's groups and governments at all levels has been so much more successful in Canada and Australia than in Great Britain. We shall also explore why by the late 1980s the Canadian political environment had become less favourable than that in Australia to feminist interventions in government.

We shall see that the ways in which feminist demands are formulated and translated into demands made on the state depends on the ideological predispositions of the women's movement and the political opportunities for feminist influence on government. Policy-makers have their own constraints to contend with. It is much easier for them to respond to demands on which there is a broad social consensus, which are presented in the familiar and non-challenging language of liberal social policy and where policy action involves little expense. Creating a women's policy machinery, addressing (though not solving) gender stereotypes and violence against women, granting maternity and parental leave, increasing women's participation in politics, and recognising systemic discrimination has been much easier to implement than afford-able quality childcare, equal pay for work of equal value, pensions for homemakers or a guaranteed income for single parents.

Several decades after the onset of below-replacement fertility, researchers and policy-makers are still uncertain as to the causes, consequences and policy responses to the scarcity of births in advanced industrial societies. Similarly, despite the formal commitments of all governments in developed countries to women's equality, the achieve-ment of this goal remains elusive for the vast majority of women. Since demographers and feminists have often seen the goals of emancipation of women and pronatalism as mutually exclusive, and since an adequate analysis of the prospects for pronatal policies requires the consideration of the costs and benefits of fertility-related measures *vis-à-vis*, or jointly with immigration measures, research into the relationship between women's equality and demography, based on cross-national comparisons, is an essential ingredient in the national debates on these issues.

Part I

Women's Equality and Women's Policy Machinery

2 Models of Women's Equality: From Equal Treatment to Positive Action

INTRODUCTION

Sex equality is a term that covers a broad spectrum of ideas and practices. The basic issues in the equality debate examined in this chapter are how equality is defined (as a formal equality of opportunity or as a substantial equality of outcome), the standard against which persons are to be measured (equal, differential or pluralistic treatment), the role of the state and the most appropriate areas of policy intervention (education and training, the labour market, the family, childcare, social security, health), and what form sexual equality should take: assimilation (women becoming like men), androgyny (enlargment of the common ground on which women and men share their lives together), or an equality that rests on sex differences and the special needs of women. As Phillips (1987: 1–2) has argued,

a commitment to sexual equality does not of itself tell us what shape that equality should take. Equal pay for the jobs women do or equal shares in the jobs done by men? Equal opportunities to compete with men or numerical equality in each sphere of life? Equal responsibilities for housework and children or better conditions for women at home? Those who describe themselves as feminists have been almost as much at odds over such issues as their opponents.

Numerous approaches can be adopted to address these sets of issues, but I shall restrict myself to the conceptual dichotomy which Mullen (1988: 256) draws between an *absolute* and a *relative* equality of opportunity. The former is based on principles of non-discrimination, equal treatment and assimilation. The latter, which goes beyond the boundaries of individual acts of discrimination, recognises systemic discrimination, has a favourable attitude to state intervention, and advocates 'compensatory' affirmative action.

ABSOLUTE EQUALITY OF OPPORTUNITY: PRINCIPLES OF NON-DISCRIMINATION, EQUAL TREATMENT AND ASSIMILATION

The liberal notion of equality of opportunity represents an attempt to create social conditions which give individuals equal access to decision-making, and to important social institutions such as education, training and jobs. Equal opportunity is explicitly concerned with the integration of individuals into various areas of public life, including elite positions. The underlying assumptions of this perspective are abstract individualism (implying classless, genderless, ageless, and colourless, that is 'socially abstracted' individuals, who have freedom to make choices); universal human rights (reflecting the Western legal principle of the fundamental equality of all human beings); meritocracy (the idea that valued goods and social institutions should be distributed on universalistic grounds, through competition based on personal efforts, talents and achievement, that is merit); and strategies of rational persuasion and legal reform (such as positive action, anti-discrimination and equal pay legislation).

From a historical standpoint, the recognition of equality between men and women in all fields of social life is a very recent development. Prior to the mid-twentieth century, two legal constructs in particular enforced the subservience of women and the dominance of men: the creation of separate spheres for men and women, and the enactment of various obstacles to women's ability to control their reproductive capacity. As Law (1984: 958–9) argues,

> assumptions about biological difference and destiny provided the prime justification for creating a separate, inferior legal status for women. The law denied women equal opportunity for wage work and participation in public life. It reinforced social and religious commitment to family-centered child rearing. Women were required, by law and custom, to care for men and children. Although women and children were and are entitled to look to men for financial support, that expectation was and is not theoretically enforceable during an ongoing marriage nor as a practical matter when marriage ends.

Laws governing sexuality and human reproduction also preserved the dominance of men, by applying double standard to 'virile, sexually aggressive' men and 'passive, monogamous' women; by restricting access to contraception and abortion; and by condemning a child born out of wedlock as an inferior bastard. Laws disadvantaging the children of an unmarried woman encouraged her sexual purity and made the social and economic status of both the child and the mother ultimately dependent upon the male (Law, 1984: 960).

It is only since the end of World War II that equality between the sexes has gradually been recognised as a fundamental principle of human rights, making the doctrine of equal treatment – that similarly situated individuals should be treated alike – also applicable to women. Treating like persons alike is a standard conception of justice, with a long legal history (from Aristotle onwards). It forms a basic feature of our democratic political and legal system, and as such has been of obvious strategic importance to women in their quest for equality.

In their egalitarian arguments, women have often laid claim to the opportunities and resources that men have had on the basis that women are the same human beings as men. Zillah Eisenstein (1981: 4) has argued that 'all feminism is liberal at its root in that the universal liberal claim that woman is an independent being (from man) is premised on the eighteenth-century liberal conception of the independent and autonomous self'. This liberal argument has worked quite well as a strategy when the feminist goals have been assimilationist: women gaining access to traditionally male prerogatives within the public sphere. It has worked less well when applied to the reality of biological, psychological and cultural sex differences, because of indeterminancy of equality analysis, and because of the way in which the equality doctrine views differences among people.

As Finley (1986: 1149, 1152) argues,

the theory of equality and the legal analysis that implements the theory cannot tell us how to define or identify what is a relevant similarity in any given situation. Equality analysis, along with much of our system of legal reasoning, rests on a proces of classifying by analogy. We are taught that to arrive at the right answer we must divide things into groups of 'similars', and then we must treat everything within each group 'similarly.' But who is to say what is a difference or similarity, in the abstract or in the particular? Every person, thing or condition will always have some qualities that are similar, and some that are different from everything else, even when there is an agreement on the category of classification. . . . The outcome of the analysis which asks whether someone is different or the same, or similarly or differentially situated, depends entirely on the characteristic or factor selected for emphasis. This selection is a highly political, value-laden choice, determined by one's world view and perspective.

The equal treatment approach tells us specifically to treat women the same as men. What this means in legal practice is a comparison and measurement of women against men, that is, from a male perspective and on male terms. Whatever is different in women from the male norm (such as sexuality, menstruation, childbearing or the caring role) tends to be suppressed or 'screened out', because these social categories do not fit into the male-focused sameness classification of equality. Feminist critics of this position have pointed out that a legal bias which treats 'unalikes' (that is, males and females with different reproductive roles) as 'the same' is inequitable and stigmatising to women, and as such is unlikely to produce egalitarian results (Finley, 1986; Morton, 1988; Vogel-Polsky, 1988, 1989). Another patriarchal bias is revealed by Smart (1989: 82), who points out that 'it is women's reproductive capacity that creates a problem for the male norm inherent in law, not for example men's abdication of the caring role'.

By suppressing sex differences, equal treatment and assimilation arguments reject conceptualisation of women as a separate group. Their underlying assumption is that biological differences should not form the basis for the economic, social and political allocation of benefits and burdens within a given society, and that women should be treated in public life in the same way as men. When women are specifically referred to as a separate group, it is only with the aim of ending existing separation or special treatment (Hevener, 1982: 2–5). The most extreme version of the 'assimilationist ideal' of sex equality envisages a society in which sex would be a wholly unimportant characteristic of individuals, having no greater significance than eye colour has in our society (Wasserstrom, 1977).

However, no programme to eliminate all public distinctions based on sex has been attempted anywhere. As Hoskyns (1985) points out, all equality laws allow for derogations (exceptions in the law) for provisions to do with maternity and for sex-specific jobs. Rather than attempting to eliminate all distinctions based on maternity, the main goal of the assimilationist model of absolute equality of opportunity has been the reduction of the traditional penalties associated with motherhood, especially the legal inability of married women and mothers to engage in paid employment.

In its traditional version, the assimilation model of sex equality is a rather one-sided plea for women to seek careers in the political and occupational world in sufficient numbers to eventually show a 50–50 distribution. The model accepts both the existing dichotomy between the public and private spheres of life, and the liberal view that the role of the law with respect to the private sphere should be limited.[1] The model generally ingores the very different ways in which women and men straddle the public and private worlds, and construct their identities. The main goal of assimilation is to offer a credible employment equity, but mainly on current male terms. The model encourages women to escape from the female-populated, but male-devalued, private sphere of the family, into the male-valued world of paid work.

Employment modifications accommodating women's life patterns which are envisaged by the model, or which have been actually implemented, are minimal. They are typically limited to maternity leaves and generally unsatisfactory provision of childcare during working hours. Experiences from both state socialist and advanced capitalist societies suggest that rather than equality for women, the most likely outcomes of assimilation are the double burden of wage and domestic work; discrimination in hiring, pay and promotion; concentration of female workers in low-paid jobs; conflict between maternal and work roles; and a wide discrepancy in terms of quantity and quality of leisure for women and men (Heitlinger, 1979, 1985; Hochschild and Machung, 1989).

In the former communist countries in Central and Eastern Europe, the prevailing strategy for industrialisation had contradictory implications for women's equality. On the one hand, the pattern of economic growth, based as it had been on a quantitative rather than a qualitative development of the labour force, required substantial increase in the full-time employment of women and relatively generous social provisions for maternity and childcare. On the other hand, the heavy emphasis placed upon increasing stocks of capital goods led to wage disparities between the 'preferred' industrial occupations, largely dominated by men, and the 'non-preferred' occupations in the basically feminised service sector. Moreover, this emphasis had meant that low priority was given to easing women's domestic responsibilities (as they have been eased in the West) by commerical provision of domestic labour-saving devices and convenience foods. Shopping and the preparation of meals were extremely time consuming and energy draining, both because goods were in short supply and because of the lack of retail outlets.

Moreover, the communist leadership conducted no educational campaigns aimed at breaking down sex-role streotypes and encouraging men to do their share of domestic work and childcare. To the contrary, the communist media, and educational institutions (and generally the state apparatus) did much to foster traditional concepts of male supremacy and feminine passivity, imparting to them an aura of socialist respectability. The pronatalist policies adopted in the early 1970s also reinforced the idea that childrearing and domestic work are 'by nature' women's work (Heitlinger, 1979, 1987a).

Women in Western capitalist countries also work in low-paid jobs in secondary, unsheltered labour markets. Because of greater availability of part-time work in the service sector and insufficient provision of child-care services, women's work lives have been characterized both by frequent departures and re-entries into the labour force, and by movements between full-time and part-time employment. As in Central and Eastern Europe, women in the West have remained responsible for most of the labour in the home. While *general* employment opportunities and child-care arrangements were superior in Central and Eastern Europe, access to elite positions was easier in the capitalist countries. For the 'male chauvinist' prejudices (or authoritarian calculations) of powerful and highly selective communist male elites were more effective in marginal-ising women's issues than were comparable prejudices of male elites in the less centralised, and less controlled, Western liberal democracies. Because of the communist party state's insistence on the monopoly of power and doctrine, an independent feminist movement of the Western type could not legally emerge in the communist countries to campaign against male domination or for fundamental changes in the gender division of labour (Heitlinger, 1979).

Jaggar (1983: 182) has suggested that

> prior to the contemporary women's liberation movement, formal equality seemed to be an adequate goal for liberal feminism. It was thought that, in the absence of legal constraints, women would quickly achieve substantive equality with men; lingering prejudice would be dispelled by rational arguments appealing both to justice and to efficiency.

Contemporary liberal feminists, however, are convinced that equal rights cannot by themselves produce sex equality, and that there is a need for a broader definition of equal opportunity, for a model of relative equality of opportunity, which addresses the issue of unequal starting point in the meritocratic competition. Absolute equality of opportunity based on equal treatment assumes that those who compete on merit have an equal starting point. However, as O'Donovan and Szyszczak (1988: 4) argue, 'this conception of equality is limited, for it abstracts persons from their unequal situations and puts them in a competition in which their prior inequality and its effects are ignored.'

The traditional model of absolute equal opportunity completely overlooks the inegalitarian consequences of the existing dichotomy between the public sphere of paid employment and the private sphere of the family and domestic relations; of the unpaid work which women perform in their capacity as housewives and mothers; and of sex role stereotyping and socialisation. Aspects of women's lives labelled as private have been generally ignored by absolute equal opportunity, yet it is these aspects that condition women's opportunities (or lack thereof) in employment and politics. Sex equality policy which is based on this limited model of equal opportunity, that is one which does not recognise that family structures and sex role socialisation are important components of women's opportunities, is doomed to fail, a fact which is now widely recognised by feminists as well as policy-makers. However, as Lovenduski (1986: 259) argues, converting this recognition into practice has been a slow and uneven process.

RELATIVE EQUALITY OF OPPORTUNITY AND 'COMPENSATORY' POSITIVE ACTION

One proposed solution to the unequal starting point problem has been the notion of relative equality of opportunity, of 'preferential treatment' in favour of racial minorities and women, as a means of correcting any *de facto* inequalities that impair their chances of success in various fields. These preferential policies have been variously termed as 'positive action', 'affirmative action' or 'positive (or reverse) disrimination'. According to Jaggar (1983: 190), the notion of 'affirmative action' refers to 'any institutional policy designed to open up fields dominated by white males to any individuals previously excluded from those fields.' Vogel-Polsky (1988: 4) defines positive action in a more radical way, as 'regulations calculated to promote equality of results', but admits that 'as far as its practical application is concerned, this new concept is poorly understood and has not been properly assimilated by the legal systems in which it has been incorporated'.

In practice, the aim of affirmative action policies is to ensure that employment practices (for example recruitment, training, promotion, working hours, firing and the over-all work environment) do not indirectly discriminate against women, and that women are represented in the occupational structure in numbers proportionate to their qualifications and availability in feeder population. The concept of affirmative action often encompasses not only measures directly related to employment practices, but also policies to facilitate access of women to the labour market, in the form of pre-employment and re-entry training programmes, support services for parents of young children, and social security and taxation structures that do not discourage women's employment. The major targets of affirmative action programmes have been the civil service and companies which receive government contracts or state subsidies (OECD, 1985: 167,179).

Though highly controversial, preferential treatment is none the less quite consistent with a broader notion of equal opportunity, which incorporates the idea of an equal starting point. Its compatibility with the idea of equality of results is more problematic, because social programmes of positive discrimination in favour of disadvantaged or less privileged groups (such as women, the working class or ethnic minorities) have been historically associated with the socialist notion of equality of outcome. However, the aims of the two sets of policies are quite different. Liberal reformers merely want to ensure that the rules of entry into the meritocratic competition are the same for all. They tend to accept the fact that the promotion of equality of opportunity in a competitive society inevitably produces highly unequal results. As Turner (1986: 37) put it, 'if we imagine society to be a competitive race, then competition inevitably results in inequality of outcome, since not every person in the race can be a winner'. Competitive success and hence competitive failure are therefore sanctioned by liberals, while socialists want to achieve equality of result regardless of the starting point and talent.

A socialist/communist programme of equality would seek to transform class, sex and ethnic inequalities at the beginning into social equality at the end, irrespective of the starting point and individual talents. Need, rather than merit, and substance, rather than procedure, would be the standards. While a programme of equality of result has formed part of the platform of most socialist and communist policies attempting to redress inequalities associated with competition and the marketplace (though this commitment has never been successfully implemented in practice), equality based on need (as opposed to merit) has never been adopted as a goal by liberals. The major objection of liberals has been the perceived incompatibility between outcome equality and personal liberty. Liberals argue that the achievement and the maintenance of equality of result would require massive economic redistribution, and coercive social and political regulation by the state, resulting in a totalitarian or an authoritarian regime (Turner, 1986: 37). Anti-discrimination legislation and affirmative action policies do not attempt outcome equality in the socialist sense. As we noted, the principles of non-discrimination and equal treatment offer absolute equality of opportunity, and ignore the problem of unequal starting point. By varying the requirements according to disadvantages suffered by one sex, affirmative action offers relative equality of opportunity. Its main goals are to redress past inequalities, to give an equal start to all market competitors for the highly rewarded male-dominated managerial and professional occupations, and to reward female-dominated low-status occupations with better working conditions, higher pay and greater upward mobility. The enlarged notion of equal opportunity therefore includes two complementary notions: the principle of non-discrimination (sometimes termed as the negative aspect of equality), and an active steering component, in which the ban on sex discrimination is complemented by special corrective measures. These recognise both the importance of differences between the sexes, and the inegalitarian effects of social structures and conditioning.

Preferential policies identify women as a separate group which requires special treatment. However, their corrective provisions are significantly different from the traditional measures associated with the special protection of women. As Hevener (1982: 2–5) points out, special treatment of women in the form of protective legislation reflects a societal conceptualisation of women as a group which either should or should not engage in specified activities. The protection normally takes the form of exclusionary provisions, which stipulate certain activities from which women are prohibited. They apply to all women or to particular categories of women (such as pregnant women), as a group. They do not apply to any men, and the special protection afforded is of unlimited duration. In contrast, the corrective provisions of positive action are inclusionary rather than exclusionary. Their aim is to alter the specific discriminatory treatment that women are receiving, thus removing a previous bar to an activity and in this way bring women to the same level as men. Since these special measures do not apply to men, they may be seen as contradicting principles of gender-neutrality and non-discrimination on the grounds of sex. However, since they are designed to be of limited duration, depending on the time period required to overcome the effects of past discrimination, they are better viewed as complementary measures.

The corrective measures are typically multifaceted, flexible, and chosen in the light of previously established objectives and priorities. Rather than emphasising compulsion and penalties for non-compliance, positive action typically relies on persuasion, on influencing opinion and on voluntary methods for achieving explicit objectives. In Vogel-Polsky's (1988: 4–5) view,

> positive action necessitates a combination of actors, forces, constraints and incentives. It must reach all who may become quilty of discrimination. It combines methods of collective self-assistance and state intervention. Positive action also necessitates the creation of a new kind of institutional machinery not only to afford protection but also to settle problems connected with discrimination.

Nielsen (1983) has described this new approach to sex equality as state feminist, which she contrasts with the traditional labour law perspective on sex discrimination. Unlike the individualistic approach of traditional labour law, state feminism looks upon sex not only as a characteristic of individual persons, but also as a social category, as gender. However, there is a conflict between the focus on the systemic causes of discrimination and the reliance on individual remedial action to correct these systemic faults. Mindful of both the difficulty of proving discrimination and of the ever-present possibility of victimisation, women have not made very much use of labour legislation on sex discrimination (Coote and Campell, 1987: 122–31). The placement of equality statutes in legal and institutional environments which were not designed for the purpose of promoting the interests of disadvantaged groups thus causes problems.

As Lovenduski (1986: 292–3) has argued,

> legal arrangements have been a particular inhibition to the effectiveness of the legislation. Equal employment law has varied in its usefulness to women by whether it is situated in an adversial or inquisitorial system of justice, by where it places the burden of proof, by the procedural forms employed, by problems to do with the collection of evidence, by the availability of information on its use, by the kind of administrative agency it has generated and by the extent to which the legal professionals actually understand the meaning of

discrimination as well as by the responses of the collective bargaining partners.

Inquisitorial systems (for example France, Italy, Belgium), where the court has a basic duty to take active part in litigation, and where the judge directs proceedings, requests documents and witnesses, puts questions to parties and applies the law to the facts of the case, may be more congenial to the application of anti-discrimination law than the adversarial system (for example Denmark, Great Britain), where procedural forms tend to heighten disputes and the complainant is virtually forced to treat her employer as an opponent, making amicable relations after the dispute nearly impossible. The placement of burden of proof on the complainant is another significant impediment to the enforcement of sex discrimination legislation, because 'proving discrimination is difficult, with necessary data and documentation often not available. Hence, laws which require employers to keep full records on their workforce are important. It would facilitate matters considerably if the burden of proof were to be placed upon the employer, as it is in unfair dismissal cases in the UK, for example.'

Another major problem with the individualistic approach of anti-discrimination machinery is the limited impact of the successful cases. As Smart (1989: 145) has argued, in Great Britain,

an act like the Sex Discrimination Act 1975 provides certain rights, yet for these to have any impact for women in general requires that vast numbers of individual women can prove that they have been denied their rights through a form of unlawful discrimination. So whilst a few women may have benefitted from taking action under this legislation, the vast majority have not benefitted from their gains.

Because cases heard by industrial tribunals set no legal precedents, British 'employers could just go on behaving as before, until the next individual brought another complaint, and her victory, in turn, affected her situation alone. This was true of most cases of direct discrimination.' (Coote and Campbell, 1987: 120).

State feminism utilises the law more broadly, as part of an active labour market policy, as a steering mechanism designed to mediate the sex factor in the labour market. While in the traditional labour law model of collective bargaining the law is seen primarily as a tool for conflict resolution, the state feminist model places more emphasis on its potential as a consensus tool. For most part, the new equality legislation and the new state feminist agencies which have been set up in conjuction with the legislation are trying to reach their goals not through conflict, but on the basis of consensus and voluntary compliance.

While Great Britain has only one agency which oversees the implementation of sex discrimination and equal pay legislation, the Equal Opportunities Commission, Canada and Australia have a whole series of separate agencies and government departments involved in the implementation of sex discrimination legislation, equal employment opportunity, pay equity, positive action programmes, and the day-to-day monitoring and auditing of all government policies and programmes for gender impact, at both the federal and the provincial and state levels. The state feminist agencies help organisations both in the public and in the private sector to understand and accept the advantages of sex equality, and encourage them to voluntarily work for its promotion.

In some cases, as a result of political pressure and in recognition that an entirely voluntary approach could not achieve the objective of equal employment opportunities for women, a more statutory approach has been adopted. For example, both the Canadian and the Australian federal governments have in recent years adopted employment equity legislation requiring the implementation of affirmative action programmes and an annual or periodic reporting on results achieved in organisations under their respective jurisdictions (for example the 1986 Canada Employment Equity Act and its companion, the Federal Contractors Program; the 1986 Commonwealth Affirmative Action (Equal Employment Opportunity for Women Act) in Australia).

However, the Australian legislation

> was a considerable disappointment to women's organisations and to the ACTU. The Act covered private-sector companies with more than 100 employees and all higher education institutions, but the only sanction for non-compliance was the possible naming of an employer in Parliament. . . . The AA Agency established to monitor compliance with the Act was established with so few staff resources (twenty people to assist and monitor compliance of some 5000 companies as well as 66 institutions of higher education) that by 1988 the Agency reported that monitoring would be conducted primarily through self-assessment supplemented by in-depth audit of about 2 per cent of company reports each year. (Sawer, 1990: 210)

When Max Yalden, Canada's chief human rights commissioner appeared on 5 February, 1992 before a special parliamentary committee reviewing the five-year-old Employment Equity Act, he criticised the federal law as being too vague and not providing for an independent agency strong enough to fight workplace discrimination. In his view, only modest progress had been made to eliminate barriers to the employment of women, visible minorities, disabled persons and native (aboriginal) people. Yalden also said that his agency would like to continue to monitor how the legislation was implemented by federal departments, agencies, Crown corporations and federally regulated businesses such as banks and airlines, but that the Canadian Human Rights Commission lacked a clearly defined mandate to tackle the problem (*Peterborough Examiner*, 6 February, 1992).

In 1987, the Ontario provincial government passed a pro-active pay equity legislation, the Ontario Pay Equity Act, requiring the implementation of equal pay for work of equal value. However, almost 50 per cent of women employed by organisations covered by the Pay Equity Act were unable to claim pay equity adjustments for lack of appropriate male comparators.[2] This flaw in the legislation was acknowledged at the time of its introduction, and the Pay Equity Commission, the new bureaucracy established to administer the legislation, was charged to come up with recommendations designed to remedy this problem. However, the Commission was unable to challenge the premise of limiting pay equity comparisons to individual establishments. As a result, the Commission could not propose recommendations that addressed the needs of women workers employed in highly feminised workplaces (Findlay, 1991).

Also crucial is the recognition that pay equity is primarily an employment standard, not a human rights matter. As Niemann (1984: 52–53) argues in her discussion paper prepared for Women's Bureau Labour Canada's series on equality in the workforce,

valuable time has been lost in many Canadian jurisdictions in disputes over where responsibility for the provision lies. It is a human right standard only insofar as unequal pay is, in Canada, a peculiar form of sex-based discrimination. Unequal pay as it relates to variations between and among valuable male-dominated occupations is not a human rights matter. Therefore, wages per se can only be properly administered, and equality enforced, with the framework of labour standards legislation. Until the issue of who is to administer equal pay provisions is decided, the objectives of such legislation will remain unclear and the effects on enforcements procedures will continue to be deleterious.

The Canadian Human Rights Commission is responsible for defining equal pay for work of equal value for all agencies under federal jurisdiction, while Labour Canada is responsible for its enforcement – a typical Canadian compromise, which has contributed to constant squabbling between the two institutions about the proper discharge of their responsibilities.

The typical organisational response to state feminism has been the appointment of an equal opportunities officer with a mandate to review the situation, institute changes, set targets, and review the equality plans annually. These have included job evaluation, implementation of equal pay for work of equal value policies (which have often resulted in higher pay for women), restructuring of career ladders open to women (such as advancing directly from clerical to a managerial position), parental leaves, and in some cases, workplace nurseries.

One result of this approach, clearly evident in the countries in which it has been adopted (that is, Australia, Canada, the United States, Sweden) has been the transformation of the terms of the debate about sex equality, from the rights and wrongs of the goal to the methods of its attainment (Vallance and Davies, 1986: 151). It is in this sense, and in this sense only, that we can agree with Vogel-Polsky's definition of positive action and regard state feminism as promoting equality of results. However, by depicting employers and women as having common interests, state feminism is promoting a resource perspective on sex equality. While feminist groups typically demand positive action as a strategy of empowerment of women, equality agencies promoting employment equity, or employers who have adopted positive action, tend to regard women as an underutilised economic resource, which should be safeguarded and developed.

For example, the Ontario Women's Directorate (undated: 5) promotes the benefits of employment equity to employers in the following terms:

Employment equity produces a human resources management system that is fairer and more efficient. Employment equity broadens the pool of candidates for jobs; it strengthens internal recruitment and hiring methods by eliminating biases; and it takes full advantage of all of its human resources – not just a portion of them.

Employers who have introduced employment equity report a number of additional benefits. Employment equity can produce a more stable labour force; a more productive labour force; and a more committed labour force. Staff turnover often drops significantly. The special measures included in an employment equity program – such as work-sharing, flexible working hours and special parental benefits – have a positive impact on both the morale and productivity of employees.

All of these benefits combine to improve both the internal and external corporate image of an organization. They also sharpen the organization's competitive edge.

In short, employment equity makes good business sense.

Affirmative action is therefore also a policy of elite recruitment and increased organisational efficiency, since its stated aim is to improve and legitimise the corporate system of decision making and policy formation (Hernes, 1987: 14). However, most employers have yet to be convinced that making special arrangements to accommodate women workers is a good management practice. In societies dominated by the consciousness of individual rights, it is highly unlikely that employers will voluntarily work for the collective rights of disadvantaged groups at the expense of what often seem to be individual rights of members of advantaged group (Burt, 1986: 543; Lovenduski, 1986: 293).

Burt (1986) found that in 1984, nine years after the Women's Bureau of the Ontario Department of Labour began advising companies on affirmative action, and five years after affirmative action programmes began operating at the federal level, most employers in her sample of 750 firms in the twin cities of Kitchener and Waterloo did not understand the meaning of affirmative action. Many of those who thought that they understood what positive action meant were mistaken. Most employers claimed to have received no information on the subject from either level of government. Moreover, Burt found that information sent to the head office was not always passed on to branch offices. Despite the emphasis of the government's literature on the positive impact of employment equity on the operation of firms, very few employers showed any interest in understanding the barriers to women's employment.

Trade union support for state feminism in Western Europe and North America has also been far from enthusiastic. The union reluctance to support state-directed equality policies has been attributed by Lovenduski (1986: 293–4) to the low priority unions tend to assign to women's issues, and to union opposition to state imposition on traditional, 'sacrosanct' preserves of collective bargaining. Since unions prefer to negotiate equal pay and opportunity in the normal bargaining process, their support for affirmative action is dependent on their direct involvement in the development of affirmative action programmes. The latter ensures that equity programmes do not transgress without union consent on issues which are directly industrial or industrially sensitive, such as criteria for promotion, the redesign of jobs and manual handling (Kramar, 1988). Needless to say, some good polices on occupational health and safety issues, parental leave, equal pay, work conditions, and promotion and training packages have emerged out of collective bargaining and union involvement in affirmative action programmes, benefiting large numbers of women (Kramar, 1988; White, 1989).

However, all too frequently women's issues have been given a low priority by unions at the local level, especially during periods of recession and high unemployment. As Coote and Campbell (1987: 162) argue, during the late 1970s and early 1980s, as the British economic crisis deepened,

> the unions became increasingly preoccupied with saving their members' jobs and defending the purchasing power of wages. The fight against female disadvantage was not a top priority. It seemed that women's economic equality had to be a no-cost benefit, which could only be sanctioned in a period of economic growth, because re-distribution of wealth between men and women was not seriously considered.

The story is quite different in Australia, where women's issues have become 'mainstream' union issues. From the late 1970s onwards, the peak union body, the Australian Council of Trade Unions (ACTU), has provided considerable support for feminist initiatives in both the industrial and the state arenas. Concrete gains were made in areas of equal pay, maternity and parental leave, childcare, and equal opportunity women's policy machinery within government. In 1984, the ACTU adopted an Action Program for Women Workers and appointed a co-ordinator directly responsible to ACTU Secretary, Bill Kelty. Based on the Working Women's Charter (which in turn is based on the British Working Women's Charter) adopted in the 1970s and the ACTU Women's Policy, the Action Program

> sets out the priorities of the ACTU and a proposed strategy to achieve each priority. These include leave and flexible working arrangements for workers with family responsibilities, improved provision of childcare, equal pay, Equal Employment Opportunity and Affirmative

Action, and increased involvement of women in the trade union
movement. It thus sets women's issues firmly within the general
strategy of the trade union movement and integrates them into the
work of most of the ACTU's officers.

(Booth and Rubenstein, 1990: 129–30)

More recent initiatives in wage negotiations have included proposals
for improved conditions in existing superannuation schemes (which
discriminate against part-time and low-paid workers, and against those
who do not stay in the same job until retirement); improving wage outcomes for low-paid workers; the extension of award coverage to groups
such as outworkers and family day care workers; and award restructuring
to provide for clear career paths and recognition of skill training. Award
restructuring is of particular assistance to women workers who are now
relegated to the lowest paid, 'dead-end' classifications. The ACTU and
relevant unions have worked closely with women's policy units within
government and working women's resource centres funded by the
government on improving industrial protection for migrant workers in
the clothing industry and improving awareness of maternity and parental
leave and anti-discrimination provisions relating to the workforce.

Booth and Rubenstein (1990) attribute the strong ACTU commitment
to feminist issues such as pay equity and the integration of work and
family responsibilities to the centralised wage-fixing system (which has
been much more successful in narrowing the gender gap in full-time
earnings than the 'comparable worth' or 'pay equity' principle adopted
in Great Britain and North America); the restructuring of the Australian
economy towards female-dominated industries; the growing unionisation
in the public sector and in clerical and service industries; the emergence
of the women's liberation movement which brought many feminists into
these industries and unions; the active participation of women workers
in their unions at all levels; the success with which they have been able
to place feminist issues within the mainstream of the union movement;
the close relationship between unions and the Australian Labor Party,
which was in power in the early 1970s and for most of the 1980s; the
expansion of union research departments, which have been increasingly
staffed by young university graduates with broad feminist concerns; and
government funding for working women's resource centres and other
such women's institutions. The largest unions affiliated with the ACTU
are now the teachers' and public service unions – both with strong
feminists among their leadership.

INDIRECT AND SYSTEMIC DISCRIMINATION

Nielsen (1983) has suggested that the twin principles of non-discrimination and positive action are best linked together by the concept of indirect discrimination. Indirect discrimination addresses effects of seemingly neutral employment conditions which have a disproportionate, and discriminatory, impact upon an indentifiable group within society. What is important is the *effects* of the action, not the intention. Like 'affirmative action', the concept of indirect discrimination was first developed in the United States, but it has now been adopted in a number of other jurisdictions, including the United Kingdom, Canada, the European Community and Australia. However, the precise legal meaning of the concept, and how it is to be proven and defended, has not yet emerged.

In an effort to clarify the issue, the European Commission asked a special network of expert lawyers from member states to draw up a typology of practices of indirect discrimination which could ultimately lead to a definition of indirect discrimination. While no generally agreed definition has yet emerged from this process, a draft covering a typology of commonly found practices which, in the view of the various network members, may be considered as constituting indirect discrimination, has been prepared. With respect to access to employment, these discriminatory practices include the way in which jobs are described and advertised, and the way in which the recruitment process relies on selection criteria which are not essential requirements for the job in question but which the majority of women cannot satisfy (for example height, age, geographic mobility, average physical strength, certain educational qualifications). As regards working conditions, indirect discriminatory practices include scheduling of work and training sessions at a time which may heavily impinge on women's domestic responsibilities. As far as promotion is concerned, the linking of opportunities for advancement to length of actual service on the job may particularly disadvantage childbearing women whose maternity leave(s) entailed career interruption(s). The generally more limited promotion opportunities for part-time workers also impact most heavily on women with children (Byre, 1988: 29–30).

Redress of indirect discrimination can have far-reaching consequences, because it can offer some challenge to the assimilationist 'embeddedness' of masculine values and power in work structures. As Eisenstein (1985) has argued, complaints of indirect discrimination, arising out of regulations governing the lifting of heavy equipment or objects, could be used both to re-examine traditional assumptions about masculinity and work expectations of male workers, and to decrease work injuries. In a similar vein, women returning from maternity leave who want to work part-time challenge dominant assumptions both about work organisation and continuity, and about the shape of the working day and the working week. Thus disputes about indirect discrimination can raise important questions about dominant work practices and structures. Are they essential, 'rational', or are they simply connected to the traditional masculine concept of the worker, presumed to be unconcerned with the details of daily life?[3]

The European Community doctrine of indirect discrimination (or the Canadian doctrine of systemic discrimination[4]) therefore recognises the connection between family responsibilities and equal opportunity in employment. In fact, reconciling family responsibilities with occupational aspirations has been given a high priority in European Community initiatives regarding women, reflecting a shift in focus from equal pay (Article 119 of the Treaty of Rome and the 1975 Equal Pay Directive) to equal treatment (several Directives and Recommendations on equal treatment in the labour market, occupational and state social security schemes, and for the self-employed, adopted during 1976–1986) to equal opportunities in working life in general (the two Community Action Programmes on Equal Opportunities for Women, 1982–85, 1986–90).

In Canada, governments at all levels formally recognise,

that labour force equality for women also requires the creation of an environment which supports and encourages the successful integration of work and family responsibilities. To this end, a joint federal–provincial–territorial effort is currently under way to develop a set of strategies to better enable Canadian workers to fulfil their employment and family responsibilities. . . . Areas to be examined include child care, parental and family leave, flexible work arrangements and hours of work, pro-rated benefits for part-time workers and the encouragement of work environments that are supportive of employees with family responsibilities.

First Ministers have directed that the development of these strategies be predicated on the premise that family and other social responsibilities should be shared by both women and men, and that workers with dependents and workers without dependents both have the right to equality of opportunity and equality of treatment in the workplace. (Status of Women Canada, 1989a: 17)

However, a word of caution is necessary, since these admirable policy objectives are well ahead of policy implementation. With respect to enhanced social provision for childcare, progress has been slow throughout the OECD (Ergas, 1987; ILO, 1988; Moss, 1988). Michel's (1986) review of positive action measures actually adopted in member states of the Council of Europe makes no mention of policies attempting to reconcile work and family life. Her study, based on answers to a questionnaire drawn up by the Council of Europe Secretariat and circulated in 1983 to the 21 member states, discusses programmes to inform girls and women about careers, education, training, employment and birth control, and to provide them with appropriate guidance and training in these areas, and attempts to involve more women in political decision-making and improve their image in the media. With the exception of birth control, these are all areas of the public sphere.

Since affirmative action programmes were designed to recognise the increasingly permanent nature of women's ties to paid work, this could hardly be otherwise. Both absolute and relative equality of opportunity are primarily labour market policies. Hernes (1987: 19) identifies three phases in the development of these policies:

Phase one encourages women (in preference to male immigrant labour) to enter the labour market. Phase two addresses problems of unequal treatment once they get there in gender neutral terms of equal access. Phase three encourages men to take over their share of family work by giving them parental leave. The goal is gender neutrality within the family and society at large.

It could be argued therefore that the ultimate goal of equality of opportunity is a new androgynous working life pattern based on a more even distribution of the sexes in all kinds of work (wage, domestic, voluntary, political and so on). However, the androgynous emphasis on role sharing masks the underlying assimilationist context in which the role sharing is to take place. The work to be shared is clearly hierarchically ordered, with paid career work considered much more important than domestic work. The implicit validation of men's market work (and its associated values of competition and achievement), and devaluation of women's traditional domestic work (and its associated values of nurturance, co-operation and altruism) clearly promotes the non-domestic lifestyles of childless women, and of women attempting to combine a career with a small family, at the expense of the traditional arrangements of domestically oriented women. The assimilationist vision of equal opportunity tends to be therefore regarded as repugnant by the 'non-working' full-time mother, who finds considerable fulfilment in her traditional unpaid work, and who knows its importance. Moreover, the assimilation vision is likely to be the source of much contemporary 'conservative' opposition to equal opportunity and to feminism in general (Jaggar, 1983: 197).

Gerson (1985: 217) summarised the deepening divisions among domestically oriented women and women subscribing to the assimilationist vision, in this way:

Across the class structure, divisions have emerged between those who opt for mothering and those who do not. Adherents to each pattern struggle to legitimate their responses to the structural contradictions between paid work and socially devalued (in terms of pay and isolation) mothering. This struggle, evidenced in battles over abortion rights, equal rights, affirmative action policy, or publicly funded day care, is likely to continue as long as the structural conditions that support them remain.

Gerson (1985: 223) even suggests that the deep divisions among traditional and non-traditional women have become as significant as conflicts between men and women. This argument is contradicted by Jones *et al.* (1990: 131), who suggest that the growing individualisation of women's lives, that is the growing variety and fluidity (in moving among employment statuses) in women's life patterns have

blurred the dividing line between 'working woman' and 'housewife'. Increasingly, women are both at the same time, whereas before 1970 few women ever were. In the second half of the twentieth century, every woman is familiar with the advantages and disadvantages of each status. This growing similarity tends to increase the feelings of solidarity among women, whether they are currently working at home without pay or in paid jobs outside.

The increasingly universal experience of paid work (however temporary) has contributed to the renewal of debates whether a concentration on the goal of sex equality in a man's world that overlooks important sex differences is an appropriate goal.

EQUALITY VERSUS DIFFERENCE AND THE SPECIAL NEEDS OF WOMEN

In recent years, 'equality versus difference' has become an important debate in American feminist theory and legal scholarship. On one side is the argument from equality which says that sexual difference should be irrelevant to the way persons are treated by the legal system, in employment, or at schools. On the other is the argument from difference which claims that an assimilationist equality in a man's world should not be an important strategic goal, and that appeals on behalf of women ought to be made in terms of the needs, interests, and characteristics common to women as a group (Buckley and Anderson, 1988: 4–5; Scott, 1988: 38).

There is also a third position, attempting to synthesise equality and difference. For example, Wolgast (1980) makes a case for a 'two-sex', 'bivalent' approach. She rejects a neutral perspective from which the concerns of both sexes can be seen 'objectively'. Her perspective attempts to accommodate sex differences by postulating two coexisting kinds of rights, equal and special. Equal rights come into play when it is clear that sex should make no difference to rights (she gives the example of jobs and promotion), while special rights come into play in the presence of special needs created by difference, be it on account of lifecycles, age, marital status, or employment. In her conclusion, Wolgast (1980: 157) comes up with the following model of rights and life situations:

> The rights needed by women in different life forms will differ. The wife and homemaker will need some special provisions for her old age; the career woman will not need these, but will need equal rights with respect to work. The woman who pursues a part-time career will need both kinds of rights less urgently; the woman whose career begins late will have a special set of needs again. The difficult problem is to formulate a programme that takes cognizance of all these needs within the framework of some reasonable social cost. To acknowledge only the claims of one group and to pursue only that set of rights is just another Procrustean bed.

The debate about equality and difference, and about equal and special rights, is by no means new. In Australia and Canada, it dates back to the beginning of the century and in Great Britain, earlier still. It was put on the political agenda by the growing entry of women into paid employment and it has been usually posed as a question of protection versus equality for women workers. The main criticism of special protective measures for women workers is their misplaced ideological bias towards women's childbearing, and their implicit view of men as the norm and of women as the deviant 'other'. As Finley (1986: 1156–7) argues,

with male as the reference point, the label 'special', or 'for women' takes on a pejorative cast because of the history of glorifying which is male and devaluing the experiences and qualities of women. Simply by focusing on women as women (as unlike men) and calling attention to their unmale needs, the special rights strategy may reinforce the stereotype of pregnancy as a woman's problem.

As an alternative way to conceptualise the issue, Finley (1986: 1169) suggests a broader approach which recognises the relational and socially constructed quality of differences. In her view, such a perspective

can lead us away from reacting to 'different' as 'unequal', or 'less'. It also requires an enlarged view of the context in which we ask the question of how to respond to the difference. Locating a difference between men and women, such as the fact that women get pregnant and men do not, in the relationship between them and in the context of the workplace, changes our view of the significance of the difference, which should affect an employer's and the law's response. The fact that pregnancy is a 'difference' between men and women does not mean that pregnancy and its consequences affect only women. Seen in this light, maternity leave may not be such a 'special' right for women only, as equality analysis portrays it to be.

Scott (1988: 43, 44, 46) comes to a similar conclusion, by arguing that 'when equality and difference are paired dichotomously, they structure an impossible choice. If one opts for equality, one is forced to accept the notion that difference is antithetical to it. If one opts for difference, one admits that equality is unattainable.' However, such oppositional pairing misrepresents the relationship of both terms, because the political notion of equality

includes, indeed depends on, an acknowledgment of the existence of difference. Demands for equality have rested on implicit and usually unrecognised arguments from difference; if individuals or groups were identical or the same there would be no need to ask for equality.

Equality might well be defined as deliberate indifference to specified differences. . . . Placing equality and difference in antithetical relationship has, then, a double effect. It denies the way in which difference has long figured in political notions of equality and it suggests that sameness is the only ground on which equality can be claimed.

As an alternative strategy, Scott (1988: 48) offers a notion of equality 'that rests on differences – differences that confound, disrupt, and render ambiguous the meaning of any fixed binary opposition', and that scrutinises the relationship between women and men as it is constructed in particular contexts.

SUMMARY AND CONCLUSION

This chapter explored the ways in which traditional liberal notions of equal rights and absolute equality of opportunity, and their underlying assumptions of abstract individualism, universal human rights, non-discrimination, gender-neutral equal treatment, and assimilation, have given way to a much broader definition of relative equality of opportunity, which ignores neither the unequal starting point in the meritocratic competition, nor indirect and systemic discrimination. This new, primarily labour market approach to women's equality, which has been described as state feminist, is characterised by broad bans on sex discrimination, positive action, strong emphasis on the need to build up monitoring systems, and a favourable attitude to active state intervention both in the labour market (for example encouraging or mandating employment and pay equity) and in working life in general (for example promoting integration of work and family responsibilities, providing childcare, supporting flexible work hours).

Positive action often encompasses not only measures directly related to the removal of discriminatory practices, but also policies and programmes that facilitate women's access to the labour market. These can take the form of pregnancy, maternity and parental leaves; retention of job security and pension coverage during those leaves; flexible hours of work; opportunities for re-entry training programmes and employment after extended parental leave; childcare services; and social welfare and taxation structures than encourage women's economic independence. As a labour market policy, positive action clearly rests upon a concept of work that is centred on *paid* work in the competitive market place, thus devaluing women's traditional unpaid work in the home and its associated values of nurturing, caring and altruism. The evident danger of masculine assimilation, and the desire to preserve at least some of the traditional women's values and lifestyles, have led many anti-feminists to oppose gender equality, and some feminists to question whether the drive for equality in a patriarchal world should be an important strategic goal.

Government initiatives on behalf of women have promoted a resource rather than empowering perspective on sex equality. If implemented unilaterally by management, from the 'top-down', without significant workers' involvement, positive action can easily become a policy of elite recruitment, since its stated aim is to legitimise and improve existing capitalist corporate structures. Despite these drawbacks, state feminism does offer an important strategic tool with which it is possible to challenge existing legitimacy (and in some cases even structures) of male power, values, and corporate practices.

For example, workers' initiated affirmative action (from 'the bottom up') can challenge, rather than legitimate, corporate decision making, and as such become an important tool of industrial democracy. Moreover, broadly conceived positive action programmes which address sexual harrasment in the work place challenge men's perceived rights of sexual access to women against their will. Positive action can also question the idea that greater average physical strength of men entitles them to better paid work, or it can debunk the presumption that no workers, or only the females ones, are concerned with the details of daily domestic life. Adoption of employment equity programmes can also shift the focus from the success stories of individual women to the impact of systemic barriers on disadvantaged groups such as women, visible minorities or the disabled. Last, but not least, positive action offers the prospects of better jobs and higher pay for women.

Childbearing presents a unique case for positive action. In Canada, feminist lawyers have persuaded the Supreme Court to use a broader definition of equality than one based on a comparison with men. They have argued that in situations such as childbearing there can be no valid comparison between women and men and for that reason equality rights must be conceived separately (Jones *et al.*, 1990: 156–7). In contrast, the tradition of 'equal rights' feminism in the US has meant that feminist organisations have not campaigned on gender-specific issues such as maternity leave. There has been a general fear than in the American context, recognition of the special needs of women workers would give rise to discrimination against them (Bacchi, 1990).

As we have seen, a rigid binary approach to gender equality and gender difference is incapable of resolving the childbearing issue. What is therefore needed is a more flexible conception of gender equality, which locates pregnancy in the network of work and family relationships rather than in biological difference from men. Thus one way out of the feminist dilemma of how to take into account reproductive difference, but at the same time not define women *primarily* in terms of their difference from men, is to scrutinise the relations between men and women as they are socially constructed in different contexts, and recognise that pregnancy and its consequences affect both women and men.

3 International Women's Policy Machinery

INTRODUCTION

Behind the various national anti-discrimination and positive action machineries lies much work done by international organisations. The most important multilateral organisations which address gender equality and the social protection of motherhood at the international level are the United Nations, associated specialist organisations such as the International Labour Organisation (ILO) and the World Health Organization (WHO), the Organisation for Economic Co-operation and Development (OECD), and the various regional organisations such as the Council of Europe or the European Economic Community (EEC). The work of these organisations can be divided into two broad categories: (1) research, analysis and sponsorship of special conferences and seminars, and (2) the establishment and monitoring of international 'instruments' – the various international treaties, conventions, directives, recommendations, declarations, and plans of actions, whose aim is to set international standards and patterns for national legislation and programmes.

International women's instruments reflect particular and historically specific understandings of gender. While the early ILO and UN instruments saw women as objects requiring special protection and rights, the more recent instruments recognise women as subjects, as 'independent, self-aware persons defining their goals and aspirations themselves, and as equal partners whenever their society and development are being designed, planned and decided upon' (Pietila and Vickers, 1990: 47). Current international status of women's instruments is rooted in the concepts of equal rights, equal opportunity, equal treatment and positive action. We shall see that international instruments have been and remain important in influencing the development of domestic gender policies, much more than the vast majority of women in the three countries under examination – the UK, Canada and Australia – realise. Canada and Australia in particular have played a major role in strengthening the various international instruments and mechanisms for the advancement

51

of women, and these in turn have provided the basis for numerous domestic initatives.

THE INTERNATIONAL LABOUR ORGANISATION (ILO)

The ILO was created under Part XII of the Treaty of Versailles in 1919. In 1946, it became the first specialised agency associated with the United Nations. Its chief aim is the promotion of high labour standards throughout the world. Most ILO Conventions and Recommendations are equally applicable to women and men. Standards adopted with respect to conditions of work, social security, industrial relations and basic human rights cover both male and female workers, without distinction. However, besides these generally applicable standards, the ILO has also adopted a number of instruments which deal specifically with women. These instruments are largely of two types, protective and promotional, reflecting the two main currents of ILO policy towards women (ILO, 1987: 1–3).

ILO protective measures for women

Some of the protective instruments were adopted very early on in ILO history, when organised labour actively sought to limit women's participation in the labour force. Trade unions at that time were concerned that women workers threatened men's jobs and wages, and to this end pursued a variety of strategies aimed at restricting women's employment, including the introduction of protective measures for women (Whitworth, 1990). Convention No. 3 on maternity protection and Convention No. 4 prohibiting women's night work in industry were adopted in 1919, the foundation year of the ILO. Both the 1919 and 1952 (Revised) Convention on Maternity Protection, and the 1919, 1934 (Revised) and 1948 (Revised) Convention on Night Work (Women) have been extremely influential, as have Conventions entailing a prohibition or restriction on women's employment in underground work, manual transport of loads, and work with dangerous substances or agents. Of the 130 countries surveyed by the ILO (1987), a majority had a large number of protective provisions applicable to women. However, the ILO publication acknowledged a trend, particularly evident in advanced capitalist countries, toward limiting or repealing such legislation. In recent years, a large number of Western countries have denounced Conventions Nos. 4, 41 and 89 concerning the ban on night work for women (ILO, 1987).

Convention 103 on maternity protection defines the exact period and conditions of maternity leave (no less than 12 weeks, compulsory postnatal leave of no less than 6 weeks, extension if actual date of confinement is later than expected), provides for cash and medical benefits during the leave, and prohibits job dismissal during such leave. It also states that employers are not individually liable for benefits, although they are required to give mothers time off for nursing. Convention 103 has had a major impact on the pattern of maternity protection throughout the world. Seventy-five countries, including all major industrial countries (with the exception of the United States), now provide for varying levels of maternity benefits through national legislation, or in the case of Australia, a centralised industrial award system (Kamerman *et al.*, 1983: 31).

ILO promotional activities on the equality of women

Promotion of equal rights and treatment of women workers was first addressed in Convention 100 (1957) concerning Equal Remuneration for Men and Women Workers for Work of Equal Value, and in Convention 111 (1958) concerning Discrimination in Employment and Occupation, at a time when no other significant international organisation addressed the issue. As Landau (1985: 15) put it, ILO Convention 100 relating to equal pay for work of equal value 'was at first in the nature of a solitary swallow that has not brought spring. Today this convention is ratified by more than a 100 States the world over and the principle of equal pay for equal work has become a universally recognised principle of labour law and is moving from recognition to implementation in practice.' The ratification often came about as a result of pressure from women's groups campaigning for equal rights and pay for women (Marsden, 1980; Sawer, 1990).

In Australia, the reformist Labor Whitlam administration used the ratification of ILO Convention 111 on Discrimination in Employment and Occupation in 1973 both as a visible occasion for meeting a major feminist demand, and as a way to clearly set itself apart from its Liberal predecessor. In addition, ILO Convention 111 gave rise to the first Australian administrative bodies dealing with discrimination on the grounds of sex and marital status. In 1978, ILO Convention 111 'was the basis of a major decision by the Conciliation and Arbitration

Commission in a case brought by the Municipal Officer's Association to prevent the sacking of female employees on marriage, a common practice in local government in Queensland. The Commission varied the Municipal Officer's Award to include a non-discrimination clause' (Sawer, 1990: 244).

The most recent developments in ILO policies on women workers concern attempts to replace special measures dealing with motherhood with gender-neutral measures dealing with parenthood, and to extend the principles of non-discrimination, equal opportunity and equal treatment for men and women workers as 'abstracted individuals' to 'actual' men and women workers with family responsibilities. In 1965, ILO Conference adopted Recommendation 123 concerning the Employment of Women with Family Responsibilities. The Recommendation provided for policies enabling women with family responsibilities to work outside the home without being subject to discrimination. It also encouraged competent authorities to facilitate, or themselves develop, services, especially childcare services, that would enable women to fulfil their responsibilities at home and at work harmoniously. Thus the main intent of the Recommendation was to facilitate women's double day.

In 1981, the 1965 gender-specific Recommendation was replaced by a gender-neutral Convention 156 concerning Equal Opportunities and Equal Treatment for Men and Women Workers: Workers with Family Responsibilities, and by an accompanying Recommendation of the same title. Preamble to the Convention recalls that the 1958 Convention 111 on Discrimination in Employment and Occupation does not expressly cover discrimination based on marital status, family situation or family responsibilities; notes the terms of Recommendation 165 and the changes which have taken place since its adoption, especially ILO and United Nations instruments on equality of opportunity and treatment; and recognises that the problems facing all workers are aggravated for workers with family responsibilities.

The Convention urges governments and employers both to ban discrimination based on marital status, family situation or family responsibilities, and to assist workers of both sexes in the fulfilment of employment and family responsibilities. Governments, employers' and workers' organisations are encouraged to facilitate entry or re-entry into employment of workers with family responsibilities by making flexible arrangements as regards working schedules, rest periods and holidays; by progressively reducing normal hours of work and overtime; by improving labour standards for part-time workers; by providing child-care services and facilities; and by improving leave provisions and social security cash benefits associated with the exercise of family responsibilities, especially the care of young children.

As of February 1990, only fifteen member states have ratified the Convention. However, by virtue of its very existence, Convention 156 is available both as an instrument of political protest and as an instrument of government legitimation. Thus women's groups and trade unions can use (and in Australia have used) ILO Convention 156 to support their gender-neutral demands for better conditions for workers with family responsibilities. Political parties and governments can use the instrument in their attempts to win women's votes. For example, ratification of the ILO Convention No. 156 became the centrepiece of the Australian federal government's commitment to women in the successful 1990 electoral campaign, although the ratification of this Convention has entered the political agenda neither in Canada nor in the United Kingdom.

THE UNITED NATIONS

Any discussion of international activity concerning the advancement of women during the last two decades is inconceivable without making reference to the United Nations and its Commission on the Status of Women. Since its inception in 1947, the Commission has been the global advocate for women's equality, monitoring the situation of women and promoting women's rights in all societies around the world. The most important accomplishments have been the design of international standards on non-discrimination (for example *Convention on the Elimination of All Forms of Discrimination Against Women*), the adoption of comprehensive international strategies to achieve women's equality (for example *Nairobi Forward-looking Strategies for the Advancement of Women*), and the promotion of the integration of women into national and international policy making.

The International Women's Year (IWY)

In 1972, the United Nations General Assembly proclaimed 1975 as the International Women's Year (IWY), which turned out to serve as a prelude to the United Nations Decade for Women (1976–85). The main purpose of United Nations International Years (of women, the child, the disabled, the families, and so on) is to increase awareness about the issue, stimulate research, and identify resources which could be mobilised to improve the situation of the designated subjects. IWY not only initiated a world-wide debate on equality of opportunity, but it made the question of sex discrimination a familiar and a respectable one. It also led to a multitude of research publications relating to the position of women in various parts of the world.

The year was also marked by several initiatives of other international organisations (for example the EEC Directive on the application of the principle of equal pay for men and women, the ILO Declaration on Equality of Opportunity and Treatment for Women Workers), and by various national initiatives, for which governments provided funding. For example, the Australian federal government provided $3.3 million for IWY projects, the Canadian government allocated $5 million, but the British Labour government provided only £10 000 for a much larger population. In Australia and Canada, expenditure on IWY activities largely took the form of grants to individuals or groups for various community projects, and for organising conferences, cultural events and educational campaigns on discriminatory treatment of women in advertising, marital property law, employment and so on. In Canada, part of the federal government's commitment to IWY also involved an Omnibus Bill on the status of women, which amended ten Acts to provide for equality of status of men and women (Lalonde, 1975; Novarra, 1980: 107; Findlay, 1987).

It is unlikely that the Australian IWY programme would have been initiated without the commitment and expertise of Elizabeth Reid, appointed by Whitlam in April 1973 as Australia's first adviser on women's affairs to the Prime Minister (Dowse, 1988: 211). Reid obtained from the Prime Minister major political and financial support for IWY 'in the hope that it would raise the consciousness of women throughout the country to feminist issues and produce a spin-off effect for the Whitlam government'. Reid also hoped that the IWY Secretariat could become a prototype feminist bureaucracy (Ryan, 1990: 76, 77). The Prime Minister himself took ministerial responsibility for IWY, which was of major importance in the face of caucus, bureaucratic and media indifference or hostility. Throughout 1975, the media potrayed the IWY programme as trivial and an unnecessary waste of money. IWY became 'a focus for all that was supposedly wrong with the Labor government' (Dowse, 1988: 212). The extreme bias of media reporting notwithstanding, IWY had a tremenduous impact on Australian society.

It not only made a significant contribution to the widespread acceptance of feminist notions about the place of women in Australian society, but many of today's women services and institutions have an origin in IWY (Sawer, 1990: 17).

The UN Decade for Women (1976–85)

At the international level, IWY culminated in the United Nations World Conference for Women, which was held in July 1975 in Mexico City. The Conference adopted the World Plan of Action for the Implementation of the Objectives of International Women's Year, and recommended that the UN General Assembly declare the period 1 January 1976–31 December 1985 as 'The United Nations Decade for Women: Equality, Development, and Peace'. The Plan contained 155 Articles as guidelines for national action over the ten-year period 1975–85.

Canada's response to the World Plan of Action was the first comprehensive federal plan of action to improve the status of women, *Towards Equality for Women*. Released to the public in 1979, the Plan stressed two major goals: equal opportunities and economic independence of women. These were to be achieved by a series of specific changes to government legislation, policies and programmes in areas of employment, family and criminal law, health promotion, income support, maternity benefits, language programmes for immigrant women, international developmental assistance, and native affairs. The Plan also raised the issues of violence against women and sexual harrasment, which were to become much more important towards the end of the decade. The issues which were not included were abortion, day care and mandatory affirmative action, which at that time were the major focus of organised feminist demands (Findlay, 1987: 46).

Another international action plan was produced at the Second World Conference for Women held in 1980 in Copenhagen. In addition to the main theme of equality, development and peace, there were also three subthemes: employment, health and education. The adopted Programme of Action for the second half of the decade paid particular attention to childcare, single parents, the role of women as food producers, and the problems of rural, young, migrant and unemployed women. The third UN World Conference for Women was convened in July 1985 in Nairobi to review and appraise the achievement of the United Nations Decade for Women. After long and strenuous negotiations, the Conference adopted unanimously a document entitled 'Nairobi Forward-looking

Strategies for the Advancement of Women' (FLS), which supersedes the earlier plans of action. It is intended as a broad-based framework for action between now and the year 2000 to remove remaining obstacles to women's equality, and to 'express women's views on world affairs' (Pietila and Vickers, 1990: 45)

The Nairobi Forward-looking Strategies

The Nairobi FLS – an ambitious document of almost 100 pages and 400 paragraphs – provides a blueprint for action on a broad range of issues affecting every aspect of women's lives: legal and political equality, human rights, family planning, development assistance, education and training, employment, health, natural resources and environment, food and water, agriculture, international co-operation and peace. The FLS document calls on governments to facilitate women's full and effective participation in all aspects of society; to promote the full participation of women in decision making; to encourage women's grassroots organisations and enhance women's self-reliance; to promote the sharing of domestic and parental responsibilities by all members of the family; to provide statistics to measure women's unpaid and paid work as well as their activity in the informal economy; and to establish appropriate national machinery to monitor the situation of women, identify the causes of inequality, help formulate new policies and projects for the advancement of the status of women, and ensure the integration of women into all policies and programmes (United Nations, 1985; Status of Women Canada, 1985).

Both Canada and Australia played an active role in drafting the FLS. The Canadian federal government has also put some effort into promoting this document. It has produced *Facts Sheets on the Nairobi Forward-looking Strategies* and provided some resources to Canadian women's groups to make the document more accessible. Within the United Nations, Canada has pushed for specific, issue-oriented discussions of the document and initiated the 1988 resolution that requires the entire United Nations system to incorporate the Nairobi Forward-looking Strategies as part of its mandates and programmes of work (Stienstra, 1988: 84). Australia was one of the first countries to translate FLS into its own National Agenda for Women. The relatively long lead time between its adoption in 1988 and the year 2000 enabled the government to push planning well beyond the time frame provided by Australia's short electoral cycle of only three years (Sawer, 1991).

The United Nations Convention on the Elimination of All Forms of Discrimination Against Women (CEDAW)

While *Nairobi Forward-looking Strategies* provides a charter for action, the UN Convention on the Elimination of All Forms of Discrimination Against Women is the only legally binding instrument that has emerged out of the United Nations Decade For Women. CEDAW covers a broad range of issues, including those covered by earlier specific treaties on slave trade, traffic in women, nationality, access to education and employment. It reiterates the principle of non-discrimination on the basis of sex, and reaffirms sex equality as a goal. Moreover, the Convention endorses affirmative action. Article 4 clearly states that the adoption of 'temporary special measures aimed at accelerating de facto equality between men and women shall not be considered discrimination as defined in this Convention'.

The Convention also includes several provisions with respect to motherhood. The Preamble of the Convention raises the twin issues of social protection of motherhood and equal sharing of parental roles as follows:

Bearing in mind the great contribution of women to the welfare of the family and to the development of society, so far not fully recognised, the social significance of maternity and the role of both parents in the family and in the upbringing of children, and aware that the role of women in procreation should not be a basis for discrimination but that the upbringing of children requires sharing of responsibility between men and women and society as a whole.

Article 4 of the Convention states that special measures 'aimed at protecting maternity shall not be considered discriminatory'. However, as Hevener (1982: 23) points out, 'maternity' is not defined in the Convention, leaving the content and applicability of the measure wide open. Would all women of childbearing years be deemed in need of special protection, and thus be excluded from a wide variety of activities assumed to be dangerous to potential mothers? The UN Convention does not address the problem of reconciling maternity protection from reproductive hazards with the goal of equal employment opportunity in any detail.

Specific maternity provisions in Articles 11 and 12 of the Convention closely resemble provisions contained in the ILO Convention on Maternity Protection. Governments are to ban dismissal on the grounds of pregnancy or maternity leave; enact maternity leave with pay without loss of employment, seniority and social benefits; promote the establishment and development of a network of childcare facilities to enable parents to combine family obligations with work responsibilities and participation in public life; provide special protection to women during pregnancy in types of work proved to be harmful to them; and ensure to women appropriate nutrition and services in connection with pregnancy, confinement and the postnatal period.

Under the terms of CEDAW, governments which have ratified the Convention are required to submit reports on measures taken for its implementation by the end of the first year and then every four years. The reports are examined by the Committee for the Elimination of Discrimination Against Women. Australia's first CEDAW implementation report was regarded by the Committee as a model of its kind, 'both in terms of the legislation, machinery and programs described and in terms of its frank and self-critical approach' (Sawer, 1990: 247).

By 1987, CEDAW has been ratified by 87 countries, including the United Kingdom. However, the British government reserved the right to regard the existing anti-discrimination legislation as constituting appropriate measures for the practical realisation of the objectives of the Convention. What this means is that the British government is required to make *no* legislative changes to comply with the Convention in the form in which it has been ratified, a fact very much regretted by the Equal Opportunities Commission (EOC, 1987: 54–64). Unlike Canada and Australia, the UN Decade for Women was 'invisible' in the UK, both in terms of the invisibility of the Decade to British women, and of the parallel invisibility of women to British policy making (Ashworth and Bonnerjea, 1985).

THE WORLD HEALTH ORGANIZATION (WHO)

The World Health Organization is a specialised agency of the United Nations with primary responsibility for international health matters and public health. Created in 1948, WHO is the only international organisation to which all countries belong. Its major focus is on research and programme development and as such it serves as a forum for health professionals to exchange their knowledge and experience. It provides technical assistance to governments experiencing a particular health problem (or problems) which they don't know how, or find politically too difficult, to handle. It can also act as 'bad consciousness' for governments and corporations, as was the case with the boycott of the Swiss multinational company Nestlé on account of its aggressive marketing of formula milk in Third World countries. WHO international instruments – goals, resolutions, strategies, plans of action – rely on voluntary compliance, but they can be as effective as the legally binding Conventions of the ILO or the United Nations.

In addition to its headquarters in Geneva, where the World Health Assemby meets annually, WHO has six regional offices throughout the world, each with its own programme geared to the particular health problems of the countries it serves. The European Region is of particular significance to this study, because a large number of its active thirty-three member states are industrialised countries with relatively high life expectancy, low maternal, perinatal and infant mortality, low fertility and advanced medical and maternity services. In fact, a report of WHO Director General to mark the ending of the United Nations Decade for Women and the 1985 Nairobi World Conference for Women identified over-utilisation of technology and over-medicalisation of pregnancy and childbirth as major health problems of both advanced industrial societies and urban areas of some developing countries. The Region of the Americas and the European Region in particular have been involved in a review of these problems (WHO, 1985a: 15–16).

The European Region's involvement dates to 1979, the International Year of the Child, when maternal and child health issues were discussed during the annual meeting of the thirty-three member states of the WHO European Region. The WHO Regional Office for Europe was requested to study and report on problems surrounding birth and birth care in the Region. In response to this request, the Maternal and Child Health Unit at the Regional Office set up a Perinatal Study Group, which issued its final report in 1985 (WHO, 1985b). While the major focus of *Having a Baby in Europe* is on the critical evaluation of medical care before, during and after birth, maternity benefits such as the duration of prenatal (during pregnancy) and postnatal (following birth) paid maternity leave, financial and other diverse maternity benefits (for example free milk and vitamins, special privileges when travelling by public transport, priorities for housing) are also discussed (WHO, 1985b: 10–13).

WHO also cosponsored an ILO (1985) publication on the protection of working mothers. The global survey (1964–84) on maternity benefits summarises existing provisions on a regional basis, and emphasises the need to extend the coverage of such provision – both in terms of the population covered and the extent of each provision (for example increase in time and facilities for breastfeeding). Occupational health risks for women, particularly regarding reproductive health, were discussed at meetings organised by WHO in Budapest in 1982 and in Tbilisi (USSR) in 1983. In 1976, WHO designated women as a 'vulnerable group' with regard to their health status, but several equal rights advocates at the Budapest considered 'different' a more suitable term. The meeting touched upon conflicts between protective health measures and sex discrimination, but the issues 'were not fully explored as they were not considered to be within the remit of the Working Group [on Women and Occupational Health Risks]' (WHO, 1983: 3). The strongest opposition to special health measures for women only came from the representative of the European Commission. All the delegates from the Eastern bloc countries strongly supported special protective measures for women, claiming that they are essential for the achievement of sex equality (WHO, 1983: 18).

THE ORGANISATION FOR ECONOMIC CO-OPERATION AND DEVELOPMENT (OECD)

The Organisation for Economic Co-operation and Development was established in 1961 as a successor body to the Organisation for European Economic Co-operation (OEEC), which was established in 1948 in connection with the Marshall Plan. All of its twenty-four member states are advanced industrial 'Western' countries, with the exception of the less developed Turkey. OECD's activities cover practically all aspects of economic and social policy. The major part of its work is carrried out in numerous specialised committees and working parties of which there exist about two hundred. Of particular significance to this study is the Working Party on the Role of Women in the Economy (WPRWE).

WPRWE was established in 1974 (in anticipation of International Women's Year) by the OECD Manpower and Social Affairs Committee with the mandate to identify problems related to the changing position of women in the labour market. Its report, which also specified some of the policy measures that could be adopted, was published in 1979 as *Equal Opportunities for Women*. After reviewing the changing role of women in the labour market, the report addresses the influence of education and training, the problems of achieving equality of pay and employment, flexibility of working time, childcare arrangments for working parents, and the impact on women of social security legislation. In the last part of the report, the main trends in member countries are identified, together with some of the policy measures that could be adopted. However, none of the conclusions on how to bring about equality of women in education, training, employment, remuneration and social security, are, of course, binding on member countries.

The High Level (that is, ministerial) Conference on the Employment of Women, which was held at OECD Headquarters in Paris on 16 and 17 April 1980, also grew out of the WPRWE study. Labour ministers and other high officials of OECD countries attending the Conference adopted a fourteen-point Declaration on Policies for the Employment of Women, pledging themselves to achieve equality of opportunity and of conditions in the employment of women as a matter of priority. Among other things, the Declaration urges governments, in co-operation with employers and trade unions, to put into practice equal pay for work of equal value along the lines of ILO Convention 100 and EEC Directives on Equal Pay; develop more flexible working arrangements; provide for part-time workers (who are predominantly women with children) levels of pay and social security benefits which are proportional to those of full-time workers, and the same levels of working conditions and standards of protection; ensure that the provisions of taxation, social security and child-support systems do not bias decisions made by men and women as to how to allocate their time between paid employment and other activities; review protective labour legislation for women to ensure its consistency with the goal of equal opportunity in employment; guarantee pregnant women and women returning from maternity leave protection from dismissal and the right to return to work without loss of earned benefits; and ensure that the special problems of migrant women are given consideration in relation to all the other aims (OECD, 1985: 153–5).

In order to encourage and monitor implementation, WPRWE has established a number of panels to monitor progress, review strategies for promoting the objectives identified in the Delaration, and publish findings. While many member countries (not identified in the report) have extended the period of maternity leave beyond the ILO minimum standard of twelve weeks, and some have introduced an extended leave which may be taken by either parent, at least one country (most likely Great Britain) actually reduced both the duration of paid maternity leave and the level of benefit. The non-European member countries with no general national maternity scheme (namely the United States and

Australia) appeared to have made little progress by the time the report was published (OECD, 1985: 171).

The Report also notes British opposition to any government initiatives in this area, because of the UK government's belief that parental leave is a matter for collective bargaining rather than for government intervention. In WPRWE's view,

> this slowing down of progress is to be regretted since the development of systems of parental leave and the introduction of more flexible working arrangements for parents are vital elements in the attainment of equality for married women . . . it should be noted in passing that the development of day care facilities for children is also essential in order to allow parents, particularly mothers, to participate in the labour force.   (OECD, 1985: 150–1)

However, all the countries that provided information on childcare facilities (over half of the member countries) concluded that current facilities for childcare are inadequate to meet demand. Lack of care facilities after school hours was also identified as a problem. Finally, the Report criticises a number of countries (not named) for adopting strategies that emphasise incentives for women to withdraw from the labour force or to work part-time in order to care for children, thus reinforcing rather than reducing sex role stereotyping (OECD, 1985).

The OECD proposals are less well known than the international instruments developed by the UN or the ILO, and national governments have made little effort to make them accessible to the general public. As an intergovernmental organisation, the work of OECD, including the Working Party on the Role of Women in the Economy, is confined to the bureaucratic level, with no direct imput from non-governmental women's organisations. As a result, OECD proposals on women's equality are strongly biased in favour of the resource perspective on women noted in Chapter 2.

Rather than developing international conventions and recommendations as standards for specific national policies, the OECD is best known for its comparative analyses of economic trends, which are often explicitly evaluative. Occasionally, they can lead to the adoption of specific Recommendations and Declarations by OECD Council or specific high level ministerial conferences. While the OECD Declaration on Policies for the Employment of Women goes a step beyond an evaluative analysis, it falls short of becoming an efffective international instrument available to women's groups as some form of leverage over their national or provincial governments. Nevertheless, like other international instruments, the OECD Declaration provides a minimum standard by which to judge a country's action (or lack thereof), and as such it is politically useful.

In Australia, WPRWE's work played an important role in legitimising several domestic equal opportunity initiatives. WPRWE's 1980 report on labour market sex segregation showed Australia to have the highest level of segregation among countries studied. This finding was to provide the underpinning for a host of programmes to increase women's access to non-traditional jobs. WPRWE's decision in 1987 to make pay equity a priority issue enabled the Women's Bureau in Canberra to expand its work in this area (Sawer, 1990: 244).

THE EUROPEAN ECONOMIC COMMUNITY (EEC)

The European Economic Community was established by the Treaty of Rome in 1957 by the Group of Six (France, West Germany, Italy, Belgium, the Netherlands and Luxembourg), who were unable to secure support for a European common market and a limited quasi-federal European political authority within the framework of Council of Europe. The aim was to intertwine West European countries in such a way as to make them economically interdependent and unable secretly to arm themselves and wage wars against each other. At the same time it was hoped that fair competition, free trade and overall economic integration would contribute to economic prosperity and improvement in working and living standards (Lodge, 1983: xiv). The Treaty of Rome is concerned mainly with creating a framework for decision making, leaving the creation of policy to the institutions it set up. The main EEC institutions for policy making – the Commission, the Council of Ministers, the Court of Justice and the Parliament – have wide discretionary powers to adopt policies in areas not specifically covered in the Treaty. This prerogative has been very important for the advancement of women's equality.

While all four major institutions of the European Community have been involved in the promotion of women's equality, the driving force behind the upsurge in EC intiatives regarding women in the early 1970s has been the Commission. The Commission is not merely a European civil service but has the important Treaty-based right of initiative in most policy matters. The Commission can hire experts and consult who it wishes in preparing policy; it has also several statutory advisory and management committees with members appointed by governments. The Commission also spends the Community budget and manages funds such as the European Social Fund (covering special operations concerning specific categories of persons, such as youth or women). Based on its role as the 'custodian of the Treaty' and Community law, the Commission has the right to take infringement proceedings against a member state failing to incorporate EEC Directives into their national law and bring the case to the European Court of Justice (ECJ).[1]

Article 119 of the Treaty of Rome

The EEC women's policy derives from Article 119 of the Treaty of Rome, which bound member states to the principle of equal pay for equal work. Although Article 119 was included in the section of the Treaty dealing with social policy, it was adopted on economic grounds. As Odile Quintin (1988: 71), the former Head of the Equal Opportunities Bureau in the Commission, argues, 'one member state (France) already had legislation establishing the principle of equal pay and it considered that it would be at a competitive disadvantage unless all member states applied the same principle'.

Thus what was at stake was not women's equality, but unfair competition and improper functioning of the market. Equal pay was therefore viewed mainly from the perspective of employers, as equal costs. The inclusion of Article 119 in the Treaty was to ensure that competition among employers of different nationalities is not distorted, as part of EEC labour market harmonisation objectives. Subsequent EC policies on equal treatment and equal opportunities have placed equal pay in a somewhat broader context, but its primary aim of achieving fair and equal competition among employers remains (Nielsen, 1983: 26).

In any case, Article 119 of the Treaty did no more than establish the principle of equal pay. In the early 1970s, with the growth of feminist movements, governments of several member states came under increasing pressure to legislate for equality (Alexander, 1985). Popular feeling over the equal pay issue in Belgium inspired feminist lawyer Eliane Vogel-Polsky to seek a test case to determine whether Article 119 enabled women to claim over and above what the law in their own country required. Vogel-Polsky eventually chose a case of Gabrielle Defrenne, a Sabena Airlines employee, who had complained that she was expected to retire at forty when men were not, and that the terms of her pension were inferior to theirs. After winding its way through the

Belgian judicial system, different aspects of the case were heard by the European Court of Justice in 1971, 1976 and 1978. The first Defrenne judgment publicised the equal pay issue and Community obligations to its achievement (Lovenduski, 1986: 282).

The second Defrenne ruling was a landmark in the development of Community law on equal pay in that it settled the question of the federal nature of the relationship between Article 119 and national legislation. The Court ruled that within certain limits, Article 119 was directly applicable to direct forms of discrimination which originated in national legislative provisions or in collective labour agreements as well as cases in which men and women received unequal pay for the same work on the same premises, and that individuals can rely on its provisions before national tribunals. Moreover, the Court also declared that Article 119 had a double purpose: economic and social. It was a mechanism both to prevent distortion of competition (by the employment of women at lower rates than men for the same work) and to improve the working and living conditions, particularly of women (Landau, 1985: 25, Nielsen, 1983: 46). Thus by the mid-1970s, the principle of equal pay for men and women had acquired a broader social egalitarian significance unforseen by the founders of the EEC.

The activities of the European Court of Justice coincided with a commission-sponsored report on the position of women in employment in all the member states. The author of the report, the reknowned French sociologist Evelyn Sullerot, highlighted the numerous disadvantages women faced in the labour market, including those associated with motherhood. Pressure also came from women within the Commission's social affairs directorate (DGV) for a stronger equal pay policy at a time when there was a growing world-wide interest in the place of women in society and when the Commission was interested in policies assisting disadvantaged groups. These concerns were at first translated into the Social Programme, initiated in 1974 and aimed at improving working conditions for disadvantaged social groups. Proposals on women prepared in DGV proved easy to slot into the Programme (Lovenduski, 1986: 283). The critical years were 1975–9, during which the Council of Ministers issued three separate Directives on equal pay, equal treatment in employment and equal treatment in matters of social security.

The EEC women's Directives

The Equal Pay Directive covers both the private and the public sector. It enlarges provisions of Article 119 in the Treaty of Rome in a number of ways. Most notably, it widens the scope of equal pay to work to which equal value is attributed (by a job classification system or by some other means), thus bringing it into line with ILO Convention 100 and making it possible to introduce equality also in segregated fields of employment. However, as it stands, the Directive has been effective only in areas where both men and women are employed, because like in North America, the courts have not accepted any 'hypothetical male' comparisons (that is, consideration of what a man would have been paid had he been employed in the particular job in question) and have required actual comparisons to be made (Byre, 1988: 22).

The other two Directives are aimed at removing discrimination at the point of entry to the labour market and in vocational training, promotion, working conditions, and social security. Directive 76/207/EEC (Article 2-1) outlaws discrimination 'on the grounds of sex either directly or indirectly by reference in particular to marital or family status'. Based on the argument that equal pay is of limited value if women's employment opportunities are restricted, the 1976 Directive was adopted to ensure that men and women have equal access to employment, training and promotion, and broadly similar working conditions. Derogations (exceptions in the law) are permitted for sex-specific jobs (e.g. actors or models), pregnancy and maternity protection, and for affirmative action provisions designed to promote equal opportunities for women.

The Social Security Directive, passed in December 1978, required the progressive implementation of equality of men and women in statutory social security schemes. The benefits covered were contributory schemes such as sickness, invalidity, old age, maternity, accidents at work, occupational diseases and unemployment. However, there were many exclusions, often in areas where the greatest inequalities are to be found: survivors' benefits, family allowances, the determination of retirement age, the granting of derived benefits to wives, or long-term increments to benefits for dependent spouses (Brocas *et al.*, 1990: 13). Despite these limitations, the Directive is important, because it confronts the traditional bias of social security schemes towards men as breadwinners, and the slow adjustment of various social security schemes to the increase of married and divorced women in paid employment (Collins, 1983: 106).

Two additional implementing Directives, extending the principle of equal treatment for men and women to occupational social security schemes and to self-employed persons, were adopted in 1986. The Occupational Social Security Directive provides for equal treatment in occupational pensions schemes for employees and self-employed people.

It covers the scope of schemes, conditions of access, the level of contributions and calculations of benefits including payments for a spouse or a dependent. The setting of the different ages at which men and women are eligible for old age and retirement pensions was again permitted, and the Directive also excluded from its provisions survivors' pensions. Taking into account women's greater life expectancy, companies were permitted to continue using for another thirteen years different actuarial data on mortality and life expectancy to set benefits for men and women. Although this new Directive was hailed by EEC ministers as a major step forward for women, Tongue and Eberhardt (1987: 2) regard it as 'the weakest of Community legislations', since 'its provisions allow existing discrimination to continue'.

The Directive on self-employed women and women in agriculture was designed to protect self-employed women and guarantee pay and social security benefits to wives working on farms and in family businesses. However, maternity protection and legal recognition of the work of the spouse stayed in the Directive only as encouragement to government action, leaving it to the discretion of each country to adopt what measures or gestures they like in recognising the work of a farmer's wife. The Directive was so weak that Tongue and Eberhardt (1987: 3) regard it as 'a step backwards as far as women's equality in the Community is concerned'.

All of the Directives emphasise comparisons between men and women workers, not the competitive relationship of employers, which, as we noted, is the basis of the more narrowly focused Article 119 of the Treaty of Rome. Women are seen in the Directives as important actors in the labour market, not as weak welfare clients – the initial focus of the 1974 Social Programme. For this reason, the EEC policy on women is clearly a steering labour market policy, not a welfare distribution policy, and as such a significant example of state feminism (Nielsen, 1983: 28). The equal pay and treatment Directives took effect almost immediately (within one to one and a half years), whilst the 1979 and 1986 social security Directives had a very long implementation period: seven and five to thirteen years respectively.

EEC women's policy machinery

A Council Directive on a specific issue automatically brings into existence a set of Commission procedures for implementing, monitoring and reviewing its application. Accordingly, a women's unit was set up within the Directorate General for Information with the responsibility of informing the press and women's groups. The Women's Information Bureau publishes a bimonthly bulletin, *Women of Europe*, which furnishes information on EEC policies that most affect women, on the changing status of women and legislation of EEC member states, and on the activities of national and international women's associations. The women's unit also sponsors seminars, conferences and training courses arranged by national women's groups on EEC themes, produces audio-visual material on women in the European community, and conducts opinion surveys on men's and women's attitudes on general and women-specific issues (Jonkheere and Gerard, 1984: 10)

The Bureau for Women's Employment and Equality was established within Directorate General for Employment, Social Affairs and Education (DGV) in 1976 with broad terms of reference. Within the Commission, the Bureau is the inter-departmental co-ordinating body on all specific aspects of Community policies affecting women. It is the body that proposes and defends proposals for various Community instruments to promote equal opportunities. It also helps to translate EEC Directives on sex equality into practice by drawing up progress reports on their implementation and preparing infringement proceedings. The Bureau also represents the Commission in dealings with the other international agencies concerned with women's employment (Jonkheere and Gerard, 1984: 12).

Consultation with the national equal status councils and commissions is provided for by the Advisory Committee on Equal Opportunities. It was set up in 1981 as part of the 1982–85 action programme on equality. The Committee meets two or three times a year and has observer status on Community bodies such as the European Social Fund Committee, the Vocational Training Committee and the Freedom of Movement Committee. Networks of independent experts within member states were also set up under the 1982–85 action programme. For example, there are networks on the implementation of Directives, on training and education, on women in television, on women in employment, and on childcare.

The application of EEC Directives at the national level involves a set of procedures emanating from the Commission, which makes steady demands on member states to monitor, reform and adjust national legislation in line with EEC provisions. As Byre (1988: 23) has argued,

> in the area of equal pay and equal treatment, this has taken the form of: (a) an initial monitoring activity, via questionnaires to and reports from member states' governments on the application of the basic

Treaty and Directive provisions in their particular countries; and (b), on the basis of this feedback and analysis (and also, more recently, of practical researches undertaken by the special independent network of national lawyers and practitioners set up within the context of the EEC's 1982–5 Equality Action Programme), action by the Commission against individual governments, via formal infringement proceedings before the European Court, to secure full implementation of the Community requirements.

Such actions against the British government forced it to amend the Equal Pay Act to include equal pay for work of equal value, and to allow women to retire at the same age as men, despite the government's avowed hostility to 'social engineering' of this kind. In July 1982 the ECJ ruled that the United Kingdom was in breach of the 1975 Equal Pay Directive because its Equal Pay Act gave a restrictive interpretation of the concept of work of equal value. The UK amended its legislation in January 1984 to conform to the Directive, nine years after its issuance. The amendment to the British Equal Pay Act has produced a flood of new cases on this issue. Similarly, both Germany and Ireland were forced to adopt equal treatment legislation because of the necessity to comply with the equality Directives. As Hoskyns (1988: 35) argues, 'such legislation would have come much later, if at all, without this intervention'.

EEC enforcement procedures of community legislation

European Community 'secondary legislation', consisting of Directives, Regulations and Decisions, is prepared and monitored by the Commission, scrutinised by Parliament, approved by the Council of Ministers, and if there is a dispute, interpreted by the European Court of Justice. Frequently, deadlines for answering questionnaires and reporting on the application of the basic Treaty and Directive provisions in their particular countries are not kept. If the Commission refers an infringement to the ECJ, the Court's decision can take a long time to reach (Buckley and Anderson, 1988: 8, Freestone, 1983: 43). This cumbersome decision-making process entails a long time-lag between adoption and final implementation of Directives, but it opens up possibilities for debate and pressure.

As Hoskyns (1988: 36) argues, in the case of equal pay and equal treatment,

> legislation which has its origins in the 1960s, and was adopted by member states in the 1970s, is now being applied in the 1980s when circumstances are quite different. Thus one of its main effects is to help keep the issue of women and employment on the agenda, at a time when governments would much prefer to let it drop. The strength of the policy derives principally from the type of Community measures which exist to enforce compliance at the national level with Community legislation, and to monitor progress in this direction. Both the European Commission and the European Court, until recently at least, have adopted a broad interpretation of the legislation on women, and have taken a severe attitude towards infringements by member states.

Politicians and civil servants in member states claim that there was little understanding at the time the Equal Treatment and Social Security Directives were adopted of what their domestic consequences would be. The extent and ramifications of the legislative change became apparent only later, at the implementation stage. Officials are now very aware of the effects of the legislation and the prevailing ethos among EEC governments is against social legislation of this kind – witness the failure of the Council of Ministers to adopt in 1982 a Directive on temporary workers, in 1983 a Directive on part-time work, and in 1985 a Directive on parental leave and leave for family reasons. (This draft Directive is discussed in Chapter 8.) The European Commission is itself giving much higher priority to industrial restructuring than to social policy. In fact, between 1979 and 1991, there were no new Directives on women's issues – the two 1986 Directives merely consolidated provisions of existing Directives.

The 1991 Directive concerns the protection of pregnant women at work, and covers such issues as the length of remunerated maternity leave, protection of employment rights during pregnancy and maternity, and physical health and safety of pregnant women at work. Although all member states have maternity legislation already in place, and the draft Directive required only minor modifications, the British government strongly opposed it. However, rather than mounting a legal challenge in the European Court of Justice against the EC authority to legislate on this issue, it worked out a compromise. While the draft Directive guaranteed pregnant women 14 weeks on full pay, Great Britain, which has the worst provision for pregnant women in the EEC, eventually agreed to the 14 weeks but at the existing lower rates than those suggested by the Commission (Palmer, 1991).

The Action Programmes on Equal Opportunities for Men and Women

The most important Community instruments on women's equality which have emerged during the last decade have been political rather than legal ones, namely the three medium-term Action Programmes on the Promotion of Equal Opportunities for Women (1982–5, 1986–90, 1991–4). The first of the Programmes was the direct outcome of a Conference, jointly organised by the Commission of the European Communities and the UK Equal Opportunities Commission, in Manchester in May 1980. The conclusions of this Conference were further developed in the European Parliament's Resolution of February 1981 on the position of women in the European Community, in which it called on Community institutions to intensify and broaden Community activity on women's concerns (Quintin, 1988: 72). The Action Programme was also inspired by demands from national women's employment or equal opportunities committees, and by similar programmes drawn up in other international bodies, especially the UN (Vallance and Davies, 1986: 77–86).

The Action Programme pursues a multifaceted policy to bring about broadly defined equality of opportunity. It brings together many aspects of gender discrimination within a single action framework. The actions to be carried out are grouped into seven categories: improved application of existing provisions, education and training, employment, new technologies, social protection and social security, sharing of family and occupational responsibilities, and increasing awareness and changing attitudes. Under the category of sharing of family and occupational responsibilities, the Community Programme on Equal Opportunities for Women recommends to member states to establish a system of parental leave (after the period of maternity leave) and leave for family reasons, promote the continuous and diversified development of pre-school and after-school childcare, provide for career breaks and flexible work conditions, and to promote, especially among young people, the acceptance of more equal sharing of family, occupational and social responsibilities (Commission of the European Communities, 1986: 15). More recent Community initiatives in this area include a new Recommendation Concerning the Sharing of Family and Occupational

Responsibilities, and two separate measures dealing with the protection of childbearing women at work.

The Women's Committee in the European Parliament

The Action Programme was introduced largely as a result of pressure from the Women's Committee of the European Parliament. An *ad hoc* Women's Committee was established almost immediately after the first direct European Parliament election in 1979 produced a record number of women MEPs, of whom many had an interest in women's issues. The eighteen-member Committee met regularly, taking evidence from the Commission, the Council of Ministers and the Commission's new Advisory Committee on Equal Opportunities, and in 1981 produced the enormous Maij-Weggen report, named after the Committee's rapporteur. The report led to the EP Resolution of February 1981 on the position of women in the European Community, and to the establishment of the EP Committee of Enquiry into the Situation of Women in Europe. This Committee published eighteen separate reports focusing on the implications for women of such things as taxation laws, parental leave, vocational training and the new technologies. Since 1981, these various reports have provided ready-made resolutions which have produced around 5 per cent of the total resolutions before Parliament. After the 1984 European elections, this pattern has been continued by the more permanent Committee on Women's Rights, the first to be established as an official committee of the Parliament (Vallance, 1988: 135).

Of particular significance to this study are the 10 March 1986 Resolution on childcare infrastructure, the 14 October 1987 Resolution on the reintegration of women into working life and 10 March 1988 Resolution on women and employment. The latter regrets that part-time work, 'a form of employment sought by many women with family responsibilities because it suits their personal circumstances', is not 'accorded the status, pay or conditions it merits', and urges Council 'to approve the directive on voluntary part-time work as soon as possible in order to prevent further discrimination against women who are forced to accept the type of work' (*Official Journal of the European Communities*, 10 March 1988, p. 79). It also decries the lack of suitable childcare facilities and urges the adoption of the draft directive on parental leave. The Resolution on the reintegration of women into working life expresses similar sentiments. Moreover, its preamble asserts that an 'increasing number of young women, particularly those with secondary and higher education, reject the idea of interrupting their working life because of the difficulties likely to result from this, and therefore either have to bear the double burden of family and work or abandon entirely the idea of starting a family' (*Official Journal of the European Communities*, 16 November 1987).

The existence of the Women's Committee and the various Reports and Parliament Resolutions emanating from the Committee have provided an important focus for pressure by women MEPs throughout the decade. As women MEPs have been more confidently asserting the importance of women's concerns, they have helped to change the whole nature of the debate on sex equality. As Vallance (1988: 137) argues, 'from the Enquiry came the realisation that equality was not to be achieved simply by fiat: that the real impediment to it was no longer (if indeed it ever had been) direct discrimination against women, but the much more complex and "indirect" forms often written into the structure of social institutions and working patterns'. 'And, perhaps most important of all', Vallance (1988: 139) adds, 'the women in the Parliament have provided a focus for the equality campaign: they could be pointed to by those in the Commission who wanted action as indicative of an enduring political commitment to women within the Parliament, and they have been a rallying point for lobbying by those outside the institutions of the EEC.'

Throughout the decade, support for women's equality in the Employment, Social Affairs and Education Directorate General (DGV) has run well ahead of the Council of Ministers, where in turn commitment has been greater than in many national governments' departments. The British government in particular has been very hostile to any form of 'social enginnering' emanating from Brussels, including policies on women's equality. It has blocked the Commission's proposal on parental leave and leave for family reasons, failed to pass most of the provisions in the Action Programme into national legislation, and was the only member state who refused to sign the EEC social charter.

It ensured that the promotion of positive action for women was adopted only as a Council Resolution (84/635/EEC). It acted on the principle of equal pay for work of equal value only as a result of ruling from the European Court of Justice on infringement proceedings brought by the Commission. While the British government is the most outspoken in its opposition against the 'social dimension of Europe', the prevailing ethos among many other Community governments is against mandatory social legislation. Like their North American and Australian counterparts, EEC national governments are nowadays more concerned with reducing public expenditure, deregulating business and 'freeing' the labour market than with promoting equal opportunities.

Despite the displeasure of many of the EEC national governments, the Commission policies on women have forced a common form of legislation on member states and have kept the issue of equal opportunities on the political agenda. By putting women on the political agenda in a way which made it difficult for member states to disregard them, EEC changed the climate of opinion on equality. As Vallance and Davies (1986: 131) have argued, positive action is no longer dismissed as a demand of a few radical feminists, but is approached in terms of whether it should be pursued mandatorily or by voluntary agreement. Indirect discrimination is seen as a reality. Without the constant pressure from the EEC, terms of debate and actual policies would not have come that far.

CONCLUSION

During the last two decades, international activity on the advancement of women has been focused largely around the United Nations-designated International Year of Women (1975) and the United Nations Decade for Women (1976–85), although the International Labour Organisation addressed issues such as maternity protection, discrimination in employment, and equal pay for work of equal value much earlier. Equal pay is also included in the 1957 founding Treaty of the EEC, but the issue is approached from the perspective of employers rather than women, as equal costs rather than equal opportunities.

All the current international standard-setting activities on women's equality emphasise equal rights, equal treatment, equality of opportunity, maternity protection, equal sharing of domestic and employment roles, and positive action. They all endorse the twin models of relative equal opportunity and state feminism discussed in the previous chapter. They differ mainly with respect to the degree to which they endorse sex differences and the special treatment of women, and the procedures they use for implementing, monitoring and enforcing the translation of their respective instruments into national legislation. The EEC has the most vigorous enforcement procedure of its legislation, and permits no special provisions for women workers with the exeption of pregnancy, childbirth and postpartum.

The WHO and ILO have been long-standing supporters of both equality and special protective measures. The UN, ILO and Council of Europe standards-setting instruments can be also legally binding, but member states are not obliged to pass such international Conventions into their national legislation. Specific Conventions, or only their parts, are legally binding only in those countries which have ratified them. However, once ratified, Conventions do create national obligations for governments to observe their terms. Traditional international law is generally regarded as a law between states or international organisations, and as such creates no rights or obligations for individuals. Whether the provisions of a treaty can be relied upon before a national court is therefore up to national constitutional law alone. Traditional international law is only concerned that states honour their treaty obligations.

In contrast, European Community law can be 'directly effective', that is it can confer rights directly on individuals in member states, thus making it possible for them to take Community law-based action in their domestic courts. Because of the direct applicability and supremacy of Community law, the relationship between Community law and the national laws of the member states in many respects resembles a relationship between federal and state (provincial) law. As we noted, this legal practice has been quite significant for the enhancement of women's equality throughout the EEC, and especially in Great Britain. Without it, enactment or extension of equal pay and equal treatment policies would have come much later, if at all.

International instruments such as the Nairobi Forward-looking Strategies, OECD, ILO, EEC or Council of Europe Resolutions and Recommendations are binding only politically, not legally, and as such have no mandatory authority. However, these international recommendations and action plans do set new standards by which to judge governmental actions and policies, and as such can be politically useful, both as instruments of political protest and as instruments of legitimation of reformist governments.

These instruments have to be generally known, however, or their usefulness is very limited. If most women's groups do not know about the various international action plans, and if women's equality is not a high government priority, as is certainly the case in Great Britain, international standard-setting activities are of little help to the advancement of status of women.

4 National Women's Policy Machinery: Canada, Australia and Great Britain

INTRODUCTION

The concept of a specialised government mechanism (or mechanisms) for integrating women's needs into government policy making – a women's policy machinery – came into wide usage during the United Nations Decade for Women. Eighty-seven (69 per cent) of the 126 countries which provided information on the origins of their national machinery to the UN Branch for the Advancement of Women gave dates between 1975 and 1984 (Sawer, 1991). The UN Commission on the Status of Women began to push for advisory national commissions as early as 1963, in the context of preparing the forerunner of Nairobi Forward-looking Strategies, the Unified Long-term United Nations Programme for the Advancement of Women. In subsequent years, the UN Commission convened a number of expert meetings on the topic in various parts of the world. By the time of the Copenhagen Conference in 1980, there had been a general shift among UN member states from a pattern of non-governmental and advisory machinery on the status of women towards government machinery (*Women 2000*, 1987: 3–6).

This chapter examines the respective evolutions of such machineries in Canada, Australia and Great Britain. The establishment of human rights, equal opportunity, affirmative action and women's policy machineries implies bureaucratisation, which in turn has led to the emergence of a new class of feminist bureaucrats, the so-called 'femocrats'. The term was invented in Australia, and it describes self-declared feminists who work within the state bureaucracy in career positions explicitly created to benefit women. The most striking thing about femocrats, Eisenstein (1990: 90–91) argues, is their

> undisguised commitment to feminism, and the acceptance of this within the bureaucracy. . . . Indeed, the requirement of a demonstrated commitment to feminism, in the form of some experience in an

activist area, had been, with some help from the Equal Employment Opportunity (EEO) programme, incorporated into job descriptions. . . . By the 1980s, there were sufficient number of femocrats at least in New South Wales, to be divided into specializations. There were health, child care, welfare, legal reform, and education femocrats, and there were also femocrats edging their way into very 'male' areas such as the Treasury and the Water Board. One element that accelerated the progress of femocratization of the bureaucracy was the impact of the EEO programme.

Summers (1986) identifies two contrasting models of femocracy: the 'Missionary model', based on public advocacy and private proselytising, and the 'Mandarin model', based on adaptation of bureaucratic techniques and structures to feminist philosophy. Most femocrats are, of course, both. Politicians and traditional career bureaucrats generally regard them as missionaries, while feminists outside the government tend to view them as mandarins. These splits between outsiders and insiders are important to bear in mind when we address a major problem posed by the institutionalisation of feminism: the ambiguous and conflictual relationship between women's policy machinery and the women's movement.

Findlay (1991: 106) suggests that the term femocrat has a merely analytic function, and does not imply 'any judgment about those who have chosen the state as a terrain of struggle'. However, when Hester Eisenstein (1990: 89–90) was first introduced to the concept in Sydney in 1981, the term 'femocrat'

connoted 'sell-out' or co-option; the 'femocrats' were contrasted with the true believers in boilersuits who inhabited the lesbian separatist communities of Glebe and Balmain, where the true heart of feminist revolution lay. The opposition, then, was between revolutionary feminism on the streets, outside the corrupt system of power and prestige, and the official feminism of the state, which created bureaucrats in its own image, painted birds whose role it was to generally contain and dissipate the energy of feminism.

The extent of femocrats' influence and the quality of their representation of feminist concerns is the subject of an on-going debate in Australia (Levi and Singleton, 1991). The politics of dress is a fascinating side issue in this debate. In the 1970s, causal dress was seen as a symbolic rejection of patriarchy and the preceding two decades of conservative government. However, from the 1980s, a recognition of the positive power of 'dressing for success' brought among femocrats a 'sisters in suits' conformity (Sawer, 1990).

Feminist intervention in government in Great Britain has been much more limited, with the possible exception of local and metropolitan levels of government in the early 1980s. The explanation can be found in different feminist ideological and strategic predispositions towards the state, oppositional and pragmatist politics, public or behind-the-scene advocacy and lobbying, litigation, and alliances with political parties and trade unions. In turn, these predispositions are related to country-specific political traditions, cultures and specific political climates, as well as available opportunities for advocacy groups to influence the processes of policy making and implementation.

WOMEN'S POLICY MACHINERY IN CANADA

The Canadian women's policy machinery is quite complex. Its main components are Status of Women Canada (SWC), the Minister Responsible for the Status of Women, the Canadian Advisory Council on the Status of Women (CACSW), their provincial counterparts, the Women's Program of the Department of Secretary of State and the few First Ministers' Conferences (FMCs) which explicitly addressed women's issues. Canada's national women's policy machinery developed primarily in response to the landmark Report of the Royal Commission on Status of Women.

The Royal Commission on the Status of Women (RCSW) and the feminist movement

The RCSW Report was tabled in Parliament in December 1970, at a time when public policy was in flux. The progressive political climate at that time encouraged the promotion of equality, justice and 'compensatory' government services for the 'disadvantaged'. There was a lot of interest in citizens' participation in public policy making, and state bureaucracies were willing to hire people with radical views, even some socialist feminists who were dedicated to extra-parliamentary opposition (O'Neil, 1990). Established during Canada's centennial year in 1967, the Commission involved thousands of women from communities across Canada in writing some 1000 letters and 468 formal briefs to advise the government on reform. The widespread involvement of women in the Commission's deliberations helped to legitimise feminism, and enabled feminists of all stripes to identify with the Commission and its report as their 'own' (Findlay, 1987: 35).

The report was predicated upon six general principles: human rights; equality of opportunity; freedom to choose whether or not to work outside the home; shared responsibility for the care of children between the mother, the father and society; special social responsibility for women on account of pregnancy and childbirth; and affirmative action (Paltiel, 1972: 2–3). When tabled in Parliament in 1970, the report contained a well-articulated, comprehensive set of recommendations on a wide range of public policy issues. One cannot stress enough the significance of the Royal Commission for the development of both an articulate liberal feminist movement, which in the 1970s became the 'public face of the women's movement', and a governmental women's policy machinery (Findlay, 1988a). Among the report's 167 recommendations were several that recognised the need for governments at all levels to set up co-ordinating bodies and advisory councils on issues involving the status of women. Early in 1971, the Prime Minister announced the federal government's response to the Commission, promising that the 167 recommendations of the report would be given priority consideration. Three measures that were adopted straight away concerned machinery initiatives. In 1971, the federal government established the Office of Equal Opportunity in the Public Service Commission, appointed a federal Minister Responsible for the Status of Women, and set up a new Office of the Coordinator, Status of Women, within the Privy Council Office. The creation of the Office of the Coordinator was linked to the formation of an Interdepartmental Committee (1971–2) whose mandate was 'to study the report and related questions and to recommend to the government a strategy for implementing the recommendations as well as other measures designed to improve the status of women in Canada' (Lalonde, 1975: 1). The Committee proposed the creation of several new status of women agencies, which would take over some of the functions previously performed by the Women's Bureau.[1] The federal government accepted these recommendations, and between 1970 and 1975 put in place a collection of status of women agencies. In later recollections about the process, Florence Bird, the Chair of the Royal Commission of Status of Women, 'reflected that the creation of multiple agencies was a mistake.

The Commission had pressed for several, hoping to get one' (Burt, 1990: 198).

None of these machinery initiatives, 'relating more to the bureaucracy's capacity to organize its response to demands than to developing policies or programs for substantive changes in women's lives', impressed the feminist movement, 'anxious for the implementation of specific policies' (Findlay, 1987: 36). By the spring of 1972, seeming government inaction provoked liberal feminists to renewed collective action. Led by Laura Sabia, a prominent radio broadcaster, the liberal feminists induced Minister of Manpower and Immigration Bryce Mackasey to give them enough money to bring women from across Canada for a conference on the future of the recommendations of the Royal Commission. Held in downtown Toronto, the April 1972 'Strategy for Change Conference' was the first national conference of Canadian feminists. The conference gave significant organisational impetus to the developing feminist movement, resulting in the establishment of the National Action Committee on the Status of Women (NAC) (Marsden, 1980: 244).

Designed as an umbrella group of 'new' feminist groups and women's centres, and 'traditional' women's organisations (such as the YWCA, National Council of Jewish Women of Canada, the Ontario Women Teachers Federation), NAC's initial mandate was to maintain communication with women across Canada (not an easy task in such a large and diverse country) and to get the RCSW recommendations implemented. Over time, NAC evolved into a national advocacy organisation with a membership of over 500 groups and a mandate to lobby the government on a variety of women's issues. NAC's annual general meetings set issue priorities, which are then presented to the federal cabinet at an annual lobby session. Thus since the early 1970s, the major feminist strategy in Canada has been reliance on reform by the state, coupled with the belief that building an autonomous movement was necessary to overcome government resistance to feminism.[2]

Over time, the majority of RCSW recommendations were implemented, mainly in areas of economic and social policy that did not involve much expense, that did not threaten the power structure and on which there was broad social consensus (e.g. maternity leave, increasing women's participation in politics, reducing barriers to women's equal employment opportunities, eliminating discriminatory provision in legislation). Recommendations which could not meet all of these criteria, such as those for a national childcare system, equal pay for work of equal value, pensions for homemakers, a guaranteed annual income for single parents and abortion on demand in the first 12 weeks of pregnancy, were not implemented, and are still on the feminist movement's shopping list today (Munter, 1990).

Status of Women Canada (SWC)

As the expertise on women's issues in government increased, and as the government's understanding of what needed to be done to make change possible became more informed by a feminist perspective, the mandates of both the Minister Responsible for the Status of Women and the Office of the Cordinator were broadened:

> In 1976, the Minister was made responsible for ensuring that the concerns of women were integrated into the overall government planning and decision-making process. This approach, which still forms the cornerstone on the federal strategy for the advancement of women, led to the creation of Status of Women Canada, a federal agency providing expertise and strategic advice to the Minister and to federal departments on issues affecting women. This was a first step in the establishment of a national machinery for the advancement of women.
> (Minister of Supply and Services Canada, 1990: 7–8)

The main mandate of Status of Women Canada (SWC) is to 'eliminate the obstacles that limit choices and opportunities for women' (Minister of Supply and Services, 1990: 8). To this end, SWC works to provide overall policy co-ordination and monitoring; to give advice to the Minister Responsible for the Status of Women and to other departments on all matters within federal jurisdiction that affect women in Canada; to co-operate with provincial and territorial governments and international organisations in the analysis and development of policies concerning women; to consult with women's groups, academics and others in Canada and abroad who are concerned with women's issues; and to provide public information on federal government priorities and programmes relating to the status of women in Canada. In the fiscal year 1987–8, Status of Women Canada had a total budget of $2.85 million (Cdn.) and a staff of 41 (Status of Women Canada, 1987, 1988). Within the federal government, SWC

> undertakes a systematic analysis of the impact on women of existing social, economic, legal and cultural policies and programs, and reviews proposals for new and revised programs, policies and legislation

with regard to their impact on women. It recommends policy changes to other federal departments and initiates policy and program proposals to meet unfilled needs. (Status of Women Canada, 1987: 2).

Integrating and monitoring government's policies

In 1975, in the context of the International Women's Year, Marc Lalonde, the Minister Responsible for the Status of Women, undertook a review of the government's record in advancing women's equality. His report led to the adoption in 1976 of a new federal policy of integration of status of women concerns. Under the terms of the policy, all sectoral departments are supposed to examine the impact on women of their proposals, to include a specific analysis of status of women considerations in all relevant Cabinet documents, and to designate an implementation mechanism (a person or a unit) to service these activities. Representatives from several federal departments are supposed to meet regularly as an interdepartmental committee on integration mechanisms to share and co-ordinate information about new government policies and developments, and to facilitate the process of integrating women's concerns throughout the federal government. The committee is chaired by SWC and its members have been appointed by the Deputy Minister of their sectoral department. They apparently have full access to the senior levels of policy decison making within their departments (Status of Women Canada, 1987).

While most federal departments now have employment equity and affirmative action programmes for their own employees, only a small number have assigned specific responsibilities to designated persons and/or units for an ongoing policy and programme analysis for gender impact. These include departments of justice, health and welfare, secretary of state, employment and immigration, labour, fitness and amateur sport and agriculture (Status of Women Canada, 1987). However, femocrats in these departments have only 'nominal power to recommend policies, and real power only to promote research and offer advice' (Burt, 1990: 198). Thus, the policy of integration of status of women concerns, that is the bureaucratic pattern of interdepartmental consultation and co-operation, to achieve early intervention in policy development and monitor for differential gender impact, has not worked very well.

As a rule, federal departments do not want to share information about their respective policy agendas with any other department, let alone with the 'Missionary' Status of Women Canada. The differential impact of policies and programmes on women is generally poorly understood by 'mainstream' bureaucrats lacking a feminist perspective, and is often confused with personnel policies of equal opportunities for women employees of the federal government. Deputy ministers in particular devote very little time to the evaluation of the impact of their policies and programmes on women (Interview, Status of Women Canada, 13 December 1989). The Neilsen Task Force on government organisation found that, with the exception of Labour Canada, no federal department systematically reviews its policies to determine their impact on women. It further concluded that the main success of Status of Women Canada was in pulling 'the provinces together for national awareness of issues relating to women and for consensus building' (Burt, 1990: 200).

Each province and territory has adopted status of women mechanisms similar to those existing at the federal level. All provinces and territories have appointed a minister responsible for women's issues and most have established policy development/co-ordinating bodies similar to SWC. Status of Women Canada holds regular meetings with its counterparts in the provinces and territories, and participates in various joint working groups to study issues and formulate policies in areas of shared jurisdiction such as education and training, the criminal justice system, health and social services, labour and human rights legislation, and immigration. In recent years, such joint working groups have addressed childcare, the role of women in non-traditional fields, family violence, and women's reproductive health (Status of Women Canada, 1987; Minister of Supply and Services Canada, 1990).

Minister Responsible for the Status of Women

The main responsibility of the Minister Responsible for the Status of Women is to ensure that the concerns of women are integrated into the overall government planning and decision-making process. To this end, the minister may raise concerns about a proposed policy, programme or piece of legislation at meetings of Cabinet committees or the full Cabinet and brief the Prime Minister on key women's concerns. As part of her/his mandate, the minister also meets regularly with representatives from a variety of women's groups across the country to discuss issues of mutual concern. Since 1982, the federal minister has been meeting regularly with her/his provincial and territorial counterparts to address issues of mutual concern (Status of Women Canada, 1987).

All Ministers Responsible for the Status of Women have simultaneously held other portfolios. These have varied, including such diverse portfolios as Labour, Employment and Immigration, Health and Welfare, Consumer and Corporate Affairs, Mines, Justice, Secretary of State, Privatization and National Defence. This dual responsibility has sometimes led to conflicts between the minister and SWC, since the ministers have tended to view their responsibilities for women through the perspective of their other portfolios. For example, Burt (1988: 151) reports that, in the early days of women's policy machinery, when Bryce Mackasey was responsible for both status of women and manpower and immigration, most of his contacts with women's issues were through the Women's Bureau in the Department of Labour rather than through the Office of the Coordinator, Status of Women. When Marc Lalonde held the post, he even proposed to reorganise the Office of the Coordinator and make it part of his other portfolio, the Department of Health and Welfare.

Thus there are some potentially negative consequences of linking women's policy mechanisms with another portfolio, though these are hardly as serious as the potential marginalisation of a completely separate Status of Women Minister. One positive outcome of the dual responsibility is the increase in awareness of women's issues of the minister and his/her colleagues. Senior cabinet ministers with no previous knowledge of women's issues who add Status of Women to their main, more prestigeous and powerful portfolio, then can, if they wish, advance the cause of women's equality directly in the Priorities and Planning Committee in Cabinet. This option is not open to the more junior ministers (such as the current Minister Mary Collins, who also serves as Associate Minister of National Defence), who are not members of the top cabinet committee. On the other hand, the more junior portfolio may enable such ministers to devote more time and energy to status of women issues and to policy monitoring for gender impact in their other portfolio.

Thus Mary Collins (1991: 3) has claimed in an interview published in *Perspectives*, the quarterly newsletter issued by SWC and distributed at no cost to 14,000 recipients across the country, that much of her effort as Associate Minister of National Defence is devoted to human resources. Collins claimed to have gained 'a great deal of satisfaction in announcing in 1989 the opening of all Canadian Forces trades and occupations to women (the sole exception being submarine duty)', and in working on improvements in 'the harmonization of the work and family responsibilities of our service personnel', since 'military life imposes special burdens on families'.

The Canadian Advisory Council on the Status of Women (CACSW)

The policy development/co-ordinating role of the less visible, 'Mandarin' SWC and its provincial and territorial counterparts should not be confused with the 'Missionary' advisory and consultative function of the Canadian Advisory Council on the Status of Women (CACSW) and comparable provincial and territorial bodies. The Council's mandate is to act as a conduit for information from women across Canada to the federal government on all issues of concern to women, carry out and publish research studies on women's issues, bring before the public matters of interest and concern to women, and present briefs to parliamentary and government committees studying issues of particular concern to women. Established in 1973 as a response to another recommendation of the Royal Commission, CACSW is in theory an independent organisation funded by the government. In the 1987–88 fiscal year, CACSW budget was $3.2 million (Status of Women Canada, 1987).

The Council is composed of a maximum of 27 part-time and three full-time members (a president and two regional vice-presidents) who are appointed by the federal Cabinet through Orders-in-Council. The only objective criterion that is used in appointments to the Council is a balanced regional representation. This has left the government open to charges of patronage, and to related criticisms that its practice of appointing Council members rewards political loyalty rather than expertise on women's issues, and as such compromises the independence of the Council. Some critics have argued that in recent years, the pro-government conservative leanings of a number of Council members have compromised the highly regarded capacity of CACSW to produce independent, credible in-depth research on a variety of women's issues.[3] Thus Sweet (1987) charges that pro-corporate political interference from Council members distorted research findings of a major resource book on women's economic status, which the Council members, appointed by the Conservative government, considered too anti-business and too much in favour of labour and unions. Such accusations were, of course, disputed by the Council's president.

A more direct case of political interference in the Council's work by the Minister Responsible for the Status of Women, which eventually backfired on the government, occurred during the process of patriation of Canada's constitution from Great Britain. In 1980, CACSW commissioned a series of papers on the implications of the proposed constitutional Charter of Rights on women, and began to plan for a national conference on 'Women and the Constitution'. On 5 January 1981 the CACSW Conference was cancelled at the request of Lloyd Axworthy, who was then the Minister Responsible for the Status of Women. Axworthy used partisan manipulation to convince the predominantly Liberal appointed Council of the political necessity to cancel the conference and instead hold a series of regional conferences.

CACSW president, Doris Anderson, the former editor of Canada's popular English-language women's magazine, *Chateleine*, and a well-known feminist and Liberal, resigned publicly, accusing the minister of interference in the autonomy of the Council. The cancellation of the conference and Anderson's resignation led to successful mobilisation of women's groups from across Canada, an alternative conference on women and the constitution, and the eventual entrenchment of women's equality in the constitutional Charter of Rights and Freedoms (Kome, 1983; Gotell, 1990).

Over the years the Council 'has experienced incredible tensions and conflicts – displayed in ongoing problems with the staff, dissention among members over Council recommendations, difficulties in setting priorities, poor relations between the Council and Status of Women' (Findlay, 1988b: 90). These problems can be attributed to CACSW's structurally marginal position with respect to both the government and the women's movement. Unlike SWC and other women's advisors within the bureaucracy, the Council has no easy access to government policy-making process. Yet, as we noted, because of patronage, the advisory body is often perceived by grass-root feminists as being too close to the government and as failing to accurately represent their views.

The Women's Programme of the Department of Secretary of State

Several other federal agencies with specific responsibility for delivering programmes to Canadian women were also created during the 1970s. The most important of these is the Women's Program of the Department of Secretary of State, whose official mandate is to administer grants to women's equal rights organisations and social service groups (e.g. rape crisis centres, women's refuges, educational counselling groups) at the national, regional and local level. The Program's official objectives are 'to promote public understanding of women's equality issues, assist in the organizational development of women's groups working toward equality for women, and encourage institutions to incorporate women's equality concerns in their decision-making structures, policies and programs'. The first budget of the Women's Program was only $223 000, but in 1989–90, over 750 women's groups received funding from a total budget of $13.2 million (Status of Women Canada, 1989b: 151).

Government funding has provided women's groups with financial stability, and improved their claim to legitimacy. However, the availability of government funding has restricted their freedom to develop their own set of policy directions. In order to obtain funding, women's groups have had to adjust their priorities according to prevailing granting guidelines set by the government. As Burt (1990: 199) has argued,

> the government controls the groups' agenda by setting a priority list of funding. For example, in 1983–84, funding priorities were violence against women, communication, and women in the economy. In addition, the government directs money to be spent in specific activity areas, requires its approval for budget transfers, and, according to some groups, discourages service providers from taking public stands on issues related to women.

Over the years, the Women's Program has been embroiled in several controversies. According to Findlay (1987: 39–40), the Women's Program's first Director, the Women's Program was set up strategically by feminists who had decided that 'the resources of the state could be used to support the development of the women's movement' in a department that had a history of creating programmes for the 'disadvantaged'. For a time, femocrats in the Women's Program were able to retain their strong 'Missionary' orientation, because,

> unlike most women who were appointed as advisors in other departments, those in what officially became the Women's Program in 1974 held themselves responsible to the women's movement rather than to government priorities. All were defined as feminists and were largely drawn from feminist groups. Liaison with the women's movement was built into every aspect of the Program's work. A feminist perspective clearly determined the Program's development, and was reflected in project definition, staff recruitment, and the Program's organization and management.

The relative autonomy from bureaucratic supervision and account-ability is attributed by Findlay (1987) to the *ad hoc* nature and relative invisibility of the Program and to the successful rescue by the Women's Program of the credibility of the government's International Women's Year Program. Over time, the Women's Program mandate became much more visible, and subject to attacks from right-wing politicians and Canada's major anti-feminist organisation, REAL Women.

REAL is an acronym standing for *Realistic, Equal, Active, for Life*. Launched in 1983 in response to the proposal of the then Minister Responsible for the Status of Women, Judy Erola, to scrap the tax exemption for dependent spouses, REAL's backlash politics has focused on the government funding for non-governmental feminist organisations. In their view, the Women's Programme funding is the 'lifeblood' of the feminist movement (Erwin, 1988). As an organisation explicitly com-mitted to *not* promoting women's equality, REAL was refused funding from the Women's Programme on several occasions on the grounds that it does not meet criteria of eligibility. With the help of several right-wing Tory MPs and media hungry for sensational stories, REAL has tried to make the most out of the fact that a lesbian organisation was offered Secretary of State funding while REAL was not. In accordance with the recommendations in the 1987 report of the Standing Committee on the Secretary of State, 'Fairness in Funding', REAL received some funding in 1989.

Partly as a result of the controversy, partly as a result of lobbying from right-wing anti-feminist Tory backbenchers, and partly as a result of government's attempts to cut budgets of all departments with grant pro-grammes in order to reduce the federal deficit, the federal government had been seriously reconsidering its policy of funding 'Missionary' activities of groups critical of the government (Interview, Status of Women, 13 December 1989). The recent thinking of the Tory govern-ment was that the public advocacy process had gone far enough and that for budgetary and partisan political reasons, Women's Program funding had to be reduced. In April 1990, core operational funding was cut from numerous feminist organisations which support and publish feminist research (e.g. Canadian Research Institute for the Advancement of Women, Resources for Feminist Research, Healthsharing), and from social services providers – groups that make counselling, referral, educa-tional, or shelter services available to women in communities across Canada.

By substituting irregular project funding for stable operational funding, the Conservative government indicated that its primary interest lies in increased state control over, rather than empowerment of, grass-roots feminist organisations. However, after a large-scale nation- wide feminist protest, and after the refusal of the provinces to pick up funding for women's shelters, rape crisis centres and other federally funded services run by the women's voluntary organisations, core funding to women's centres was restored. The feminist service providers won largely on economic grounds, because they were able to demon- strate that their programmes, run to a large extent by volunteers, save the government a lot of money. Organisations which support and publish feminist research could not resort to such an argument, and their core funding was not restored.

Thus, it would appear that feminism within government functions best when there is a sympathetic government, reacting to strong pressure from feminist groups outside the government and its own civil servants. In turn, external feminist advocacy is most effective when there is an organisational structure within the government which can follow up on feminist demands and translate them into policy. Internal pressure by SWC and external lobbying by various women's organisations can take credit for the initiation of enlightened policies for government-funded services related to wife battering, child sex abuse and other form of family violence; for insisting that 50 per cent of recipients of the Canadian Scholarship Program must be women; for changes in the Canadian Jobs Strategy (a vocational traning and continuing education programme); for upgrading programmes and services offered to feder-ally sentenced women; and for placing the issues of women's economic equality and the integration of work and family on the agenda of annual First Ministers' Conferences, the top national policy-making body (Status of Women Canada, 1987; Minister of Supply and Services Canada, 1990).

At the provincial level, feminists inside and outside the government successfully influenced the development of Ontario's 1987 Pay Equity Act. According to Findlay (1991: 94),

it was the Equal Pay Coalition that led the feminist struggle for pay equity reforms – defining and coordinating the response to govern-ment proposals and articulating compromises that were acceptable to the majority of feminists. It was femocrats in the Ontario Women's Directorate who organized the development of legislative proposals for pay equity within the state as well as the public consultations on them.

First Ministers' Conferences (FMCs)

Chaired by the Prime Minister and attended by the leaders of government of each of the ten provinces and, as observers, the two territories, FMCs are held twice a year on a wide range of subjects. In 1984, two provincial Premiers, who were simultaneously also the Ministers Responsible for the Status of Women in their provinces, successfully lobbied the Prime Minister to hold in 1985 a First Ministers' Conference on Women and the Economy. The conference was also presented as an occasion to mark the end of the United Nations Decade for Women (1976–85). In February 1985, part of the agenda of FMC was devoted to the theme of 'Women and the Economy', with specific emphasis on the impact on women of national economic policies on investment, trade, regional economic development and job traning.

The November 1985 FMC on the economy endorsed an omnibus document prepared by the Status of Women Canada entitled *A Framework for Economic Equality for Canadian Women*. The document identified labour force equality as key to economic equality, and directed Ministers Responsible for the Status of Women and ministers responsible for labour market matters to develop a strategy and mechanisms to facilitate on going co-operation on issues related to labour force equality. Improving women's educational and training opportunities, and specifically their job skills, was singled out as a first step to women's ability to compete effectively in the labour market. Accordingly, another document, *Towards a Labour Force Strategy: A Framework for Training Women*, containing nineteen specific measures and a commitment to four specific data collection and evaluation measures, was prepared for the November 1986 meeting of First Ministers. Several lower-level ministerial meetings were held subsequently on implementation of measures outlined in the framework. A progress report was considered at the November 1987 FMC (Government of Canada, 1987).

The integration of work and family responsibilities was identified as another important measure which could be undertaken to improve women's disadvantaged position in the labour market. An SWC background paper on the topic, *Integration of Work and Family Responsibilities: Report on Strategies*, was endorsed by the November 1989 FMC. The document is of particular relevance to this study, because it deals with the development, consolidation and monitoring of policies and programmes in areas such as childcare, parental and family leave, flexible work arrangements, part-time work, and gender-neutral division of labour. The proposed integrative strategy will be discussed in more detail in Parts II and III of this study.

Thus state feminist commitment to broadly defined women's equality and positive action seems to be well entrenched in Canada, and women's policy machinery at both federal and provincial levels enjoys strong bi-partisan support. Canada's women's policy machinery has made an important contribution to the acceptance of women's equality as a legitimate issue on the economic and social policy agendas of the state, and to the development of policies and services that have addressed the specific needs of many women. The network linking women's groups with the state has evolved from a largely state-directed policy network in the 1960s, to a clientele relationship in the 1970s, and a pressure pluralist network in the 1980s. In the 1960s, when there were few vocal feminist groups drawn into the network of government funding and policy participation, women's policy initatives came primarily from government agencies, such as the Women's Bureau or Health and Welfare Canada. The emergence of strong liberal feminism inside and outside government in the 1970s created an effective clientele relationship. Status of Women Canada developed close links with feminist groups, especially NAC and the National Association of Women and the Law. In turn, these liberal feminist groups underwent organisational development that equipped them to move from policy advocacy to policy participation (Burt, 1990).

As the groups have become more diverse and fragmented, partly as a consequence of government funding, the policy network based on clientele relationship broke down, and was replaced by a pressure pluralist network. Combined with the plurality of interests represented within women's groups is the new climate of privatisation. Since the election of the Conservative government in 1984, economic rationalism and privatisation have become as important as the equal rights mentality in setting policy limits. Burt (1990: 209) predicts that in the future, the Canadian government

> may be reluctant to act on status of women issues, or may move away from feminist positions in its policy directions . . . it will become increasingly easy for governments to refuse to act, on the grounds that the 'women's lobby' is divided. Alternatively, governments may select policies that correspond with their own pre-set goals, comfortable in the knowledge that, within the new plurality of interests represented among groups, they can find support for their actions.

As we shall see in the next section, the same scenario may be emerging in Australia, despite the fact that in the 1980s Australia had become *the* model of how to introduce feminism into government.

WOMEN'S POLICY MACHINERY IN AUSTRALIA

Australia's women's policy machinery is in many respects similar to that of Canada. The Minister Responsible for the Status of Women, SWC, the policy integration mechanisms in sectoral departments and CACSW have their Australian counterparts in the Minister Assisting the Prime Minister on the Status of Women, Office of the Status of Women (OSW), women's desk officers and women's bureaux in various functional departments, and the National Women's Consultative Council (NWCC). Provincial equivalents have their state counterparts. Other similarities between the two countries include the strong influence of liberal feminism, manifested in the establishment of major lobbying organisations (NAC in Canada, Women's Electoral Lobby in Australia) and in the alliance between 'new' feminist and 'traditional' women's organisations; government funding for a large number of women's voluntary community groups; and the lack of an effective anti-feminist opposition to the feminist influence in government. The most important features which distinguish Australia from Canada include extensive debates within the women's movement and the Australian Labor Party (ALP) on the most appropriate form of machinery, and the development of distinctive monitoring mechanisms such as the Women's Budget Program and longitudinal gender equality indicators.

Women's Electoral Lobby (WEL) and femocrats

The Women's Electoral Lobby (WEL) was formed in Melbourne in February 1972 to prepare for the Australian federal election due later that year. Modelled on the National Organization of Women (NOW), the liberal reform-oriented strand of the US feminist movement, WEL's main concern was to place the six basic demands of the Australian Women's Liberation Movement (WLM) – free, safe abortion on demand; free contraception; 24-hour childcare; equal employment opportunity; equal pay; and equal access to education – on the political agenda of the federal campaign.

Following the electoral guide published by *Ms* magazine in

preparation for the US Presidential campaign, candidates in the Australian federal campaign were surveyed, interviewed and graded according to their (generally poor) knowledge of, and attitudes towards, the six basic feminist demands. By the end of the campaign, WEL had established important contacts with the major political parties, yet it remained an autonomous non-partisan organisation, with no constitution or hierarchical structure, and with members from across the political spectrum. Most women joined WEL 'to gain political experience in lobbying, writing submissions and press releases, speaking in the media and generating interest in the WEL objectives. By the end of 1972 WEL had a membership of about 1700' (Ryan, 1990: 73).

In time, WEL proved highly effective in translating the demands of the women's movement into a public policy agenda and in providing a political training ground for many women who moved into important political and bureaucratic positions. A survey of state and federal women MPs in 1985 found that 28 per cent had been, or were still, WEL members. In 1990, two out of the three women cabinet ministers in South Australia were former WEL activists, and three out of the four in Western Australia, including the state Premier (Sawer, 1991). The Canberra-based WEL branch in the Australian Capital Territory (ACT) played a particularly important role in the lobbying of parliamentarians, government ministers and their staff, and in supplying its own members for policy-making positions. According to Ryan (1990: 73), many members of WEL ACT,

had lived in the US where they had joined the National Organization of Women (NOW). Now they were underemployed or even unemployed without any opportunities to test their skills and experience. . . . It was WEL ACT which lobbied for the appointment of a women's adviser, for anti-discrimination legislation and for equal opportunity programmes. Between 1973 and 1975, WEL ACT maintained strong pressure upon the Whitlam government to pursue an integrated child care policy, to introduce the supporting mothers' benefit and abortion legislation. . . . As a liberal feminist organisation concerned with equal opportunity, its goals suited the Whitlam government's radical liberal concerns, and fitted the national mood. At a time when Aboriginals were demanding land rights and the White Australia policy was being laid to rest, Women's Liberation as the stormtroopers and Women's Electoral Lobby as the pragmatic face of feminism found a space in the political agenda that had previously not existed.

Women's adviser to the Prime Minister

The decision to appoint a women's adviser to the Prime Minister was the result of a suggestion made by Gail Radford (Wilenski), then convenor of WEL ACT, to Peter Wilenski, then principal private secretary to the Prime Minister, Gough Whitlam. The selection of Elizabeth Reid – a feminist activist and a senior tutor in philosophy at the Australian National University (ANU) in Canberra – as women's adviser in April 1973, 'was the first step in the evolution of the current Office of the Status of Women. As with all such victories, WEL had to follow up immediately with lobbying for adequate resources for the new position' (Sawer, 1990: 8–9).

Reid's position was a political rather than a career bureaucratic appointment, since it was held at the whim of the Prime Minister. According to Sawer (1990: 10), the position was originally envisaged as

one of a number of positions in the Prime Minister's Office providing private advice to the Prime Minister. Instead it became a very public position, because of press interest, the expectations that were raised, and Reid's own conception of her role. Whitlam allowed this development, whereby a staffer took on a highly visible (some said even quasi-ministerial) role.

Reid's combined consultative and co-ordinating function resulted in an enormous workload. During the first two years of her appointment, she was involved in travelling across Australia and listening to women talk about their problems; changing the direction of the pre-school and childcare programme; arranging the monitoring of Cabinet submissions and their impact upon women; committing the government to major political and financial support for International Women's Year; and answering the huge volume of correspondence that her appointment had generated. She was seen as a major point of access to government by women in the community, and received more letters than anyone else in the government other than the Prime Minister. She was also faced with tremendous press hostility, and vocal opposition to her appointment by the more radical wing of the women's movement (Ryan, 1990: 75; Sawer, 1990: 9–20).

Not only could the 'PM Supergirl' do nothing right for the press, but her appointment and her high salary were seen by many feminists as a sellout to feminism. Her successors would face similar accusations. As Summers (1986: 60), herself a subject of feminist abuse for wearing makeup, put it, 'there has been an almost unwholesome eagerness to find fault with such appointees, to criticize them for what they say, for their silences, even for their clothes'. In her view, one outcome of these consternations had been 'a divided and consequently weakened women's movement, one which politicians can more easily ignore'.

In 1974, the Department of Prime Minister and Cabinet (PM&C) agreed to establish a small Women's Affairs Section within its Welfare Division – incidentally the same location where the Office of the Coordinator, Status of Women Canada, started out. The mandate of the Section was 'to attend to Elizabeth Reid's correspondence, some of which formed the basis of policy initiatives, to prepare briefings and speech notes for her and for the Prime Minister on women's issues, and to monitor Cabinet submissions as they affected women' (quoted in Ryan, 1990: 75).

Sara Dowse, another feminist activist associated with WEL ACT, became the head of the Women's Affairs Section. Following the abolition of the women's adviser position and Elizabeth Reid's resignation in October 1975, Dowse was appointed to head the upgraded Women's Affairs Branch. She was to make a lasting contribution to the development of the distinctive women's policy machinery that characterises Australia to this date.

Introducing feminist machinery of government

The question of how to introduce a feminist machinery of government was the subject of much discussion by WEL members and the first femocrats who were brought into the Whitlam government during the years 1973–75. The answer, presented as a paper by Dowse at the International Women's Year Women and Politics Conference in 1975, was a centre-periphery model of women's affairs machinery. Conceived as a network rather than as a hierarchy, the centre-periphery model was seen as more appropriate to the non-hierarchical philosophy of the feminist movement than a traditional vertical integration. The proposal was sometimes also expressed in terms of a wheel, of which the Women's Affairs Branch formed the hub and the units in the sectoral departments formed the spokes.

This novel approach to administration was endorsed by both the outgoing Whitlam government and the incoming conservative administration of Malcolm Fraser. Early in 1976 Fraser accepted the proposal that the Women's Affairs Branch (WAB) would become the nucleus of a network of women's policy units to be established in various policy departments.

By 1977 ten such units were established in the Departments of Health, Education, Attorney-General, Social Security, Aboriginal Affairs, Immigration and Ethnic Affairs, Environment, Housing and Community Development, the Schools Commission and the Australian Development Assistance Bureau. These units supplemented the already existing Women's Bureau in the Department of Employment and Industrial Relations. Fraser also authorised the establishment of a co-ordinating mechanism for the women's units, the Interdepartmental Working Group on Women's Affairs, chaired by the Women's Affairs Branch (Dowse, 1988: 215–16; Sawer, 1990: 35–36).

Thus the period of the first Fraser administration was one of consolidation and growth of women's policy machinery, at both the federal and the state level. In June 1976, Fraser appointed the first Minister Assisting the Prime Minister in Women's Affairs. The federal Labor opposition allocated a shadow portfolio in this area only in 1979, when Senator Susan Ryan became Shadow Secretary for Women's Affairs in addition to her other portfolio responsibilities. Unfortunately, Fraser's support for an effective wheel of women's machinery did not last very long. Following the 1977 federal election, the renamed Ofice of Women's Affairs was transferred to a newly created Department of Home Affairs and Environment, the second lowest ranking ministry. Sara Dowse resigned in protest, thus making the location of the Office a political issue and paving the way for its eventual return to the PM&C after Hawke Labor victory in 1983.

The relocation of the Office to such a low-ranking ministry made it very difficult to gain access to and comment on Cabinet submissions, and to have a guaranteed voice in the budget process. Having been downgraded from a central co-ordinating department to a peripheral one, the Office of Women's Affairs was no longer able to play an effective role as the hub of the women's affairs wheels, and the Interdepartmental Working Group gradually became moribund as women's units in sectoral departments became weaker. Gradually, only specific 'women's issues' were referred to them,

> to be dealt with in isolation from overall departmental policy development and planning. This marginalisation ran contrary to the intent that adequate monitoring of all policy take place at its point of origin, placing an increasing burden on the Office. Often women's policy advisers did not hear of important submissions before they were picked up by the head of the Office. (Sawer, 1990: 49)

The co-ordinating role of the Office increasingly depended on the bureaucratic politicking of its director. Its focus became more and more restricted to attempts to develop and influence increasingly 'elusive' social policies (Dowse, 1988: 219).

Despite predictions that the Office would disappear, it survived and had some resounding successes, especially towards the end of the Fraser period. The survival of the Office owes a great deal to the political skills and capacity for lateral thinking of Kathleen Taperell, who took over from Dowse as the Head of the Office (Sawer, 1990: 48). Faced with a hostile political environment, the Office had to maintain a low profile. Taperell's goals were

> to keep the Office and the women's units alive, to develop networks outside the bureaucracy, to liaise with feminist bureaucracies in the States, to promote sex discrimination legislation, to promote Australia's role in relation to women in the international sphere and to support the extension of EEO in the Commonwealth Public Service.
> (Ryan, 1990: 81)

While the low profile of the Office secured the desired minimal attention from the hostile Right, it exacerbated tensions between feminists inside and outside the bureaucracy. Feeling cut off from its natural constituency in the women's movement, many femocrats felt isolated and without a political base. In turn, the apparent lack of a strong constituency made the Office and the women's units a natural target for cuts when the small government faction became more influential after the 1980 election. In 1981, the Review of Commonwealth Functions (Razor Gang) recommended the dismantling of the machinery. In the event the machinery survived, but the wheel (that is, the Office) lost most of its spokes (that is, departmental women's units), though only temporarily.

In 1983, the Fraser government was replaced by a new Labor administration, which came to power with the most developed women's platform of any Australian government to date. The women's electoral platform was set out in the 1982 policy document *The ALP and Women: Towards Equality*. Drafted by Sara Dowse, it included promises of immediate anti-discrimination legislation, a programme of affirmative action in public and private sector employment, and a relatively high status, well-resourced Office of the Status of Women within the Department of PM&C.

Senator Susan Ryan, as Minister Assisting the Prime Minister on the

Status of Women from 1983 to 1988, and as a senior Cabinet Minister of Education, was to play a vital role in translating the Labor platform into reality. Labor's swift implementation of several of the major planks of its women's policy was undoubtedly also guided by the recognition that women swing voters had helped to deliver electoral victory (Summers, 1986: 63–4; Sawer, 1990: 62–6, 69).

The Office of the Status of Women

The Office of the Status of Women (OSW) was given its current title in 1982, to bring it in line with the terminology used by the UN. Since its return in 1983 to the Department of PM&C, and its upgrading to a Division, the Office has been engaged in a broad range of activities. Its key function has been to provide relevant policy advice to the Prime Minister and the Minister Assisting the Prime Minister for the Status of Women, and to monitor Cabinet and budget material for its impact on women. The central location of OSW in the Department of PM&C makes it relatively easy for the Office to monitor all departmental proposals and submissions to Cabinet, and to analyse the cumulative impact of such proposals on women.

However, influencing policy at such a late stage is quite difficult. By the time a policy proposal reaches the Department of PM&C, it usually cannot be significantly altered because there are too many vested interests involved. Thus regular networking with women's desk officers (WDOs) and women's bureaux in sectoral departments is often more important in effecting policy than the monitoring role at the central office. The Hawke government decided in 1984 that all Commonwealth departments should have women's units or their equivalents. The function of these units is the same as that of 'integrative mechanisms' in Canada: to ensure that all departmental policies, not just those specifically designed for women, have a positive impact on them. Regular meetings of WDOs with OSW were inaugurated in 1986 to strengthen the day-to-day co-ordination function of women's policy machinery and to provide support for sometimes isolated WDOs.

The Women's Bureau in the Department of Employment, Education and Training (DEET), the oldest women's unit (established in 1963), with its own grant and publications programme, co-operates quite closely with OSW (Commonwealth of Australia, 1989). However, the major economic departments are quite hostile to OSW, thus hampering its co-ordinating function. The low priority attached to gender impact evaluation by these rival co-ordinating departments is reinforced by the absence of women from key forums for economic decision making such as the Expenditure Review Committee of Cabinet. The tripartite formula favoured by the Hawke government for consultations (unions, employers and government) also tends to work against women's interests (Sawer, 1990: 90; Interview, Victoria Women's Policy Co-ordinating Unit, 20 February 1990; Interview, OSW, 27 February 1990).

OSW's mandate also involves the co-ordination of the annual preparation of the Women's Budget Statement (one of the budget-related papers tabled on Federal Budget night each year); the communication and consultation with community groups on a variety of issues of importance to women; sponsorship of various research projects aimed at improving the status of women (e.g. a cost benefit study of employer-provided childcare, a commissioned research on financial and retirement planning by women at different stages of their life); the maintainance of an ongoing register of women able to serve on various boards and advisory bodies, so as to increase their representation; co-operation with international bodies concerned with the status of women; convening and chairing special advisory or consultative bodies (e.g. the National Working Party on the Portrayal of Women in the Media, the Commonwealth/State Domestic Violence Task Force and the Task Force on Non-English Speaking Background Women's Issues); publishing a quarterly newsletter, *OSWOMEN*; and providing secretariats both for the National Women's Consultative Council (NWCC) and for the Secretaries' Taskforce on the Status of Women (made up of the heads of Commonwealth departments and chaired by the Secretary of the Department of PM&C) (OSW, 1989a). OSW also administers a grants scheme providing annual operational grants to twelve national women's organisations and project grants for small-scale programmes of activities or research. In 1988–9, $100 000 was given in operational grants and $200 000 was allocated for 37 projects throughout Australia. The funds available are considerably smaller than the $12.4 million (Cdn.) budget of the Canadian Secretary of State's Women's Program. However, women's centres and services, which in Canada are funded mainly by the federal government, are in Australia funded by the states.

As in Canada, these local services are run by women for women. They make community resources more accessible to women, especially to those who are isolated at home and lack self-confidence to approach the 'government', but are happy to speak to women who may have had experiences similar to their own (Commonwealth of Australia, 1989: 28). Feminist activists who staff these agencies encourage women to consider as unacceptable circumstances to which they had long acquiesced, such as domestic violence or the demeaning treatment of single mothers (Levi and Singleton, 1991). Women's health centres have empowered women to regain control over their own health. Government funding has been also made available for re-entry, confidence-building, training and education programmes for women who have left the workforce (Sawer, 1990: 251).

Over the years, there has been a general shift of machinery activities from a pattern of active lobbying for new women's policies, programmes and approaches towards a pattern focusing on the co-ordination and monitoring of existing departmental programmes and policies. Relying on administrative mechanisms and assuming the mantle of bureaucratic respectability is very much the 'Mandarin' approach (Summers, 1986: 63). This drift towards 'Mandarin' state feminism has been reinforced both by the drop in grass-roots feminist activism, and by its fragmentation into a variety of specific causes such as the environment, health, racism, immigrant women, poverty, violence against women, feminist research and publishing. The links among these various groups are quite weak, with the result that the political pressure needed for broad pro-active lobbying, and for the consolidation of feminist gains in government, is not always available. Like Status of Women Canada, the Australian OSW is generally perceived to be far removed from the lives of ordinary women, a perception reinforced by OSW mandate to co-ordinate but not directly deliver specific services to women.

Women's units in functional departments, such as the Women's Bureau in DEET, are closer to the day-to-day problems of employed women, and as such perceive themselves to be more radical and client oriented than OSW, but even DEET's Women's Bureau is involved in policy advice and co-ordination. The policy advisory/co-ordinating role is confusing to most people and even the government does not fully understand it, let alone women's groups. When grass-roots feminists (negatively) evaluate femocrats, they often forget that femocrats are civil servants rather than protest politicians. Femocrats are generally not free to operate independently of their host agency or government department. They cannot take on the role of autonomous politicians and publicly demand, defend or denounce (as the case may be) specific government policies relating to women.

OSW also chairs quarterly meetings of Commonwealth, State, and Territory women's advisers, who are the heads of central women's policy units. Recently, the head of the Ministry of Women's Affairs in New Zealand has also attended these meetings. In the late 1970s and early 1980s, the then twice-yearly meetings were genuinely co-operative, and

an important source of mutual political support. A great deal of time was
devoted to mutual sharing of information, and to informal strategising.
When specific policy problems arose, the advisers would lobby and/or
write joint or individual letters to the various levels of government on
the specific issues of concern. However, in recent years, federal issues
have tended to dominate the agenda. There is a perception on the part
of the state women's advisers that OSW is less interested in genuine
sharing of information, and more interested in getting strategic information from the states (Sawer, 1990: 141; Interview, Victoria Women's
Policy Co-ordinating Unit, 20 February 1990).

In 1989–90, OSW had a budget of $3 571 400, of which $2039 was
spent on programmes and the remainder on salaries and administration.
Among its staff of 37, most were based in Canberra. There were two
regional information offices in Hobart and Brisbane, the capital cities of
the two states without a women's policy machinery. However, by the end
of 1989 both Tasmania and Queensland were in the process of setting
up their own machinery, planning to absorb the current OSW information services into their own structures (OSW, 1989a; Commonwealth of
Australia, 1989).

Women's Budget Statement

At the same time as the Hawke government upgraded OSW, it
established the special Task Force on the Status of Women, made up of
heads of departments whose policies most affected women. The Task
force has been instrumental in securing some key machinery initiatives
such as the restoration of women's units in sectoral departments and the
introduction of the women's budget process.

The Women's Budget Program (later renamed Women's Budget Statement) requires all public sector agencies to produce annually detailed
assessments of the impact of their programmes and activities on women,
for release as a Budget Document on Budget Night. The preparation
of the document (running to 300 pages) is co-ordinated by OSW in
conjuction with departmental desk officers. In addition to the analysis of
gender outcomes of past and future expenditures, the document also
outlines the government's progress in implementing the *National
Agenda for Women*. Largely the initiative of Anne Summers, Head of
OSW during 1983–6, the Women's Budget Program (WBP) was introduced on a trial basis in 1984, when it covered thirteen departments.
From 1985 onwards, all federal departments and agencies became

accountable for the gender equity impact of their programmes and policies.

For departments with large female clientele, such as education or welfare, both the collection and the disaggregated analysis of data on a gender basis posed few problems. However, for many 'mainstream' bureaucrats, who had traditionally regarded public administration as gender neutral and who did not give much thought to differential gender outcomes of policies and programmes, the exercise presented something of a challenge. At the beginning, a number of the economic departments resisted producing disaggregated analysis of the impact of their policies, claiming that their policies and programmes were gender neutral.

However, over time even the Treasury became more sensitised to issues of gender equity. While the early Treasury contributions to WBP provided no analysis of differential impact of the taxation system on women and men, a recent statement mentions a review of taxation laws for consistency with the Sex Discrimination Act, an amendment to the law concerning the taxing of maintenance payments so as to remove its discriminatory features, benefits to one-income families in tax rebates, and the recognition of the cost of children through increased family allowance (Sawer, 1990: 230–1; OSW, 1989b: 223–6).

The comprehensive disaggregated analyses presented in the annual Women's Budget Statements are now regarded as exemplary within the UN, Commonwealth, and OECD bodies concerned with the status of women. However, the women's budget process is unlikely to be emulated in Canada. The dominant view in Status of Women Canada is that the adoption of such a mechanism would merely give rise to a large, self-perpetuating bureaucratic industry, which would produce a lot of self-justifying documents without being able to exert much pressure on the government to reorient its policies (Interview, SWC, 13 December 1989). Such fears are not completely without foundation.

While in the early years the WBP played an important educational role in sensitising departments to their impact on women in the community, in recent years the WBS has become less of a critical exercise in departmental evaluation and more of a public relations exercise in departmental self-justification. Moreover, because so many recent budgetary decisions have been taken at the last minute by the Expenditure Review Committee of Cabinet, they were either not included at all in the WBS, or only briefly mentioned, with no accompanying analysis of their disproportionate effect on women. For example, in 1986 WBS made no mention of $1.3 million (over 25 per cent) cut to Human Rights Commission's Budget, affecting its ability to promote and implement the

Sex Discrimination Act. Also, several decisions with a particularly deleterious effect on women (such as the means testing of family allowance adopted in May 1987) were taken in May mini-budgets. No gender impact analyses were prepared for these budgetary decisions, although they were eventually included in subsequent WBSs (Sawer, 1990: 233).

The WBSs are public documents which are made widely available to various women's organisations. However, because WBSs have so far lacked cross-portfolio analyses of the cumulative impact of government policies on women, they have not been widely used by non-governmental organisations in analysing the impact of budgets on women. The dry bureaucratic style has also prevented WBSs from becoming an effective mechanism for providing easily digestible information to the general public, or for selling government women's policy achievements (Sawer, 1990: 235).

The National Agenda for Women

Underpinning much of OSW work is the *National Agenda for Women*, based on the Nairobi FLS. As we noted in the previous chapter, Australia was one of the first countries to translate Nairobi FLS into a national plan of action till the year 2000. The Prime Minister, Bob Hawke, presented a first outline of the *Agenda* in Parliament in November 1985. Its major themes were 'a say, a choice, a fair go'. An extensive period of consultation followed, with some 25 000 women filling out questionnaires, making submissions, or participating in meetings or conferences, some subsidised by the government. A report of the result of these consultations, called *Setting the Agenda*, was published in 1987 (Sawer, 1990: 241–2).

The *National Agenda* was launched by the Prime Minister in February 1988 as a comprehensive umbrella document covering government achievements, specific objectives for the year 2000, and action plans for the next five years. It also included national programmes to be developed in areas of shared jurisdiction such as education, employment and health (OSW, 1989c; Commonwealth of Australia, 1989). However, the specific budget initiatives associated with the agenda were relatively small, amounting to $1.6 million for a three-year national domestic violence campaign and $5.1 million for health initiatives relating to breast and cervical cancer screening, also over three years. Women's groups have criticised the *National Agenda* for its lack of specific commitments in the area of childcare and pay equity (Sawer, 1990: 242).

One of the most important and innovative aspects of the *National Agenda* was the inclusion of statistical gender equity indicators for measuring women's economic and social progress. Presented in the form of bar graphs, the gender equality indicators track the situation of women relative to men in various areas such as educational attainment, labour force participation, occupational segregation, representation in management and parliament, income distribution, access to super-annuation, and consumption of analgesics. The fifteen gender equality indicators include two that measure the use of formal childcare and the availability of childcare for women who want to work. Both the value of the indicators and their rate of convergence to a value of 1 (which re-presents gender equality) are important in monitoring women's progress and the effectiveness of the Government's plan of action (OSW, 1989d).

An annual implementation report of the *National Agenda for Women*, together with an annual update of the gender equality indicators, are now included in WBSs. The annual monitoring against the objectives established in the *National Agenda* and against gender equality indicators provides a useful mechanism for measuring government performance on a longitudinal basis. However, as Sawer (1990: 243) argues, 'like other performance measures, it will be effective only if it is used as a lever by women in the community as well as by women within government'.

The National Women's Advisory (Consultative) Council

The National Women's Advisory Council (NWAC) was established in 1978, after a period of national consultation conducted by a working party. As Sawer (1990: 42) argues, 'it was recognised (after the sacrifice of Elizabeth Reid during the Whitlam period) that it was unwise to com-bine the policy development/co-ordinating roles with the consultative functions. The provision of a separate mechanism for public consultation was intended to deflect public controversy from the Office and enable it to get on with policy work.' After some discussion within the Office, it was decided to let the government make the appointments, 'and to rely on these relatively conservative women being radicalised by prolonged exposure to the issues during consultation processes'.

In fact, many of the appointments were made on the advice of the Office of Women's Affairs. As in Canada, members were chosen on the basis of regional representation – there was a woman from each state. Each member was also an informal representative of a major women's organisation and of an important sectoral interest. Thus the first Council included an Aboriginal woman, a migrant woman, the president of the Family Planning Association (also a leading member of WEL), a prominent member from the Country Women's Asssociation, and an ACTU representative (Ryan, 1990: 82).

The Convenor of NWAC from 1978–82 was Beryl Beaurepaire, a prominent Liberal (she was Vice-President of the Victorian Division of the Liberal Party). Under her astute leadership, the Council played an important role in converting traditional women's organisations towards supporting feminist demands, in raising the public profile of women's affairs in a much more positive way than had occurred during the controversial activities of IWY, in maintaining bi-partisan support for women's policy machinery, in effectively lobbying against federal attempts to withdraw medical benefit funding for abortions, and in sponsoring pioneering social research relevant to the needs of migrant women, mothers of disabled children and other disadvantaged women. NWAC also commissioned an important study by Meredith Edwards (1981) on financial arrangements within families. Edwards challenged the widely held belief that families pool resources, and provided valuable evidence for resisting policies that assumed that fiscal welfare extended to a male breadwinner will be as a rule equitably shared with the rest of the family.

NWAC also played an invaluable role in deflecting anti-feminist criticism of women's policy machinery. Most of the effort of the major Australian anti-feminist organisation – Women Who Want to be Women (WWWW), founded in 1979 to oppose feminist influence in government – was focused on the abolition of NWAC, and on disruptive activities relating to the UN Decade for Women. The influence of WWWW peaked in 1980–2, when its anti-feminist message coincided with the views of the small government faction within the Coalition government. Like WWWW, the latter stressed the need for 'strengthening the family' as an alternative to 'expensive' state provision of welfare, childcare and care for the aged. However, the extremist views of WWWW were not palatable to most Australian conservative politicians, and the political influence of WWWW was quite marginal and short-lived (Sawer, 1991).

After the election of the Hawke Labor government in 1983, WWWW and other such anti-feminist groups were excluded from advisory bodies or grants programmes designed to promote the status of women. As we noted, the Hawke government came to power with the most fully developed women's platform of any Australian government to date. Because of this, it saw little need for an advisory women's body and only reluctantly established in 1984 National Women's Consultative Council (NWCC). However, NWCC had little independence and was seen largely as a means of promoting government initiatives among women rather than as conveying the views of women to the government. The Hawke government favoured relatively passive modes of consultation, such as the *National Agenda* questionnaires. Made up of representatives of major women's organisations rather than on the basis of political patronage, members of the Consultative Council have not had the same access to government as the political nominees of its predecessor, the National Womens' Advisory Council (Sawer, 1990: 84–9).

The relationship between the Council and the Office has been characterised by an on going tension over the demarcation of their respective roles in consultative work and the work of policy development and co-ordination. For the most part, OSW is perceived to be inward looking and bureaucratically respectable, promoting women's issues *in* government, without much public visibility; in contrast, the National Women's Consultative Council (NWCC) is regarded to be more outward looking towards the broader community. However, the internal/external orientation is not always clear-cut, because NWCC has been known to want to be directly involved in the formulation of policy. Moreover, part of the mandate of OSW is to consult with women in the broader community. Sharing the Council's secretariat with the Office has tended to reinforce rather than ease these tensions (Interview, OSW, 27 February 1990). As we noted, the confusing demarcation between the broad consultative and the specific policy development function has led to similar tensions in Canada.

In comparative terms, Australian feminism has been remarkably successful in effecting change in government policies and in fostering bureaucratic innovation. Australian feminist commentators attribute this success to: (1) the dominant political climate, which, as in Canada, fosters the view of a 'neutral' and 'benevolent' state, whose services should be extended to the disadvantaged; (2) the political tradition whereby radical social movements have looked to the government to satisfy their social demands and service their needs; (3) the emergence in 1972 of WEL, an influential liberal feminist political organisation; (4) the election in December 1972 after twenty-three years of conservative rule of a reformist Labor government particularly receptive to addressing – if perhaps not fully meeting – feminist demands; (5) bi-partisan support for gender equity issues; (6) the alliance between newer feminist organisations such as WEL and 'traditional' women's organisations such as YWCA, Nursing Mothers and a host of others; (7) lack of effective anti-feminist opposition to feminist influence in government; and (8) the existence of a centralised wage-fixing system and a powerful, legitimate trade union movement supportive of feminist workforce initiatives and of women's policy machinery within government (Dowse, 1988; Ryan, 1990; Sawer, 1990, 1991).

WOMEN'S POLICY MACHINERY IN GREAT BRITAIN

Feminist interventions in the bureaucratic and political arenas in Great Britain have been much more limited than in Canada and Australia, with the possible exception of local and metropolitan levels of government in the early 1980s. At the central administrative level, autonomous feminism has not been accepted as a legitimate political force that can set a political agenda, participate in a dialogue about specific policy initiatives, monitor the implementation of relevant policies and otherwise engage in interest politics on behalf of women. The British feminist failure to gain meaningful access to the political process can be attributed both to the unfavourable political opportunity structure and to the localised, fragmented, left-wing socialist character of the women's liberation movement. For the most part, British feminists have been more concerned with changing consciousness than with changing public policy (Bouchier, 1984).

The closed and inflexible nature of the British political system, the strong emphasis in the feminist movement on sectarianism and ideological purity, and the general ambivalence among feminist activists about 'playing the state' and engaging in pragmatic reformist politics, have inhibited the development of liberal feminism. The building up of women's coalitions and networks across a broad spectrum of issues and ideological orientations, the creation of links with traditional women's organisations, and the lobbying of the national government are much less developed in the UK than in Canada and Australia. In turn, these systemic constraints have inhibited the development of an effective women's policy machinery capable of putting forward feminist concerns and building government support for them, translating specific women's demands into policies, and monitoring all new and existing government policies for gender impact (Meehan, 1983; Gelb, 1989).

British political opportunity structures

The British political culture favours government secrecy and bureaucratic neutrality. Politicking 'behind the scenes' and networking within the upper levels of government is far more prevalent than interaction with the grass roots. Legal advocacy on behalf of oppressed groups is also highly restricted, since the courts define themselves more as defenders of the state than as defenders of individual rights. Because of its unwritten constitution, Great Britain has no distinct concepts and rules that the courts can use to interpret (rather than simply apply) the law. Class action suits used to aid reform movements in the United States, or the recent constitutional challenges under the Canadian Charter of Rights and Freedoms, are virtually non-existent in the UK.

Judicial recourse is further limited by the role of industrial tribunals, which hear most discrimination-related cases. Industrial tribunals are seen as part of the collective bargaining process, and as such are comprised of representatives of industry and labour. Their personnel are generally overworked and undertrained, and lack an understanding of sex discrimination cases. Moreover, tribunals do not create case law, with the result that their rulings tend to 'get lost' in a plethora of *ad hoc* decisions. There is no general right of appeal from industrial tribunals (Atkins and Hoggett, 1984: 27–33; Gelb, 1989: 94).

The strong antagonism to feminist viewpoints and issues of a powerful female prime minister, Margaret Thatcher, has also worked against the interests of women, as has the existence of mostly covert procedures governing appointments to 'quangos' (quasi-autonomous non-governmental organisations), which include the Equal Opportunities Commission (EOC). Quangos are autonomous, non-governmental bodies with advisory, executive, and policy-making functions. Because they are not subject to direct parliamentary and government control, quangos have the potential of an alternative loci of power. In the post-war period, quangos were viewed as mechanisms for inadequately represented interests to gain a voice in government, but as Gelb (1989: 20) argues, 'they have in fact been hard pressed to play such a role'.

Appointees to British quangos are chosen according to rules designed first and foremost to satisfy the interest groups which carry the most weight with the government (that is, the two political parties, representatives of labour and business, regional representatives from Scotland and Wales), and only secondly to enable the organisation to perform its statutory duties. Confidentiality prevails, and there is virtually no opportunity for group activists to influence such processes

(Coote and Campbell, 1987: 133; Gelb, 1989: 17). Persons regarded as 'radicals' tend to be excluded from these secret processes of nomination and appointment to public bodies, which are conducted behind closed doors by the Civil Service in consultation with ministers. In the case of the EOC, several suggestions for appointees with feminist views were rejected by the Home Office (Meehan, 1983: 181).

While in Canada and Australia, femocrats and women's groups routinely consult each other and often offer mutual support, EOC femocrats have lacked the supportive political constituency which is neccessary for a successful bureaucratic confrontationist stance. There is no powerful national women's lobby to press for specific reforms across a range of women's issues and for greater access to elite institutions. Since the emergence of the 'second wave' of feminism in the 1970s, the British women's movement has been strongly influenced by Marxist writings with an uncompromising view of the state as an instrument of capitalism and patriarchy.

Publications such as *In and Against the State* exorted feminist activists to build a culture of opposition and create alternative institutions and practices (Watson, 1990: 4). Attempts to work within state structures were viewed with suspicion, and tended to be dismissed as co-option. In contrast to Canada and Australia, little effort was put into creating a 'mainstream' voice for feminism to seek legitimacy, and into devising strategies pursuing the advancement of women in existing political structures (Wilson, 1986: 98). In turn, the ideological tendency discouraging pragmatic reformist activity contributed to the marginalisation of feminist issues on the British political agenda.

Since the British political system is so inhospitable to interest group politics, women's groups have had to choose between political isolation and working through the mediation of political parties, unions and the European Community. According to Gelb (1989: 108),

> the passage of the Equal Pay Act (EPA) and subsequent Sex Discrimination Act (SDA) owed more to the parties, the TUC, and also the EEC (whose Article 119, promulgated in 1957, provided for equal pay for equal work) than it did to the women's movement. Women's groups have played an auxilliary – but not central role – in creating support for legislative enactments.

The TUC support for equal pay legislation, and for the EOC set up in connection with the two pieces of legislation, owed more to its fear that lower women's wages would undercut those of men than to its concern for feminism and discrimination against women.

The Equal Opportunities Commission

Based on the American Equal Employment Opportunities Commission (EEOC), the British Equal Opportunities Commission was created by the Labour government in 1975 to work towards the elimination of discrimination on the ground of sex, to promote general equality of opportunity between men and women, and to enforce and review the working of the Equal Pay and Sex Discrimination Acts. The EOC meets this mandate by pursuing educational, research, investigative, lobbying and law enforcement activities, though it is not involved in the kind of integrative and policy evaluation activities that define the work of Status of Women Canada and the Office of the Status of Women in Australia.

As a result of the rules governing the nomination and appointments of individuals to British commissions and 'quangos', the commissioners that emerged out of the appointment process were not individuals most noted for their enthusiasm and ability to work for women's equality. They were people who 'had prior and sometimes conflicting allegiances, who were busy with other commitments and saw their work on the Commission as peripheral to the rest of their lives, and who approached their statutory task with a passionate caution' (Coote and Campbell, 1987: 133). They routinely referred controversial policy documents to their parent organisations before deciding on what position to adopt at the EOC.

Moreover, defending the sectoral interests of the parent organisation was often more important than defending the interests of women. For example, a TUC representative who declined to sign a TUC-approved dissenting report on an EOC document on protective legislation was subsequently removed from her senior post in the TUC and not allowed to serve for another term on the Commission (Meehan, 1983: 182). There has been even an allegation 'that the commissioners from the TUC and CBI tended to combine forces to prevent the EOC meddling in industrial affairs' (Coote and Campbell, 1987: 135). On the other hand, the continuation of TUC representation in the EOC may suggest just how unimportant the Tory government considered the EOC to be, since TUC representation was removed from many other public bodies during the Thatcher years (Interview, TUC, 20 July 1989).

While being very relaxed about confidentiality among themselves, EOC commissioners had insisted on confidentiality among EOC staff.

For example, at the end of 1977, Dr Byrne of the Commission's education section was dismissed for discussing with the press a supposedly confidential report by the Home Office, which stated that there was no need for an education section in the Commission. However, a tribunal later held her sacking to have been unfair (Meehan, 1983: 186). EOC staff have been repeatedly told to behave 'like administrators' and to leave their 'feminist hats at home'. The tradition of bureaucratic neutrality, the idea that civil servants can and should keep public and private hats completely separate, has led to numerous tensions in the EOC between non-feminist commissioners and feminist staff. During the first five years of its operation, the EOC had four Chief Executives. In 1978, staff turnover was 38 per cent – more than three times that of an average office. These massive defections suggest to Coote and Campbell (1987: 134) that the organisation was 'severely at odds with itself, unable to reconcile the grand scale of its mission with the disabling knots of its constitution'.

EOC's law enforcement powers enable it to provide legal advice and legal representation directly to individuals. The EOC can also bring actions against employers, or it can finance and provide legal representation for employees to do so. However, the House of Lords has prevented the EOC from mounting formal investigations into the general workings of organisations, restricting the scope of such investigations to actual acts of discrimination. Overall, the EOC has placed limited emphasis on enforcement and sanctions, and has been involved in few, if any, dramatic court cases. Of the few cases that have been won, at least two have been won on appeal to the European Court (Corcoran, 1981; Meehan, 1983: 175–6; Atkins and Hoggett, 1984: 38–42). *The Sunday Times* alleged in 1977 that the women's officer of the National Council for Civil Liberties seemed to be doing more to enforce the Sex Discrimination and Equal Pay Acts than the whole of the EOC, with a tiny fraction of the Commission's budget (quoted in Coote and Campbell, 1987: 136). The restructuring of the EOC initiated by Johanna Foster when she assumed the EOC chair in 1988 is unlikely to change the low priority given by the EOC to its statutory function. Unlike feminist and trade union activists, the EOC leadership prefers to rely on persuasion and voluntary agreements of employers not to discriminate against women rather than on enforcement and monitoring mechanisms (Interview, EOC, 4 October 1988; Interview, TUC, 20 July 1989).

The EOC is financed by an annual grant from the Home Office. The grants have failed to keep pace with inflation, forcing the EOC to engage in periodic staff and programme cutbacks. Throughout the 1980s, the

EOC has not publicised its concern over shrinking resources, hoping that behind-the-scenes pressure would eventually pay off. However, with the restructuring and streamlining of its activities into fewer areas, the EOC launched in early 1989 a public campaign to galvanise support for its work. Apart from asking for more cash, the EOC also singled out child-care and other work and family issues as priority concerns (Hague, 1989). The prioritisation of childcare corresponds to the government's concerns over the prospect of skill shortages in the 1990s and the need to recruit more women into the workforce – an issue discussed in more detail in Chapter 9.

Additional components of national women's policy machinery

Another potential institutional base for women's advocacy is the Women's National Commission (WNC). Established in 1969 by the Labour government, it has a strictly advisory role. Despite its broad base and traditionalism, which make it quite legitimate from the government standpoint, the WNC is institutionally quite powerless. It consists of fifty people, who are the representatives of various traditional establishment-oriented organisations, such as townswomen's guilds, women's in-stitutes, Salvation Army, or the Federation of Army Wives. The latter remained a member even after a review to bring the WNC more up to date and include some new organisations with younger membership (Interview, TUC, 20 July 1989). Most of the feminist groups are excluded from WNC because they cannot meet the requirement that member groups must have a national membership and presence. Women's sections of unions and the Labour Party are the only feminist groups that can meet the requirement (Gelb, 1989: 97–8).

The WNC has several working groups which examine a variety of issues, often in response to government consultative Green and White papers. However, unless the WNC submissions correspond to govern-ment objectives, they are ignored. Thus the WNC submission to the government to increase child benefits (supported unanimously within the WNC) was not acted upon by the Tory government (Interview, TUC, 20 July 1989). The government's own rudimentary machinery – Department of Employment Advisory Committee on Women's Employment and the Ministerial Group on Women's Issues – has also been largely in-effectual. The Advisory Committee meets only three times a year and so far has placed nothing of real significance on its agendas.

Since its inception in 1986, the most notable achievement of the

Ministerial Group on Women's Issues has been the resolution to 'proof' equal opportunities legislation to safeguard against the inadvertent discrimination in laws and regulations. However, without an agency set up to monitor and evaluate the legislation, the commitment to women's equality will remain largely rhetorical. In a similar vein, a rather brief review of childcare policies published in 1989 was high on rhetoric, but short on new proposals and new government funding (Jones, 1989).

Feminist intervention in local government

British feminists have had more luck with local levels of government. In the early 1980s, several Labour-controlled local councils established women's committees to take up issues of equality, the representation of women and other women's interests (Goss, 1984). The greatest resources were those of the Women's Committee of the Greater London Council (GLC), which by its fourth (and final) year had a budget of almost £90 million to set up feminist structures and fund local women's groups and projects. Aided by its own support unit, which in 1986 consisted of 96 posts, the Committee attempted to involve a wide spectrum of women by holding open meetings, and by setting up working parties on employment, childcare, visible minority women, lesbian women, women with disabilities, and violence against women (Goss, 1984; Coote and Campbell, 1987: 105–7).

A women's unit set up at the London borough of Camden funded a 'women's bus' to travel around housing estates, workplaces and shopping centres to initiate women's discussion groups and advice sessions. Such bureaucratic innovations, designed to allow women greater access to decision making and to establish closer links with women's organisations outside the council structure, challenged the traditional relationships of local authorities to the communities they served, as well as the traditional distribution of power between men and women at the local level of government. There was a determined shift of emphasis towards Black and ethnic minority women, working class women, women with disabilities, lesbians and older women. According to Coote and Campbell (1987: 107),

> this was based not so much on a new theoretical analysis where the roots of oppression lay, as on a critique of the white, middle-class character of the women's movement of the 1970s, and on the simple

observation that groups which had been deprived and disregarded in the past should now be empowered and recognized.

The distinctive feminist style of the GLC Women's Committee received a generally hostile media reception (Flannery and Roeloffs, 1984). In a smililar vein, the GLC funding to the Greenham Common Peace Camp and to the feminist magazine *Spare Rib* created a great deal of controversy, and raised a political outcry from opposition members (Goss, 1984: 113). The abolition of the GLC in 1986 and the fiscal crackdown on local government by the Thatcher administration towards the end of the decade put a quick end to these feminist experiments in government.

CONCLUSION

The comparative experiences of Canada, Australia and Great Britain suggest that state feminism works best in countries with an open and flexible political structure and a strong 'mainstream' feminist movement able and willing to engage in pragmatic reformist politics. The building of effective networks and coalitions to press women's demands both outside and inside the government and the judiciary appear to be far more significant than the simple creation of an administrative agency (or a set of agencies) to promote women's equality and monitor sex discrimination. The British Equal Opportunities Commission is an administrative body with wide-ranging powers, yet it is politically isolated and institutionally quite powerless, much more so than its counterparts in Canada and Australia.

Australia and to a lesser degree Canada have well-established political traditions of using the state to achieve important economic, social and demographic goals. Consistent with that tradition, reformist feminist movements in those countries have looked to the state as the main agency capable of redressing a whole range of women's grievances. Since the 1970s, various levels of the state have responded favourably, both by creating distinctively feminist political and bureaucratic structures, and by placing broadly conceived women's equality on their economic and social policy agendas. International bodies such as the UN regard Australian and Canadian women's policy machineries as exemplary, and as models for other countries. Indeed, when success of state feminism is measured in terms of the sophistication of a distinctive feminist bureaucracy, Australia and Canada are the leading countries in the world. The very existence of this machinery has given women's issues (e.g. employment equity, equal pay for work of equal value, social provision for maternity and childcare, violence against women, integration of work and family) a much greater degree of visibility and legitimacy than has been the case in the UK.

However, distinctive feminist political and bureaucratic structures are quite meaningless without some substantive policy outcomes. Since the main purpose of this study is to explore the intersection of demographic and gender equality policies, the rest of this book focuses on shifting policy responses to women's needs as mothers. Part II examines the increasing compatibility between broadly defined demographic and women's equality policies, and the costs and benefits of fertility-related measures *vis-à-vis*, or jointly with, immigration measures. The egalitarian components of demographic policies or the demographic implications of policies pursuing women's equality are the subject of Part III. Chapter 7 reviews protective legislation as a contentious strategy designed to reconcile the ideal of women's equality with the reality of reproductive difference. Chapters 8–10 focus on maternity and parental leave policies, children's policies and family support policies. We shall see that like state feminism, maternity/parental leave benefits and publicly supported childcare provision are much more developed in Canada and Australia than in the UK

Moreover, throughout the 1980s, Canadian and Australian maternity/ parental leave provisions *improved*, while the UK witnessed a steady erosion in maternity benefits and employment protection. However, as Canada and Australia follow Great Britain in moving their political spectrum to the right, these gains may be lost. Privatisation, economic rationalism and selectivity have become as important as equality of opportunities in setting policy limits.

Part II

Demography

5 Pronatalism and Women's Equality Policies[1]

INTRODUCTION

The major goals of this chapter are: (1) to examine the various definitions of pronatalism, and (2) to determine which specific pronatalist policies are most compatible with policies pursuing women's equality, and vice versa.

CONCEPTUALISING PRONATALISM

Although pronatalism is hard to define in an absolute and unequivocal way, it is safe to suggest that it implies encouragement of all births as conducive to individual, family and social well-being (de Sandre, 1978: 145). Pronatalism can then be seen as operating on several levels: culturally, when childbearing and motherhood are perceived as 'natural' and central to a woman's identity; ideologically, when the motherhood mandate becomes a patriotic, ethnic or eugenic obligation; psychologically, when childbearing is identified with the micro level of personal aspirations, emotions and rational (or irrational) decision making (by women or couples); on the cohort level, when changes in the birth rate are related to the size of successive generations; and on the level of population policy, when the state intervenes, directly or indirectly, in an attempt to regulate the dynamics of fertility and to influence its causes and consequences.

COERCIVE PRONATALISM: RACISM AND EUGENISM

The cultural, and especially the ideological, meanings of pronatalism have been historically associated with right-wing coercive ideologies, laws and practices that overemphasise natalist goals, reinforce the traditional family model of father as breadwinner and mother as homemaker, and severely limit reproductive freedom of choice. Moreover, coercive ideological pronatalism has been variously linked with strong nationalism, explicit racism, fascism, imperialism and eugenism. Many of its measures have been highly selective, combining strong pronatalism for some with strong anti-natalism for others. For example, Nazi Germany was characterised by an intrinsic connection between pronatalism promoting 'desirable' births among healthy married women of an 'Aryan' ethnicity, and anti-natalism imposed on 'undesirable' women who did not meet the specific ethnic, eugenic or social standards. These included Jewish and Romany women, lesbians, single mothers, and women with physical or mental disabilities (Bock, 1984).

In Australia, women as 'breeders of the white race' have been a central preoccupation in population and immigration policies. Under the legal and ideological restrictions imposed on 'unassimilable' immigrants under 'White Australia' immigration policies until the 1960s, most settlers have been White. While some women have migrated independently, the majority came as dependents of men, expected to marry and reproduce within the nuclear family. In contrast, Asian and Melanesian immigrants, introduced to the Australian colonies in the last century, were prevented from establishing families and reproducing themselves and their 'race'. Nor were Aboriginal people always permitted to raise their children in their family forms. However conceptualised, as breeders of the White 'race'/nation in the nineteenth and early twentieth centuries, or as reproducers of multicultural Australia today, these conceptualisations are both racist and sexist (de Lepervanche, 1989a, b).

Racist and eugenic attitudes towards procreation have not completely disappeared. For example, at a recent forum on drug and alcohol abuse, the community relations officer of the police force in Dartmouth, the second largest city in the Canadian province of Nova Scotia, felt free to suggest that people on social assistance should be forced to practice birth control, partly because their 'limited genetic pool' results in 'welfare breeding welfare' (*Peterborough Examiner*, 30 April 1990). Instances of sterilisation of welfare mothers without their knowledge, or of xenophobic outcries against immigrants or 'undesirable' ethnic minorities, who allegedly 'breed like rabbits', can be found in most developed countries. However, it is worth emphasising that explicit, state-sponsored eugenic or racist pronatalism is usually not tolerated by 'mainstream' democratic political elites. Thus a few days after he made his derogatory statements about welfare recipients, the Dartmouth policeman was removed from his position as community relations officer

Pronatalism and Women's Equality Policies 123

(though not from the Dartmouth police force as such) on the grounds that his views 'are not the views of the police department or the city government' (*Peterborough Examiner*, 3 May 1990).

PRONATALISM AND THE MOTHERHOOD MANDATE

It is also worth noting that the coexistence of selective pronatalism with selective anti-natalism is not limited to eugenism or racism. In most cultures, the pronatalist cultural prescription of motherhood varies according to the marital status and sexual orientation of the individual involved. As MacIntyre (1976) points out, contemporary social norms are characterised by 'two versions of reality': the equation of marriage with motherhood, and non-marriage with non-motherhood. Thus in married women, pregnancy and childbearing are seen as normal and desirable, while a desire not to have children is seen as aberrant and in need of an explanation. In contrast, pregnancy and childbearing of single or lesbian women are regarded as abnormal and undesirable, and the wish of these women to have a baby is accordingly seen as aberrant, selfish, and in need of an explanation. In a similar vein, infertility is generally perceived as a much greater problem for a married person than for a single one.

Another dominant theme in feminist literature on pronatalism is its controlling effect on individual reproductive decision making. Blake (1974), Russo (1979), Gimenez (1983) and Spakes (1989) have all argued that broad pronatalist assumptions that focus women's individual worth and the derivation of meaning in life primarily on motherhood allow neither complete freedom of reproductive choice, nor the free pursuit of other occupational roles. As Russo (1979: 7) put it, 'motherhood is on a qualitatively different plane than other sex roles for women in our society. It is a mandate that pervades our social institutions as well as our psyches.'

While Gimenez (1983: 290) agrees that women have increased their reproductive self-determination with respect to number and timing of births, and whether or not to enter the paid labour force, she also suggests that women are still not free to choose not to have children. 'Given the present material conditions', Gimenez (1983: 300-1) argues,

pronatalism compels women to handicap themselves, sometimes very early in their lives, and a similar argument could be made with respect to men. . . . Pronatalist reward structures impel women and men marginally committed to parenthood to form families because that is the price to be paid for normalcy, respectability, credibility, and fulfilment of adult sex role expectations. The high incidence of child abuse and battered wives, the high divorce and remarriage rates, the high increases in illegitimacy and teenage pregnancy, and the growth of female-headed households are phenomena which should highlight the importance of investigating the negative consequences of prescriptive parenthood.

One can counteract this argument with evidence suggesting that the cultural prescription of parenthood is not as universal as is claimed, especially for the more educated women. After all, liberal democracies practice political pluralism, in which pronatalist notions such as 'children make life meaningful' or 'motherhood constitutes the fulfilment of womanhood' coexist with anti-natalist ideologies promoting the environmental advantages of 'zero population growth' or the individual advantages of a 'child-free lifestyle'.

PRONATALISM AS GOVERNMENT POLICY

Pronatalism at the other levels raises a whole series of questions about the relations between the state, the individual and the family. Could/should procreation be regulated in liberal democracies at all? If so, how and where could/should the nation state intervene? What categories of individuals and institutions should the design and realisation of a pronatalist policy be aimed at? What should be the balance between 'quantitative' pronatalist measures (attempting to stimulate higher fertility, especially marital fertility) and 'qualitative' ones (designed to reduce the incidence of unwanted births and of birth defects), and between fiscal and legal/administrative measures?

In Romaniuc's (1989) view, a government policy, if any, which may arise from the current debates on population, will greatly depend on the prevailing intellectual outlook. He identifies three contrasting intellectual frameworks addressing changes in fertility: evolutionary, self-equilibrating, and social engineering. The first two frameworks leave no room for government intervention in procreation. Within the evolutionary perspective, Romaniuc (1989: 265) argues,

> low, subreplacement fertility is seen as a chronic condition, an inescapable feature of advanced societies. The policy response to such an outlook would be to rely on immigration in order to achieve the population growth if such growth is deemed desirable. If the latter is not desirable in itself, then social and institutional adjustment to an environment of demographic no-growth and aging must be sought as a policy response.

The self-equilibrating perspective is based on the assumption that the economic doctrine of *laissez-faire* is also applicable to demographic processes. A central element in the demographic auto-regulation thesis is the belief that the 'invisible hand' of the market, as opposed to state intervention, is the key mechanism capable of restoring higher birth rate. The notion that fertility policies are unnecessary because populations will correct their demographic developments 'automatically' on their own is an attractive one in developed societies. Not only is there lack of consensus as to what is demographically desirable, but most Western governments, faced with high deficits, are more interested in cutbacks and privatisation than in costly new policies and programmes.

However, such complacency about the efficacy of *laissez-faire* in demographic matters may not be warranted. Demeny (1986a: 473, 476–7) stated in the opening remarks of his Presidential Address at the 1986 Meeting of the Population Association of America in San Francisco: 'the essence of the population problem, if there is a problem, is that individual decisions with respect to demographic acts do not add up to a recognized common good – that choices at the individual level are not congruent with the collective interest.' The very fact that demographic processes are the result of a very large number of uncoordinated individual decisions,

> renders population processes, and most notably fertility behaviour, a legitimate object of attention for collective and, in particular, governmental action. When socially advantageous modification of demographic behaviour is beyond the capacity of private markets to provide, it assumes the character of a public good that must be acquired, if at all, through the political market place. Demographic change becomes a matter for public concern whenever it can be

plausibly assumed that such modifications are both desirable and possible.

Chesnais (1983: 387) also believes that fertility is not self-regulatory, and that, 'the political alternatives are to boost the birth rate today or to allow a more massive influx of foreign migrants tomorrow'.

Thus one is left with the social engineering perspective, although the very nature of demographic change is not likely to produce immediate governmental action. In comparison to economic and social matters, demographic issues are more stable, less contentious and easier to plan for. This is so at least in part because of the time-lag involved between a prolonged decline in the birth rate and an effect on the workforce or on population ageing.

Demographers tell us that exact population replacement occurs when the total fertility rate (TFR) is 2.1 children per woman, that is, when an imaginary, abstracted cohort of 1000 women end their reproductive lives having given birth to 2.1 children. A replacement level TFR is higher than exactly one child for each parent because not all children born will survive to their reproductive years. In poorer countries with high infant and child mortality rates, a TFR of 2.1 would be insufficient therefore to ensure population replacement in the long run. Moreover, a stationary or declining population will not be achieved for two or three generations after a TFR at or below 2.1 has been reached, because of the effects of the age structure of populations. High levels of fertility in the past will have resulted in a large number of women still reaching their fertile years, and these women will continue to bear children well beyond the point at which a TFR of 2.1 is achieved.

In other words, even if parents of today have only small families, there are still more children being born than there are people dying. Thus the current age structure of the population, a consequence of past demographic trends, distorts the impact of current crude death rates and birth rates, with the result that crude rates of natural increase are positive and are expected to remain so in most developed countries for the remainder of this century (Frejka, 1974; Wulf, 1982). Canada, Australia and the United States will maintain population growth well into the next century because of the reverberating impact of the tremendous post-World War II 'baby boom' (which lasted well into the 1960s) and because immigration levels have remained high.

Politicians naturally seek refuge in these less disturbing short-term prospects. If a particular issue can be removed from the political agenda for several decades then it typically is not a problem to which politicians have to respond in their election programmes. Even if demographic trends (such as below-replacement fertility) are taken seriously as an issue for governmental action, politicians still may shy of overtly pronatalist policies on the grounds that they cannot guarantee results and involve major public expenditure at a time when other pressing demands are made on the government purse. Thus much population policy is coincidental, without an explicit demographic rationale.

CLASSIFICATION OF PRONATALIST POLICIES

Various typologies can be used to classify pronatalist policies. One such typology draws a distinction between direct and indirect pronatalist policies, that is between policies that explicitly intend to influence fertility, and broader policies which might also have some pronatalist effect. However, as Demeny (1986b: 349) points out,

the absence or presence of pronatalist objectives and the stridency or tentativeness with which such objectives, if any, are articulated are in fact poor predictors of the scope and generosity of the services made available to the population. . . . Scandinavian countries, for example, declare themselves satisfied with existing levels of fertility; yet provision there of the types of social services that would be classified . . . as pronatalist is among the most generous.

Indeed, in a complex modern state, there are hardly any measures which comprise the 'welfare state' that do not bear at least indirectly on women, the family and children.

Since so many pronatalist measures are simultaneously components of social welfare, economic and equal opportunity policies, this study discusses pronatalism in the broader context of indirect policies 'with population effects', as opposed to the narrower context of policies that are explicitly designed to influence population problems, in this case a below-replacement fertility. It is also worth noting that governmental decisions ostensibly taken for reasons not directly connected to demographic considerations (such as means-tested housing or social security policies whose principal aim is to alleviate poverty) may none the less have an impact on family size. Thus, as Klinger (1987: 388) argues, 'a policy designed to reduce inequalities of income, but not to change family size, may yet be regarded as a "population policy", because it may incidentally modify fertility, and not always in the desired direction'.

When cash benefits are dependent on some demographic criterion (for example third child in a family), pronatalism may be the primary objective, as has been acknowledged to be the case in France, Hungary, Czechoslovakia and Quebec. Relatively few of the developed countries have such explicit policies. However, almost all have legislation, social services and income transfers providing some form of assistance to families with children, and as such can be regarded as at least partly pronatalist. Moreover, in recent years there has been a noticeable shift in emphasis from 'child quantity' to 'child quality', with the result that the broad population policies are for the most part directed towards improving the quality of lifestyle of a near-stationary population rather than towards increasing the size of the population (Young, 1989a: 42–46). Thus speaking of pronatalist policies in the Western world is 'by and large, merely a fancy way of describing social policies which might also have some pronatalist effect' (Demeny, 1986b: 349). One way to resolve the dilemma between direct and indirect pronatalist policies is to reserve the term 'pronatalist' for cases where the intention to raise the birth rate is explicit. The greater range of policies which happen to make childbearing/rearing easier without increase in the birth rate being an explicit objective could perhaps be described as 'pronatal', 'enabling' or simply 'family' policies.

Another relevant typology is that of Livi-Bacci (1974), who classifies governmental measures attempting to influence demographic trends according to broad policy objectives. These include:

1. Provisions directed to extend, modify, and guarantee individual human rights.
2. Measures designed to increase social justice and equality.
3. Legal or economic measures designed to encourage or to discourage certain types of behaviour.

Other typologies pay more attention to the specific measures which might be introduced. Andorka (1978: 347–8) draws a distinction between:

1. Measures using coercion, primarily the prohibition and prosecution of induced abortions, and sometimes also a prohibition on the sale of contraceptives.
2. Measures using no coercion, but incentives, primarily different social

benefits given to families with children. These measures might also be differentiated by their monetary or 'in kind' character, the monetary benefits being given in cash to families who may use them as they like, while the benefits 'in kind' are provided directly to the children (for example free meals at schools, cheap milk and so on).

Andorka (1978: 348) acknowledges that in practice, 'most concrete population policies do not belong to these "pure" types, but utilize a mixture of such measures', but none the less argues that 'the impact of population policy depends very much on the type of it'. In his view, Romanian coercive measures have had only temporary effects, while the non-coercive French and Hungarian population measures produced a 'certain rise in the level of fertility' (Andorka, 1978: 352, 358).

Recent reviews of population policies in advanced industrial societies (for example van den Brekel, 1983; McIntosh, 1983, 1986; Leeuw, 1985; Demeny, 1986b; Heitlinger, 1987a; Klinger, 1987; Lodh, 1987; Höhn, 1988, 1989; Young, 1989a) have identified ten major pronatalist approaches taken either separately or in conjunction with each other:

1. Family founding loans (made to couples at the time of marriage at low or no interest, with the provision that part of the loan will be written off with the birth of a child or children within a certain time period after marriage).
2. Birth grants.
3. Child allowances.
4. Tax exemptions for children and/or for dependent spouses.
5. Guaranteed income for mothers (parents) who care for their children instead of working for wages.
6. Work-related measures, addressed to women or couples through extended maternity (parental) leaves, flexible work schedules and leaves for family reasons (such as child's sickness).
7. Subsidised housing, childcare and/or recreational facilities for children.
8. Pronatalist propaganda campaigns, educational programmes and psychological inducements.
9. Restrictions on abortions and in some cases also on contraceptives.
10. Emphasis on infrastructural changes in order to create an environment more 'friendly' to children.

These incentives have been introduced in Eastern and Western Europe in packages with various emphases. For example, France has put the emphasis on direct financial assistance, especially for the third child, whereas the West German government has been more prone to stress the creation of urban environments 'friendlier to children' (Lodh, 1987). In Central and Eastern Europe, pronatalist policies have been more explicit, and have relied on a combination of coercive measures (for example restricting access to abortion), ideological propaganda, and various benefits 'in kind' (for example preferential allocation of apartments to couples with children in a context of severe housing shortage) as well as fiscal incentives (Heitlinger, 1987a).

The classification of pronatalist and family policies adopted in this book builds upon these typologies. It employs a threefold distinction between (1) coercive policies limiting access to abortion and/or contraception, (2) 'facilitative' measures associated with the 'social protection of motherhood' and (3) 'positive' fiscal incentives. Moreover, these policies are also classified according to whom they are supposed to benefit or regulate: women, men, or married couples. 'Coercive population policies' (for example state regulation of access to abortion), and 'facilitative' measures associated with the 'social protection of motherhood' (for example protective labour laws for women, pregnancy and maternity leaves) concern exclusively women.

'Positive' fiscal incentives (for example family allowances, tax deductions for children, low-interest loans to newlyweds) usually concern couples, but typically benefit the individual with the higher income, usually the man. As such, these policies tend to reflect an empirically incorrect assumption that *per capita* income is shared and pooled equitably within families. As Edwards (1981) demonstrated in her study on financial arrangements within Australian families, increasing the fiscal welfare of the male breadwinner need not automatically increase the resources of all family members. Pahl (1980) provides similar evidence for Great Britain, and demonstrates considerable 'hidden poverty' of family dependents. However, some of these cash transfers, namely child (or family) allowances, are sometimes paid directly to mothers. Correspondingly, wives tend to value family allowances more than husbands, since for some of them this is the only money over which they have direct control (Eichler, 1988: 185). Childcare services should in principle be included under the 'couple' category, but in practice are usually discussed under the rubric of 'women's needs'. Of particular significance to men are the various tax deductions for children or for dependent spouses, and parental leaves.

The distinction as to whom pronatalism is supposed to influence and regulate (women, couples or men) enables us to integrate Livi-Bacci's

(1974) classificatory scheme based on broad policy objectives with classifications based on the types of specific measures adopted. Moreover, broadly defined pronatal policies can also be classified according to their emancipatory component (Niphius-Nell, 1987). When evaluating specific policies, we can establish (1) whether the measures are based on or reinforce traditional sex roles of the 'breadwinner' father and the 'stay-at-home' mother, (2) whether they promote women's paid employment while retaining some emphasis on sex differences and the special needs of women, or (3) whether they can be described as androgynous or gender neutral. Potential integration of pronatal and sex equality policies can then be conceptualised in terms of six sets of specific policies as outlined in the Appendix.

Not all policies can be neatly classified. For example, European, Canadian and ILO maternity policies have tended to emphasise the need for special treatment of pregnant employees – hence the inclusion of these policies under the rubric of 'sex equality based on sex difference'. The state of California also regards pregnancy as a 'unique' condition, and to this end has established a separate set of standards and provisions for women. In comparison, the US federal legislation on childbearing has been informed by the equal rights perspective. Attempts to eliminate sex-based discrimination in medical coverage of pregnancy and child-birth have been translated into the requirement that birthing women *cannot* be treated differently from other workers temporarily unable to work. In 1978, Congress passed the Pregnancy Discrimination Act as a direct rebuff to the Supreme Court ruling that employers' disability plans (which excluded pregnancy but covered all other medical disabilities, including male-specific ones like vasectomies and prostectomies), did not discriminate against women on the basis of their sex. Designed to entitle pregnant and birthing women to healthcare benefits, and to provide a few weeks of maternity leave, the legislation transformed gender-specific childbearing into a gender-neutral 'disability' and fringe benefit (Law, 1984; Vogel, 1987).

With some exceptions, the federal courts have followed the same course of gender neutrality. They have not only treated men and women equally under the Pregnancy Discrimination Act, but they have also treated pregnancy as analogous to a broken arm or pneumonia. As Lucie (1988: 235) argues,

the results of this 'assimilationist' approach to pregnancy are good for men, but may not serve women so well. . . . Only a few court decisions insist that adequate leave for pregnancy is mandated by the

Pregnancy Discrimination Act, independent of leave arrangements for other workers. Pregnant women have also been excluded from jobs where 'disabled' men would have been excluded.

Historically, childbearing has had a unique importance in justifying pervasive social and economic discrimination against women, and as Lucie (1988: 236) argues, 'it remains at the very front line of the battle for equality'. However, it is doubtful whether denying the uniqueness of pregnancy is the most effective way to achieve this goal. It would seem that accommodating the workplace to childbearing (such as shifting pregnant workers from hazardous jobs, providing adequate maternity leaves and benefits, safeguarding women's jobs and seniority) is a better strategy, and more compatible with pronatalism, than extending the terminology of equality into comparison of pregnancy with 'other disabilities'. The language of disability assigns pregnancy a negative value, which is in complete contradiction to the positive meaning with which childbearing is imbued by pronatalism. Pregnancy is neither an illness nor a disability, and is best treated in a manner consistent with its uniqueness.

Coercive pronatalist policies are excluded from the matrix of integrated pronatal and sex equality policies. Reproductive coercion infringes upon the individual reproductive rights of women and couples to determine the number and spacing of their children, and as such, policies of reproductive coercion cannot be seen in any way as being compatible with the goals of women's equality. The types of policies that *are* included in the matrix are aimed at both ensuring equality of employment opportunities, and providing more options for mothers (or couples) to choose how to balance their commitments between paid work and family.

Not only do these policies differ in terms of how they regard male and female relationship to paid work and parenthood, and how they conceptualise equality, but they also translate into different policy concerns. Thus policies based on the premise that traditional gender roles are the most effective in minimising the strain between paid work, family life and equality tend to translate into concerns how to best subsidise one or a lone parent to remain at home to fully concentrate on home and family responsibilities. Policies supporting the opportunity for all healthy adults to manage work and family roles simultaneously tend to focus on questions connected with parental leaves and adequate provision of out-of-home childcare services. Finally, there is also the option of supporting parents to decide for themselves whether to patronise a day care, employ a baby sitter, or provide the service themselves (Kamerman, 1980a). How are we to treat these choices? As we noted, traditional pronatalism considers full-time motherhood as vastly superior to women's attempts to combine career with a (small) family. Conversely, an equal employment opportunity policy implicitly devalues women's traditional unpaid work in the home. While the pitting of women in the labour force against 'stay-at-home mothers' may be popular among the general public,[2] it is uniformly accepted neither in feminist circles, nor in the more conservative European women's and family organisations. Thus the resolution of the Steering Committee of the EPP Women's Organisation[3] emphasises that 'instead of polarizing working women and women at home, we should envisage a family policy that caters for everyone, without making any value judgments of their individual choices' (European People's Party, 1988: 149)

Moreover, the choice between motherhood and a job is hardly ever all or nothing. As Joshi (1989: 6–7) argues for Great Britain, it is full-time employment which is difficult to combine with motherhood, but not part-time. The first birth provokes exits from full-time jobs, but the presence of children increases the chances of part-time employment'. Joshi (1989: 8–9) also argues that

the cash opportunity costs of a given set of births are not fixed. Families can adapt not only by avoiding births, but by buying commodities and help to substitute for the demands of children on unpaid time. Opportunity costs can be converted into direct cost. If child care is purchased, especially if it is subsidized, the links of the argument from female employment to fertility behaviour are weakened.

Thus advanced industrial societies are increasingly characterised by diverse family and work arrangements, and by variations in the degree to which women are primarily defined in terms of their reproductive role and their relationship to men. These variations stem from differences among women as regards their educational and occupational attainment, marital status, age at first birth, the spacing and number of children, employment opportunities, the location and cost of their homes and so on. Hence there must be a recognition of the need for a range of pronatalist policies to cater to the growing individualisation of women's lives.

SUBSIDISING THE 'STAY-AT-HOME MOTHER'

Feminists have traditionally regarded the sexual division of labour between breadwinning fathers and stay-at-home mothers as enforcing women's subordination and dependency rather than as a form of women's equality. As we noted in Chapter 2, traditional assumptions about biological sex differences provided the prime justification for creating a separate, inferior legal status for women. The law denied women equal opportunity for wage work and participation in public life, and reinforced social and religious commitment to family-centred child-rearing.

While the commitment to family-centred child-rearing is something traditional family organisations would like to see preserved, they too have identified the economic hardship suffered by women who stay at home with young children as a problem. Various forms of guaranteed income for mothers who care for children instead of working for pay have been suggested therefore by both feminist and more traditional groups. These include 'wages for housework' (put forward by elements in the Italian and British feminist movements), a 'maternal salary' (proposed in 1973 by The National Union of Family Associations in France), and independent right to social security payments (included in the recommendation by the Canadian Royal Commission on the Status of Women, and in a European family proposal put forward by the European People's Party-Christian Democratic).

Burch (1986: 8) has argued that guaranteed income plans need further investigation,

> as a promising alternative to subsidized day care. If governments are willing, as increasingly they seem to be, to pay third parties to take care of a couple's children, then it would seem to make sense to pay one of the couple (or some other close relative – for example, a young adult son or daughter) an equivalent amount to stay home in a household-management as well as childcare role. Government policy might in effect create a new occupation, which could be described using the time-honoured term *steward/stewardess*, as in 'household steward'.

In 1990, a Canadian group called Kids First mounted a challenge to Section 63 of the Canadian Income Tax Act under the equality provisions of the Charter of Rights and Freedom. Section 63 provides for annual deductible childcare expense of up to $4000 per child under age seven and $2000 for other eligible children (since increased to $5000 and $3000, respectively). Childcare payments made between spouses are not allowed as an expense, and the spouse with the lower income must make the deduction. Kids First argues that these provisions discriminate against one-income couples. In the two test cases picked by the group, the husband – who has the higher income – has contracted the wife to provide childcare services and has claimed the childcare expenses as a tax deduction. The group, which says it has a membership of 5000 across Canada, is in favour of a tax system that would replace the current benefits with a single refundable tax credit dependent on family income. The maximum credit would be $2500 per child per year for children up to the age of five, then $1000 per child per year for children aged six to twelve. The group is not against day care, because it is 'tolerant of other people's choices' (*Globe and Mail*, 28 April 1990).

The two main sets of problems with such schemes are the low level of financial reward relative to the costs of both child-rearing and the loss of one income, and the reinforcement of the sexual division of labour. Non-employment of either parent is currently an important source of poverty for children (Joshi, 1989). Since guaranteed incomes for stay-at-home mothers would be very low, there is little hope that this pattern would be reversed. As Gro Harlem Brundtland (1983: 18), Chairman of the 1982 European Population Conference, stated in her opening remarks, 'it is financially almost impossible to imagine benefits that are high enough to compensate the family for the lack of one income'. Paying women to stay at home to raise their children may also provide additional legitimacy to the idea that raising children is primarily women's work, and that fathers' interaction with children is not very important.[4]

Single mothers would find it, of course, quite impossible to stay at home on only $2500 a year (should the Kids First scheme be accepted). The majority of single mothers live in poverty, due in part to the partial, and all-too-frequently total absence of the father and his economic resources; in part to the mother's limited earning capacity, reflecting the disadvantages women, and especially mothers with children, face in the labour market; and in part to low levels of social security payments. Reconciling paid work and other family obligations presents special difficulties for lone parents. Part-time employment may seem a sensible solution to combining the roles of a caring and a breadwinning parent, but in most developed countries, the income available from part-time employment would not finance independence for a single person, let alone for a single parent family, nor would it better the income available from social assistance (Joshi, 1989). The majority of lone parents are thus caught in the welfare poverty trap.

Unlike other welfare recipients, lone parents are typically exempt from the requirement to look for work, reflecting the official belief that mothers of young children ought to stay at home. However, special benefits attached to lone parent status make single mothers vulnerable to attacks that the benefits actually promote lone parenthood, and to threats to withdraw these benefits. For example, in 1986, the then Queensland Minister for Welfare Services, Yvonne Chapman, suggested that sole parent benefits be stopped for unmarried mothers with more than one child. Many Queenslanders were sympathetic to that suggestion (Sawer, 1989: 24).

Single mothers on welfare benefits are often subject to unpleasant policing of their living arrangements. The special welfare benefits can be, and often are, withdrawn when the mother is found to be no longer single, even if she is just cohabiting with no sharing of financial resources taking place. When their children leave home, welfare mothers lose any special treatment which they enjoyed while their children were still living at home, making it that much harder for them to be able to find work after so many years spent in full-time mothering.

The only way to end welfare dependency is to have access to afford-able, state-supported childcare. The welfare view of childcare funding is quite logical since it is less expensive for the state to pay the childcare costs of the low-income parent than it is to pay her costs of subsistence through the welfare system. In the UK, childcare allowance of £50 a week is now available to unemployed single mothers taking part in the Government Job Training Scheme (Cohen, 1988a: 18). However, the introduction of the selective childcare allowance brought the government into conflict with its own anti-discrimination laws. In an important test case, the Bedford industrial tribunal ruled that the Training Commission's practice of allowing only single, divorced or separated parents to claim the childcare allowance constituted discrimination against married people under the 1975 Sex Discrimination Act (Davies, 1989).

Another subsidy to the 'stay-at-home mother' can be effected through income splitting between married couples. Income splitting is a form of family taxation that favours single income families. It tends to benefit the individual with the higher income, usually the man, and to penalise the secondary earner, usually the wife, as her income, when aggregated with her partner's, attracts a higher rate of taxation. This can act as a disincentive for married women to enter the paid workforce, or to increase their participation. Moreover, increasing the resources of one family member need not automatically increase the resources of *all* family members. In Australia, many 'stay-at-home mothers' are unaware whether or not the Dependent Spouse Rebate is received by their spouse, or what its value is (Sawer, 1989).

Some supporters of income splitting have promoted it as a pronatalist measure, on the grounds that it encourages women to stay at home and have children. 'There are indications, however,' Maas and McDonald (1989: 37) argue,

> that policies such as income splitting may have exactly the opposite effect. Where the combination of paid work with child-rearing is made more difficult, as with income splitting, more women may opt to have no children at all. Indeed, in West Germany where labour force participation rates of women with dependent children are low and where income splitting is in place, the birth rate is the lowest in the world. In contrast, Sweden, which has high labour force participation rates for women together with policies which enhance the combination of child-rearing and paid work, is the only country in the Western world in which the birth rate has risen significantly in recent years.[5]

PRONATALISM AND EQUAL OPPORTUNITY POLICIES

While pronatalism is conventionally regarded as a conservative cause, one can find several historical examples when national political concerns over falling birth rates coincided with implementation of progressive policies supporting women's equality, reproductive freedom, and state assistance to families with children. Thus the Swedish pronatalist policy, adopted in the 1930s to forestall what was then viewed as a precipitous and destructive decline in population, is best known both for its emphasis on voluntary parenthood, and for its extensive provision of government services for parents and children. While these provisions were originally developed to encourage fertility, as time went on, they have gradually become part of a general social policy, with their demographic policy attributes presently unclear.

Conversely, the explicit pronatalist policies adopted in Central and Eastern Europe in the late 1960s and early 1970s, built upon rather than repudiated the various egalitarian measures adopted earlier (in the

1950s) on social and humanitarian grounds. Family allowances, tax deductions for families with children, free antenatal medical care, maternity leaves, day care facilities and so on were originally introduced in the name of social justice, emancipation of women and to affirm the responsibility of the state for the welfare of the family, especially families with larger numbers of children. With the arrival of explicit pronatalism, many of these measures were amplified and expanded to meet explicitly pronatalist objectives (Heitlinger, 1979, 1987a).

In recent years, pronatalism and sex equality have been linked also in France. The French socialist government, which includes a Ministry for Women's Rights, has been at pains to dissociate itself from the position of the former conservative Gaullist Primer Minister, Michel Debré, who would like the state to pay women 'family salary' to stay at home and look after children, and thus also help to reduce unemployment. In contrast, the current French socialist *politique familiale* accepts both the modern woman's dual role as mother and worker, and reproductive freedom (Tomlinson, 1984).

COFACE, the confederation of some sixty traditionally conservative, largely Catholic, and mainly pronatalist family organisations in the member states of the European Community, also opposes the Debré-type argument, on the grounds that it is ineffective in the fight against unemployment, and, above all, that it is contrary to the principle of integrating work and family responsibilities. COFACE (1985, 1986) sees women's equal rights and opportunities, reproductive freedom and pronatalism as mutually compatible objectives.

Measures aimed at enabling women and men to reconcile employment with family responsibilities also characterise contemporary family policy in Quebec, where the government sees family policy as a 'particularly suitable vehicle for dealing with the birthrate'. However, 'the goal is always the quality of family life rather than reaching a particular birthrate' (Clichet, 1984: 84). Moreover, measures offering economic support for families, day care services, working time adjustment and pregnancy/maternity/parental leaves are seen as important components of both women's equality and family policy (Government of Canada, 1989: 19–23). However, Quebec pronatalism is also linked to attempts to increase public support for nationalist policies. As Baker (1990: 19) argues, the falling birth rate 'has become a rallying point for action to increase Quebec's power within the Canadian federation and to prevent further erosion of culture and language'.

Thus what the above policies have in common is their underlying nationalist, or in the case of COFACE, continentalist, orientation. As

Steiner (1984: 214) has argued, 'without the explicit tie between pro-natalism and the national interest, intensification and redirection of all social policy to provide more appropriate social conditions for parenthood becomes a policy objective in search of a justification'. I shall argue that the broadly conceived women's equality policy discussed in Chapter 2, that is the multifaceted, 'corrective' measures of positive (affirmative) action, can provide such a justification. As we noted, the concept of affirmative action often encompasses not only measures directly related to employment practices, but also policies attempting to facilitate access of women to the labour market, in the form of pre-employment and re-entry training programmes, support services for parents of young children, and social security and taxation structures that do not discourage women's employment.

Initially, the main emphasis of affirmative action policies has been on increasing the opportunities and options for women. As Russell (1984: 1071) argues,

> such an approach appears to overlook the possibility that women might have some *responsibility* to provide financial support for others. . . . An emphasis on choices for women, rather than on responsibilities, however, can be taken to imply that men have a greater responsibility for breadwinning. This approach could in fact help to limit women's employment opportunities by reinforcing traditional ideas about divisions of labour.

Similar criticism has been levelled against the notion of a 'mommy track'. The notion of a 'mommy track' refers to the slower, lower paid promotional route reserved for working mothers with children who are willing to trade off the pressure of fighting to the top of the corporate ladder for more free time with their families. Women without children, perceived as being more dedicated to their job, are placed on a fast career track with men. Thus, two categories of women employees are created, where bearing children becomes a liability to career advancement. Instead of highlighting the needs for employers to develop a work environment which accommodates work and family responsibilities for both sexes (as recommended in ILO Convention 156), 'mommy track' places the emphasis on individual women having to choose between having children or a career. There is no suggestion for a comparable 'daddy track'.

However, the recent Canadian and EEC positive action policies reviewed in Chapter 2 suggest a shift in focus from expanding employment options for women to more general, and more gender-neutral, concerns with the interface between family and employment. Thus, a broadly conceived equal opportunity policy, which attempts to reconcile family responsibilities with occupational aspirations, can provide a new, quite powerful justification for policies which in other contexts may be called pronatal or pronatalist. There is, of course, no guarantee that attempts to create more appropriate social conditions for parenthood in the workplace will effect the birth rate. As Brundtland (1983: 18) argues,

these types of measures are largely untried. They are however, the only possible options that I can see. They are worth trying, because they will in important ways contribute to a more humane and pleasant society. And they are not financially impossible to implement in our affluent societies.

Young (1989a: 44) has also argued that

many of the measures which would benefit young, educated women are of relatively low cost: part-time work; unpaid parental leave; the ability to continue a career without loss of status or pension rights after a break for childbearing; and high quality child care. In fact, it has been found that in Australia the benefits accruing to the government from the taxes of the additional female workers actually outweigh the costs of the provision of additional child care places.

The pronatal potential[6] of these policies is of particular importance to women who have postponed their childbearing. The longer women postpone childbearing, the more likely they are to be well educated and committed to long-term continuous participation in the labour force and to sex equality. With the postponement of first births from the early to mid-20s (or later), women increasingly are in the paid labour force when they are making decisions (often in conjunction with their spouses) as to whether and when to have their first child. Their decision is likely to be rationalised by the constraint of the poor availability of dependable, inexpensive childcare (Presser, 1986).

How does the availability of childcare affect fertility? To the extent that childcare availability increases women's entry into paid employment, it may be anti-natalist, but to the extent that it reduces the burden of child-rearing for those who are, and will remain in the labour force, it may be pronatalist. In Presser's view, in industrialised societies with large numbers of mothers with young children already in the workforce, and with fertility desires often exceeding actual behaviour, subsidising childcare for employed mothers (or parents) would seem to be pronatalist, as would a reduction of the caring burden after women (or parents) come home from work. Presser also suggests that both aspects of child care become problematic with the increase of the women's age at first birth, because women are more likely to want to remain in the labour force with minimal interruption after their first child is born. Furthermore, they will be making subsequent childbearing decisions while they are employed and experiencing these difficulties. Heitlinger (1987a) notes that mothers in Czechoslovakia who were finding it difficult to place their first-born children in day care tended to postpone their subsequent child, often indefinitely.

Thus, pronatalist health, family, taxation, social security and labour market policies that do not attempt to reconcile demands of parenthood with those of participation in the labour force, are unlikely to succeed in stimulating a higher birth rate. Needless to say, making the role of a mother (or parent) more compatible with that of a wage earner closely corresponds to the goals of sex equality, as viewed both from the traditional socialist perspective and the affirmative action framework discussed in this book. The effect of these policies is likely to be felt in the creation of more favourable social conditions and attitudes towards parenthood rather than in a direct incentive to have more children.

CONCLUSION

Pronatalism is a term that covers a broad spectrum of ideas and practices. In its most extreme, and most discredited version, pronatalism has been associated with imperialism, racism, eugenism, reinforcement of the traditional family model of father as breadwinner and mother as economically dependent homemaker, severe limitation of reproductive choice, and a selective combination of strong pronatalism for some with strong anti-natalism for others. At the other end of the ideological spectrum, pronatalism has been associated with policies supporting women's emancipation (by attempting to make the role of a mother more compatible with that of a wage earner), and with various forms of state assistance to families with children. The underlying rationale for these very different policies has been the belief that below-replacement fertility is socially undesirable, and that its reversal would serve the 'national interest', however that may be defined.

Relatively few of the developed countries have explicit pronatalist policies. McIntosh (1986) has identified four major barriers to the formulation and implementation of pronatalist policies: lack of public demand; distinct limits to governments' ability to finance all of the services and cash benefits deemed necessary by pronatalist proponents; doubts about the efficacy of financial incentives as a means of encouraging women, especially married women, to have more children; and, apart from few exceptions (for example France, Quebec), a weak nationalist rationale. As McIntosh (1986: 319, 320) put it, 'today, demographic factors carry less weight. . . . Governments appear loath to use the possibility of future crisis as the justification for measures that do not command broad popular support.'

However, almost all of the countries in the Western world can be described as welfare states. They have legislation, social services and income transfers that provide some form of assistance to mothers (and increasingly also to fathers), and to families with children, and as such, can be seen at least partly as pronatal.

It is the thesis of this book that broadly conceived women's equality policy, which encompasses not only measures directly related to employment practices, but also policies attempting to facilitate access of women to the labour market, offer a more compelling rationale for broad indirect pronatal policies than the traditional demographic and political arguments. Various support services for young children and their parents, flexible work arrangements, re-entry training programmes, and social security and taxation structures that do not penalise women for motherhood have been promoted as measures of equal opportunities for women, yet they are quite compatible with pronatalism. While it is quite conceivable that broad equal opportunity policies will have no effect on fertility (after all, increase in fertility is not their explicit objective), it is equally plausible that they may at least prevent further fertility decline.

6 Immigration as Substitution for Higher Birth Rates and Pronatalism

INTRODUCTION

Immigration is a complex area of public policy. It touches upon questions of population size and distribution, economic development, labour recruitment, nation building, culture, language, ethnicity, race, human rights, international relations, and the discriminatory treatment of women as dependants of their migrating husbands, foreign domestic workers or the physical reproducers ('breeders') of specific ethnic and national collectivities. Unlike Great Britain, which regards immigration negatively, as a potential threat to national integration, Canada and Australia have long promoted immigration as a positive feature of national development.

During the inter-war period, World War II and its immediate aftermath, when Great Britain exhibited considerable despondency and alarm over the low birth rate, both past and future as anticipated by demographers,

> one possible 'solution' to the so-called 'population problem' that was firmly ruled out by the British state was encouraging immigration to Britain by the non-Anglo-Saxon inhabitants of the British colonies. This was in spite of the fact that official concern about population *growth* in some of the colonies was being expressed at this time.
>
> (Klug, 1989: 25)

Since the 1960s, the preoccupation of successive British governments has been to restrict rather than encourage immigration, especially by those without British ancestry. Successive British governments have implemented a wide range of restrictive social and immigration policies to curb the entry of non-White British subjects from former colonies. Ethnic composition rather than the nation's birth rate, size and age structure has been the dominant concern of British post-war immigration policies.

In contrast, successive post-war Canadian and Australian governments have issued several statements and reports which have outlined the positive economic, demographic, social, humanitarian, cultural, international and defence benefits of immigration. However, until the 1970s, none of these statements envisaged that immigration may have to compensate for deficit in fertility, and thus prevent population decline and population ageing. By the early 1970s the post-war baby boom had ended, and fertility had fallen below the replacement level. As the decade progressed, the prospect of future population decline and population ageing began to cause some alarm, mainly in academic and government circles. By the mid-1980s, both Canada and Australia began to adjust their immigration policies to this demographic phenomenon, planning to admit much larger numbers of immigrants. Below-replacement fertility thus became an important new element in the legitimation of immigration. However, this is not to imply that the shift towards higher immigration levels was directly influenced by the results of demographic research.

As we shall see, immigration policy is not formulated on demographic grounds alone. Policy formulation, and to a lesser extent implementation, are primarily political processes, which are guided by a political rather than demographic rationality. The findings of research compete with the frequently unfounded claims of more vocal pressure groups, to which the government must respond. One also has to realise how often demographers have been wrong in their predictions. As Teitelbaum (1990: 19) suggests, the baby boom

> should introduce a certain modesty among demographers since none predicted either the boom nor its reversal. At a time when 90 per cent of fertility is under the rational control of women, demography has (paradoxically) much difficulty in rationally anticipating their behaviour. While demographic change can be forecast more reliably than economic or political change, fertility predictions cannot go beyond some 10 or 20 years.

Moreover, demographers typically provide policy makers with various scenarios (for example if fertility remains below, at or slightly above replacement levels) without knowing which of the senarios presented is likely to predict the future, because they often have insufficient social, political or economic knowledge to make that judgment. Population projections made in Canada in 1970 predicted that the Canadian population in the year 2001 will be either 41 million (if fertility and immigration are high) or 30 million (if fertility and immigration are low). 'How useful', asks Marsden (1972: 111), 'are projections that range from 30 to 41 million? How is rational planning advanced when there may be a several million person difference either way?' And what if both projections are wrong? More recent estimates expect Canada to reach its 'peak' population, 31 million, 'only' in 2026. At that time, the Canadian population is projected to begin a long, slow decline, reaching 25 million after 2086, ultimately reaching a stable population of 18 million, comparable to the size of the country in the late 1950s (Health and Welfare Canada, 1989).

In these circumstances of uncertainty, research findings are often used selectively, as retroactive justification for policy decisions that have been determined in the broader political context. Moreover, research findings that are supportive of existing policies (for example immigration can slightly delay population ageing) are usually given more prominence than findings which are not seen as politically relevant (for example immigration has no impact on population ageing in the long run). This is another way of saying that governments tend to use demography when it appears to their political advantage (McIntosh and Finkle, 1985; Richmond, 1987).

The major goals of this chapter are to examine: (1) the ways in which declining birth rates and the prospect of population decline and population ageing have been used in Canada and Australia to legitimise immigration; (2) whether immigration can and needs to offset the ageing of the population and the decline in population size; (3) the benefits and costs of immigration policies *vis-à-vis*, or jointly with, pronatalist policies; and (4) the relationship between demographic data and policy.

CANADA

Below-replacement fertility and immigration in the 1970s

The potential of immigration to compensate for long-term deficit in fertility was put on the national agenda during the preparation of the 1976 Canada Immigration Act. The Act was the product of extensive work by a government task force, an inter-departmental drafting committee, and a parliamentary committee which held public hearings across Canada. Both the Green Paper on Immigration Policy (produced by the task force), and the Special Joint Committee of the Senate and the House of Commons on Immigration Policy (appointed to examine the Green Paper and to hold public hearings on it across Canada), noted that immigration seemed likely to become increasingly important as a determinant of population growth in view of Canada's declining birth rate and continuing losses through emigration.

One of the recommendations of the Special Joint Committee's ex plicitly suggested that,

> immigration should be treated in future as a central variable in a national population policy. A country as large and thinly populated as Canada cannot afford the declining population which is indicated by current trends in fertility, and must continue to welcome a minimum of 100 000 immigrants a year as long as present fertility rates prevail. Major efforts should also be made to forestall a further decline in Canada's French-speaking population.

Throughout the national debate on immigration and population, im migration issues of planning and management, racism, and the selective admission of different classes of immigrants were discussed with much more care and in greater depth than demographic issues of the size, distribution and the rate of growth of the Canadian population (Hawkins, 1991: 63–70). In the end, Canada's declining birth rate and the prospect of future population decline did not become the significant issues they were to become a decade later. The outcome of the debates, the 1976 Immigration Act, is regarded by Hawkins (1991: 70) as 'an innovative, liberal and effective piece of legislation and a vast improvement on its 1952 predecessor'. The Act explicitly affirmed in law the various objectives and principles of Canadian immigration policy: family reunion, non-discrimination, concern for refugees and the promotion of Canada's demographic, economic, social and cultural goals.

The Act contained several important new provisions relating to the planning and management of Canadian immigration. It established three principal classes of immigrants who could be admitted to Canada: (1) independent immigrants selected on the basis of the points system (first introduced in 1967), which measures the applicant's education and training, job opportunities, language ability, age and personal suitability; (2) family class immigrants sponsored by a relative in Canada; and (3) refugees. The Act also required an annual announcement of future immigration levels in Parliament, an extensive consultative process, and specification of demographic considerations in immigration planning.

Canadian immigration policy in the 1980s

The deep and prolonged recession of the early 1980s created unemployment, and produced sharp reductions in both planned and actual landings. In May 1982, a requirement was imposed on independent applicants in the economic stream to have a prearranged job to be eligible for landing. This requirement reduced total landings to just over 84 000 in 1985 from 128 000 in 1981. By 1985, only 6500 selected immigrant workers were landed in comparison to about 60 000 in 1975. As Taylor (1987: 10) argues, this downward trend in immigration 'represented a continuation of a short term "tap-on, tap-off" approach to immigration planning based on fluctuations in unemployment levels'.

However, it is worth noting that Lloyd Axworthy, who was the Liberal Employment and Immigration Minister during this period, remained supportive of the demographic rationale for immigration. Adamant that a short-term economic recession should not deflect the country from its long-term immigration goals, Axworthy suggested in an interview that 'immigration provides a very useful component in maintaining a level of growth, because as the birth rates decline and as the age of the population becomes older, immigration is one way of continually providing new people' (quoted in Hay, 1982: 56). A similar view is presented in a study of Canadian fertility by Anatole Romaniuc (1984: 94):

> The current regime of low fertility, and the consequent aging and slowdown of growth in the Canadian population, are creating an historically new situation which may affect long-term immigration strategies. Indeed, if the fertility rate does not increase substantially and if population growth is a national goal, then large-scale immigration is the alternative.

Romaniuc's study was published just prior to the election of a new Conservative government, which took office in September 1984. His study gave an added impetus to growing concerns in government circles about the need to re-establish the linkage between immigration and demography (Romaniuc, personal communication). In January 1985, Flora MacDonald, the new Employment and Immigration Minister, launched a special immigration policy review. Its results were set out in a special Report to Parliament on the Review of Future Directions for Immigration Levels, which was tabled by the Minister in the House of Commons in June 1985.

This was the first time since the introduction of forward planning by the 1976 Immigration Act that an immigration levels document other than the regular autumn report had been tabled in Parliament. The special report indicated the Mulroney government's determination to reverse the trend to declining landings by moderate, controlled increases in immigration levels; to restore the balance between the three main immigration streams by increasing the intake of independent economic immigrants; and to address the impact of migration on future demographic characteristics of Canada. The special report also provided the federal government with an opportunity to acknowledge the work of the House of Commons Standing Committee on Labour, Employment and Immigration. Its 1985 reports focused on current demographic concerns and their relationship to the immigration programme. Among other things, the Standing Committee recommended using immigration policy to smooth out the current age imbalance in the Canadian population.

The relationship between immigration levels and the nation's demographic future was considered even more explicitly in the regular 1985 *Annual Report to Parliament on Future Immigration Levels*. The required chapter on 'Demographic Considerations' suggested the following:

> Demographic projections indicate that the Canadian population would begin to decline shortly after the turn of the century if fertility continued at its current below-replacement level of 1.7 and if net immigration continued at the low levels experienced in recent years.
>
> Immigration is the available mechanism for shaping future population of Canada's demographic future.
>
> There is need to consider the broader economic and social implications of Canada's demographic future.
>
> (Employment and Immigration Canada, 1985: 11).

In May 1986, the government announced a new multidisciplinary demographic study. The special Review of Demography and Its Implications for Economic and Social Policy, initially established for three years but subsequently extended until mid-1992, was appointed under the direction of Jake Epp, Minister of Health and Welfare Canada and Chairman of the Cabinet Committee on Social Development.

The Demographic Review

The Review of Demography and its Implications for Economic and Social Policy was very broadly conceived. It was supposed to generate empirical evidence on the following issues: population projections for Canada for the next forty years (1985–2025); the prospect of population decline nationally and regionally within this time horizon; the impact of Canada's changing age structure during the next forty years on federal policies and programmes; the relationship between Canada's projected population growth and economic growth, including the long-term benefits and costs of immigration to and emigration from Canada; the impact of immigration to Canada on internal patterns, urban/suburban/rural growth and the Canadian labour market; the relationship between changes in fertility rates and changes in the family; and comparative policy and programme response of other countries. However, this broad focus was not sustained. Apart from an optimistic assurance that the demographic problems are not as serious as previously thought and that there is no 'demographic crisis', the final Report of the Demographic Review, *Charting Canada's Future*, had little to say about demographic implications for economic and social policy.

The final report is a relatively short, but 'an interesting and informative document, presented in an attractive diagrammatic form that, as intended, makes its demographic materials easy to understand' (Hawkins, 1991: xxiii). Judging from the nature of Members of Parliament questions upon the release of the report, it needed to be quite simple. Some MPs knew nothing about demographic trends (Maureen Baker, personal communication). This reality was appreciated much more by journalists than by academics. While journalists generally liked the report, academic commentators found it short on analysis, forecasts, proposals for policy or action, and lacking in explanations and data necessary for the support of some of its arguments (Fisher, 1989; Hay, 1990; Beaujot, 1990; Federation of Canadian Demographers, 1990).

The basic two themes of the report are (1) the description of demographic trends in Canada and other prosperous developed countries, such as Sweden, whose population ageing is more advanced than in Canada, and (2) an optimistic assurance that the demographic problems are not as serious as was previously thought. Neither population decline or stagnation, nor the ageing of the population (both correctly seen as the result of declining fertility) are regarded as causes for alarm. The current age structure with a large proportion of women in the childbearing ages would ensure that the population would grow until the year 2026, although immigration rather than fertility is regarded as the main component of population growth:

> As the effects of the current age structure disappear, Canada's population tends toward a constant size, a size that depends solely on the level of immigration. With fertility at 1.7 and with 130 000 immigrants per year, the population would peak at 31 million and then would decline to a stable 18 million. With immigration of 200 000 a year, it would peak at 35 million and later could decline to a stable level of 33 million. With zero net immigration, the population peaks at 28 million in 2011, and eventually, eight hundred years from now, disappears. (Health and Welfare Canada, 1984: 44)

However, as Sharir (1990: 23–24) argues, 'the claims that population levels peak and stabilize according to the level of immigration, and that zero net migration spells the disappearance of Canada, hold only if the current below-replacement fertility rate continues indefinitely'. In Sharir's view, a declining population will lead to various social adjustments, which 'may be expected to change society's values by placing a premium on rearing children. All these adjustments, except for the rise of females' wage rates, can be expected to raise fertility at least to its replacement level. Thus, the Canadian population is likely to stabilize even without immigration, contrary to the impression left by the report.'

The Demographic Review is best viewed as a legitimation exercise used by bureaucrats and politicians to secure retroactive rationalisation and justification for past decisions – in this case the 'moderate, controlled' increases in immigration levels during the mid-1980s. During the second half of the 1980s, annual intakes more than doubled from the low of 84 000 in 1985 to a high of 189 200 in 1989. Even higher immigration levels are planned for the 1990s.

The planning of the 1991–5 immigration levels

The majority of ethnic minority, multicultural and refugee support groups who were consulted during the planning of the 1991–5 immigration target levels extolled the benefits of immigration. Many favoured immigration level target of 1 per cent of the Canadian population, which amounts to about 265 000 immigrants a year. However, there were other groups, such as the House of Commons Standing Committee on Labour, Employment and Immigration, business groups, municipal governments and researchers from the Ottawa-based Institute for Research on Public Policy, who urged caution. Rather than seeking to simply increase the overall intake levels, these groups favoured a shift in immigration policy away from family-sponsored immigrants, over whom Canada has limited discretion, to independent immigrants, who are selected under the stringent points system on the basis of their education, language and job skills. Municipal governments in the cities most affected by immigration and refugee claimants also pointed out that they had to shoulder increased costs for services immigrants require without assistance from the federal government. Finally, there was also the government of Quebec, which wanted to increase Francophone immigration.

The five-year immigration plan announced in October 1990 tried to balance all these concerns. Annual immigration levels were increased by 50 000 above current levels, up to 250 000 annually; the government tightened up on the types of people who are admitted as family members, using the notion of dependence on the Canadian family as the determining factor in admission; and an additional $200 million was promised for language training during the next four years to ease immigrants' adjustment to the country. In announcing the plan, the government returned to the demographic rationale. When asked about the immigration increase on television, Michael Wilson, the Finance Minister, talked about the need to compensate through immigration for low fertility and the ageing of the population. However, the argument which carried the day in cabinet internal debates was not one of demography but one of politics. Ethnic minority voters in Canada have long been regarded as partial to the Liberals. By responding positively to lobbying from ethnic groups to substantially increase immigration, the Tories were hoping to make significant inroads in the ethnic communities and obtain sustained electoral support from grateful ethnic minority voters (Winsor, 1990).

AUSTRALIA

Below-replacement fertility, population ageing and immigration in the 1970s

The issues of below-replacement fertility and its significance for immigration were first put on the national agenda by the National

Population Inquiry, which was established by the federal government in 1970 to look into all aspects of Australian population growth, including natural increase and immigration. The Inquiry was set up in response to growing concerns in the late 1960s among some people who 'began to question the value of large-scale immigration on the grounds of pollution, development, quality of life, the selection of immigrants and the world population explosion' (National Population Inquiry, 1975: vi). The Inquiry was a joint enterprise between the federal government and Australian National University. The Inquiry was chaired by Professor W. D. Borrie, the then Head of the Department of Demography. The Inquiry investigated Australia's demographic situation in considerable depth and held public hearings in all states. Its first report was produced in 1975, followed by a supplementary report and a series of shorter research reports three years later. The scholarly examination of future desirable population size concluded that the levels of population growth implied in the fertility and immigration trends up to 1971 were no longer appropriate. A marked downswing in fertility, together with a deliberate reduction of migrant intake to 80,000 new settlers a year by the Whitlam government (1972–5), slowed down population growth. With fertility soon expected to decline to replacement levels, natural growth was expected to be very modest in ensuing years. The Inquiry then presented three population outcomes for Australia, showing the impact of three possible levels of net immigration: 50 000, 75 000 and 100 000 per annum (National Population Inquiry, 1975: 724–5; Hawkins, 1991: 111–14). The Supplementary Report of the National Population Inquiry (1978) recommended 50 000 as the preferred net immigration level, but this did not prove to be the view of the Fraser government, when it came to power in 1975.

The new government's priorities were worked out during the final months of the Whitlam administration (Hawkins, 1991: 116). In March 1976, three months after the Liberal National Country Party Coalition took office, the new Minister for Immigration and Ethnic Affairs, Michael MacKellar, made a Ministerial Statement in the House of Representatives, explicitly linking immigration with below-replacement fertility. Australia, he said, was in a period of significant fertility decline. The decline in the birth rate and immigration had led to a considerable drop in the rate of population increase and to the ageing of the population. Not responding to this situation would mean a transfer of economic resources from education, training and investment in productive processes to the needs of the aged. As it was neither acceptable nor feasible to increase fertility, external migration was the only major instrument available to the government to influence the level and composition of Australia's population, and the government was committed to using it. The Labor Opposition accepted the demographic argument that slower growth and a more mature age composition were grounds for anxiety (Betts, 1988: 123–4; Hawkins, 1991: 125). The minister then announced the reconstitution of the Australian Population and Immigration Council (APIC) created by the Whitlam government a year earlier. One of the APIC's first tasks, according to the minister, would be the preparation of a Green Paper on immigration and population matters. Drawing on the findings of the National Population Inquiry, the Green Paper examined the implications of recent demographic trends and prospects for population growth in Australia. It was tabled in Parliament on 17 March 1977 and led to a protracted debate about the economic and demographic costs and benefits of immigration. According to Betts (1988: 127),

> the success of the demographic argument about the ageing of the population was illustrated by the fact that only one speaker questioned it. In an emphatic attack on growth policies Cass [who was then Shadow Minister for Health] pointed out that the aged need not be a burden on society, and that the spectre raised by the Government of increasing hordes of elderly dependents was in conflict with the Government's retirement policies. But this scepticism was not shared and some Labor speakers gave definite support to the Government's position and had fears of their own to contribute.

Thus the two traditional justifications for immigration in Australia – defence and economic growth – were in the mid-1970s joined by a third, a need to offset future population decline and to help achieve a more balanced age structure of the Australian population. As Betts (1988: 28–9) has argued, the need to forestall population ageing,

> became a strong theme in the justification of the immigration programme. Growth lobbyists did not necessarily argue that a more mature age structure was undesirable in itself, rather they made links between demographic ageing and economics. A growing number of frail elderly people would seriously strain the capacity of a diminishing pool of taxpayers and would waste the scarce resources needed for economic recovery. The numbers of the aged could not be reduced but they could be offset by adding more people to the younger age group categories. There was no point in trying to increase the birth

rate with higher family allowances, child care programmes, or other forms of social supports for parents. This was too costly. The easy and obvious solution to the 'problem' of lower birth rates was immigration.

Below-replacement fertility, population ageing and immigration in the 1980s

Labor returned to power in 1983 under a new leader, Bob Hawke. Its first major statement on Australian immigration policy and on the 1983–4 immigration programme was delivered on 18 May 1983 in the House of Representatives by Stuart West, the new Minister for Immigration and Ethnic Affairs. The statement signalled significant reorientation of immigration priorities and a temporary reduction of migrant intake in response to economic recession and high levels of unemployment. After suggesting that immigration was needed neither for population growth nor as a major supplier of skilled labour, the Minister stated that the major purpose of immigration should be 'to serve a social and humanitarian purpose, emphasizing family reunion and the admission of refugees who should be drawn from a wider area of need'. West also emphasised that the government is committed 'to the continued development of the Business Migration Program with the specific objective of introducing new and improved business technology, the creation of jobs, and the stimulation of exports (quoted in Hawkins, 1991: 250).

However, the downgrading of demographic considerations did not last very long. By 1985, Australia's low fertility and prospect of population decline re-emerged as important justifications for expanded immigration. In 1985, during the announcement of 1986–7 immigration levels in Parliament, Chris Hurford, who replaced West as Immigration Minister, once again linked immigration with the problems of population decline and ageing that face Australia as a result of low level of fertility, 'currently 10 per cent below the long-term population replacement level with little chance of recovery'. Immigration, he said, must now be seen in the context of Australia's population and economic development needs. The Government was concerned to 'awaken Australia's interest in an appreciation of the population dimension'. Its vision of future was one of 'managed, gradual expansion of the migration program', growing to 95 000 in 1986–7, 110 000 the following year and 125 000 in 1988–9, from 89 000 in 1989. Subject to community support, these levels could represent 'a return by managed steps to historical intake levels of 160–

Immigration   155

170 000 or about 1 per cent of the population of that time' (quoted in Hawkins, 1991: 272–3).

Hurford expanded on these themes in his opening address to the Third Australian Population Association Conference, held in Adelaide on 3 December 1986. Hurford (1986: 5) paid particular attention to a commissioned report entitled *Greying Australia*, which was prepared by Hal Kendig and John McCallum of the Australian National University for the National Population Council:

> In announcing the current immigration policy earlier this year I made reference to the ageing of Australia's population. Since then the 'Greying Australia' Report has been released. One of the findings was that immigration can postpone the impact of population ageing. Immigration, of course, cannot reverse the process but it can have a small but significant retarding effect, particularly when the cost implications of an older population are related to the financial burden of taxpayers. The government does not use immigration's impact on ageing as the rationale for increasing the intake but it does regard such impact as beneficial.

Hurford (1986: 7–8) also explained why the Government was not considering the adoption of a pronatalist policy:

> The government shares the community's general feeling that a return to higher fertility levels is unlikely in the foreseeable future and that any intervention by the government to encourage people to have larger families is neither appropriate nor likely to succeed. Accordingly, population and economic growth will have to be substantially underwritten by managed, economically driven, expanding immigration programs.

In Hurford's (1986: 7) view, demographic justifications go hand in hand with economic ones:

> This government is committed to restoring Australia's international competitiveness and to raising real living standards for all. I cannot contemplate any economic or social strategy towards these ends which would not embrace a central role for population growth and expanded immigration of the right blend.

Critiques of the demographic rationale for immigration

The argument that the aged cost more than the young rests solely on the *public* costs of caring for dependents. Restricting the costs to what is covered by taxpayers is an incomplete way of considering the social costs of dependency, because it ignores private costs incurred by families, especially women. Once the *total* costs (that is, both public and private) of youth and aged dependency are taken into account, supporting a child far exceeds the total costs of supporting an elderly person. As Betts (1988: 30) put it, 'a two-year old child requires far more care than her 67-year old grandmother. The grandmother probably needs no more care than any other adult and may well be helping to look after the grandchild and a range of other people as well.'

Intergenerational flows of economic and emotional assistance are by no means all in one direction. As Day (1988a: 183) points out, 'the aged, in addition to doing a lot for themselves and one another, frequently also lend support to younger elements in the population. Among other things, they care for children, extend financial assistance (with school fees, for example, and equity for home purchases), provide counsel and emotional support. It is assistance no less real for its not being allocated through some marketplace.'

In her review of myths and misconceptions concerning the demographic effects of immigration, Young (1988, 1989b) found that with current fertility rates 10 per cent below replacement and zero net immigration, the Australian population would continue to increase by about 3 million to a level of nearly 19 million in 2026. It would remain above its present level of 16 million for about 95 years. Young (1988: 222) also questions the idea that 'a stationary population is undesirable, and that Australia's population can keep on growing forever. Obviously, in the interests of quality of life, limits of resources and so on, the population cannot grow indefinitely, and a time will have to come when a stationary population is the wisest choice.' Young (1988: 227–8) also stresses the need to consider the very long-term effects of the demographic decisions that we make today:

> We cannot simply say, let's bring in a net of 100 000 migrants each year to achieve a total population of 23 million in 2021. We also need to know that if we keep on with such a high intake the population will increase by another four million by the middle of the century. We also need to know that if we suddenly decide that 23 million is indeed quite enough people, and reduce the annual net immigration to zero

beyond 2021, the population would still continue to increase for several decades.

In another publication, Young (1989b: 11) suggests that higher levels of immigration may actually reduce fertility, because a high level of immigration increases demand for housing, thereby creating a shortage and forcing up both house prices and rents. In turn, the lack of affordable housing 'may prevent young couples from settling down and starting a family, thus reducing the numbers of births'.

Finally, Young (1990b: 57) suggests that there is no need for increased immigration to offset deficit in fertility because 'the decline in fertility in Australia is not as serious as some alarmists claim'. Demographic projections based on the longitudinal measure of the total lifetime fertility of generations of women in Australia suggest that fertility will not fall below replacement level until women born since 1959 complete their childbearing, which will be beyond the year 2000. In contrast, the cross-sectional annual TFR has been below the replacement level (though only just) since 1977. However, Young (1990b: 57) concludes, 'because the decline has now reached the level of just below-replacement fertility among generations of women, it is desirable that no further decline in cohort lifetime fertility occurs'.

None of the environmentalist, demographic and social security arguments have had any effect on immigration policy making. An official at the Department of Immigration, Local Government and Ethnic Affairs (DILGEA) remarked to me in an interview in February 1990 that the Department carefully monitors demographic characteristics of the three major migration categories – family, skill and humanitarian – but that demographic considerations drive neither overall programme levels nor the relativities of the categories. While demographic consequences of the programme levels might be subsequently taken into account, government immigration policy is not formulated on demographic grounds alone. The government must also respond to vocal business, ethnic and refugee advocacy lobbies, which all favour much larger immigration intakes. What this means is that immigration policy makers in Australia have to balance politically the economic and humanitarian arguments for growth against the ecological and demographic arguments whether Australia can, or should, support that many people. Demographers tend to play a rather marginal role in this negotiating process. Demographic research is rarely cross-disciplinary in its orientation, and it seldom addresses the politically important economic, social and humanitarian criteria. As a result, demographic research tends to be marginalised, unless it is seen as politically relevant.

Migration versus pronatalist policies

In her comparative review of population policies in developed countries, Young (1989a: 49) argues that 'none of the European nations, which are facing older populations, below-replacement fertility and the prospect of declining populations in the next century, sees immigration as the solution to its situation'. According to data compiled by the United Nations, 'only the United States, Australia and Canada intend to maintain their high levels of (legal) immigration. All other countries, including those which consider their level of fertility to be too low, wish either to lower the current intake of migrants, or to maintain an existing insignificant level of immigration.' Young (1989a: 51) also suggests that 'the United States, Canada and Australia are unique in that they are the only countries which have no overt policy to maintain their level of fertility and at the same time support a significant level of immigration'.

Betts (1988: 31–2) argues that broadly defined pronatalist policies are more justifiable than expanded immigration:

> Changes in the age structure of the population are very much an outcome of changes in fertility and mortality; immigration makes a substantial difference to total numbers but has only marginal effect on age. Seventeen per cent over the age of sixty-four is rather more than the 14 per cent which is normal for a post-transition society. But attaining the balanced age structure of a demographically mature society requires not immigration but more assistance to parents so that fertility can move to slightly higher levels. Rising housing costs, longer formal education, and the hard work involved in bringing up children in congested cities have increased the heavy responsibilities of parents. Children are not simply their parents' private hobby. The wider society has an interest in their health and education, and an obligation to help the people who shoulder the greater part of the rising costs of child rearing.

In Europe, France is the only country which has at various times in its history promoted both pronatalist and immigration policies. However, the risk (and the reality) of racial and ethnic tensions between in-digeneous and immigrant workers, and the recognition that immigrant workers are not necessarily cheap workers,[1] have convinced officials involved in population policy formulation that 'it is more sensible to try to raise the birth rate rather than to leave oneself entirely dependent on immigration' (McIntosh, 1983: 104).

Lesthaeghe (1988) regards immigration as an inefficient instrument to solve Europe's demographic problems. 'If migration is to compensate for the currently highly deficient reproduction of their nationals,' Lesthaeghe (1988: 17) argues,

> the EC-12, including the five member-states that now have hardly any non-EC nationals, would have to attract and absorb an immigration stream of the order of 2.5 to 3.0 immigrants per thousand population every year . . . they would also have to accept that one-third of all EC-residents would be aliens or descendants of aliens by the middle of the next century. Since migration is likely to be unevenly spread, some areas (particularly urban areas in the northern member-states, which already have sizeable alien populations) would undergo even more marked and rapid transformation.

Immigration could counter population ageing only

> if a 'guestworker' policy was applied extremely strictly, that is if all immigrants came on strictly limited-duration visas and were required to return to their country of origin after a few years. However, the experience of the 1960s and 70s in Europe (and the rising numbers of illegal immigrants in the US in the 80s) illustrates the difficulties of applying such a policy. And, at any rate, the physical departure of an immigrant does not remove him or her from the population entirely when, for example, her or she has acquired pension rights through his/her contributions to the unfunded pension schemes typical of western Europe. (Lesthaeghe, 1988: 18)

The idea that very low fertility can be countered by a steady influx of young migrants pays little attention to the ageing of immigrants themselves and to the future course of immigrant fertility. Once immigrants adjust their fertility to that of their host population, no significant immigrant-induced population rejuvenation occurs. Moreover, Lesthaeghe (1988: 19) argues, 'the ultimate stationary population resulting from a regime with a fixed influx of young aliens who adopt sub-replacement fertility, would be *older*, not younger, than the present population'. Lesthaeghe (1988: 17, 24) suggests that 'a gradual restoration of replacement-level fertility among nationals during the next 25

160   *Women's Equality, Demography and Public Policies*

years would be just as effective as the combination of record immigration and continued below-replacement fertility among nationals',
and that 'in the longer run, an effective pro-natalist policy for EC-
nationals would be more effective with respect to aging than would
massive immigration'.

Lesthaeghe's conclusions are broadly similar to those reached by
Charting Canada's Future. Increases in Canadian immigration to levels
as high as 600 000 per year, have, in the long run, no impact on the age
structure. An increase in fertility to replacement levels has only a minor
impact. Only a significant (and highly unlikely) increase in the fertility
rate, from the current 1.7 to at least 3.1, would reverse the long-term
trend towards an older demographic age structure. As we noted,
Charting Canada's Future implies that population ageing is not a
serious problem. Moreover, it makes no specific proposals for policy
action, pronatalist or otherwise.

Pronatal and pronatalist policies have the advantage of providing
social justice for parents in comparison with childless couples or
individuals. As Höhn (1988: 477) argues,

> this alone is a sufficient objective of a policy that requires no further
> demographic justification. The precondition of such a generally
> accepted policy is that measures are not coercive, but that they
> facilitate realization of procreative wishes. The greater efficacy of
> coercive measures is not a sufficient motive for adopting them because
> they create social tensions, frustration and a potential for political
> instability.

As we noted in the last chapter, the major barriers to the formulation
and implementation of active fertility policies are lack of public demand;
the negative connotations associated with government attempts to
encourage women to have more children; distinct limits to governments'
ability to finance all of the services and cash benefits that are deemed
necessary by pronatalist proponents; doubts about the efficacy of
financial incentives as a means of encouraging women, especially married women, to have more children; and an already ageing population.

The influence of the latter is evident in an increasing competition for
resources between advocates of expenditures in social security and those
aiming at policies supporting families with children. The outcome has
been largely at the expense of children and their parents, in part because

the elderly are voters while children are not (Kernaghan, 1982; Preston, 1984; McIntosh, 1986; Coale, 1986; Höhn, 1988). A similar argument is applied by Young (1990b: 62) to a situation 'where the provision of funds for families and children is in competition with funds to maintain a high level of immigration at a time when the electoral power of ethnic groups is increasing'.

Viewed from a simple quantitative perspective, migration strategies are by far the easiest way to increase the total numbers in the population. However, as we noted, immigration has only a marginal effect on the age structure of the population. To the extent that immigration is viewed as making up for deficit fertility, it raises an important question about the meaning of procreative choice. As Taylor (1987: 18) put it, 'if fertility decisions continue to remain voluntary, will Canadians view increased immigration as a negation of their voluntary choice to have fewer children?'

Immigration as a demographic recruitment policy can have many undesirable ecological and social consequences. In Australia, researchers (and many ordinary people) are concerned about the effect of population growth on congestion, urban sprawl, and encroachment on farming and forest lands resulting from the expansion of Australia's major cities. Because immigration is a major component of Australian population growth, this has led to the questioning of the continued high levels of immigration (Betts, 1990; Young, 1988; Joske, 1989). In contrast, policy makers such the Immigration Minister Chris Hurford (1986: 6) claim that 'Australians are becoming progressively more accepting and supportive of larger immigration programs. They patently see the benefits in population growth, they would like to see greater fertility but are pessimistic about it happening and they do not foresee population increases having a serious impact on the environment so long as a balance is maintained in their management.' Thus Australians are quite divided on the benefits of high levels of immigration, much more than their Canadian counterparts.

The impact of population growth (sustained by high migrant intake) on the environment has received considerably less attention in Canada. While the final report of the Demographic Review reported the growing ethnic diversity of immigrants, and the tendency of immigrants to settle in a limited number of ethnic neighbourhoods in large metropolitian areas such as Toronto, Vancouver and Montreal, it failed to address any potentially negative implications of these developments either for the environment or for race relations. This ommission is criticised by Sharir (1990: 24):

As the number of minority groups, their population sizes, and their concentrations in major cities increase, one expects racial intolerance and social tensions to increase as well. This is more likely to occur during periods of recessions. While this issue brings us close to dangerous waters, society cannot benefit from pretending that the issue does not exist. It is, therefore, disappointing that the report does not deal with the issue. Canadian society has to decide whether the immigration of minorities should be curtailed.

However, as we noted, the dominant view among the numerous participants in the extensive immigration consultations that took place between November 1989 and March 1990, is that immigration is good for Canada and that admission levels should be increased during the next five years. There are no Canadian equivalents to the vocal environmentalist anti-immigration groups such as the Australian Conservation Foundation, Australians for an Ecologically Sustainable Population, Writers for an Ecologically Sustainable Population or Australians Against Further Immigration. These lobbyists have over the years repeatedly called for a reassessment of the federal migration program on ecological as well as economic grounds, first attacking the growth lobby's claims on the benefits of population growth, and more recently explaining the benefits of lower numbers and stability (Betts, 1990).

In fact, the Australian federal Cabinet agreed to a fairly substantial reduction in the numbers of new settlers for 1990–1. The government had decided on a balanced reduction from the 1989–90 planning level of 140 000 to the new planning level for 1990–1 of 126 000. According to Hawkins (1991: xvii), 'this decision was applauded by conservation groups and condemned by ethnic group leaders, with some politicians, academics, journalists, and others taking sides in a continuing debate. There was further reduction to 111,000 in 1991–92, but there are plans to bring this level up to 128,000 in 1993–4'.

In Canada, the contribution of immigration to the growth of the English-speaking at the expense of the French-speaking population has been politically much more significant. In recent years, in an attempt to reverse this trend, increasing the birth rate and retaining more Francophone immigrants have become the rallying points for action for Quebec nationalists. Their major goal is to increase or at least retain Quebec's power within the Canadian federation, and to prevent further erosion of culture and language. However, as Baker (1990: 19) notes in her analysis of benefits and costs of Quebec pronatalist and immigration policies, an increased population does not guarantee the retention of a society's culture. In fact, increasing Francophone immigration could lead to more third-world immigrants whose customs might alter substantially the nature of Quebec society. Furthermore, direct pronatalist policies might prove to be more effective among certain ethnic minorities rather than Quebec-born Francophones, as appears to be the case in 1989. In addition, incentives to raise the birth rate might be most effective among families with insufficient funds to raise their children, which would place more pressure on social services.

In Europe, immigration has been blamed for growing racial and ethnic tensions. As Höhn (1988: 477) has argued,

the resistance toward immigration should not be underestimated. Moreover, the problems associated with immigration will become more not less serious in the future because of increasing cultural distance between natives and immigrants. Since all Western populations will start to decline sooner or later, the pool of eligible migrants will shift away to remoter parts of the world; migrants will have to be recruited increasingly from less developed countries. At the same time population pressure from LDCs will increase.

The success of any European migration policy, therefore, lies in 'the proper recruitment and the decided effort to integrate those recruited as soon as they arrive' (Höhn, 1988: 475). European countries can learn a great deal from Canada, Australia and the United States in this respect. These countries have been relatively successful in their management of pluralism and

particularly in their capacity to welcome, take in and absorb immigrants and refugees from almost every part of the globe, who arrive today under their universal immigration policies. Not the least part of this effort is their evident capacity to make the majority of these newcomers begin to feel a part of this society within a reasonable period of time, and to identify with it to a considerable extent in due course. (Hawkins, 1987: 101)

Thus immigration can be a viable strategy, provided there are sufficient policies and procedures to facilitate the arrival and integration of diverse groups. Indeed, the scale of demographic imbalances and economic inequalities between the poor, high-fertility countries of the Third World and the rich, low-fertility Western countries, makes migration virtually inevitable. Since the demographic rationale for immigration to developed countries is so weak, and the economic justification so controversial, migration should be supported primarily on humanitarian grounds.

CONCLUSION

We have noted that below-replacement fertility entered the Australian and Canadian political agendas as a 'problem' requiring a policy response through immigration in mid-1970s. It played a more prominent role in Australia, where the reorientation of migration policy of the Fraser government in 1976 towards growth was justified by the need to forestall the negative economic effects of declining fertility. A similar rationale re-emerged in 1985, when the Hawke government also opted for expansion in immigration.

However, as I learned during my interviews with Australian officials involved in immigration policy formulation and management, it is highly unlikely that fears associated with the negative consequences of below-replacement fertility were the main reason for the decison to expand immigration. As we noted, the relationship between demographic data and policy is relatively weak in Australia (and elsewhere), and the decision to use below-replacement fertility as an additional legitimation for expanded immigration was governed by a political rather than a demographic rationality.

A similar political process has been at work in Canada, where the resort to a demographic justification for immigration has been less frequent and more inconsistent, despite the fact that the Canadian population will start declining somewhat earlier than its Australian counterpart. While the special parliamentary committee on immigration policy appointed in March 1975 listed declining fertility as one of several justifications for Canadian immigration policy, there is no evidence suggesting that this recommendation in any way influenced actual policies in the 1970s.

Declining fertility and the prospect of population ageing and population decline became more of an issue after the 1984 election of the Mulroney government. The new Conservative government not only re-established the linkage between immigration and demography, but it also used the dramatic decrease in Canada's fertility in the 1960s and 1970s as the main rationale for the 'moderate, controlled' increases in immigration levels in the late 1980s. The Mulroney government also launched in May 1986 a special federal assessment of the changing makeup of Canada's population, the Review of Demography and Its Implications for Economic and Social Policy. While the Demographic Review had a broad mandate to address policy implications of a variety of population questions, it ended up not resolving any of the questions raised. The final report, *Charting Canada's Future*, simply, and politically conveniently, concluded that the population 'problems' are not as serious as previously thought. This conclusion allowed the federal government to temporarily abandon the demographic–immigration linkage as the main rationale for immigration, and to return instead to traditional economic and humanitarian justifications. However, when the substantial increase in immigration intake for the 1991–5 period (up to 250 000 a year, compared to the annual average of 87 240 for the 1980s) was announced in October 1990, the role of immigration as a means for compensating for low fertility re-emerged as an important, though by no means the only, justification for the shift in policy.

Individuals and groups most likely to make use of demographic data supporting stationary population and a smaller immigration programme have tended to be less powerful than business groups or ethnic and refugee lobbies which have favoured larger immigration programmes. It remains to be seen whether the growing importance of environmental issues will move such considerations into a more central place in immigration policy making than has been the case so far. As Richmond (1991: 88) has argued,

> during the 1980s, affluent societies became increasingly aware of the harmful ecological and environmental impact of their own life-styles, including the wastage of non-renewable resources and the dangers of pollution. These concerns related directly to population problems and lead to support for 'zero population growth' and an anti-immigration lobby, particularly strong in Australia.

The demographic rationale for immigration is viable only in a context in which population growth is seen as desirable, and as necessary to offset population ageing. Yet, with proper planning, adaptation to an older population should not be all that difficult. After all, in the 1950s and the 1960s, both countries adapted with remarkable ease to a very young population, created by the baby boom and large-scale immigration of young adults. However, given the historical novelty of below-replacement fertility, and misunderstandings and anxieties which continue to surround this issue, the very different long-term and short-term impacts of immigration on population size, rate of growth and age distribution are not about to completely disappear from the political agenda.

Part III

Egalitarian Components of Demographic Policies or Demographic Implications of Policies Pursuing Women's Equality: Canada, Australia and Great Britain Compared

7 Protective Legislation and Equal Employment Opportunity

INTRODUCTION

Of all the concerns raised by the implementation of anti-discrimination and affirmative action policies, none has been as problematic as those associated with the selective protection of women workers. Historically, exclusionary protective measures for women developed for a wide range of reasons. Throughout the nineteenth century, the main preoccupation was with the perceived indecency and immorality of a woman performing a man's task in male company. Women were viewed as more fragile and, like children, were seen as needing protection both of their morality, and from long hours and dangerous and arduous work. During this century, the case for protective legislation has been argued more in terms of the need for married women to devote themselves wholeheartedly to home and family, than in terms of feminine morality (Lewis, 1983). In recent years, exclusion of women of childbearing age, or of pregnant women, from jobs involving potential exposure to toxic substances has been justified primarily on the grounds of possible damage to the developing foetus.

A twofold distinction can be made between protective measures that are based upon historically specific (and outmoded) views about women's capabilities and appropriate roles in society, and those aimed at protecting women's reproductive and maternal functions. Conflicts between equal employment opportunity and protective legislation are easier to solve when the latter aims to 'protect' women as the weaker sex or as persons who bear the primary responsibility for domestic work than when the concerns are reproductive and foetal health.

PROTECTIVE LEGISLATION, DISCRIMINATION AND EQUALITY

An historical review of protective legislation reveals that most of these laws were restrictive. They either barred women from certain occupations or industrial processes (such as underground mining, lead processing or the handling of heavy weights) or limited their hours of work (such as restricting night work and shift work or instituting maximum hours of work). However, some protective laws granted women benefits which males did not enjoy, such as the provision of special amenities and facilities, or the entitlement to a minimum wage, or to lunch or rest breaks (Stellman, 1977; Bertin and Henifin, 1987; Labour Canada, 1989: 3; Bacchi, 1990: 136–7). Proponents of equal treatment have attacked special protective measures for women workers for their selectivity and double standard, and on the grounds that they inhibit equality of opportunity and treatment in employment. Protective legislation prohibited women from dangerous well-paid 'male' jobs in mining, construction or heavy industry, yet no such restrictions were implemented in female-dominated, poorly paid jobs in non-factory settings such as hospitals or laundering establishments, where working conditions were equally arduous and unhealthy. Exponents of equal treatment have also pointed out that night work prohibitions on women's employment were aimed specifically at industrial work in factories, ignoring major areas of women's work such as nursing, waitressing, domestic work, or telephone operations, where evening and night work were standard features (Bertin and Henifin, 1987; Labour Canada, 1989).

During the late 1960s and early 1970s, the negative impact of protective legislation on women's employment and promotion prospects was increasingly acknowledged also in governmental and inter-governmental circles. Several international organisations, notably the United Nations, the ILO and the Commission of the European Communities, called for protective measures to be reviewed and brought up to date with a view to 'revising, supplementing, extending, retaining or repealing such measures according to national circumstances' (ILO, 1987: 6). In the United States, the Equal Employment Opportunity Commission (EEOC) declared in 1969 that state protective laws discriminated rather than protected women, and as such were illegal under Title VII of the Civil Rights Act.

The favourable state response to the liberal feminist argument that any special legislation is discriminatory, and therefore should not be allowed as it limits women's employment opportunities, fits well with the resource perspective on equality and with the liberal notion of an open, competitive market system accessible to all. Indeed, as Bacchi (1990: 138) argues,

in America, the subject of protective laws was debated in the 1960s largely as a result of buoyant economic conditions which produced an increased demand for labour. Women had to be 'freed' from 'restrictive' labour laws because their labour was needed. That Britain did not follow America's path in removing most protective laws was due largely to the role played by the British Trade Union Congress (TUC).

In the United Kingdom, the 1975 Sex Discrimination Act explictly exempted protective laws. The decision not to repeal these laws received considerable support from many of the same human rights, trade union and women's groups that supported women's equality and the Sex Discrimination Act (Coote, 1975; Gunningham, 1986: 263; Bacchi, 1990: 138–41).

State socialism also has a history of insisting that special protection of working women is essential to gender equality. While acknowledging some negative effects of protectionism,

> notably, the concentration of women workers in lower-paid, lower-skilled occupations, and the risk of confirming prejudices against the appropriate roles of women

the Hungarian communist government none the less regarded these as being of 'transitory nature'. Hungarian communist officials also emphasised that

> in a socialist country like Hungary – where the means of production are state-owned, the national economy is centrally planned and one of the fundamental human rights, the right to work, has been implemented to the full – special protective measures for working women do not prejudice women's prospects for employment. These do not depend on ups and down in the labour market, since there is no unemployment. (Quoted in ILO, 1987: 139,140)

Since the collapse of communism in Central and Eastern Europe in 1989, this argument no longer applies, if it ever did. For the state socialist 'concentration of women workers in lower-paid, lower-skilled occupations' was neither transitory nor any different from the effect protective legislation had on women workers in capitalist market economies. The latter have also relegated women to the bottom half of the segregated dual labour market, thus making them more dependent on male earners. Once protective laws determine what types of jobs women (but not men) may or may not do, they inevitably discriminate against women and contribute both to the legitimation of the sexual division of labour and to the persistence of wage differentials between the sexes (Heitlinger, 1987b).

Protectionist policies directed only at women clearly collide with equality legislation which says that women and men must be treated the same, not differently. As we noted in Chapter 2, anti-discrimination legislation typically requires treating likes alike. In the United States, the late 1960s and 1970s saw the virtual elimination of protective legislation in response to laws prohibiting discrimination against women in employment. Similar trends toward repealing or limiting protective legislation have been also observed in Canada, Australia, Japan, New Zealand and the countries of the European Community (ILO, 1987: 2).

REPEALING PROTECTIVE LEGISLATION IN CANADA

Many changes in Canada's protective legislation occurred in the 1970s, largely in response to the work of the Royal Commission on the Status of Women and the high visibility of women's issues during the International Women's Year in 1975. The establishment of the Royal Commission and the UN Decade for Women gave the concept of equal rights for women a new legitimacy. The 1970s and 1980s were then marked by increased attention from government, business and unions to the issue of equality in the workplace.

The Royal Commission on the Status of Women noted that protective legislation for women has the effect of restricting their job opportunities, and recommended that protective legislation be applicable to both sexes. Various provincial women's organisations took up the issue and successfully pressed for removing women-specific prohibitions against industrial night work, work in mining operations, and work involving the manual transport and lifting of heavy loads. The removal of legislative restrictions was also supported by many employers, who in the 1970s were facing labour shortages in industries such as mining and textile manufacturing. Another factor was the recognition (by women's groups, employers, unions and the government) that technical advances made the manual work less arduous.

In May 1978, Canada renounced its previous ratification of ILO Convention 45 'On Underground Work (Women)' explicitly on the grounds that it is incompatible with gender equality (Labour Canada, 1989: 14). However, the removal of legislative prohibitions on women in mining appears to have had a limited impact on their employment. For example, the 1971 and the 1981 census figures for mining and quarrying reveal an increase of 300 per cent, but the actual increase in numbers was quite small – it went from 380 in 1971 to 1625 in 1981. The limited progress women have made has been attributed to the boom-and-bust cycles common to resource industries, lower demand for labour caused by increased mechanisation of both underground and surface operations, and continuing discrimination against women in non-traditional areas of employment (Labour Canada, 1989: 14–15).

Very few workplace-oriented measures specific to women remain in Canadian law. Of those still in place, most are aimed specifically at pregnant women or women of childbearing capacity. They generally attempt to limit exposure to hazardous substances, such as lead and radiation. The current emphasis is on general protective measures applicable equally to men and women, although employers have continued to argue that implementation of stringent occupational health protection for all workers would be either too costly or technically too difficult (Labour Canada, 1989).

CHANGES IN PROTECTIVE LEGISLATION IN THE EUROPEAN COMMUNITY

The developments within the European Community and its member states have paralleled those in Canada. The obligation of the European Commission to examine protective legislation and practices of member states stems from the 1976 equal treatment directive. While the directive explicitly exempted 'provisions concerning the protection of women, particularly as regards pregnancy and maternity', it also required that 'those laws, regulations and administrative provisions contrary to the principle of equal treatment when the concern for protection which originally inspired them is no longer well founded shall be revised' (Commission of the European Communities, 1987: 1).

The Commission's review of the various national and international protective measures took more than a decade. The final report on the issue takes the view that protective legislation should in principle be consistent 'across sexes and across occupational areas', and that the only exception to this principle are measures 'strictly necessary to protect the special biological condition of women'. Instead of laying down general principles as to what work, if any, should be banned for women, the Commission (1987) divided protective legislation into two basic categories: humanitarian measures (which were subdivided into measures associated with family commitments, night work, strenuous and arduous work, and mines) and health and safety provisions, and then recommended specific action for each category and subcategory.

A whole list of jobs presently barred to women were found to be against the equal treatment directive. The Commission urged the repeal of national provisions restricting women on the navigation of internal waterways and on board of ships, in customs control, in work on machines that are running and in work on compressed air caissons. The Commission also wanted governments to repeal provisions protecting women from strenuous or arduous work. On the issue of shifting heavy loads, the Commission recommended the lowering of levels to improve conditions for all workers. It also suggested that relevant vocational training for this type of work be extended to women.

The Commission also urged the repeal or generalisation to all workers of provisions that have been based on women's traditional domestic responsibilities. The long list of these women-specific measures includes limits on night work in industry, maximum daily or weekly working time, provision of hygiene at the place of work, ban on shift work, extra annual leave and family leave, an extra leave to do housework, and ban on Sunday work. For restrictions on jobs in the army, police force, gendarmerie, fire brigade and jobs outside the Community involving EEC organisations or companies, the Commission advocated gradual abolition so that these institutions get used to 'the idea of having more women' (*CREW Reports*, vol. 7, no. 2, February 1987).

Researchers associated with the Centre for Research on European Women (CREW) do not expect that convincing member states to change their discriminatory provisions will be easy, though they stress that the European Commission can threaten EEC countries with court action to fully implement the equal treatment directive (*CREW Reports*, vol. 7, no. 4, April 1987). A strong opposition to the repeal of protective legislation is expected from the trade unions, especially if the Commission's warning that 'equality should not be made the occasion for a disimprovement of working conditions for one sex' is ignored, as has been the case in Italy. According to CREW, Italy is the only member state to have abolished all its protective legislation, but the repeal has had the effect of women being recruited mainly for the worst jobs.

BALANCING EQUAL AND SPECIAL TREATMENT

Feminists, liberals and socialists have been divided as to which approach – equal or special treatment – they should pursue. On the one side are liberal feminists and the US government who argue that any form of special treatment is discriminatory and as such an obstacle which limits women's opportunities to participate fully in the workforce. On the other are governments (mainly in Central and Eastern Europe), numerous international organisations (such as the ILO), trade unions (such as the British Trade Union Congress) and women's groups which regard the double burden of domestic and paid work as a compelling justification for continuing certain protection. A third position, supported by socialist feminists, the Australian Council of Trade Unions and the Australian National Occupational Health and Safety Commissions Advisory Group on Women's Issues, wants to make special occupational standards for women effective standards for all workers. If all workers had reasonable working conditions, women would be required neither to emphasise their particular vulnerability nor deny their sex-specific needs (Bacchi, 1990: 142).

Selective restrictions which are based on outdated views of women as 'fragile creatures' (such as legislative restrictions on the maximum weights which may be lifted by women, or legislative exclusion of women from work with explosives or in underground mines), or which want to 'protect' women's (but not men's) family obligations, are manifestly discriminatory. Such measures unduly restrict women's employment opportunities, contribute to women's inability to earn equal pay and, as such, are inconsistent with a commitment to equal employment opportunity. The solution should be to level up rather than down, that is, to extend to all workers rather than repeal provisions that have been based on women's traditional domestic responsibilities. The adoption of ILO Convention 156 concerning Equal Opportunities and Equal Treatment for Men and Women Workers: Workers with Family Responsibilities could then become an important strategic tool with which to challenge existing legitimacy of male norms, power, and corporate practices. As we noted in Chapter 3, ILO Convention 156 debunks the presumption that no workers, or only the females ones, are concerned with the details of domestic life.

In 1979, Melbourne's Working Women's Centre discussed the impact of shift work on family and social life, and concluded that the absence of a father is just as disruptive as the absence of a mother. According to Bacchi (1990: 142), a recent tripartite Conference on Legislative and Award Restrictions . . . heard a paper which concluded that the 'adverse occupational health and safety effects of shiftwork affected men and women equally' and called for a national code of practice on forward rotation and maximum number of continuous night shifts and workload. The ACTU and the CAI (Confederation of Australian Industry) agreed, however, *only* to the '*removal of outdated restrictions on the hours of employment for women*'. [emphasis was added by Bacchi]

The modification of weight-lifting standards for women has been more successful. According to Bacchi (1990: 142),

the ACTU has endorsed a 'preferred standard' on manual handling which advocates a limit of sixteen kilograms on unaided lifting for *both* men and women. The larger goal, as declared, is to 'reduce the burden for workers' and to 'secure safe work practices that apply regardless of sex'.

In Australia, existing occupational standards governing the lifting of heavy equipment and objects were identified as a form of indirect discrimination. Their modification has become an aspect of affirmative action to improve employment opportunities for women, re-examine dominant assumptions about masculinity and work expectations of male workers, decrease work injuries, and challenge the idea that greater average physical strenghth of men entitles them to higher paid work (Eisenstein, 1985).

Conflicts between equal employment opportunity and protective legislation that safeguards women's reproductive role pose a more difficult challenge for public policy formulation, but even in this case the preferred solution is to 'level up' and make women's occupational health and safety standards effective standards for all workers.

PROTECTING WOMEN AS POTENTIAL MOTHERS

Because of their childbearing role, women are more vulnerable to reproductive hazards than men, although in the case of several substances, male fertility may also be at risk. The assumption that reproduction and women are coterminous has meant that scientific inquiries have almost completely ignored the male reproductive system (Bacchi, 1990: 146). Lead, benzene, and ionising radiation, which can cause miscarriage, foetal abnormalities and developmental defects, are probably the best documented reproductive hazards. As Gunningham (1986: 242–3) points out, occupational exposure to lead may occur in over 100 occupations, such as lead smelting, manufacturing of lead storage batteries, solder manufacture, shipbuilding, car manufacturing, and printing. Inhaling of airborne lead or ingestion of lead can cause nerve, blood or kidney damage. In Great Britain, lead is the single biggest cause of reported poisoning at work. Lead may also affect male reproductive capacity, and that of wives of workers exposed to lead. As one of the oldest industrial toxic hazards, lead was one of the first to be regulated.

ILO Convention No. 13 (Concerning the Use of White Lead), adopted in 1921, prohibits women's employment 'in any painting work of an industrial character involving the use of white lead or sulphate of lead or other products containing these pigments'. More recent ILO Conventions and Recommendations prohibit the employment of women of childbearing age, pregnant women or mothers of small children in work involving exposure to benzene (Convention No. 136, adopted in 1971) or ionising radiation (Radiation Protection Recommendation No. 114, adopted in 1960; Nursing Personnel Recommendation No. 157, adopted in 1977). While Canada has ratified neither of these Conventions, most Canadian jurisdictions have regulations for these hazarduous substances. Moreover, these occupational health and safety regulations require or could be interpreted as requiring special treatment for women in the labour force, particularly pregnant women and women capable of bearing children (Labour Canada, 1989).

In contrast, the US lead standard, promulgated in 1978, is gender neutral. The precedent-setting provisions concerning permissible exposure level, monitoring of these levels, medical surveillance and workers' knowledge of the potential reproductive as well as other health hazards from exposure to lead, recognise that harmful effects can be transmitted from either or both parents to the embryo/foetus. In addition, the standard contains statements that specifically prohibit sex discrimination (Williams, 1988: 121). In a similar vein, the European Parliament's Directive on Lead demanded 'that the directive set a "single low standard" of exposure for women and men, "not only because men's reproductive health was at risk by the higher standard but because to set a dual standard would be discriminatory"' (Bacchi, 1990: 148).

There are many other chemicals that are either suspected or known to affect adversely workers' reproductive health. These include certain metals (smelter workers), solvents (laboratory workers), anaesthetic gases and viruses (hospital workers), low-level radiation (most white collar workers working with microcomputers and video display terminals), certain pesticides and mercury. However, the state of our knowledge about which agents cause reproductive damage and of what kind is rather uneven. This leads to a dilemma as to how to make policy decisions in the face of scientific uncertainty. It is a problem of risk assessment and risk management. The former is concerned with amassing and analysing the scientific data while the latter deals with its economic, social and legal ramifications (Williams, 1988).

Since there is no such thing as zero risk, policy makers also have to decide how to apportion the health risks and economic costs among women, men, employers, taxpayers and the future generation. Should employers be required, or permitted to prohibit all women, or certain categories of women (that is, fertile or pregnant women) from holding jobs believed to be particularly dangerous to them or to their offspring? Should concerns for maternal exposure to toxic agents and hazardous conditions take precedence over concerns for the effect of paternal exposure? Is it economically and technologically feasible to insist that the hazards, rather than women, are removed from the workplace? And what about the issue of privacy – should male and female workers be required to communicate to their employers that they are planning to have a child? Finally, there is also the issue of discrimination masquerading as protection.

In the United States, the typical response in industries involving exposure to lead and other known reproductive hazards has been to 'protect' women from such exposure by refusing to hire them or by forcing them to prove their inability to become pregnant. Beginning in the mid-1970s, certain American corporations, such as General Motors, Exxon, St Joe Minerals and Allied Chemical, began to transfer or fire women employees who were of childbearing age from jobs involving exposure to chemicals deemed harmful to their reproductive system. When transferred, these women often lost their seniority, and were forced to accept lower-paid jobs, such as janitorial work, in order to remain employed. Women were also told that they could retain their jobs upon proof of sterility.

Needing their jobs more than their fertility, many of these employees were sterilized and many complained subsequently to their unions.

(Felker, 1982)

THE DOUBLE STANDARD OF FOETAL PROTECTION POLICIES

Felker (1982: 11) also noted that there were no instances of male employees given a 'choice' of job loss versus sterilisation, though it is known that some chemicals men work with mutate sperm. The same pattern has been observed in Canada. Thus General Motors in Oshawa, Ontario, required female workers in a lead storage battery division to take a transfer to a lead-free area of the factory or to show proof of sterility. Findings that male exposure to lead could cause abnormal sperm, low sperm count, and decreased sex drive were ignored (Chenier, 1982: 42). The move to exclusionary policies in Canada has been also criticised on the grounds that these policies only concern women's employment in non-traditional areas of work, leaving women to continue their employment in hospitals, dental offices, laundries, dry cleaning establishments, and other female-dominated workplaces with potential hazards (Labour Canada, 1989: 5).

Similar criticism has been voiced in Great Britain and in the United States. As Fletcher (1981: vi) argues in her report sponsored by the British Equal Opportunities Commission,

> when the evidence emerged in the 1970s that miscarriage and birth defects were associated with exposure to anaesthetic gases during pregnancy (with weaker evidence there was also some evidence of a link with paternal exposure before conception), the option of excluding women from this (poorly paid) employment was not considered. Instead the, at first sight, better option of reducing the hazard at source was (eventually) advocated. However, the hazards were played down in the only official move, a DHSS circular in 1976 and the action was undertaken rather half-heartedly. The notice warned, somewhat cautiously, that there may be a risk.

The same double standard characterises foetal protection policies in the United States. As Bertin and Henifin (1987: 103) argue,

> health care professionals, 75% of whom are female, are exposed to radiation but are rarely subject to fetal protection policies, whereas women are commonly excluded from the employment in the nuclear power industry. Likewise, women have been excluded from jobs involving exposures to solvents such as toluene and benzene in male-intensive industries, but textile and apparel workers (46% and 81%

female, respectively) and electronic workers (75% female or more) have not been similarly excluded.

The Canadian Labour Congress rightly condemned the double standard of exclusionary policies, as well as its underlying motive – the corporate drive for profitability: 'Different safety standards for women and men protect corporate profits by avoiding the need for costly changes to the work environment. Meanwhile, women are forced into unemployment or low-paying, often equally hazardous work. Men are left to face the hazards' (quoted in Labour Canada, 1989: 57).

From a business perspective, excluding women but not men from high-paid hazardous jobs is a cheaper alternative than potential legal liability for foetal damage or the reduction of hazards at source. For the most part, governments in Canada have conceded employers' arguments that the cost of imposing more stringent health protection measures for all workers would be too costly or technically too difficult (Labour Canada, 1989: 59).

REPRODUCTIVE HEALTH OCCUPATIONAL POLICIES
IN GREAT BRITAIN

Reproductive hazards, especially those arising from exposure to ionising radiation and lead, have received a lot of attention also in the UK. Since the mid-1970s, there have been several reports on the subject in the UK by the Health and Safety Commission, the Equal Opportunities Commission, the Chemical Industries Association and the Association of Scientific, Technical and Managerial Staff. In its 1979 report, *Health & Safety Legislation: Should We Distinguish Between Men and Women?*, the Equal Opportunities Commission did not demand a single low standard applicable to both sexes if it were not *reasonably practicable* (whatever that means), thus clearly siding with the corporate viewpoint.

However, the EOC rejected the crude definition of reproductive capacity adopted by a number of US employers and by the British Health and Safety Commission, which regarded all women between the ages of 15 and 55 as 'women of reproductive capacity', unless they had a doctor's certificate stating that they were incapable of bearing a child. Instead, the EOC advocated a more flexible definition of this term, which would not exclude from the definition 'the very large group of women who have no intention of bearing children and if necessary take active steps to prevent pregnancy' (p. 170).

The issue of reproductive health also appeared on the agenda of the chemical industry. In 1984, after four years of preparatory work, the British Chemical Industries Association (CIA) published a report entitled *Employment and Reproductive Health*. The report warns that the issue is likely to grow in importance and that individual firms have to develop appropriate policies. Moreover, the report takes great care to point out that the issue is not exclusively an issue about women in the workplace. It notes that while past emphasis has been solely on the mother's exposure to harmful substances, employers today must also recognise the father's role in reproduction and the potential damage from his exposure, and accordingly include male reproductive health in all employment policies. The CIA suggests that companies should not only write a reproductive health policy applicable to both sexes, but also keep records on reproductive health of all its employees of reproductive capacity (*Health and Safety Industrial Bulletin* 122, 4 February 1986).

Studying reproductive health is unfortunately fraught with numerous methodological difficulties that range from the limitations of using questionnaires to the inability of individual firms to establish adequate control groups of normal pregnancy outcomes against which to judge the findings of its own corporate monitoring. Obtaining reliable data about miscarriages is especially difficult because spontaneous abortions can be caused by a variety of factors. The best data on abnormal reproductive outcomes which may be a result of occupational exposure have been so far collected in the Scandinavian countries (*Health and Safety Industrial Bulletin* 122, 4 February, 1986).

Under British law, responsibilities to protect health and safety take precedence over anti-discrimination legislation, and in principle the duty of employers to provide a safe place of work is more important than implementing policies of equal employment opportunity (Fletcher, 1981). However, prior to 1974, reproductive health regulations covered only a limited number of industrial sectors, with the result that women were excluded from smelters but exposed to lead in the pottery industry. Health and safety standards are now set for all workplaces (*Health and Safety Industrial Bulletin* 123, 4 March 1986).

The 1980 Health and Safety Commission Approved Code of Practice on the control of lead at work requires women to notify employers if they become pregnant and no pregnant women are allowed to continue with work exposing them to lead (*Health and Safety Industrial Bulletin* 123, 4 March 1986). However, such self-monitoring policy of first trimester pregnancies may not be very effective in protecting the foetus, 'because it is not known how early in the course of pregnancy central nervous system damage can be caused by lead, and because elevated levels of lead in tissues persist for several months after the cessation of exposure' (World Health Organization, quoted in Gunningham, 1986: 253). Hence the adoption of protective policy that excludes women of childbearing capacity.

While dismissing a woman on the ground of her pregnancy constitutes discrimination under the British Sex Discrimination Act, such employment protection can be overridden if another statutory instrument, such as the Control of Lead at Work Regulations, requires that a woman be excluded from work in certain circumstances. Moreover, a woman who only *may* become pregnant faces the same prospect. Under British law, an employer can dismiss a woman of childbearing capacity if he *reasonably* believes that her workplace is hazardous to a potential foetus. Under equivalent American sex discrimination law, employers have to show that the exclusion of women was *necessary* for the protection of unborn children of female workers, that males do not face the same risk and that there were no other alternatives. Thus courts in the US have gone much further in ensuring that discriminatory treatment of women workers is properly justified (*Health and Safety Industrial Bulletin*, 4 March 1986; Walsh and Kelleher, 1987).

BALANCING EQUAL OPPORTUNITY WITH REPRODUCTIVE HEALTH

Safeguarding childbearing capacity therefore raises difficult legal, scientific, economic and moral questions about women's and men's rights, employers' costs and responsibilities, the interest of the unborn and the role of the state. On one side of the ideological spectrum are liberal individualists, who assert that pregnancy is a voluntary condition, and if a woman wishes to take a reproductive risk and work in hazardous jobs, that is her business and not the state's. Proponents of this view also argue that women are more than perpetual baby machines, and that health protection far too frequently focuses solely on women's reproductive functions, to the detriment of other health needs. Since the average woman nowadays bears only two children, childbearing occupies a relatively short period of a woman's working life. Many women choose not to have any children at all, and as such they should not be discriminated against merely because they have a reproductive capacity (Stellman, 1977; Gunningham, 1986: 257).

On the other side of the spectrum are exponents of special treatment, who argue that women work in ghettoised jobs where they face hazards specific to those jobs (such as repetitive strain injury); that women workers face special health problems as a result of their dual roles as wage workers and mothers/housewives; and that on account of their childbearing function, women have specific health needs in the workplace (Chavkin, 1984). Exponents of the state socialist viewpoint argue that childbearing is a social rather than an individual matter. According to Fina Kaloyanova (1976: 32), a Bulgarian author writing for *World Health*, the WHO monthly publication, the 'protection of women from hazards in the work environment is a vital safeguard not only for present but for future generations'. Kaloyanova also suggests that the gender-specific 'restrictions can in no way be considered discriminatory, nor do they result in the underemployment of women. Our country has in fact a continuing lack of manpower.' Thus the socialist/communist argument is that protecting women's reproductive and maternal function is essential both for women's equality and for the safeguarding of the 'quality' of the new population.

All these arguments have merit. The liberal position that wants women to be wary of legislation that may have the latent effect of denying them access to certain jobs draws our attention to the discriminatory potential of protective legislation. However, to suggest that no legislation is therefore necessary is like throwing the baby out with the bath water. The special treatment argument highlights the particular difficulties faced by childbearing women in paid employment, but downplays the ways in which women's special needs have been used against them in discriminatory ways. Combining protection of women's reproductive health and the foetus's health with equality for women sounds like a fine solution for a planned communist economy with chronic shortages of labour, but it does not get around the problems of scientific uncertainty and business profitability. Balancing equal opportunity with reproductive and foetal health in a capitalist economy is difficult because of conflicts between scientific uncertainty, state enforcement of employers' responsibility for occupational health and safety, equal employment opportunity, business profitability and the interests of the unborn.

The only sure way of eliminating reproductive risk is to remove the hazard at source. However, among the 500 000 chemicals in use today only 3 per cent have been rigorously tested for potential carcinogenic or reproductive effects. There are 3000 new chemicals being synthesised each year and for the most part, their testing for reproductive effect is not required by law. Although further regulatory legislation in Ontario is pending, the process is extremely slow and cannot realistically deal with the mass of chemicals already in use, let alone the additional ones being introduced at a rate of almost ten a day. Enforcement of such legislation also poses a problem. At present there are only 25 government health and safety inspectors monitoring some 25 000 industrial establishments in Toronto, Canada's largest city (Jones and Nunn, 1986: 14).

In the United States, the effectiveness of the Occupational Safety and Health Act (OSHA), passed by Congress in 1970, has been hampered by stiff resistance from business organisations and, during the Reagan administration, by anti-regulatory mood in Washington. There are more than 59 000 chemicals on the *Registry of Toxic Effects of Chemical Substances*, but OSHA standards have been developed for only twenty-three chemicals. Industry groups have succeeded in having the courts invalidate two of these chemical standards (benzene and cotton dust) as well as selected provisions of other regulations. Litigation over some standards is still proceeding (Bertin and Henifin, 1987: 100).

The OSHA Act is enforced by inspectors who may issue citations and fines to employers who are not in compliance. In 1983, fewer than five out of every 1000 establishments received a health inspection. Female-intensive industries are inspected particularly infrequently because OSHA inspectors have targeted construction, oil-well drilling, and grain elevator operations for special attention. None of these industries employs large numbers of women (Bertin and Henifin, 1987: 100). Moreover, the average penalty for *serious* violation of the provisions of the OSHA Act (that is, violations that create substantial probability of death or serious physical harm) was only $172. Thus it is often cheaper for employers to ignore OSHA standards than to comply with them. The chances of being caught are quite low, and even if they are cited for violations of the law, the penalty may be insignificant in comparison with the costs of correcting the hazards (Bertin and Henifin, 1987: 100).

Thus in the current situation, the removal of hazards (as opposed to women workers) from the workplace would appear to be an unattainable objective. If business profitability and scientific uncertainty prevent the creation of a risk-free work environment, and if blanket exclusion of all women from well-paid industrial employment is in conflict with the legal requirement of equal employment opportunity, what practical steps can be taken towards the solution of the question of protection or equality for women workers? In Bacchi's (1990: 142) view, the first step is to recognise that it is misleading 'to present sex-based specification of occupational safety standards as incompatible with the pursuit of equal opportunity. The solution to this "conflict of principles" is to make so-called "women's standards" effective standards for all.' As an example of such an approach, Bacchi quotes from the Working Women's Charter of the Australian Council of Trade Unions, which suggests that protective legislation should be reviewed with one aim in mind – 'protecting both female and male workers' health'.

Given the way in which anti-discrimination law is currently interpreted, arguing that women and men are equally vulnerable to toxic substances 'forecloses the possibility that women will be excluded from the work on the grounds that they are "different". The "equal vulnerability" argument is also likely to win many male trade union supporters who are concerned about male worker's health.' However, Bacchi (1990: 147–8) also points out that the suggestion to extend the protections currently enjoyed by women to men is based on the problematic assumption that in order to address *women's* problems, they have to be shown to be men's problems as well.

> In cases where it is difficult to prove equal vulnerability or in cases where it is clear that the fetus is affected only through the woman, the door to exclusion reopens . . . while it is useful to show that men are also disadvantaged by work rules which treat employees like childless people, it is vital to keep women as primary actors.

Unlike the United States, where many feminists fear that any acknowledgement of women's specific needs will be used against them, in Australia it does not seem quite so necessary to avoid references to women's particular needs (Bacchi, 1990: 150). In Canada, the subject of special measures to protect women's reproductive capacity remains a 'major area of disagreement' (Labour Canada, 1989: 65). As long as feminists are torn between their desire to meet women's specific needs and at the same time avoid confirming stereotypes which can then be used against women, this disagreement is likely to continue, forcing feminists (and policy makers) to make what are essentially negative choices between sex discrimination and potentially hazardous work environment. Thus in the area of radiation exposure, 'a long-standing tradition of differential protection for women of reproductive capacity has shifted to focus only on pregnant women' (Labour Canada, 1989: 65)

The balancing of equal opportunity with reproductive health would then imply the coexistence of legal requirements for equality of opportunity with legal requirements for the special protection of pregnant women and not, as previously, of all women of childbearing capacity. The female worker would then have to assume the responsibility of informing her employer about her planned or actual pregnancy.

PROTECTING REPRODUCTIVE HEALTH OF PREGNANT WORKERS

Protective legislation in the form of permanent exclusionary provisions that apply to women of childbearing capacity should not be confused with the more temporary special rights for women who are pregnant or nursing. While there should be no dispute about the need to protect the health of pregnant women and the developing foetus, only a few jurisdictions have addressed this issue in a legislative framework. Among all the provinces in Canada, only Quebec's 1979 Occupational Health and Safety Act gives a pregnant woman the right to request reassignment to safe work she can reasonably perform. With a medical certificate verifying that the working conditions are hazardous, pregnant workers can seek a transfer to a position that does not involve such danger. If this request is not immediately met, she may stop working until she is reassigned or, if that is not possible, until the date of delivery.

An employee exercising the right of job reassignment retains the rights and benefits of her regular employment and must be returned to it after her maternity leave. Under this Act, a female worker may also request job reassignment on medically certified grounds that there is danger to the child she is breastfeeding. If this reassignment is delayed she may stop working until she receives such reassignment or until the child is weaned (Labour Canada, 1981: 33). The compensation, based on 90 per cent of the woman's net earnings, is to be paid by La Commission de la santé et de la securité du travail (Chenier, 1982: 70).

The adoption of the *Occupational Health and Safety* was a significant victory for the Quebec labour movement. In 1972, the three major labour bodies formed the Common Front for joint negotiation on issues deemed crucial to their public sector members. Of the 200 000 workers in this sector, more than two-thirds were women, and issues related to women's childbearing responsibilities quickly became a priority. By 1979, there was a concentrated union effort to improve maternity leave benefits, parental leave and workplace safety during pregnancy and the Party Quebecois government eventually conceded these demands.[1]

However, there have been continuing tensions between corporate and labour perspectives, which are reflected in the way in which the Quebec legislation was (improperly) implemented. All too frequently, the protective reassignment was implemented as a protective layoff. Since the programme is jointly funded by employers and the provincial government, it is often cheaper and more efficient for each of the contributing partners to lay the woman off. However, overall costs of the programme have soared, with the result that the issuing of medical certificates verifying workplace reproductive risks has been tightened. La Commission de la santé et de la securité du travail, which is responsible for the financial compensation, has increasingly insisted upon relying on its own physicians rather than on doctors chosen by the pregnant worker. This practice has obviously been very unpopular, both among individual women and among union officials (Interview, Women's Bureau, Labour Canada, 12 December 1989). Somewhat similar experiences have been reported from state socialist Czechoslovakia (Heitlinger, 1987a: 61).

CONCLUSION

We have drawn a basic distinction between three types of special 'protective' legislation for women: (1) exclusionary measures which are based upon historically specific, and outmoded, views about women's capabilities and appropriate roles in society; (2) corrective provisions of affirmative action designed to redress direct and indirect discrimination against women in the workplace; and (3) measures aimed at protecting women's reproductive and maternal function. Western policy makers have become increasingly sympathetic to feminist claims that traditional protective legislation limits women's access to the labour market, and have repealed many of the exclusionary provisions. However, the removal of legislative prohibitions in Canada has had limited impact on women's employment in traditional male-dominated areas such as mining.

The modification of restrictive weight-lifting standards in Australia has been more successful, because it was linked to affirmative action and led to a reformulated labour standard benefiting both male and female workers. A New South Wales sex discrimination case concerning regulations governing the lifting of heavy objects and machinery revealed that management at Australian Iron and Steel used the women-specific weight-lifting limitation of sixteen kilograms in a cavalier and discriminatory fashion. The management kept women in certain tasks, excluded them from others, and refused them promotion (Bacchi, 1990: 142). Affirmative action arising out of the discriminatory effect of these regulations then became an important strategic tool which addressed traditional assumptions about masculinity and femininity and work expectations of male and female workers, and in the process also decreased work injuries.

Conflicts between equal employment opportunities and protection of reproductive and foetal health are more difficult to solve, mainly because providing full and effective protection from hazards for women and men would cut into business profitability and there is considerable scientific uncertainty about what a risk-free environment would look like. Within the context of developed capitalist market economies, characterised by industrial use of as many as 500 000 chemicals, lack of reliable knowledge about their reproductive effects, less than satisfactory regulation of known hazardous substances in the workplace, and a weak enforcement of existing legislation pertaining to occupational health and safety, the gender-neutral removal of hazards (as opposed to gender-specific removal of women workers) from the workplace appears to be an unattainable objective.

We can identify several key concerns with respect to foetal protection legislation. The first set of concerns stems from the fact that the scope of the 'protection' is not sufficiently broad – men as well as a whole range of potentially hazardous jobs in the feminized sectors of the economy are excluded. An opposite concern stems from the fact that protective foetal legislation narrowly overemphasises women's reproductive role to the detriment of other health needs. Foetal protection then can lead to unnecessary exclusion of women not planning to have children from areas where they would like to work.

Moreover, it is clear that protective legislation for women is not just a foetal protection issue. If this were the case, then we would not have the double standard which excludes women from the nuclear power industry but not from health care jobs where radiation exposure also exists. Women have been excluded from jobs involving exposure to such hazardous solvents as toluene and benzene in male-dominated industries, but women textile, apparel and electronic workers have not been similarly 'protected'. This double standard suggests that foetal protection may, in fact, have to do less with any real concern for foetal safety, and more with general patterns of employment discrimination against women. The selective rationale for protection in some industries but not in other equally harmful industries can only be understood in terms of stereotyping of women (that, is the first reason given for protective legislation) rather than in terms of genuine concern over potential health risks to the mother and the foetus.

Moreover, if the rationale of the current protective legislation is the health protection of future generations, it is curious that there is no corresponding legislation protecting male reproductive capacity, despite increasing evidence that work environments of fathers may pose considerable risks to their future children. While the economic costs of implementing such legislation would be prohibitive, its absence suggests that the intent of at least some of foetal protection legislation is not to protect future generations but to provide acceptable grounds on which to discriminate against women workers.

Thus both the intent and the consequences of any protective legislation must be examined in order to fully assess its impact on women. We need to separate exclusionary protective legislation based on outmoded stereotypes of fragile women from inclusionary provisions of affirmative action policies. Legislation and policies recognising the sex-specific needs of women need not suggest that women are weak and vulnerable, nor exclude them from better paying jobs. Thus one way of resolving the debate about protection or equality for women workers is to determine whether any special legislation does, in fact, promote equity, or whether it merely further discriminates against women.

8 Maternity and Parental Leaves and Benefits Programmes

INTRODUCTION

Because childbearing women need to take a break from work during the pre-, intra- and postnatal period, they are at high risk of experiencing discontinuity of employment, and suffering adverse consequences such as loss of income, downward occupational mobility and social isolation. As we noted in Chapter 3, the first, and by far the most influential, international standard recognising the special needs of working mothers – the ILO Maternity Protection Convention (No. 3) – was adopted in 1919, the foundation year of the International Labour Organisation. The Convention laid down the basic principles of maternity protection, which are as relevant today as they were in the early part of this century: a woman worker's right to maternity leave, a cash benefit during absence from work, nursing breaks, and the right to retain her job throughout pregnancy, confinement and early childrearing. Thus the Maternity Protection Convention recognised that maternity is an important social function, for which women should not be penalised by discriminatory employment practices.

A general right to maternity leave now exists in all industrialised countries except the United States, where the political culture with its emphasis on free enterprise, privacy and the self-sufficient family poses 'an almost insuperable barrier to necessary reform in the area of maternity' (Bacchi, 1990: 131). In the context of a weak trade union movement, poor welfare structure, general distrust of state intervention, and strong preference to achieve change through litigation rather than legislation, American liberal feminists and federal policy makers have tended to reject the gender-specific maternity protection approach, regarding it as discriminatory. Instead, they have appealed to a gender-neutral, equal rights model. Thus under the Pregnancy Discrimination Act and the Disability Benefits Act, gender-specific pregnancy and childbirth were turned into gender-neutral disability. In a similar vein, gender-specific maternity leave became gender-neutral parenting leave. Under the Clinton administation, an unpaid family leave of 12 weeks became a statutory right. However, the mandatory legislation only covers companies with 50 or more employees. Prior to 1993, only women in favourable labour market positions (that is, those with valuable skills and those employed in large organisations) – approximately 40 per cent of the female labour force – could obtain a job-protected leave and some income support immediately before and immediately after childbirth as a fringe benefit negotiated during collective bargaining between employers and employees. The remaining 60 per cent were without any coverage or job security whatsoever. Thus gender-neutral provisions in the United States are generally worse than the equivalent gender-specific provisions in the rest of the developed world (Hewlett, 1986; Bacchi, 1990).

The distinction between gender-specific maternity leave and gender-neutral parental leave has emerged also in Europe, Canada and Australia. However, the distinction is being made in a context in which 'special treatment' and 'equal rights' are seen as complementary rather than as mutually exclusive strategies. Maternity leaves are regarded as health protection measures for working mothers and their children, and as measures of equal opportunity and income replacement. Maternity leave benefits designed to meet the health needs of pregnant and birthing women are clearly gender specific, while programmes concerning income replacement and the care of small children can apply to either parent.

Thus the provision of maternity and parental leave benefits is a complex area of public policy. It involves health protection for working mothers and their children, equal opportunities for women workers, equal rights for men, family income replacement, the responsibilities of employers and the state towards parents and children, the care of young children, and a whole range of employment issues. From a feminist perspective, the fundamental components of an optimal maternity policy for women in the workforce are access to adequate antenatal and birthing care (a health policy, gender-specific issue); occupational health and safety, protection against unfair dismissal, the right to be transferred during pregnancy and in the early postnatal period to easier work without loss of pay and seniority, job-protected leave from work for the pre-, intra- and postnatal period during which the mother (or, in the case of parental leave, the father) is unable to perform her (his) regular job (gender-specific as well as gender-neutral employment issues); and a cash benefit while the parent is on leave (social security issue, in theory gender neutral). Such a policy also needs to promote a general social consensus that childbearing and the rearing of the next generation concern the whole society rather than just the parents. A climate of opinion which regards pregnancy as simply a private decision with private consequences would not be very conducive to a successful implementation of maternity policies and programmes.

My comparative survey of maternity and parental leave benefits in Great Britain, Canada and Australia will focus on: (1) the ways in which the current maternity and parental benefits have emerged as 'minimal' social packages of the welfare state, as outcomes of wage and fringe benefit agreements reached in collective bargaining between employers and employees, or as results of court litigation; and (2) the various policy justifications for these social packages, such as the enhancement of equal opportunities, the desire to recruit and retain skilled women workers, and the demographic need to ensure population replacement.

GREAT BRITAIN

Statutory maternity leaves

The legal right to maternity benefits was introduced by the 1975 Employment Protection Act. A number of maternity rights were also included in the Employment Protection (Consolidated) Act 1978 and the Employment Act 1980. Technically speaking, employment protection legislation does not guarantee a statutory maternity leave. Instead, it provides for a right to stop work 11 weeks prior to the expected date of birth and to be reinstated up to 29 weeks following the actual birth, provided the employee meets a number of qualifying conditions. This period of absence 'does not constitute a break in employment but is not leave and this has implications for the treatment of some contractual arrangements such as contributions to occupational pensions' (Moss, 1988: 60).

Coussins *et al.* (1987: 1–2) summarise the basic rights of pregnant workers in Great Britain as follows:

1. A pregnant woman has the right to any necessary time off for antenatal care without loss of pay. This applies to all women whatever the hours of their work, the length of time they have been employed or the size of the workforce.

2. Dismissal purely or mainly on the grounds of pregnancy is unfair dismissal.
3. A woman has the right to be reinstated in her job, or a similar job, for up to 29 weeks after the birth of her baby.
4. A woman has the right to statutory maternity pay.

Entitlements to job protection, maternity leave and maternity pay by no means apply to all pregnant workers, because the entitlements vary with the length of service, hours worked, average weekly earnings and the size of the firm. Women with at least two years' full-time continuous service (defined as at least 16 hours a week) with the same employer, or with five or more years of part-time service (defined as 8–16 hours a week), are entitled to six weeks' paid leave at 90 per cent of the normal pay (known as the Higher Rate Statutory Maternity Pay) plus an additional 12 weeks on a considerably lower flat rate, which in 1993 was £47.95 a week. Thus out of the total leave entitlement (that is, the maximum length of time women retain the right to return to work) of 40 weeks, benefit payments are made for only 18 weeks. Moreover, the cash benefits are earnings related for only six of these 18 weeks; payment for the remaining 12 weeks is made at a low flat-rate level.

Women with more than 26 weeks' but less than two years' service at the 15th week before their baby is due, and whose average weekly earnings exceed the national insurance lower earning limit (£43 in April 1989), are only entitled to 18 weeks' maternity pay at the flat-rate level. Employers can claim back the six weeks' maternity pay from the Maternity Pay Fund, which is financed by a supplement to employers' national insurance contributions. The 12 weeks' flat-rate maternity allowance is paid from and funded as part of the national insurance system (House of Lords, 1985: xv). Moreover, women in this category have no statutory right to return to work (*IRS Employment Trends* 439, 10 May 1989). Under the pressure from the European Community, Great Britain agreed to a 14-week leave, but at lower rates than those suggested by the European Commission (Palmer, 1991).

Since the election of the Thatcher government in 1979, statutory maternity rights have beeen gradually eroded. For example, the years of service requirement for protection against unfair dismissal have twice been increased, from six months to a year in 1979 and to two years in 1985. Moreover, the 1980 Employment Act exempted small firms with fewer than six employees from granting women the right to return to work after having their babies, if the firm could show that it was not 'reasonably practicable' to do so. The Act also allowed larger firms to offer women different jobs, which the new mothers had to accept or risk dismissal for 'unreasonable' rejection of a suitable alternative (Coussins *et al.*, 1987: 26; Carter, 1988: 103).

By international standards, the 40-week period of maternity leave is quite generous. However, the numerous qualifying conditions and the low pay attached to the leave make it one of the worst provisions in the European Community. As Coussins *et al.* (1987: 26–7) argue,

> the 'years of service rule' for eligibility for higher rate maternity pay and the right to reinstatement excludes thousands of working women. Many women have to keep interrupting their employment because of *lack of childcare and play facilities* during the school holidays, which forces them to stop and start work several times during the year. This pattern can last for years. . . . The rule also discriminates against those women who will be in their early or possibly mid-20s by the time they have completed their further or higher education or some kind of professional training, but who, for one reason or another, wish to have children while they are still in their twenties. . . . *Part-timers* have even less chance of fulfilling the service requirement . . . 85% of Britain's four million part-time workers are women and one working woman in six works less than 16 hours a week. . . . Hardly any women qualify for maternity rights on the basis of five years' part-time service. This discrimination against part-time workers particularly affects women expecting their second or third child.
>
> [italics in the original]

It should come as no suprise that the majority of working women in Great Britain do not return to their previous jobs after the birth of their child. Daniel (1980) found in his nationwide survey of 2400 mothers of babies born during February and March 1979 that of all women who worked during pregnancy, only 24 per cent were at work again within eight months of birth of their child. A further 14 per cent were looking for work, mainly on a part-time basis. Moreover, of those who returned to work, only 20 per cent went back to jobs in conformity with the statutory requirements. Mothers were unable to resume full-time paid work because of lack of childcare facilities, especially for very young children, rigidity of working hours, and widespread hostility to working mothers by coworkers.

The widespread hostility to working mothers is also reflected in other studies. For example, Martin and Roberts (1984) found in their 1980 national study of women and employment that 85 per cent of British women thought that mothers of pre-school children ought to stay at home when children are young. This high percentage was remarkably constant across the class structure, and varied very little according to whether or not the respondents were themselves employed. Brannen's (1987) smaller study of 185 London women on maternity leave who were planning to return to work revealed that most women in the study neither expected nor received approval for their decision. The respondents saw their return to work as an individual problem to which they had to find an individual solution.

A study of women's experiences of going on maternity leave and returning to work sponsored by the Maternity Alliance[1] has found that for many women,

> the negative responses of colleagues and employers to their pregnancy, maternity leave and return to work greatly diminished the benefits they should have derived from decent leave and maternity pay provisions. Maternity leave, it seems, is often regarded as a 'skive' or as extra, undeserved holiday. Women returning to work after having babies are seen by some as taking jobs which should be held by men, and no longer deserving of promotion or training.
>
> (O'Grady and Wakefield, 1989: 1–2)

Employers' experiences with maternity leave have been more positive than those of women, largely because so few women have returned to work after maternity leave. When the right of women to return to their previous jobs after childbirth was first proposed, employers expressed fears that such maternity legislation would result in administrative inconvenience, disruption and additional costs, and that it would lead to reluctance of employers to hire women of childbearing capacity, especially in smaller firms. However, none of these consequences manifested themselves.

Only 1 per cent (5 per cent among smaller firms) of employers were reluctant to take on women of childbearing capacity. Only 18 per cent of employers had experienced a problem over maternity rights, and the difficulties 'were regarded as general irritants rather than serious problems' (Daniel, 1981: 81). When asked more specifically whether they had been caused any particular difficulty by a woman employee exercising her right to resume her job after having a baby, only 5 per cent said that they had. Thus the impact of maternity rights legislation on employers had far fewer negative effects than expected.

None the less, the British Conservative government continues to believe that any extension of maternity provisions

> would add to employers' costs and could therefore affect their competitiveness, their willingness to recruit and promote young women and the total level of employment they could offer. . . . The compulsory introduction of parental leave would also damage competitiveness, undermine job prospects and ultimately be detrimental to the welfare of working parents and their children.

However, the Government recognises that

> there is a range of measures – including flexible working time, personal leave arrangements and workplace childcare facilities – which can be of help to working parents in reconciling career and family responsibilities, and it commends to employers the advice on these matters contained in the Equal Opportunities Commission's Code of Practice.   (Central Office of Information, 1987: 3)

A number of British employers, faced with a shortfall of skilled young males (a consequence of low fertility), have turned to women, the fastest growing section of the workforce, for a solution to labour shortages. A survey by the British Institute of Management has revealed that during the 1980s the number of women working as managers more than doubled in the construction, textile, technical and financial service sectors. This increase coincided with a number of initiatives to attract and retain skilled women employees. These initiatives have included improved maternity rights and long-term unpaid maternity leaves, usually described as career break schemes (Devine, 1989).

Career breaks and 'fringe benefits' maternity rights

Daniel (1981) found that only 5 per cent of British employers were hostile in principle to mothers returning to work after six months of maternity leave. Moreover, one-third of employers actively encouraged women, both skilled and unskilled, to return to work. However, only six per cent of private sector employers provided better maternity pay or leave than the statutory minimum, and only 15 per cent of private firms reported that they made special provisions (such as flexible working hours) to help mothers of young children to continue to work for them. A more recent survey of 120 public and private sector employers found the situation only slightly improved. Only one in five (24) of the organisations surveyed offered maternity benefits beyond the statutory minimum. Yet, the survey also showed that while 25 per cent of women going on maternity leave returned to work in organisations offering statutory minimum maternity provision, almost twice as many (49 per cent) returned to work in organisations offering more than the statutory minimum (*IRS Employment Trends* 439, 10 May 1989).

Improved maternity benefits have been made available mainly to middle-class executives and professionals in banking, teaching, law, the oil industry, computing, civil service and local government. The pioneering 'career break' programme was introduced by the National Westminster Bank, Great Britain's largest bank. The Bank offers a career re-entry programme, which allows women with middle or senior management potential the chance to be at home with their children on an unpaid maternity leave for as long as five years. Open mainly to young executives, the NatWest's 'career break' programme is also open to men, but the emphasis is clearly on women (Rudd, 1988).

The Midland Bank and Barclays Bank have followed suit. The Barclays scheme requires five years of service plus banking examinations for an employee to qualify. A seven-year career break has been also negotiated between the National Union of Teachers and the local authorities in Kent. Anyone taking advantage of the scheme (a woman or a man who wants to leave her or his job temporarily for 'domestic reasons' such as the need to look after a child or an elderly relative) is guaranteed a full-time teaching post within the county when they return, provided they have done at least 10 days a year supply teaching in the interim. An official of the Tory-controlled council said that 'it was difficult to recruit teachers from outside the South East because of high housing costs. It was hoped that the initiative would encourage more staff to return to permanent jobs after their career break' (Marston, 1988).

ICI and Unilever – both large private corporations – have also announced career break schemes for up to five years for skilled employees who wish to look after a pre-school child or a dependent relative, with guarantees of return to the same or a similar job at the same grade. The ICI scheme is available mainly in areas where there is a 'tight labour market' such as information technology and legal functions. ICI has also announced that all eligible female employees, not just those in a 'tight labour market', will be able to increase the statutory period of maternity leave and right to return by 17 weeks. Alternatively, there will be the option of a period of part-time work for those who return before the end of the extended period of leave.

Unilever maternity initiatives are part of an affirmative action aimed specifically at increasing the supply of women managers. The company has also raised maternity pay from the statutory minimum to full salary for the women who are eligible for the career break scheme. Littlewood's maternity initiative has reduced the service requirement for full maternity pay from two years to one. Employees returning to work after maternity leave will have the option of returning on a full- or part-time basis subject to the availability of jobs. Paternity leave was increased from five to ten days. Several government departments faced with staff shortages have also offered up to five years' unpaid leave to staff with family responsibilities (*EOR*, no. 25, May/June 1989).

While the British government is resolutely refusing to improve statutory parental rights, provide state creches or aid workplace nurseries, it is attempting to help women who want to return to work after having a family. The Women Returners Project, funded by the government's Training Agency, has launched an ambitious scheme to provide advice to such women from a computer database about training, education and career opportunities. The system, designed by IBM, was first demonstrated in April 1989. It was hoped that it will be made available throughout Great Britain at places easily accessible to women (Devine, 1989). The Thatcher government clearly regarded individual counselling of mothers who have left the workforce as ideologically preferable and financially cheaper than the improvement of social provision for maternity and childcare.

With few exceptions, the long-term unpaid maternity leaves are enjoyed by a highly select group of middle-class professionals and executives who have postponed having children to build their careers, and who are employed in large organisations interested in attracting and retaining skilled female labour. The benefits are usually not available to couples who want to have children when they are young or who want to have larger families. Provisions tied to length of service, skill and shortages of labour are of necessity divisive, ensuring that lower paid, less-skilled women or women with a larger number of children remain at a disadvantage.

Parental leave

Parental leave (not to be confused with paternity leave[2]) is time off work for either parent, to care for a young child. The leave was first introduced in Sweden in 1974, when fathers became entitled to ten days' paid paternity leave plus an additional period of six months of parental leave. Parents themselves could decide how to divide the latter, though both could not be on leave at the same time. In addition to the six months after birth covered by the basic parental leave, a further six months of special parental leave may be taken at any time up to the end of the child's first year at school. This may be taken as a full-time, half-time or quarter-time leave, with the period of leave extended accordingly. The basic parental leave and the first three months of the special parental leave are paid at 90 per cent of gross income; the last three months of the special parental leave are paid at a basic flat rate. The leaves are funded as part of the national health insurance scheme, which is financed from taxes and employers' contributions.

The Swedish parental leave scheme was adopted as part of a policy designed to promote equality between women and men in the home, on the job and in public life (House of Lords, 1985: 192). The EEC Proposal for a Directive on Parental Leave and Leave for Family Reason was justified on the same grounds, as 'a tangible step forward in the achievement of greater equality of opportunity in practice between women and men in the labour market'. Docksey (1987) suggested that the Directive would also have very tangible benefits for employment policy, by freeing parents from work to care for their families and thus opening up valuable temporary employment and work experience opportunities for young people and the unemployed: 'If workers are not given concrete encouragement to take leave, they will not take it, and we can wait for ever for places to open up for young workers and the unemployed.' Docksey (1987) also hoped that as a result of the Directive, 'it would no longer be necessary for women and men to choose between bringing up children and the world of work. There is considerable potential here for encouraging family life and, in particular, for reversing the present disturbing demographic changes in our societies.'[3]

The European Commission's involvement in parental leave dates back to 1980, when the British Equal Opportunities Commission, in conjuction with the European Commission, organised a conference in Manchester to assess from a broad perspective the obstacles that continue to block the achievement of equality for women throughout the European Community. That conference, which was attended by delegates from all member states, called on the EEC to introduce a Directive on parental and family leave as part of its broader Action Programme on Equal Opportunities for Women. Released in November 1983, and amended in 1984 to take account of the opinion of the European Parliament, the proposed EC Directive included the following features:

1. Minimum period of leave of three months per worker per child. In a two-parent family where both parents are gainfully employed this would mean a total entitlement of at least six months' full-time leave, to be divided equally between mother and father.
2. Parental leave would not have to be taken immediately after maternity leave, but must be taken before the child is two years old (five years for a handicapped child).
3. With the agreement of parent and employer, the leave may be taken part-time, with the leave period extended accordingly.
4. Both parents may not be on leave at the same time.
5. The leave entitlement may not be transferred from one parent to the other.
6. Leave entitlement may be extended for single-parent families or for both parents of a handicapped child.
7. The question of payment is left to member states, but any payment would come from public funds and not from employers.
8. Family leave would entitle women and men workers to a minimum number of days leave for pressing and important domestic reasons such as the illness of a child or spouse or death of a near relative.

The British Government, local authorities and the Confederation of British Industry opposed the proposed Directive on the grounds of cost, that it was not an appropriate area for legislation, that it may be counterproductive to achieving equal opportunities, that it would cause rigidity in the labour market and contribute to unemployment, and that its subject matter is best pursued by voluntary negotiations between employers and employees. In contrast, the Equal Opportunities Commission, numerous trade unions, several voluntary organisations (such as the Maternity Alliance or the National Council for One Parent Families), and some professional health organisations (such as the Royal College of Nursing) strongly supported the proposed Directive.

The House of Lords Select Committee on the European Communities which considered the draft Directive also supported the idea of a statutory parental leave. Reviewing all the evidence, and noting that 'the arguments against introducing parental leave are similar to those raised when maternity leave was being proposed in the 1970s', the Select

Committee concluded that 'parental leave will promote equal opportunities for women', that 'it will also improve childcare', that it 'should be paid', and that 'there is no convincing evidence one way or the other that parental leave would raise industry's costs. But because parental leave will achieve important social objectives, any increased costs should be met in part by government' (House of Lords, 1985: xxv, xxxvii)

Subsequent research sponsored by the Equal Opportunities Commission concluded that statutory parental leave would not be very costly relative to other social welfare costs associated with employment. Sally Holterman (1986), a former Senior Economic Adviser with the Government Economic Service, estimated that between 120 000 and 170 000 parents might take parental leave in any one year, 80 per cent of whom would probably be women. The women taking the leave would account for about 1–1.5 per cent of all female employees, while the men would represent 0.1–0.15 per cent of all male employees. The extra costs from disruption and recruitment would add between £10 million and £15 million to employers' costs, which is less than 0.01 per cent of the total wage bill. The net cost to the Government would be between £31 million and £45 million, but some 6000 to 9000 people a year could be taken off the unemployment register as a result of jobs created by a parental leave scheme, with savings of £15 to £25 million.

Thus far from creating unemployment, the parental leave scheme would actually create jobs. In fact, several European countries have already used extended periods of full- or part-time leave to promote temporary withdrawals from the labour market and the hiring of temporary replacement workers from the ranks of the young and the unemployed. Since 1985, all employees in Belgium have been entitled to time off work for a period of six months to a year, subject to employer agreement. In theory, the statutory sabbatical is not a parental leave, because it can be taken for variety of reasons by all employees, not just parents. However, mothers of small children have been the main beneficiaries of the scheme. Eighty-seven per cent of employees on leave in May 1986 were women, and 63 per cent were women aged 25–35. A low, flat-rate allowance is paid during the leave (1054 BF a month in 1986). The first two months of operation of the sabbatical leave scheme in late 1985 saw the creation of some 2500 replacement full-time and part-time jobs, including 1200 private sector jobs and 1000 new jobs in teaching. The 10-month parental leave established in 1986 in the Federal Republic of Germany (increased to 12 months in 1988) was expected to create 200 000 one-year contracts for currently unemployed people (Docksey, 1987; Moss, 1988: 63).

Like all EEC Directives, the adoption of the Directive for Parental Leave and Leave for Family Reasons required unanimous support from all member states. Because of British veto, the Directive was not adopted. However, since it was first proposed in 1983, parental leave has become available in the majority of EEC countries. The Directive has made an impact even in Great Britain, where, as we noted, it has provided an impetus for many trade unions to demand provisions for parental leave in their collective agreements. Several employers in sectors faced with shortages of labour have designed various 'career-break schemes', increasingly available to either parent. However, in the foreseeable future, the major beneficiaries of such schemes will continue to be women.

AUSTRALIA

Maternity leave benefits

The general right to a maternity leave in Australia has become available through both national legislation and wage agreements reached in collective bargaining. Starting with the Maternity Leave (Australian Government Employees) Act 1973, which gave right to maternity leave to federal civil servants, maternity benefits have been progressively extended through industrial awards and state legislation. However, benefits vary greatly between the public and the private sector, and even within the public sector itself.

The real watershed in the development of a quasi-national maternity leave policy was an industrial test case on maternity leave, which was brought in 1978 to the Australian Conciliation and Arbitration Commission by the Australian Council of Trade Unions (ACTU) and five unions. When the ACTU presents a 'test case' to the Commission, it does so for a particular award or awards, but on the understanding that if the case is successful, it will benefit all employees in Australia covered by awards. Thus the 1979 decision of the Australian Conciliation and Arbitration Commission, which granted women employees the right to unpaid maternity leave, initially covered only six federal awards. However, the maternity clause which accompanied the decision was subsequently incorporated in all federal and state awards, and is now recognised as a standard provision. Ninety-four per cent of female wage and salary earners in Australia are covered by such awards (ACTU, 1979, 1989; Glezer, 1988: 15).

The maternity leave clause grants a period of up to 52 weeks of unpaid, unbroken leave to both full- and part-time employees with at least 12 months continuous service with the employer before taking the leave. Casual and seasonal workers are, however, excluded from coverage. The maternity leave clause protects women against dismissal on account of pregnancy or maternity leave, entitles them to a transfer to a safe job or leave in lieu of a transfer (without, however, protecting their earnings), and guarantees them their original job or a comparable one at the end of their leave. The maternity leave clause also grants special maternity leave and sick leave in cases of miscarriage, stillbirth and illness related to pregnancy. The employer, whether in the public or the private sector, bears the cost of any income support indicated in the award (ACTU, 1979).

Maternity leave provisions within the public sector usually offer more than the minimum entitlement. Thus for Commonwealth and Victoria civil servants, 12 weeks of the total 52 weeks' leave period are paid. In New South Wales, civil servants are entitled to six weeks' paid leave before the expected date of confinement, half pay for six weeks after childbirth and unpaid leave for the remaining 40 weeks. However, the regulations require employees to return to work for at least 62 days after leave before payment is received. What this implies is that the benefit is seen less as a form of income replacement, and more as a reward or incentive to return to work. Maternity benefits in the remaining state public services include no paid component and as such are not markedly different from those prevailing in the private sector. However, Tasmania offers teachers three years' unpaid nurturing leave. The equivalent entitlement for teachers in Victoria is up to seven years of unpaid family leave. Education departments have offered these additional leaves in order to retain more teachers. The marked differences between public and private sector maternity leave benefits are regarded by many women as unfair and unjust. The special benefits for teachers have drawn a lot of criticism, as has the fact that some women are paid for part of their maternity leave while others are not (Glezer, 1988: 16, 89, 140).

Provisions for job security and the length and flexibility of the maternity leave appear to be more generous in Australia than in the United Kingdom. The total period of leave is 52 weeks (as opposed to 40 weeks in the UK) and the leave is less rigidly defined. In the UK, mothers of babies born prematurely who have not taken all, if any, of the 11 weeks required before the expected date of confinement are still only entitled to 29 weeks after the birth, rather than the 40 weeks available to a mother whose pregnancy goes to term. In Australia, the only restrictions are that six weeks of the total 52 weeks of leave must be taken after birth, and that an employer may require the employee to commence maternity leave up to six weeks prior to her expected date of confinement (ACTU, 1979; Phillips and Evans, 1987).

The eligibility requirement of 12 months of continuous service for both full-time and part-time workers is also more generous than the British equivalent of two years of unbroken service with the same employer for full-time and five years for part-time workers. However, this does not mean that Australia has universal coverage. Out of a nationwide sample of 921 women who gave birth during the last week of May in 1984 and who were in employment during their pregnancy, 24 per cent were ineligible for maternity leave (Glezer, 1988). Thus nearly one in four women workers in Australia (compared to nearly one in two in the UK) is ineligible for maternity leave either because she is a temporary casual worker or because she has been insufficient time with her employer.

In the public sector, 76 per cent of employees take maternity leave, compared to a mere 21 per cent in the private sector. The 1984 sample revealed that 69 per cent of private sector employees eligible for maternity leave did not take it, either because they did not want to return to paid employment while their children were very small, or because they had no information about their maternity leave entitlements. Forty-four per cent of private sector employees in managerial/professional occupations took maternity leave, compared with 23 per cent in clerical or industrial jobs (Glezer, 1988: 46).

The lack of information about maternity leave provisions found in the employee survey was matched by similar ignorance among private sector employers, particularly small business. Glezer (1988: 9) found that 'not only did small business have no information, but many had erroneous views of maternity leave, assuming they would have to pay their employees for the twelve month period'. The survey of private sector employers, which was based on 1252 establishments of five different business sizes and eleven industry sectors, found that only 35 per cent of the total sample had ever experienced an employee taking maternity leave. Only 16 per cent of establishments with fewer than 100 employees had ever experienced an employee taking maternity leave. Maternity leave was a more common occurrence in larger organisations. As in Great Britain, it was regarded as a minor irritant rather than as a major problem. Many employers saw the provision as a valuable tool in enhancing their ability to retain skilled women workers and valuable expertise. However, 14 per cent of employers admitted that they respon- ded to the mandatory maternity leave provision by using discriminatory employment practices. Among those who acknowledged their discrimi- nation, 36 per cent stated they used more casual workers (who are not eligible for maternity leave) and 10 per cent employed fewer women in the childbearing years (Glezer, 1988: 120)

On a more positive side, the overwhelming majority of private sector employees who were eligible for maternity leave reported positive reaction from their employer to pregnancy. Just under a third of private sector employers gave the respondents lighter duties and more flexible working hours. Although Australian employers are not required to provide time off for antenatal care, almost half the employers did so. The relatively few complaints about poor employer reaction concerned illegal dismissals (Glezer, 1988: 49–50).

Seventy-three per cent of those who took maternity leave returned to work after their leave; sixty-five per cent returned to the same employer. The majority of maternity leave takers (63 per cent) were satisfied with the amount of time they had off; 35 per cent would have liked more. The main reason for returning to work was financial (56 per cent of the sample), and the next most important given was an enjoyment of work (18 per cent). Very few women (5 per cent) said 'continuing career' was the main reason for returning to work. The major reasons given for not returning to work were negative attitudes towards combining work and child-rearing, the cost and lack of suitable childcare, desire to breast- feed, partners who preferred their wives not to work, and the feeling that there was no economic necessity to be in the workforce (Glezer, 1988: 51–5).

Among women employed during pregnancy, those who were having their first child were less likely to return to the workforce than those having second or subsequent children. Examination of maternity leave status by number of children revealed that 57 per cent of those who took maternity leave were having a first child. The remaining 43 per cent were having their second or subsequent pregnancy. However, the overall proportion of first-birth mothers in the total sample (n = 696) who took maternity leave was 31 per cent; 17 per cent were expecting a second child, and seven per cent a third or subsequent child. Thus maternity leave provisions have the greatest impact on women's first pregnancy. As Glezer (1988: 69–70) argues,

substantially fewer women were in the workforce after the first birth which is the major exit point; therefore, there were fewer women taking maternity leave for second births. However, as the retention rates given above illustrate, women who have demonstrated commitment to workforce participation by returning after the first birth are more likely to return after second or subsequent births. From an employer's point of view, women with children who return to work are likely to remain in the workforce. The problem for employers is to retain women after the first birth.

Whereas all those who returned from their maternity leave were working full time before the birth, only 44 per cent of those who returned to work after the birth were working full-time. There is a strong preference for part-time work amongst the majority of women with a pre-school child, be they employed or not. Amongst women who are not in the workforce, 47 per cent prefer their current status to working, but 49 per cent would have liked to have part-time jobs. Thus every other woman with a pre-school child not working could be regarded as a 'discouraged' worker due to lack of jobs with suitable working hours. Data from the employers' survey also indicate that women often prefer to work part-time when their children are very small (Glezer, 1988: 7–9).

Findings from a smaller scale 1986 study of 112 women on maternity leave from a large public sector organisation in Melbourne confirmed the strong preference mothers have for returning to work on a part-time basis. Of all the women interviewed, only about 20 per cent were planning to return to full-time positions. The majority were either not planning to return or hoping to return to a part-time position. One-third of the respondents named financial reasons, one-third cited career and self-fulfilment issues, and the remainder identified family responsibilities and the demands of parenting as the factors to which they gave primary weight in their decision making about returning to work (Castleman *et al.*, 1989).

In summarising the results of the study, Wulff (1987: 17) suggests that

> maternity leave did serve as a time for child-bearing and early infant care, and as a time for decision-making about returning to work – all with guarantee of job security. But for many women, it was maternity leave with the possibility of returning to a part-time position that attracted them back to the workforce. . . . For many respondents, part-time work is a strategy for maintaining attachment to the labour force without bearing the full brunt of the demands of full-time work. This strategy is, of course, not without problems. Although the possibility of permanent part-time work, with pro rata salary and

benefits, has been introduced, it is still poorly integrated into the mainstream career structure and is seen to be particularly unworkable at higher levels of responsibility and status. There are a number of practical problems including the organisation of work tasks, maintenance of staffing levels and the design of meaningful jobs on a part-time basis. A larger problem is that, until such time as fathers share in early child care and family responsibilities, part-time work may come to be seen as secondary work, largely engaged in by mothers of young children.

Parental leave

Like maternity leave, parental leave provisions evolved through gradual extension of legislation and industrial awards. In 1985, the federal government introduced for its own employees entitlement to parental leave. The Australian Public Service provision gives men and women the right to 40 weeks' unpaid leave after the public service provision of 12 weeks' paid maternity leave. Similar provisions are available for civil servants in New South Wales, South Australia and the Northern Territory, ranging from one year in New South Wales and South Australia to six years in the Northern Territory. Extended parental leave for fathers is also available to teachers in all states except Queensland.

The ACTU became involved in parental leave as a result of its 1984 'Action Program for Women Workers'. The Program included measures to assist workers with family responsibilities, such as provision of childcare, flexible working hours and a series of test cases on parental leave. The first of these test cases was presented to the Arbitration Commission in 1985. It dealt with adoption leave. The ACTU won the case, with the result that the right of maternity leave was extended to adopting mothers in all federal and state awards. The Arbitration Commission also granted two days per adoption application for both mothers and fathers to attend medical examinations and interviews relating to an adoption (ACTU, 1989).

In 1989, the ACTU presented a national test case for two types of parental leave: 52 weeks' unpaid leave for fathers, similar to maternity and adoption leave, and five days' annual 'special family leave' for both parents to care for a sick child or for school requirements. The parental leave after birth was to consist of three weeks of 'short paternity leave' available immediately after childbirth, and 'extended paternity leave', which could be taken by either parent at a time of their choice, up to the child's second birthday. The 'special family leave' would not threaten existing paid sick leave or emergency leave entitlements of either parent. It was to apply for children up to the age of 18. Since the claim was for an unpaid leave entitlement, there was no provision that parents cannot take the leave at the same time.

The ACTU (1989: 3, 8) believes that 'it is discriminatory to deny a man the right to unpaid leave to care for his child, when this right is available to women through maternity and adoption leave'. It also believes that

> by allowing both parents to take their leave up to the child's second birthday, the provision will allow parents to share more equally in child-rearing and to give the child a longer period of time in the home in the care of its parents, if that is their wish. The optional part-time provision in the claim will give parents more flexibility in regard to caring for the child and working part-time if they wish.

As far as benefits to employers are concerned, the ACTU (1989: 12) suggests that 'the provision of parental leave can improve staff morale, reduce absenteeism, and lift productivity'.

On 26 July 1990, the Federal Industrial Relations Commission granted most of the ACTU demands. Subject to a qualifying condition of 12 months of continuous service, all male employees covered by industrial awards are now entitled to one week unpaid paternity leave at the time of confinement of their spouse. Male workers are also eligible for an additional period of up to 51 weeks' unpaid paternity leave, which has to be taken by the child's first birthday. Paternity leave is reduced by any period of maternity leave taken by the employee's partner and, except for the week at the time of the birth, may not be taken concurrently with her maternity leave. The total period of leave available to adopting parents is also 52 weeks, which may not be taken concurrently, except for three weeks which may be taken at the time of placement of a child. The right to work part-time during the parental leave ceases on the child's second birthday and 'may only be worked by agreement with an employer' (Glezer, 1990).

Thus the ACTU and the Australian Conciliation and Arbitration Commission have played a major role in advancing women's equality. In its 1969, 1972 and 1974 decisions, the Arbitration Commission endorsed the principle of equal pay. The general principle of maternity leave was endorsed in 1979. In 1985, maternity leave was extended to adoptive mothers and in 1986, to outworkers in the clothing industry. Another important decision handed down by the AIRC was the 1988

National Wage Decision, which emphasised the need for award restructuring to remove indirect discriminatory practices. These include practices that discriminate against workers with family responsibilities (OSW, 1990).

In 1987, the Office of the Status of Women organised a special workshop on 'Women and Award Restructuring'. One of the issues addressed by the workshop was the constraints faced by workers with family responsibilities. Using the experiences from career-break schemes that were developed elsewhere, officials from the South Australian Department of Labour's Women's Adviser's Unit argued that such schemes 'would allow workers, who are taking a break from the workforce in order to care for children or dependent relatives, to keep in touch with employer organisations, to retain skills and perhaps provide a pool of skilled labour to be called upon for holiday relief or peak workloads. This could be supported by a graduated return-to-work option following longer periods of absence from the workforce' (OSW, 1990: 17).

CANADA

Maternity leave benefits

Before 1971, the majority of employed women in Canada were required to resign from their jobs during pregnancy, with no guarantee of re-employment after the birth of their child, and with no income provision while they were away from work. The real watershed in the development of a national maternity leave programme was a recommendation to that effect made by the Royal Commission on the Status of Women in 1970. The following year, the Canada Labour Code was amended, prohibiting dismissal on the grounds of pregnancy in all organisations under federal jurisdictions (for example banks, communications, transportation and other interprovincial enterprises). The new code also granted all women with one year of continuous employment with the same employer 17 weeks of unpaid maternity leave. At the same time, the Unemployment Insurance Act was changed to include provisions for 17 weeks of unemployment insurance maternity benefits, at 60 per cent of an employee's regular salary, up to a maximum benefit, and with a two-week waiting period before any money can be collected. In 1993, the maximum benefit for the 15 weeks of paid leave was $437.00 per week.

The main reason for grouping maternity with unemployment was that unemployment insurance (UI) comes within the jurisdiction of the federal government and, as such, was the only way to extend coverage to most working women throughout Canada (Bennett and Loewe, 1975: 91). However, the inclusion of maternity benefits under the provisions of unemployment insurance led to various anomalies. For example,

> it was soon discovered that teachers could not receive maternity benefits during the summer because of Section 158 of the UI Act that prevented teachers on summer vacation from applying for unemployment benefits. After three court rulings that Section 158 was null and void, and with other appeals pending, the UI Commission stopped applying this provision to maternity benefits in 1976. . . . Other women found themselves ineligible for all or part of their maternity benefits because of a technicality around the benefit period, or because maternity benefits could be obtained only 8 weeks before and six weeks after the expected date of confinement. Amendments to the UI Act that resolved these difficulties were introduced in 1975 (Bill C-69 and Bill-16). The latter bill permitted women to claim their 15 weeks at any time within a 26 week period around birth.
>
> (White, 1990: 157)

Another set of anomalies was brought to light by Stella Bliss and her appeal against Section 46 of the UI Act. Since the UI Act made eligibility requirements for maternity benefits more stringent than for regular unemployment benefits, it was possible, as in the case of Bliss, to be ineligible for maternity benefits, eligible for regular UI, yet denied those UI benefits under Section 46. The latter prohibited a woman from collecting regular UI during the period of eligibility for maternity benefits – defined as eight weeks before the expected birth to six weeks after – on the grounds that she would be unavailable for work. Stella Bliss was ineligible for maternity benefits, but fulfilled the less stringent eligibility requirements for regular unemployment benefits (10–14 weeks of previous employment). She applied for unemployment benefits six days after the birth of her child, stating that she was available for work. Her application was denied on the grounds that she was ineligible under Section 46. She appealed and her case eventually appeared before the Supreme Court of Canada in June 1978. The case was lost, but it created considerable publicity and created an opportunity for women's groups to pressure the government to amend the legislation.

'When the UI Act was passed in 1971', White (1990: 156–7) has argued,

maternity leave was included as an incidental part of the package. However, criticism of the provisions was immediate and became increasingly vocal over the following years, one element of the emerging women's movement and its focus upon discriminatory legislation. . . . It was not only the UI Act that came under discussion during these years. Women's organisations also criticized provincial legislation on maternity leave. As late as 1976 four provinces and the two territories had no provision for security of employment during maternity leave.

However, by the end of the decade all of the provinces and the territories had enacted labour laws entitling women employees under their jurisdiction to a maternity leave of 17 weeks or longer, prohibiting their dismissal on the grounds of pregnancy, and in some cases, guaranteeing the same or comparable work on return after childbirth. Protection against dismissal or layoff because of pregnancy and against discriminatory practices related to pregnancy and childbirth were also included in federal and provincial human rights legislation. In many provinces, however, students, domestic workers and farm labourers were explicitly exempt from coverage.

The federal and most of the provincial jurisdictions tie the reinstatement and job protection aspects of maternity leave to a minimum period of previous employment. The length of employment required to qualify for the leave had ranged from six months in the federal jurisdiction to 12 months plus 11 weeks in Ontario. The norm is 12 months of continuous employment for the same employer. The qualifying period in Canada is therefore less stringent than in the United Kingdom, and broadly similar to that in Australia. The main justification for the requirement is a corporate one, 'to protect the employer in instances where an employee had not established a serious work commitment' (Labour Canada, 1984: 1).

The requirement for previous continuous employment excludes most part-time workers who work irregular hours. Townson (1983: 45) notes that

only about 45% of potential maternity benefit claimants actually receive benefits. In 1981, for example, there were 365 000 births in

Canada. Based on a 68% labour force participation rate for women in the main childbearing years (age 20–34), it may be assumed that approximately 248 000 new mothers were in the labour force and might have applied for maternity benefits. In fact, only about 113 000 claimants actually received benefits through the unemployment insurance program in 1981. This represents a 'take-up' rate of only 45% of women. Employment and Immigration Officials estimate that about 15 000 applicants were disqualified for one reason or another. The remaining potential claimants do not even apply for benefits. This may be partly because they are aware that they could not meet the eligibility criteria. But officials believe that other reasons for low take-up may be the possible stigma attached to the unemployment insurance generally, and lack of awareness that the maternity benefits program even exists.

Qualifying for maternity *leave* and qualifying for cash *benefits* are two completely separate processes in Canada. As we noted, the qualifying period for a job-protected maternity leave under the various federal and provincial employment standards legislation typically requires 12 months of continuous work for the same employer. In contrast, the qualifying period for maternity cash payments under the Unemployment Insurance Act is 'only' 20 weeks of employment in the last 52 weeks. The cash benefits are available for up to 15 consecutive weeks in the period surrounding the birth, provided the woman is receiving no other cash benefits during that period.

Under the UI legislation, the woman is free to start collecting benefits any time during the period that begins 11 weeks prior to the expected delivery date and ends 17 weeks after the actual delivery. This flexibility in benefits entitlement is particularly helpful to women who have premature babies. Throughout the 1980s, the length of the leave and the level of financial compensation have been gradually increased, and extended to adoptive parents and natural fathers, as a result of collective bargaining, lobbying by women's groups and legal challenges under human rights legislation. Collective bargaining significantly improved benefits for federal civil servants, who since 1981 have been entitled to 37 weeks of maternity leave, with up to 11 weeks permitted for prenatal leave and up to 26 weeks for postnatal leave. The postnatal leave is also available as 'paternity leave without pay' to male employees. The leave may begin on the day of childbirth, not before, and it may extend up to 26 weeks after the birth.

In 1976, the Canadian Avisory Council on the Status of Women had recommended that employers be permitted to top up the difference between UI benefits and the woman's regular wage under the Supplementary Unemployment Benefits Plan (SUB). When first introduced, SUBs only applied to supplementary coverage for illness and temporary lay-off. In 1978, SUBs were altered to permit coverage also for maternity leave. By 1981 there were 1241 SUB arrangements in existence, of which the majority, 1220, covered only payments for maternity (White, 1990: 158). Most female public servants who take maternity leave are covered by SUBs entitling them to a bridging benefit for the two-week period before UI payments begin. The amount is the same as that paid under unemployment insurance – up to 60 per cent of the woman's insured weekly earnings to a specific maximum amount.

To compensate for the loss of 40 per cent of income, several public service collective agreements have provided for additional cash benefit during maternity leave, known as maternity allowance (Public Service Commission of Canada, 1984: 5). The first provincial breakthrough on this issue occurred in Quebec, where the public sector is more highly unionised and more militant than elsewhere in Canada. Moreover, since the formation of the Common Front in 1972, Quebec public service unions representing government, education and health workers bargain jointly rather than individually on priority issues. Throughout the 1970s, these priorities focused on women's health and equality issues, and on broader issues of family and parental rights.

In the 1979 collective agreement, the Common Front negotiated 20 weeks of maternity leave at full pay, 10 weeks of paid adoption leave, five paid days for paternity leave, continuous accumulation (rather than mere retention) of annual leave, pension, seniority and other such benefits, and the previously mentioned (in Chapter 7) health protection for pregnant women. This collective agreement covered 20 per cent of all employed women in the province of Quebec. It soon became the model for negotiation elsewhere, especially in the federal public service (White, 1980: 109–14).

The demand for fully paid maternity leave was successfully put on the national agenda by the Canadian Union of Postal Workers in the 1981 round of negotiations. Prior to 1981, a woman CUPW member taking maternity leave was entitled to up to six months of unpaid leave, during which her employer's superannuation contributions, sick leave and annual leave credits ceased to accumulate. UI benefits were the only income available during the leave. When the 1981 negotiations broke down, the union went on a 42-day strike, with paid maternity leave remaining as one of the central issues. At the end of the strike, CUPW became the first national union to win for its female members a 17-week supplement to UI benefits, which brought the earnings of a woman on maternity leave up to 93 per cent of her regular pay.

As White (1990: 160–1) has argued,

> while paid maternity leave was generally supported by the membership as a demand, it was a lot more controversial as a strike issue. . . . Men complained that there was nothing in this for them and that it was discriminatory, older women felt that they had managed without it and that younger women wanted everything, and even some young women did not support it, feeling as one woman expressed it that it was a 'nice benefit' if you could get it, but 'ludicrous' to be out on strike over it. . . . The negotiating team was aware that it would not be an easy issue, because it affected only a small number of members and minority issues are never easy. . . . There could not have been a strike over just maternity leave because it would not have been crucial enough to sufficient members to obtain the necessary support. However, the strike also involved health and safety demands, the use of closed circuit television, vacation and statutory holidays, issues that affected most or all of the members.

White (1990: 162) also suggests that

> the importance of the issue in the initial negotiations was related more to the commitment of the union's leadership and their recognition that paid maternity leave was a demand likely to muster public support and therefore create pressure on the government to provide the benefit. Thus, the attention focused on the issue by women's organisations over the previous ten years was important in creating a climate in which such a struggle would be successful. The union leadership saw the opportunity that had been created and was prepared to take advantage of it, despite the fact that it might be controversial among their own members. It was important that CUPW had a tradition of being a generally progressive union, concerned with broader social issues rather than just the more narrow concern of wages and strictly work-related benefits.

The first private sector employer who agreed to at least partially close the gap between the UI benefits and regular pay was the telephone company Bell Canada. The arrangement, effective on 1 January 1984, in the third year of a three-year agreement, made up the difference between unemployment insurance and 75 per cent of regular pay, up to a maximum of $1000 for each eligible employee. The benefit was therefore of greater value to the low-paid switchboard operators than to the higher paid female technicians (List, 1982). However, not all SUB plans are the result of collective agreements. Some employers have developed SUBs as a way of paying additional maternity benefits to valuable professional and managerial employees, whose earnings are considerably higher than the maximum insurable earnings limit imposed on UI benefits, and who would otherwise suffer a significant drop in income during the maternity leave period (Townson, 1983: 92–3). Unlike Australia, where unpaid leave predominates, a substantial proportion of maternity absence in Canada is paid, with UI benefits constituting the most common form of financial compensation. In 1987, 92 per cent of all maternity leave taken was compensated, with 20 per cent receiving full or partial pay from their employers or group insurance in addition to, or instead of, UI benefits (Moloney, 1989).

Throughout the 1980s, there has been a dynamic interplay between federal and provincial legislation, lobbying by women's organisations against discriminatory statutes and for improvement in maternity benefits, legal challenges by individual women (and men) under human rights legislation, and collective bargaining. The interaction among these processes also characterised the progressive extension of maternity benefits to adoptive parents and to natural fathers.

Adoption and parental leave benefits

Adoption benefits were incorporated into the Unemployment Insurance Act system in 1984, allowing adoptive parents (mother or father, but not both) to apply for up to 17 weeks of adoption benefits starting with the week of the child's placement, provided the parent could meet the normal UI qualifying requirements. However, because of the split juris-diction of the federal UI system and the provincial labour standards, not all adoptive parents could take advantage of the new benefit. By the end of 1988, only the federal Canada Labour Code, employment standards of five provinces and some private sector collective agreements had laws that made it mandatory for employers to grant adoption leave (Canadian Advisory Council on the Status of Women, 1988). As with maternity leave, not all of the provinces reacted instantaneously to changes in the unemployment system.

By adding adoption benefits into the UI scheme as a separate category, and by making them gender neutral, the federal government explicitly recognised for the first time the crucial feminist distinction between gender-specific maternity benefits for childbearing on the one hand and gender-neutral benefits for childrearing on the other. However, since the parental gender neutrality was not extended to natural fathers, a new gender-specific anomaly was created. The criticism of the exclusion of natural fathers from UI parental coverage emerged almost immediately, and soon resulted in a series of highly publicised legal challenges under the Charter of Rights and Freedoms. In turn, the publicity surrounding the male discrimination cases led to broader debates about parental rights, and served as an opportunity to remind Canadians that most European countries, though not the United States, offer much better provisions for maternity and parental leave than Canada does (Rauhala, 1988).

The least controversial case, and the one which received the greatest public sympathy and the swiftest governmental response, was that of John McInnis, whose daughter was born at the end of 1987 after her mother's brain death. When the new widower and single parent applied for maternity leave benefits, 'he was told that maternity benefits were for women only. It was even suggested he adopt his own child because adoptive fathers are eligible for the benefits. McInnis, a shy and reserved man who shunned attention, felt he had to fight. With the help of men's rights activist Ron Sauve, he took his concerns first to the Human Rights Commission, and then straight to Parliament Hill' (Fruman, 1988). McInnis's also met with the Employment and Immigration Minister Benoit Bouchard, who was clearly touched by McInnis tragic fate. Aware of the minimal cost involved, Bouchard responded quickly and decisively. The UI Act was amended to allow payment of benefits to fathers who are widowed or whose wives are disabled and cannot care for infants, provided the father can meet the normal qualifying conditions for UI special benefits. The amendment was made retroactive effective 29 March 1987 (Employment and Immigration Canada, 1988).

Another successful complaint of sexual discrimination against fathers was launched in 1985 by Shalom Schachter, an arbitration officer of the Ontario Nurses Association, after he was denied paternity leave benefits following the birth of his second son. Schachter first took his complaint to the Canadian Human Rights Commission, which acknowledged that the UI Act discriminated against natural fathers, but that it was power-less to do anything about it. In its special report on the issue tabled in Parliament on 2 November 1987, the Commission urged the federal government to extend the 15 weeks of UI maternal benefits to all fathers.

The report also pointed out that the cost of parental benefits would be approximately $500 million, which may explain why the federal government, which is under no legal obligation to respond to a commission report, chose to remain silent (Fruman, 1988; Smith, 1988).

Schachter then took his complaint to court. Since his legal challenge was based on the constitutional Charter of Rights and Freedoms, there was a genuine risk that rather than extending benefits, the court could decide that the current 15-week period of benefits must be shared by both parents. To avoid this happening, the Women's Legal Education and Action Fund (LEAF), a feminist organisation that addresses legal equality issues of interest to women, sought, and obtained, an intervener status in the case. During the court hearings in May 1988, LEAF brought in expert witnesses to convince the court not to strike out maternity leave. LEAF's most authoritative witness, Dr Marsden G. Wagner, a World Health Organization maternal and child health official, testified that 'Canada's provisions for new parents and babies are at the low end of the scale when compared to those in other industrialized nations'. Dr Wagner also said that 'he knew of no jurisdiction in which parental leave was given at the expense of the mother's leave, nor of one in which the leave to the father depended on whether the mother was disabled or dead' (Rauhala, 1988).

In June 1988, Judge Barry Strayer of the Federal Court of Canada ruled that the section of the Unemployment Insurance Act which denies benefits to natural fathers on parental leave while giving them to natural mothers and adoptive parents is unconstitutional, and rooted in sex-role stereotyping. The judge also said that the discrimination in benefits should not be remedied by taking away existing benefits of biological mothers. Women's groups and opposition MPs in the House of Commons welcomed the decision and urged the government to accept the ruling and accordingly amend the Unemployment Insurance Act. However, business groups warned that the granting of parental leave would disrupt the workforce and seriously drain the unemployment insurance fund (MacQueen, 1988; Rauhala and Delacourt, 1988).

In the end, the federal government both appealed the ruling to the Supreme Court of Canada, and amended the Unemployment Insurance Act with the Federal Court of Canada ruling in mind. Stalled for almost a year in the Senate, and introduced within the broad context of a radical overhaul of the unemployment insurance scheme,[4] the new Unemployment Insurance Act came into effect on 18 November 1990. It left maternity benefits intact, and provided an additional 10 weeks of shared parental UI benefits, five weeks fewer than adoptive parents used to enjoy. Thus new parents in Canada are currently eligible for 15 weeks of UI benefits payable only to the biological mother, and an additional 10 weeks of parental benefits which the natural or adoptive parents can divide between them any way they want. The federal government expects that 80 per cent of eligible mothers but only 5 per cent of eligible fathers will apply for the 10 weeks of UI parental benefits (Jones, 1990). The number of parents applying, though not the gender composition, will ultimately depend on when all the provinces amend their employment standards to provide for paternal or parental leave.

In Ontario, the September 1990 election of the first social democratic NDP government in the province's history ensured an immediate response. Exceeding the federal provisions, in November 1990 the new NDP government brought in legislation that allows mothers 35 weeks and fathers 18 weeks of unpaid job-protected leave, during which seniority, pension benefits, life insurance and extended health care benefits are maintained. The qualifying period for the job-protected leave was reduced to three months of previous employment (McInnes, 1990). Similar legislation was unveiled at the same time in Quebec, where the amended Labour Standards Act allows parents to take up to 34 weeks of unpaid leave to care for a newly born or adopted child, and requires no qualifying period for the leave.

The respective federal and provincial legislative changes were enacted in recognition of gender equality, and to make it easier for parents of both sexes to reconcile their work and family obligations. However, the Quebec legislation is also part of a family policy 'aimed at encouraging couples to have more children in the government's overall drive to reverse the province's demographic trend' (Violette Trepanier, the Minister Responsible for the Status of Women and for the Family, quoted in Séguin, 1990). Thus in addition to promoting maternal and infant health, gender equality and integration of work and family roles, Quebec parental leave policies are also designed to raise the birth rate.

CONCLUSION

The provision of maternity and parental leave benefits is a complex area of public policy. It touches upon questions of health protection measures for working mothers and their children, equal opportunity measures for women workers, equal rights for men and adoptive parents, income replacement for mothers or fathers in the labour force, the optimal care of young children, measures by employers to attract and retain skilled labour force, the creation of temporary employment and opportunities for work experiences for young people and the unemployed, and an attempt to increase the birth rate. Regardless of the different philosophical bases and policy objectives, all maternity/parental leaves recognise child-bearing as a social function rather than as a private decision. However, beyond this common framework, variables such as women's labour force participation, the structure of the welfare state, the strength of the trade union movement and its responsiveness to women's concerns, the division between federal and provincial (state) jurisdictions, the presence or absence of a pronatalist policy, and the role of litigation in the formulation of public policy are all important influences in how maternity and parental leave benefits are structured and funded.

The maternity and parental leave benefits in the three countries reviewed here have been introduced in the 1970s through different mechanisms. While Great Britain relied (in a descending order of importance) on national legislation, collective bargaining and employers' desire to attract and retain qualified staff, in Australia most parents get maternity and parental leave benefits under the terms of industrial awards rather than through legislation. The Canadian maternity and parental leave and benefits programme emerged as a result of interplay between the federal unemployment insurance system, federal and provincial labour legislation, lobbying by women's groups, collective bargaining and legal challenges under constitutional human rights legislation.

Employer groups in all three countries have tended to oppose maternal and parental leave on the grounds that such leave would impose on them extra financial and administrative burdens. However, research has shown that maternity leave is not a major problem for employers, largely because it occurs so infrequently. Maternity leave provisions tend to favour workers with strong attachment to the labour force, especially middle-class professionals and executives who have postponed having children to build their careers, and who are employed full-time in large organisations interested in attracting and retaining skilled labour. Couples who want to have children when they are young, domestic workers, farm labourers, regular part-time and casual workers are often excluded from coverage, either by statute or because they cannot meet stringent qualifying conditions tied to the length of service.

The periods of maternity leave in the United Kingdom (40 weeks) and Australia (52 weeks) are considerably longer than the 25 weeks available in Canada. However, the British statutory maternity leave period is rarely taken in full (Brannen and Moss, 1988: 80). Since so little of the leave period is paid, British women tend to return to work five months after childbirth, which is not very different from Canada. More than 90 per cent of eligible maternity leaves in Canada are paid, with 20 per cent receiving full or partial pay from their employers or group insurance in addition to, or instead of, unemployment insurance benefits. In contrast, the majority of maternity leaves in Australia are unpaid, largely because employers are solely responsible for any payment. Paid maternity leave is available only to federal and to some state civil servants, and then only for 12 weeks of the total 52 weeks' leave period.

Throughout the 1980s, the length and the level of pay of maternity leave in Canada have been increased, mainly as a result of collective bargaining. A successful court challenge under the Canadian Charter of Rights and Freedom gave men access to 10 weeks of shared parental benefits under the federal Unemployment Insurance scheme. By leaving existing 15 paid weeks of maternity benefits intact, the 1990 legislation reaffirmed a conception of gender equality which views gender-specific maternity leave benefits and gender-neutral parental leave benefits as complementary rather than as mutually exclusive strategies. The gender-specific component of the Australian parental leave provision is only one week at the time of childbirth, but it is hard to imagine a situation in which a couple allocates maternity and paternity leave in such a way that the breastfeeding mother ends up with only one week's leave. In fact, the take-up of the long-term parental leave by males is expected to be low, largely because the leave is unpaid.

Since the election of the Thatcher government in 1979, statutory maternity rights have been eroded. Despite research findings to the contrary, the British government has continued to insist that any extension of maternity provisions would add to employers' costs, and thereby affect their competitiveness and their willingness to recruit and promote young women. While some British organisations have vol-untarily adopted parental leave schemes, they are not common and are most likely to be found only in sectors with shortages of skilled labour such as banking, teaching, computing and local government.

Parental leave is an important step towards gender equality, but its implementation can be expected only with the equalisation of female and male wages. As long as parental leave is unpaid, or set at a low flat rate, fathers are unlikely to take advantage of parental leave, because the financial costs of withdrawing from the labour force are so much greater for them (and their families) than is the case for mothers. In the foreseeable future, it is likely to be mothers who will remain solely responsible for the care of young children.

9 Childcare Policies and Programmes

INTRODUCTION

Childcare is an umbrella term that covers a whole spectrum of care-taking arrangements mothers (parents) make when they engage in paid work. Childcare ranges from a privatised, informal, unregulated in-home care by a relative, friend, childminder or a live-in nanny to a public, licensed, professional group care in a day-care centre, nursery school, kindergarten or 'outside school hours' centre. Many definitions of services which complement or supplement parental care equate childcare with services required by infants and pre-schoolers. However, the need for childcare does not end when a child begins school, at five years of age in the United Kingdom and six years in Canada and Australia.

Neither the school day nor the school year are synchronised with schedules that govern most full-time employment. The school day is considerably shorter than the typical work day, and if schools have no special supervisory service at meal times (as is the case in many Canadian schools), the school day cuts right into the hours of work. The various school holidays also cause numerous childcare problems. The crunch often comes after the birth of a second or subsequent child, when it becomes extremely difficult to try to co-ordinate the conflicting schedules of two working parents, a day-care setting, and after-school arrangements for the older child(ren).

Childcare, like maternity and parental leave, is a highly complex area of public policy. It touches upon questions of public and private as well as direct and indirect costs of raising the next generation; the invisibility and low value attached to women's work of caring; labour market requirements; the employment needs of mothers (parents); the developmental needs of children; the class, migrant and ethnic status of childcare providers; pay and work conditions of childcare workers; child and family welfare; overlapping jurisdictions of 'care' and 'education'; state intervention in the family and in the informal sector of the economy; gender equality; and pronatalism.

This chapter examines: (1) the legacy of the ideology of 'mothercare' and its impact on post-war childcare policies; (2) the potential impact of affordable childcare on fertility; (3) the current childcare policy-making process, which in all three countries under review has fragmented the issues of childcare, education and parental employment among a multiplicity of administrative and government authorities, a plurality of childcare advocacy groups, and among a variety of 'mixes' of informal, public, voluntary sector, commercial and employer-sponsored childcare services; (4) the advantages and disadvantages of demand and supply subsidies for childcare services; and (5) the costs of *not* providing public support for childcare.

THE LEGACY OF THE IDEOLOGY OF MOTHERCARE

The mothercare 'ideology' favours the view that young children should be cared for only by their mothers, and, conversely, that a woman with a pre-school child should stay at home rather than work for pay. Reflecting a (pre-war) world in which most married women did not engage in paid employment, the mothercare ideology was powerfully strengthened in the post-war period by psychoanalytic theories of maternal deprivation. John Bowlby's writings on child development emphasised both the central importance of the mother–child relationship, especially in the first three years of the child's life, and the dangers of separating mothers and children.

The ideology of maternal deprivation was extremely influential in determining the major thrust of post-war childcare policies, which had discouraged provision of day-care places except for children with special needs. Public debates about childcare services focused only on the needs of children; little was heard of the employment needs of the mother or the parenting needs of the father during this period. The mother–child relationship was synonymous with 'family life'. Fathers wishing to look after their children received far less state support than mothers. Traditionally, single fathers have found it much more difficult than single mothers to recieve social assistance to care for their children at home (Eichler, 1988). As we noted in the previous chapter, the eligibility for parental benefits under the Canadian Unemployment Insurance Act was implemented only in 1990, after a successful legal challenge under the equality provisions of the Charter of Rights and Freedom.

Post-war policies which took for granted that mothers stop paid work when they have children took no account of the large indirect costs of raising children at home, paid mainly by women in loss of employment and income. These indirect childcare costs to women have been the subject of much recent feminist research. The main findings of this research have been that: (1) by far the largest amount of care of pre-school children is by mothers at home and by others in informal settings; (2) whatever the setting, it is women, not men, who care for dependent children; (3) many informal care providers are foreign migrants and/or members of visible minorities who are frequently subject to exploitation; and (4) women's care-giving work is neither adequately recognised nor remunerated (Pascall, 1986; Eichler, 1988; Arat-Koc, 1990; Ferguson, 1991).

This socio-economic reality rests on the ideology of mothercare, on the belief that women's caring for young children is 'normal' and 'natural'. As New and David (1985: 13) put it, 'women are given caring work on the grounds that they are mothers, or may become mothers, or should have been mothers'. Since the childcare component of women's domestic work is the most difficult one to combine with wage work, the lack of affordable and reliable childcare, and the absence of adequate financial compensation for maternal (parental) childcare, continue to surface as significant factors preventing the achievement of women's equality. The allegiance to the theories of maternal deprivation was never complete. Demand for day-care places, far from declining as expected after the Second World War, has steadily risen in all developed countries as more women with small children entered paid employment. The greatly increased proportion of mothers of small children who are employed outside the home; the diminishing pool of caregivers remaining at home and willing to care privately for children of others; the looming labour shortage (a result of the low fertility during the last two decades); and the growing political influence and institutionalisation of feminism, eventually forced governments at all levels to take the needs of working mothers into account and acknowledge the need for an expanded, affordable, formal childcare system. In recent years, many OECD governments have 'initiated, modified or even redefined their child care polices, sometimes linking them explicitly to questions concerning women's labour force participation and/or family status' (Ergas, 1987: 1).

However, reliance on maternal labour force participation as the main indicator of childcare needs perpetuates a narrow employment-based definition of childcare. While parental involvement in employment and employment-related activities is a major factor in determining family needs for childcare, families need and use childcare for a variety of reasons (Lero, 1991). The recognition of families' needs for a variety of childcare supports has led to the *concept* of a comprehensive childcare system, but to the *reality* of a fragmented and underfunded childcare (non)system.

CHILDCARE AND PRONATALISM

Existing evidence on the impact of reliable and affordable day care on fertility is sporadic and speculative. To the extent that childcare availability increases women's entry into paid employment, it may be anti-natalist, but to the extent that it reduces the burden of child-rearing for those who are, and will remain in the work force, it may be pronatalist (Presser, 1986). A British study of first-time mothers who intended to return to full-time work revealed that some women begin the search for childcare 'before they conceive; becoming pregnant may indeed be conditional on having arranged childcare' (Brannen and Moss, 1988: 61). In Canada, several of the best day-care centres in Toronto have 'fat preconception files of applications from would-be parents' (Fillion, 1989: 25).

A submission by the Canadian Advisory Council on the Status of Women (1986: 2) to the Legislative Committee on Bill C-144, the ill-fated Canada Child Care Act, has made the link between day-care provision and pronatalism quite explicit:

> For women, child care is the *sine qua non* of their work lives. Knowing that arrangements for their children are complicated, inadequate, often random, sometimes unsafe, some women are choosing not to have children. Driven by economic fear, women are on strike against reproducing. That choice is often a sad one for individuals, and a disaster for the economy. By the 1990s, with births well below replacement rate, employers will be desperately, and unsuccessfully, seeking employees.

However, very few Western governments have taken natalist considerations into account. One of these is the highly pronatalist provincial government of Quebec, which several years ago conducted a survey asking women what should be done to enable them to have more children. Seventy per cent of the respondents said that there is nothing the government could or should do. Of the remaining 30 per cent, half said that paying homemaker-mothers would make a difference, and a third of them suggested providing day care. The provincial government acted on both of these suggestions. Its May 1988 budget announced that the number of day-care spaces had increased by a third in the past three years, and would double in the next seven years (Shifrin, 1988). The biggest change, though, was the highly publicised new fiscal bonus for the third and subsequent child in a family, which will be discussed in the next chapter.

CHILDCARE PROVISION IN CANADA

Childcare as a welfare service

The view of childcare as a welfare service for children from disadvantaged families is embodied in the legislation which has provided the main support for the development of state-supported childcare in Canada, the Canada Assistance Plan (CAP). Initiated in 1966, the Plan is a major piece of federal welfare legislation that established one of the central tenets of Canadian post-war social policy: that the cost of looking after the poor was shared 50–50 by Ottawa and the provinces. The CAP is an open-ended, shared-cost agreement[1] enabling the central and provincial governments to split the operating costs of social assistance (aid to persons in need of basic services such as food, shelter, clothing, fuel, utilities) and eligible welfare services, including childcare. Although funding a public childcare system was not CAP's major objective, most public day-care services in Canada are, in fact, funded through it.

The introduction of the Canada Assistance Plan produced an initial spurt in the number of subsidised places available. While in 1966 there were 2025 such spaces available in Ontario, by 1974 this figure had increased sixfold, to 12 152. Provincial expenditures on childcare also grew, both within and outside the CAP (Abbott and Young, 1989). The welfare approach to childcare funding is quite logical, since it is less expensive for the state to pay the childcare costs of the low-income working parent than it is to pay the full cost of subsistence. It is also ideologically supportive of the work ethic. The emphasis on state support for childcare as a way of ending welfare dependency characterises not only the policy orientation of the federal government, but also the attitudes of the general public (Fine, 1990; Vienneau, 1991).

Ironically, most low-income families who qualify for subsidised care do not get the childcare services they are entitled to because eligibility for government assistance varies among the provinces, and there are simply not enough licensed spaces available. In Metropolitan Toronto alone there were in 1989 5000 eligible children waiting for subsidised spaces; the Ontario government said at that time that it would pay for only 1000 new ones (Fillion, 1989: 25). The National Council of Welfare (1988: 11) reported that in 1987 only 10 per cent of the children eligible for either a full or partial subsidy in Ontario received it.

Fiscal support for childcare: demand and supply subsidy

State support for childcare can take two broad forms – supply subsidy and demand subsidy. The former involves direct public funding of *services*, while the latter involves public subsidy of *parents*, to help them increase resources with which they can buy childcare services in the open market. While the majority of EEC member states have relied on supply subsidy, governments in Canada have favoured the development of publicly regulated but privately provided childcare services. Federal, provincial and territorial governments do not, as a rule, establish childcare facilities themselves. Rather, under the terms of the Canada Assistance Plan, they provide full or partial means-tested subsidies to families using services provided by profit-making commercial enterprises, voluntary agencies or municipalities. As Ergas (1987: 7) put it, 'the private provision of care is thus encouraged through public franchising of its delivery'.

The 1986 federal report of the Task Force on Childcare concludes that the method by which services for children are financed in Canada places good-quality licensed services beyond the means of most parents, unless their incomes are so low that they can qualify for a subsidy, or their incomes are so high that they can afford to pay the full cost. The private provision of childcare in Canada is also stimulated by fiscal arrangements which allow parents to deduct from their personal income tax documented childcare expenses. In 1993, the maximum ceiling was $3000 per school-aged child between 7 and 14, or $5000 for a child aged six and under. If the parents are married, only the one with the lower income, usually the mother, is eligible to make the claim.

Critics of the Child Care Expense Deduction (CCED) have pointed out that the maximum allowable deduction comes nowhere close to the real cost of childcare; that it does nothing to increase the supply of childcare; that it is of little use to parents who have to pay user fees up front; and since it is a deduction from taxable income, that it favours higher-income over low-income earners. It also fails to provide any subsidy to the majority of working parents who cannot produce receipts for expenses incurred. Most informal caregivers – up to 85 per cent by one estimate – do not declare their income and are therefore reluctant to issue tax receipts (Brown and Power, 1986: 54).

One result of these problems is a very low take-up rate of CCED. In 1984, the deduction was claimed by 420 000 women (and 82 000) men, with the average claim being $1487 (the maximum then was $2000 per child); yet there were 1 624 000 women in the labour force with children under 15 years of age. Thus relatively few Canadians are benefiting from CCED, and those who do are likely to be at the higher end of the income scale. Aside from being regressive, tax deductions are also unlikely to perform the supply-side miracle the federal government is hoping for. Providing childcare is simply not profitable for the private sector, unless some ongoing operating funding is provided directly to the centres. Such direct grants involve significant state intervention in what is supposed to be a free market.

The main advantage of demand subsidy is the choice that it is supposed to give to parents, at least in theory. As Ferguson (1991: 95) notes, 'studies of parental preferences in child-care arrangements indicate that parents' wishes vary for their children. Some prefer group care with more structure and professionalized input, others value the family home model's personal attention and flexibility, and still others choose to provide most of the care themselves.' In practice, however, the parental choice is more illusory than real, since, as we noted, basic principles of demand and supply do not apply to child services. It is very hard to operate a self-sustaining quality day care if parental fees are to be kept affordable, and as Fillion (1989) argues, private entrepreneurs are not lining up to open day-care centres.

In 1986, there were nearly two million Canadian children aged 12 and under, whose parents worked or studied a substantial part of the week, but only 150 000 spaces in licensed day-care centres across Canada, one-third of them in Ontario. Forty-eight per cent of these centres were operated by voluntary, non-profit groups; 14 per cent were run by municipalities, and 38 per cent were operated for profit by commercial enterprises. An additional 22 000 spaces were available in licensed family homes, two-thirds of which are located in Ontario and British Columbia. There are virtually no licensed care spaces to accommodate children of part-time or shift workers.

Over 80 per cent of Canadian children – two-thirds of pre-schoolers aged three to five, 90 per cent of infants and toddlers under age three, and 97 per cent of school-aged children – receive non-parental care in unlicensed arrangements, the quality and dependability of which are unknown. Licensed day-care spaces serve only 9 per cent of children whose parents work or study 20 or more hours each week (Task Force on Child Care, 1986). What is then the point of boosting demand through tax breaks and other forms of subsidies for parents if the supply is not there? Another problem with the user fee demand subsidy is the objective conflict of interests between the users of care (parents and children) and the providers of care (day-care owners and workers). The user fee system of care leads to a Catch-22 situation, in which any rise in profits of day-care operators or of wages of day-care workers (virtually all women) is contingent upon increase of parental fees. Staff salaries account for approximately 80 per cent of day-care operating costs. In order to attract and hold skilled staff, many centres have had to increase salaries, which in 1990 still averaged only $17 800 a year. High turnover of underpaid staff and programme cutbacks tend to reduce the quality of care, which in turn may affect demand, especially if fees are increased at the same time. The dramatic implications of this dilemma were vividly demonstrated in Toronto at the beginning of 1991, when at least four day-care centres closed their doors because of financial problems, while dozens of others had to lay off staff, cut programmes or dramatically increase fees just to survive. As fees skyrocketed by 20 per cent or more, to as much as $250 a week, many middle-class parents could no longer afford to keep their children in Toronto's 730 government licensed and regulated day-care centres. The sudden and mass withdrawal of middle-class children created 3600 empty day-care spaces. Centres that were unable to recruit enough new children to fill vacant spots had no choice but to lay off staff or pass on a higher percentage of their costs to the remaining parents, thus forcing more of them to withdraw their children. At the same time, there were more than 7100 parents on Metro Toronto's waiting list for day-care subsidies but no government funding available to meet this demand (Pigg, 1991).

Commodified childcare purchased in the open market tends not to be of high quality. A free market in childcare typically contains a large number of small-scale, under-resourced, fragmented, cottage-industry producers, whose product is relatively invisible to working parents, its frontline consumers. Many parents have no idea what is happening to their children while they are at work. With demand mulitiplying every year, quantity not quality of service is the driving imperative, both for parents and for the government. Most parents take what they can find and hope for the best. Fillion (1989) found many working parents relatively inexperienced as consumers, and quite confused about what childcare quality means and how much they should pay for it. Gifford (1989) reports the same difficulty from Australia. 'Parents frequently have little idea of what to look for in a centre, and often rely on physical features and their own "gut reactions" which may stem more from the way staff interact with them and make them feel than from an accurate assessment of the child's needs.'

The Canadian state has not served parents and children well in this respect. Over the years, there have been various charges that private commercial day-care operators have been allowed to provide poor quality care in unsanitary and even unsafe conditions (Johnson and Dineen, 1981; Fillion, 1989). The Ontario 1989 provincial audit found that day-care inspectors do not monitor the province's centres properly, often ignoring the rather minimal licensing standards developed by the Ministry of Community and Social Services. The audit found several commercial centres with chronic problems of understaffing, unsafe supervision, unsanitary facilities, poor meals and so on, yet the centres were allowed to operate for at least three years before they had to comply with the ministry licensing requirements. In most cases, parents were not informed of the infractions of provincial standards (Canadian Press, 1989). A public health consultant with the Toronto health department told a meeting of the Canadian Institute of Public Health inspectors that 'some dog kennels are often better run than some day-care centres in Ontario' (Brazao, 1989). However, a genuine state crackdown on health and safety violations would jeopardise 40 per cent of day-care spaces in the country, which is an unacceptably high proportion (Fillion, 1989).

Feminists generally favour a strategy of supply subsidy, which could eventually guarantee public childcare services for all parents who want them. In their view, childcare services should be financed in the same way as most education and child health services, out of the general tax revenue. Parents would contribute to the cost of these services through taxes paid over their adult lives rather than at the time of use. As Moss (1988: 258) has argued, charging childcare user fees puts working parents

at a financial disadvantage compared to workers without children, who have the added advantage of not carrying the other expenses associated with bringing up a child. Furthermore, childcare costs are most often paid for by women, from their earnings; they can become a disincentive for women to work, especially when they have more than one child needing to be paid for, and they can increase inequality in net income between men and women.

However, nobody expects full supply subsidy to be implemented in the current economic climate. Within the context of social services, childcare programmes are in competition for supply side funding with basic 'safety-net' programmes such as social assistance, child welfare, and services for the elderly (a growing proportion of the population) and the handicapped. Within the larger economic context, these social services are competing against the demand for increased state funding of housing, education, and health care (Lero and Kyle, 1990: 69). Thus the best one could hope for is a combination of a demand and supply subsidy. If the user fee system is to continue, more attention should be paid to the development of a coherent system for charging, with clear and common principles about what proportion of net family income should go on childcare. Parents of very young children should not pay more than parents of older children, as often happens at present (Moss, 1988: 259).

Employing a live-in nanny: the Canadian Foreign Domestic Movement Program

Employing a live-in nanny is often cheaper and more convenient than using a day-care centre, but the work conditions of live-in domestics are so undesirable that it is very difficult to find Canadians willing to do the job. As a result, the Department of Employment and Immigration has devised mechanisms to bring to Canada domestic workers from abroad, usually from the Third World, on temporary work permits. Since the mid-1970s, between 10 000 and 16 000 foreign workers a year have been issued temporary work permits. An overwhelming majority of these workers (96 per cent) are in live-in domestic service. The employment of domestic servants, a rare practice since the 1920s, may be therefore on the increase (Arat-Koc, 1990).

The Foreign Domestic Movement Program allows foreigners, mostly women from the Philippines and the Caribbean who otherwise would not qualify as immigrants, into the country on temporary work permits. The terms of these temporary employment visas oblige these women to work continuously as live-in domestics for at least two years. Their residence in Canada depends on their stay in domestic service, and it is in this sense that the temporary employment visa system has been rightly called a new version of indenture (Arat-Koc, 1990).

At the end of the two-year indentured period, the domestic is eligible to apply for permanent residence in Canada, provided she has taken upgrading courses, done volunteer work and built up some savings. Critics of the Program have pointed out that it is difficult to afford both the time and the money to meet these requirements, that the employment of immigrant domestics places the burden of childcare on the most vulnerable group of workers, and that no other group of immigrants is brought to Canada on a probation of this type, during which they must earn the right to be allowed to stay permanently (Flavell, 1990).

Many female employers hire live-in nannies because they need more than the nine-to-five help that day-care centres can provide, and because their husbands will not help them with domestic work. Hiring a live-in domestic enables high-income women to avoid a confrontation with their husbands about sharing domestic work. Moreover, the considerable class inequality and social distance between the domestic worker and her employer are likely to act as a barrier to gender solidarity (Arat-Koc, 1990: 90). In fact, working mothers – the very group most likely to fight for other women's rights – have been quite hostile to domestic workers' struggle, regarding their plight as a fair price for the privilege of living in Canada (Landsberg, 1991).

Immigrant domestic workers are also caught up in jurisdictional conflicts between the 'care' and the 'education' of young children. When the Canadian government introduced in January 1992 a new requirement that prospective domestic workers must have grade 12 education and at least six months of full-time training in a field related to live-in care, the Association for Early Childhood Education (AECE) welcomed the decision. As Scott A. Macpherson, Executive Director of AECE, put it in a letter to the national newspaper *Globe and Mail*, 'it is high time that a greater respect and compensation accrued to child-care workers and early childhood educators. The raising of educational standards for foreign trained adults who immigrate to work with our infants and young children must be further encouraged. A far greater value on early childhood education must be nurtured in our society.'

In contrast, the Chair of the Women's Committee of the Canadian Ethnocultural Committee condemned the new regulations as racist, since they placed Third World women at a competitive disadvantage:

Grade 12 equivalency would be a college degree in those countries and no one with a college degree would be a child-care worker. Further, those countries do not have training programs for child-care workers. Yet these domestic workers have, on the whole, been nothing short of excellent. They have provided years of care and love for Canadian children. . . . So here we have a case where the policy is not overtly racist. The outcome will be to favour those from Europe and discriminate against non-white workers – a racist result. It is only the motive that is a matter of speculation. One thing is clear. Few Canadians are willing to work for minimum wages as child-care workers and nurses for the elderly. (*Globe and Mail*, 15 February 1992)

As early childhood educators seek to improve the status of their occupation through professionalisation and an emphasis on the educational component of care, the 'care' component of the work of foreign domestic workers is devalued, and the hostility between the two advocacy groups intensified. Moreover, it is not clear how 'the raising of educational standards for foreign trained adults who immigrate to work with our infants and young children' can be reconciled with the continuation of the indentured work conditions of live-in domestics.

The privacy of childcare versus the public responsibility assumed for education

The historical divisions between childcare and pre-school education are based on different perceptions of the child. Childcare provided through the family assumes that the child belongs to the parent, while education provided in the public domain assumes that the child is a citizen in her or his own right (Ferguson, 1991: 87). The devaluing of women's work of caring has had an important influence on the way we have organised our public childcare services.

Day-care centres and licensed family day care are designed to perform the primarily custodial function of 'care'; kindergartens are deemed to be exclusively responsible for 'education'. The childcare sector relies heavily on parental fees, is staffed by workers with a two-year diploma in early childhood education from a community college, and the typical staff–child ratio is 1: 8. The educational sector is state funded, relies on university-trained teachers better equipped to teach school-aged children than pre-schoolers, and its staff–child ratio is 1: 20. Whereas regulated childcare services may also perform an educational function (after all, the required qualification for day-care workers in Ontario is a diploma in early childhood education!), educational institutions only rarely take the custodial needs of children of working parents into account. Most junior and senior kindergartens offer only half-day programmes, which, as we noted, cause enormous problems for working parents and children alike.

Comparison of the monetary values attached to caring for children reveals that the most highly valued form of care is that labelled as education. The substantially higher salaries of school teachers are a function of a universal education system, university credentials, and a successful organisational fight for better wages and working conditions. As childcare workers seek to improve the professional status of their work, there is a real risk that the distinctions between education and care will increase rather than diminish. Ferguson (1991: 83–4) also notes that the differing values attached to caring for children have reinforced competition between childcare settings and their supporters, thus undermining efforts to develop integrated rather than fragmented childcare provision. Instead of developing a united front, we have mutually hostile, resentful and feuding advocacy groups 'appearing to support licensed care over unlicensed, non-profit care over profit, and mother-at-home care over day care. These divisions make it easier for the issue of the underfunding and undervaluing of all child-care labour to be avoided in the political arena.'

These conflicts among childcare advocates are paralleled by jurisdictional fragmentation between social services and education. The Ontario government has encouraged boards of education to offer a full-day senior kindergarten programme, but so far few local school boards have been willing or financially able to allocate the required funding. In some areas of the province, full-day kindergarten programmes have been introduced, but they often resulted in the closing down of local day-care centres or nursery school programmes. Because education is free while childcare charges fees, day-care programmes cannot compete with kindergartens, irrespective of whether or not kindergarten programmes may be the most appropriate service for the community. There are now two major service systems in place in Ontario – childcare and education – that are expanding services for essentially the same target group of young children (Lero and Kyle, 1990: 65).[2]

The 1990 Ontario Select Committee on Education report on early childhood education recommended that every elementary school in the province should offer day-care facilities. Feminist childcare activists have welcomed this recommendation, arguing that a mass service provision through the education system is the only way in which universal childcare will become a reality (Colley, 1990). The current childcare advocates' preference for the bureacratic, professionalised and relatively inflexible education system, at the expense of the more utopian and community- and caring-oriented concepts of childcare, is regarded by Prentice (1988) as an important indicator of the 'mainstreaming' and institutionalisation of the childcare advocacy movement.

However, the Ontario recommendation and a similar recommendation from the British Columbia Task Force on Child Care (1991) are unlikely to be implemented either provincially or nationally. An expanded and properly funded national childcare programme conflicts with the number one priority of the federal government: significant cutback in federal spending. While the federal government spent most of the 1980s drafting plans for a new national childcare programme, developments in the 1990s suggest that Ottawa is unlikely to ever play a leading role in the field. In February 1992, the federal government abandoned an eight-year-old promise to create a national childcare programme in favour of a revised child benefits package and a campaign against child abuse. The axing of the long-promised programme was a bitter defeat for the Canadian women's movement.

Childcare advocacy, feminism and the Canadian state

Like other measures of equal opportunities for women, the need for an extensive, publicly financed childcare system was first put on the Canadian political agenda in 1970 by the Royal Commission on the Status of Women. The National Action Committee on the Status of Women (NAC) included state provision of universal non-profit day-care centres on its initial policy action list, but Status of Women Canada offered no leadership on the issue. As we noted in Chapter 3, Canada's response to the World Plan of Action adopted at the 1975 United Nations World Conference for Women in Mexico City, the National Plan of Action, did not include day care. The then co-ordinator of Status of Women attributed the omission of day care to the federal–provincial character of day-care funding (Burt, 1990: 207).

None the less, by the 1984 and 1989 federal elections, all three national parties found it necessary to make day care a campaign issue and acknowledge the need for a reform. During the 1980s, the Canadian state had declared its support for childcare through changes in its rhetoric (increasingly acknowledging the need for day care and a new government policy on the issue), its willingness to sponsor a variety of commissions and task forces to study the topic, increase in funding, as well as through co-optation of childcare activists. As the 1980s progressed, childcare advocates became increasingly visible in the social policy process. Several childcare advocacy groups (for example Can adian Day Care Advocacy Association, Ontario Coalition for Better Child Care) received state funding through the Women's Programme. This enabled them to employ staff, establish offices, produce news letters, prepare various policy materials and participate in a range of municipal and provincial advisory groups, task forces and other consultative bodies. According to Prentice (1988: 59),

in Ontario, childcare advocates now hold daycare development jobs with boards of education and municipal and provincial governments. The distinction between childcare advocates and state bureaucrats is a fine one as advocates work both directly and indirectly as consultants and researchers for the state.

At the national level, the Canadian Day Care Advocacy Association (CDCAA) has developed impressive skills in analysing policy, preparing press releases and lobbying politicans. As Burt (1990: 206) argues, CDCAA

relies heavily on NAC for lobby support, and many day care activists are involved in NAC work. Most of its bureaucratic contacts are with the lead ministry, Health and Welfare Canada, 'but when that isn't working, Barbara McDougall (Minister responsible for the Status of Women Canada) has been an ally in Cabinet.' And Status of Women Canada has provided beneficial information about the government's intentions and publicized the group's position within the bureaucracy. But help has not been available from the Status of Women's Adviser in Health and Welfare.

As we noted, one outcome of this institutionalisation of childcare in and by the state has been the 'mainstreaming' of the childcare movement. The original feminist vision of a non-sexist, transformative, community-based childcare now receives far less attention than the bureaucratic vision of policy development and implementation of what is essentially commodified childcare. The Canadian state has been more receptive to demands for commodified service presented in the familiar and non-challenging language of liberal social policy promoting 'equal opportunities' or 'parental choice' than for demands for radical trans-formative care. Moreover, the political rhetoric promising a more comprehensive childcare has been much bolder than actual funding and service delivery mechanisms, which have retained their earlier welfare orientation.

At the national level, Abella's (1984) Royal Commission on Equality in Employment, the Task Force on Child Care (1986), the Special Parliamentary Committee on Child Care (1987), and Canada Employ-ment and Immigration Advisory Council (1987) have all issued reports on the need for state support for childcare. The Liberal-appointed federal Task Force on Child Care carried out Canada's first comprehensive study of the issue. Its twenty background papers and a final report documented the need for childcare in every part of the country. The Task Force recommended that the government spend up to $11 billion by the year 2001 to make day care free and universally accessible.

However, no one in Ottawa took these recommendations seriously, because their implementation would have been in conflict with the free market and fiscal restraint philosophy of the newly elected Conservative government. Instead, a new parliamentary Special Committee was ap-pointed to tour the country, study the Task Force recommendations, and look for a solution within its own terms of reference. The Conservative majority on the Special Committee ensured that its March 1987 report was more in tune with government fiscal policies and its philosophical commitment to privatisation.

In December 1987, the federal government announced its new National Strategy on Child Care. The short-lived Strategy called for the end of childcare funding under the Canada Assistance Plan and its replacement with a new Child Care Act which would allocate $6.4 billion to childcare over seven years. A sum of $2.3 billion was allocated through the tax system on increased Child Care Expense Deduction and a tiny tax credit of $200 a year for stay-at-home mothers and working parents without receipts. Another $100 million was to be spent on special projects supporting innovative approaches to providing childcare services. The remaining $3 billion was earmarked but never actually allocated for joint expenditures with the provinces to create 200 000 new childcare spaces. In a speech to Parliament on 11 August 1988, Prime Minister Brian Mulroney called childcare the 'centrepiece' of his government's commitment to social justice. Mulroney claimed that 'the Canada Child Care Act will be regarded as perhaps the most important social innovation of the 1980s', and that 'child care will be regarded by all Canadians as a fundamental right' (Goar, 1992).

The Strategy placed no restrictions on the ownership of childcare facilities, and fell short of providing for the estimated 750 000 spaces (Friendly and Rothman, 1988; Burt, 1990: 208). Moreover, total expenditures proposed under the Child Care Act were to be capped, whereas spending under the CAP was at least until 1989 open ended. The proposed Canada Child Care Bill C-144 had neither declared policy principles nor any national standards. Thus women's groups, who for years objected to CAP's welfare orientation, found themselves in the paradoxical position of defending CAP against the proposed 'universalist' Child Care Act (Prentice, 1988: 60). Health and Welfare Canada participated in drafting of the proposal, but it was Finance who drew up the basic design. Many Health and Welfare officials considered the federal proposal far too restrictive (Haddow, 1990: 231). In the end, the Child Care Act was not passed. Five days before calling the 1989 election, Prime Minister Mulroney sent the childcare legislation to Senate, demanding instant approval. The Liberal-dominated upper house refused to rubber-stamp the bill, and it died.

As Goar (1992) argues,

> it was no secret that many Tory MPs were glad it died. As far as they were concerned, subsidized day care was an unwelcome concession to the feminist lobby. They had agreed to create 200,000 non-profit child-care spaces, only when the government promised to enrich the tax breaks for families with a stay-at-home parent. The collapse of the Child Care Act gave them what they wanted; the tax breaks went ahead, but the expansion of child-care facilities did not.

During the next three years, the re-elected Mulroney government repeatedly promised a national childcare programme to create 400 000 new day-care spaces, but the commitment to day care seemed to have withered. In February 1992, the childcare promise was abandoned to provide money for an enriched general income support for low-income families and for a campaign against child abuse.

The decision was justified by the results of private opinon polls and six 'focus-group' sessions with 'ordinary Canadians'. According to the private polls, Canadians no longer see childcare as the first priority for children – childcare was ranked sixth out of seven possible priorities for the federal government on children's issues. Health and Welfare Minister Benoit Bouchard told journalists at a briefing that 'day care is a priority for women earning $30 000 to $40 000, whereas providing direct relief for the 1 million children living in poverty is a priority for most Canadians' (Goar, 1992).

Childcare advocates denounced the decision to pit child abuse and child poverty against childcare as shameful and irrational, since, as we noted, access to affordable, state-supported childcare is an effective way for parents with young children to end welfare dependency and poverty. As Goar (1992) argues, 'no modern society should be forced to choose between giving women a fair break and giving children a decent start in life. . . . It is little wonder that Canadians, given a choice between putting food on a child's table and giving his or her mother a chance to build a better life, would elect to provide a short-term relief. It is human nature. But that does not make it good public policy.'

The defeat of the women's movement on the childcare issue is illustrative of the problems feminists outside and inside the national government are likely to face in the future. As a result of the proliferation of women's groups and the status of women advisers, women's policy making has been dispersed among several agencies within government. Buraucrats and femocrats who staff these agencies, and Status of Women Canada, have sometimes offered contradictory policy advice. At the same time, the plurality of childcare advocacy groups (involving women's groups, childcare providers, educators and for-profit day-care operators), most of them well organised, have presented government with conflicting demands (Burt, 1990). The plurality of interests represented within the childcare lobby, and the competition for supply-side funding from programmes attempting to combat child poverty and abuse, have made it relatively easy for the federal government to refuse to act on the childcare issue.

Politically, the use of the federal 'spending power' to establish a major national programme in an area of provincial jurisdiction would have contradicted the current momentum towards a more decentralised Canadian federalism. Moreover, Ottawa clearly lacks the money to use its federal spending power. As the *Globe and Mail* editorial on 28 February 1992, entitled 'Why Day Care Died' put it,

with a $31.5 billion deficit this year and a $420-billion accumulated debt, Ottawa's 'spending power' is almost an oxymoron. . . . Day care is an important policy issue that should allow for considerable regional variety in values and approaches. (The issue does not outlast a child beyond the age of six, however, and will soon pass as a personal concern for many baby boomer parents.) Provincial capitals are the appropriate forum for the determination of what the proper policies should be, and where the political debate should continue.

CONCEPTUALISATION AND PROVISION OF CHILDCARE IN AUSTRALIA

Introducing childcare to the federal political agenda

Prime Minister John Gorton was the first federal politician to promise during the 1970 Senate election campaign to establish some form of public childcare for children of working parents. The proposed 'pre-school cum childminding centres', facetiously referred to as 'Gortongartens', sparked off some controversy, but by May 1971 the debate died down as the government shelved its plans, ostensibly on the grounds of economic restraint. However, only a year later public childcare re-emerged on the federal political agenda and the McMahon Liberal–County Party government passed the Child Care Act. The Act provided $5 million for the establishment and operation of non-profit childcare centres and for fee subsidies for low-income parents (Brennan and O'Donnell, 1986: 22–3; Cox, 1988: 199).

The parliamentary debates surrounding the legislation made it clear that the government had introduced the Child Care Act reluctantly, as a response to employers' demands for female labour rather than as a gesture towards women's rights. The government argued defensively that it was not encouraging mothers of young children to enter the workforce, and that it was merely facing the reality of modern industrial society. Its main concern was the contribution childcare centres could make towards reducing absenteeism and improving women workers' morale and productivity. Significantly, the overseeing of the Child Care Act was placed with the Department of Labour and Immigration (Brennan and O'Donnell, 1986: 23–4; Cox, 1988: 199; Franzway, *et al.* 1989: 71).

Before any funding under the Child Care Act could be disbursed, the Liberal–County Party government lost the election and the first Labor administration in twenty-three years took office. The Whitlam government was elected on a platform of strong commitment to social reform, in which the role of education, especially 'compensatory' pre-school education, was strongly emphasised as an instrument of social change. The concept of 'compensatory' pre-school education was borrowed from overseas, especially from the British Plowden Report and from Project

Headstart in the United States. Both advocated expansion of pre-school education as a means of upgrading the life opportunities of poor and other disadvantaged children (Burns, 1981: 9).

The Australian Labor Party (ALP) was very receptive to such ideas. Whitlam's policy speech during the 1972 electoral campaign described preschool education as 'the most important single weapon in promoting equality and in overcoming social, economic and language inequalities'. Whitlam also stated that 'a woman's choice between making mother-hood her sole career and following another career in conjunction with motherhood depends upon the availability of proper childcare facilities' (quoted in Brennan and O'Donnell, 1986: 24).

Conflicts between childcare and pre-school education advocacy under the Whitlam administration

The ALP was confident that its educational proposals also met women's demands for childcare.

> Having responded to pressure from the Australian Pre-School Associ-
> ation, the party's policy was one year's free pre-school for every
> Australian child within six years. There was also a commitment to
> childcare for working parents. Yet when Labor politicians attempted
> to explain their policy it became obvious that they did not really
> perceive the difference between the two kinds of services. Unhappily,
> this confusion was to become a serious impediment to the develop-
> ment and implementation of the Whitlam government's children's
> services policy.   (Dowse, 1988: 208–9)

Related to this unresolved tension was the long-standing split between the philosophies of the pre-school education lobby and the childcare services lobby. The former was well established, especially at state levels, having its roots in the long-lived kindergarten movement.

The Australian kindergarten movement was founded in Sydney in the 1890s 'in a period of philanthropic interest amongst educated women to improve poor living conditions in the inner city slums'. The view of kindergartens as a tool of urban reform 'originated in Germany, through the work of Froebel, who saw social change as being possible through changing the nature of education, starting with the young child, letting it grow and unfold like a flower in the garden. This was viewed as a way of changing the nature of adults, and therefore eradicating behaviours which would prevent the social improvement of the poor' (Cox, 1988: 195).

Thus kindergartens were aimed at enhancing the child's upbringing, not relieving the working class mother from daily childcare or freeing her for the labour market. After World War II, 'the middle class co-opted pre-school/kindergarten provision for their own children, defining it as an education service to enhance the child's school attainments' (Cox, 1988: 198). The pre-school movement was strongly supported by male professionals in child development and education who, like their mentor John Bowlby, believed that a mother should stay at home while her child is young. Their contention was that small children are best served by a type of care which minimises mother–child separation (that is half-day kindergarten), and 'that they are ill served by substitute day-care' (Cox, 1988: 200).

By 1973, Australia had over 2000 pre-schools/kindergartens but only 867 day-care centres, with $14 million spent by the states on the former and only $1.2 million on the latter (Brennan and O'Donnell, 1988: 61; Cox, 1988: 197). Most of the long-day-care centres were run as commercial enterprises, and often lacked any trained staff or educational programmes. For the most part, they were custodial places, charging fees on a profit basis. Some provided good standards of care, others complied with fairly minimal health and building standards but otherwise offered little more. In contrast, most of the pre-school centres were 'parent-established and, therefore, it was more likely to be middle class children who had access to the services originally devised for poor and assumedly disadvantaged children. There was pressure mounting from many sources to provide a government-finaced, free pre-school year for all children' (Cox, 1988: 198).

These contradictions between childcare and pre-school education led to bitter wrangling between advocates of the two different types of services. Three successive reports on services for young children were produced, each with different ideas about the direction which the government's childcare policies should take. The first, *Care and Education of Young Children*, was issued by the Australian Pre-Schools Committee under the chairmanship of Joan Fry. The Committee was established in February 1973, just ten weeks after Labor assumed office, as an advisory body to the new government on implementation strategies for its electoral promise to make pre-school education universally available. There were neither feminists nor 'lay' working parents on the Committee; seven of its nine members were educationists, one was a psychologist and one a professor of child health (Brennan and O'Donnell, 1986: 25).

Released in November 1973, the Fry Report was received with considerable public criticism both for its bias towards the professional interests of pre-school educators and for its neglect of services for working parents. The report recommended that pre-school education in the form of three half-day sessions per week be provided for 70 per cent of all four year olds. Only 10 per cent of children were expected to be cared for by professional staff in day-care centres, with the remainder having access to non-professional childminding in family day care. For the most part, the Report simply bolstered existing provision at the state level. As Cox (1988: 200) put it, 'there was a strong emphasis on the professionalisation of services, rather than their extension'.

The Fry Report was successfully challenged by an alliance of feminists in and outside the state bureaucracy, although success ultimately depended on Elizabeth Reid, Whitlam's personal adviser on women's affairs. Reid advised the Prime Minister that the Report was 'biased in its approach', 'insensitive in its analysis', and 'unimaginative in its solutions' (Brennan and O'Donnell, 1986: 28). More importantly, Reid successfully persuaded the cabinet to act in a typical bureaucratic fashion and refer the Fry Report 'to the Social Welfare Commission and the Priorities Review Staff before committing itself to the policies the Pre-Schools Committee recommended' (Dowse, 1988: 211).

The Social Welfare Commission was an independent statutory body whose role was to advise the government on social welfare policy. The SWC issued its report, *Project Care*, in 1974. Unlike the Fry Report, *Project Care* argued against further expansion of traditional pre-school education. Instead, it recommended that the Commonwealth government sponsor a mixture of locally chosen early childhood services such as pre-school, day care, play groups, babysitting clubs, and support services for private childminders. The SWC report emphasised the need for parental and community participation in both the planning and the provision of services. The report also recommended that capital and operating grants be distributed in favour of the most needy. Local government was given a crucial role in implementing this policy. Most of the SWC recommendations were supported and endorsed by the Priorities Review Staff (PRS) (Brennan and O'Donnell, 1986: 31–2).

During the election campaign, the government pledged itself to a $130 million childcare programme. Upon its re-election it attempted to scale down the proposed programme to $34 million, but after strong political protest by the Women's Electoral Lobby, $75 million was made available in the 1974–5 budget. An Interim Committee for the Children's Commission (ICCC) was established to develop and administer the new children's services programme on a submission-based model of funding. The new programme 'was no longer under the ageis of the Education Minister or his department, but under the close watch of the prime minister's women's adviser and the Women's Affairs Section' (Dowse, 1988: 211).

The Whitlam government's support of user submission at the expense of centralised bureaucratic planning was in keeping both with Labor emphasis on community development and participation, and with the constitutional limitations on federal involvement in areas under state jurisdiction. However, the devolutionary mode of budget allocation greatly disadvantaged those who lacked the skills and resources to write complex submissions for funding. Such submission had to demonstrate the extent and type of need, identify a site, address legal requirements for staff and buildings, and translate the plans into language amenable to bureaucratic interpretation. 'All costs had to be met at first by the group and were not recoverable if the submission were unsuccessful' (Franzway *et al.*, 1989: 73).

The well-established pre-school education organisations and state education departments had an enormous advantage over the rest of the childcare community, because of the ease and confidence with which they could write submissions, their access to and representation on state-level committees, and their general knowledge of how bureaucracies work. In fact, 80 per cent of the $45 million that was allocated by the ICCC ($30 million was left unspent) was siphoned off through state block grants to pre-schools (Dowse, 1988: 214). Thus 'services which were relatively new at the time, such as family daycare, occasional care and neighbourhood children's centres, as well as daycare centres providing full-time care, fared very poorly in comparison with preschools despite the intentions of many people within the Labor government' (Brennan and O'Donnell, 1986: 38)

The feminist childcare lobby was relatively weak and uncoordinated, partly because so many activists became absorbed in writing submissions for the $2.2 million International Women's Year programme, announced at the same time as the childcare programme. 'With hindsight', Dowse (1988: 214) argues,

it is clear that the movement was fobbed off with a poorly funded public relations exercise that deflected its energies and obscured what was happening in an area involving substantial structural change and redistribution of resources. The divisiveness engendered by the availability of IWY funds could not have been more effective if it had been cynically instigated by an actively hostile government. But the fact is that this occurred through the good intentions of a sympathetic government advised and assisted by committed feminists – a sobering experience.

In Dowse's view (1988: 211), the Whitlam children's services programme could not have been initiated without the commitment and expertise of femocrats. 'For while the demand for childcare came from the women's movement, it took a particular type of activity and concentration of effort to take advantage of the opportunities the Labor government provided.' None the less, the strategic opportunity to develop an innovative and accessible childcare on a national basis was lost. 'The women's movement was able to react quickly when the returned Labor government announced a $96 million cut in the proposed children's services in its mini-budget of July 1974. But come September the movement, under the impression that the new ICCC and its $75 million programme would look after childcare, turned to IWY' (Dowse, 1988: 213).

The welfare model of childcare under the Fraser administration

The latter part of the 1970s and early 1980s saw a changed economic and political climate, which was much less favourable to state institutionalisation of childcare. The second half of the 1970s brought economic recession, financial stringencies, rising unemployment and inflation, and the return to power of the Liberal–National Country Party coalition government committed both to cutting public expenditure in social wage areas and to devolution of financial responsibility to other levels of government. Among the seven budgets introduced by the Fraser government during its term of office (late 1975 to early 1983), all but the last one reduced expenditures on children's services in real (that is inflationary-adjusted) terms. By 1981–2 there had been a real reduction of 30 per cent from the Whitlam's government peak allocation in 1975–6 (Brennan and O'Donnell, 1986: 39).

Within a few months of assuming office, the Fraser government abolished the interim Children's Commission. Responsibility for children's services was reassigned to the Department of Social Security, which established a separate Office of Child Care. This move signalled a philosophical shift towards the welfare model of childcare. Other changes introduced by the Fraser government included a formal split between education and care services, and the devolution of much of pre-school funding to the states. While under the Whitlam government 82 per cent of total funds was spent on pre-schools, the Fraser government turned this situation around. By its last year in office more than two-thirds of the children's services budget was devoted to childcare services other than preschool (Brennan and O'Donnell, 1988: 43).

The decision to switch priorities from pre-school education to day care was taken despite the perception in the Liberal Party that it

> meant redistributing funds away from the children of Liberal supporters to the children of Labor supporters. Economic arguments were used by the Women's Affairs Branch to buttress the needs argument for switching priorities. The provision of child care would enable women to move off pensions and benefits – an important consideration for those in government concerned about 'wasteful' social expenditures. (Sawer, 1990: 39)

The conservative shift to a welfare model of childcare 'was actually closer to women's needs than the unclear priorities of the previous reformist government' (Cox, 1988: 203). The category of children classified as being 'in need' included not only children with sick or incapacitated parents, handicapped children, children at risk of mal-treatment, and Aboriginal or migrant children, but also children from low-income families, especially single-parent families, and children from families with both parents in the workforce.

However, there was a significant shift away from day-care centres to family day care. Whereas in 1975–6 day-care centres received 87 per cent of childcare funds, by 1981–2 their share was down to 45 per cent (Brennan and O'Donnell, 1986: 44). Between 1976 and 1981, 1500 centre-based places were established in contrast to 10 000 family day-care places. Family day care was preferred for its alledged cost-effectiveness, flexibility, the ease and speed with which it could be established, and compatibility with the conservative ideologies of the family and of mothercare. However, the much praised flexibility of family day care was 'achieved only by the exploitation of the caregivers' goodwill and their weak industrial position' (Brennan and O'Donnell, 1986: 46).[3]

The Fraser government conducted two reviews of children's services, the 1979 Programme Effectiveness Review and the 1981 Spender Review. The Canadian-style recommendations to substantially increase parental fees and to provide demand subsidies for users of commercial day-care centres aroused particularly strong opposition and became the focus for vigorous political activity. The Spender Report suggested that users of childcare services whose family income is greater than the average male weekly wage should pay for the service 'in full, directly, and at the time of use' (Davis, 1983: 88). The Liberals believed that the government should provide services and subsidies only for those in need, not for all who wanted them.

Opposition to the commercial childcare proposal was particularly intense. As in Canada, it was pointed out that the profit motive was incompatible with the provision of high-quality service; that standards and industrial conditions in many private centres were appalling, with many young girls being employed and then dismissed when they became eligible for adult wages; that there was no parental involvement; and that it would simply transfer resources from the public to the private sector without increasing the number of children with access to subsidised care. Feminists within the Liberal Party 'publicly warned the government that it was likely to lose votes at the next election if it went ahead with the proposals to subsidise private centres' (Brennan and O'Donnell, 1986: 51).

In spite of the lobbying which followed the leaking of the Spender Report, the government went ahead and introduced new fee arrangements, a standardised income testing, and a pilot project offering subsidies to users of commercial day-care centres. However, the March 1983 election of the Hawke Labor government brought these initiatives to an end. The centrepiece of the ALP electoral platform was its Prices and Incomes Accord with the trade unions. Under the terms of the Accord unions agreed to wage restraint in return for restraint on prices and non-wage income, modest tax reform and a gradual increase in the social wage. The latter included Labor commitment to childcare as a *right* for all families (Brennan and O'Donnell, 1986: 54).

Expansion of childcare under the Hawke Labor administration

The Hawke government embarked upon a major expansion of childcare services. The 1983–4 budget provided $10 million for new services and the following year $30 million was made available. As a result, the number of childcare spaces funded by the federal government increased by almost 60 per cent during Labor's first two years in office. The

Hawke government also introduced new funding arrangements for Commonwealth-sponsored services, thus making more families eligible for reduced fees. The submission model of funding was finally abandoned and replaced with a planning approach. Planning committees were established in each state and territory to give advice on funding priorities.

The composition of these committees varied, but generally they included representatives from each level of government, community organisations, ethnic groups and women's advisory units. Under its new arrangements the Commonwealth was able to attract significant contributions from other levels of government. In 1984–5, for example, some $14 million, 140 blocks of land and a number of buildings were provided by State, Territory and local governments.
(Brennan and O'Donnell, 1986: 54–5).

Childcare became a high priority also during the 1984 election campaign. The Hawke government promised to create 20 000 new childcare spaces by June 1988 at a cost of approximately $100 million. This was the biggest spending item promised during the election campaign. The childcare commitment was a great victory for the Office of Status of Women, and in particular its Head, Ann Summers (Sawer, 1990: 80). Following Labor's return to power, the Office of Child Care was relocated to a newly established Department of Community Services. This move was generally welcomed by childcare groups since it promoted a more positive image of childcare as a general social service (Brennan and O'Donnell, 1986: 55).

However, these positive developments were soon halted. The 1985 mini-budget brought massive cuts to children's services.

The cuts were twofold: complete withdrawal of the $33 million preschool block grant and a reduction of $30 million from the 1985–6 estimates for recurrent child care subsidies. Given the size of the children's services budget ($153 million in 1984–85) these represented a massive overall reduction – indeed, the child care cuts were the biggest, in proportional terms, of all those announced in the mini-budget. (Brennan and O'Donnell, 1986: 55)

The drastic cutbacks in overall funding were accompanied by significant restructuring of the funding formula, which shifted in emphasis from supply subsidy for childcare programmes to demand subsidy for fee relief. The new funding formula saw approximately 50 per cent increase in maximum fees, a much higher proportion of users being eligible for fee relief, and an emphasis on cost containment (Cox, 1989). The Hawke government also moved away from the goal of universal access. By April 1986, subsidised childcare spaces were selectively allocated according to a list of priorities favouring children of parents in paid employment, training for work or seeking it, children with disabilities, and children at risk of abuse or neglect. This priority list is quite progressive in gender terms, because it shifts emphasis to working parents (mothers) away from care as welfare. However, it is negative in class terms, because it buttresses class divisions. Tanya Sweeney contends that the prioritised access of working parents to state supported childcare,

> results in child care becoming part of the social wage for middle-class families. By contrast, poor families, 'without parents in the workforce or under the surveillance of welfare authorities have no, or limited, access to stigma-free child care but have access or are forced to use clearly defined residual welfare services'.
>
>   (quoted in Franzway *et al.*, 1989: 81)

The programme cutbacks and the resulting search for cheaper solutions renewed debates about commercial and work-based care, about trade-offs between quality and quantity, and about the cost of *not* providing adequate childcare. In late 1987, the rationale for the whole childcare programme was thrown into question when the Finance Minister Peter Walsh attacked publicly funded childcare. In Walsh's view, state-supported childcare was too expensive, inefficient and biased in favour of the wealthy (Cox, 1989). However, a report by Ainstee *et al.* (1988), commissioned by the respected Centre for Economic Policy Research at the Australian National University suggested that the approximately $200 million expended by the Commonwealth government might well generate for the federal government $300 million in extra tax revenue and savings on social security payments. The paper also stressed the importance of childcare for skills maintenance and return on human capital investment. The report proved 'invaluable to femocrats and to women's organisations, because this time familiar feminist arguments were being put by some senior male economists' (Sawer, 1990: 82–3).

In the end, partly as a result of pressure from the ACTU, the federal government announced in its 1988 budget funding for 30 000 new childcare spaces over the next four years. By far the largest proportion – 20 000 – of these spaces were earmarked for outside school hours care, which, while needed, is very cheap when compared with all-day care. Four thousand spaces each were allocated for family day-care and child-care centres, and 2000 went for occasional care. One thousand places – equivalent to 25–30 childcare centres – were set aside for employer-supported childcare (ACTU, 1988b: 4–5).

The debate on state-supported childcare received a new boost in October 1989, when the opposition Liberal Party released its economic action plan. The Liberal proposal, which became an important feature of the 1990 federal election campaign, offered a combination of income-related spouse rebates, child tax rebates, as well as childcare rebates. The latter, costed at $820 million in the first year, involved up to $20 a week per child for children under school age and $10 a week for school age care. Since polling suggested that the proposal for rebates gained considerable approval from women voters, the Hawke government was forced to match the offer in the ALP electoral manifesto (Cockburn, 1990; Cox, 1990).

As an alternative to the Opposition's popular $20-a-week childcare tax rebate – available regardless of income – the ALP promised voters a package of supply and demand subsidies costing up to $400 million over three years to create 78 000 new childcare spaces, increase fee relief ceilings and eligible income threshold, and extend means-tested fee relief to parents using privately operated childcare centres. The latter has been strongly pushed by the ACTU, which has argued that working parents who are required to use private centres because of unavailability or higher cost of non-profit day care should not be financially dis-advantaged. To allay union and childcare advocates concerns that private operators do not offer sufficiently high quality care, Labor promised to introduce a special system of accreditation to ensure quality services are provided (Clark, 1990).

Funding for more than half of the 78 000 new places outlined in the electoral package was dependent on reaching cost-sharing agreements with the states. The latter were asked to share the capital and operating costs for 10 000 of the new centre-based places, and for 30 000 outside-school-hours places, including vacation care. Elsewhere in his policy speech, Mr Hawke said that the federal government expected an additional 28 000 places to be be created in employer-provided and commercial childcare centres. This would be achieved through the extra demand created by the extension of subsidies to families using commercial services, as well as through other inducements to companies to establish their own childcare facilities.

Employer-sponsored childcare

Hawke also committed the ALP government to an expanded employer-supported programme. The programme was initiated in 1988 as an incentive to private sector employers with a high proportion of low-income earners requiring childcare. The funding arrangement required employers to provide capital facilities (that is, the actual day-care centre) including equipment. Operating costs were to be shared between users, the federal government and employers, with the Commonwealth contribution taking the form of fee relief for low-income earners. The Commonwealth contribution automatically increases as the number of low-income users increases (ACTU, 1988b).

Hawke's policy speech promised to extend this arrangement from the private sector to government departments and government business enterprises, which are generally more interested in workplace day care. Employer-provided childcare is highly attractive to the federal government, because using employer-provided space can save the government the high cost of capital funding involved in setting up more and more community-based day-care centres. Some employers have excess space capacity, and the capital cost of setting up a day-care centre on their own premises is relatively small. However, in many cases available space could not be adapted for childcare purposes because the work premises could not meet all of the current licensing day-care requirements, which include a ground floor location, an outside playground, and an open green space.

The Women's Bureau of the Department of Employment, Education and Training (DEET) sees some of these licensing requirements as unnecessarily rigid and restrictive. According to Ruth Doobov, the Director of the Women's Bureau at the DEET, the Children's Services Program is too wedded to the traditional notion of a free-standing community childcare centre near people's homes to be sufficiently flexible and enthusiastic about employer-provided childcare. The pilot scheme for industrial childcare initiatives was apparently set up only grudgingly (interview with Ruth Doobov, 26 February 1990). The ACTU (1988a: 2) also regards the current guidelines of the Children's Services Program as too narrowly geared towards the specific needs of community-based day-care centres. In ACTU's view, the guidelines should be amended so that planning indices reflect 'employment populations (for example industrial estates, transport routes, work patterns) and extended hours provision where the need is demonstrated'.

The ACTU has had a progressive policy on childcare since its adoption of the Working Women's Charter in 1977. At the 1983 Congress, the ACTU endorsed the view that children's services are a central trade union concern. An explicit Child Care and Children's Services Policy was adopted at the 1987 ACTU Congress. Following the parental leave test case victory, the ACTU made work-based childcare one of its top priorities. Employer-sponsored childcare in Australia tends not to be employer controlled, because as a condition of Commonwealth funding, the centre has to be operated by a non-profit incorporated body. The ACTU (1988a: 6) favours the use of an incorporated management committee to operate the employer-supported childcare centre as a means of reducing the inevitable conflict between the employer's profit motive and the best interests of children.

State provision of childcare is now firmly established on the Australian political agenda. The women's adviser to the Prime Minister periodically underlines the importance of childcare to working women and to gender equality, and childcare provision figures prominently in the 'National Agenda for Women'. Both the Labor and Liberal parties routinely include commitments on childcare in their election manifestos, with childcare frequently constituting the biggest single item of proposed expenditure. However, we have also seen that both Labor and Liberal parties have reneged on their electoral promises soon after they gained office. The increasing emphasis on employer-supported childcare indicates that the government would like to shift the cost of raising the next generation elsewhere.

None the less, it has to be recognised that state expenditures on childcare have increased significantly in Australia. In 1972 the children's budget was $5 million; by 1984 it had reached $158 million. While less than 10 per cent of Australian children have access to Commonwealth-funded day-care services, less than four per cent had access in 1982 and fewer still a decade earlier when the Commonwealth government first got involved in childcare. Femocrats were early advocates of state provision of childcare and without their commitment and expertise the childcare programme could not have been initiated. The feminist childcare lobby within and outside the government remains quite influential, and as in Canada, the dividing line between childcare advocacy and femocratic childcare bureaucracy is not sharply drawn.

CONCEPTUALISATION AND PROVISION OF CHILDCARE IN GREAT BRITAIN

The influence of theories of maternal deprivation have enabled successive British governments to largely ignore both the increase in women's employment and the implications of their own espousal of equality of opportunity, and to limit pre-school programmes to part-time provision (Cohen, 1988b). The 1967 Plowden Report gave strong support to nursery education as a means of providing young children with an educational experience. However, this was to be achieved through part-time provision on the grounds that young children should not be separated from their mothers for too long a period each day. It is not clear whether the continuation of part-time provision is still a matter of fear of maternal deprivation or whether it is now used as a rationing and cost-saving device (Cohen, 1988a: 18–19).

Informal and privatised childcare

Childcare provision in the UK is regarded as a private matter between parents and private and voluntary services, and as an area in which the state should not intervene. What this means is that the majority of children with working mothers are placed with private childminders, a care arrangement about which there is much uncertainty. Inadequacies in childcare provision also directly contribute to the very low rate of employment for mothers of under-fives, which is much lower in Great Britain than in most other developed countries. In 1985, 28 per cent of mothers of under fives, but 45 per cent of those with children aged 5–9, were gainfully employed. However, most of these women were in part-time employment, earning extremely low wages. Their work is often restricted to evenings or nights when their partners are available to provide care (Cohen, 1988b).

The main forms of childcare in the UK are relatives and childminders. Relatives are the main providers of care, accounting for more than two-thirds of care. Maternal grandmothers are the most important source of care for women working full-time, but aunts and older children are also important. Fifty per cent of women working part-time and 13 per cent of women working full-time use husbands to care for their children (Cohen, 1988a: 23). American data also suggest that a significant number of parents of young children choose to 'off-shift' their work hours so that one parent is always available as a caretaker (Lero, 1991:

115). While off-shifting saves money, and avoids difficulties if non-parental care is unsuitable or unavailable, it has negative effects on parental health, marital satisfaction, and other indicators of personal well-being. Moreover, many studies regard care provided by a father while the mother is working as a form of childcare arrangement. Yet, as Lero (1991: 115) argues, 'care by mother while father is working is simply considered normal parenting – not child care. Is care by a father not parenting?'

Childcare services: serving the welfare mother

Cohen (1988b) identifies four general functions of childcare services in Great Britain: welfare, education, play and substitute care for working parents. The welfare function is served by local authority nurseries, which have been explicitly earmarked for socially underprivileged children. Serving fewer than 2 per cent of all children aged 0–4, public day nurseries provide part- or full-day care for children considered to be in need of help because of some developmental delay or some social disadvantage. Because most of the parents are in 'need', fees are very low and cover only 8–20 per cent of the operating costs. As the name indicates, nurseries are staffed by nurses, not teachers, and thus offer custodial care rather than purposeful education. The emphasis on physical needs over developmental ones sharply separates day nurseries from other pre-school programmes such as nursery schools, nursery classes or playgroups,[4] which all offer services that are more developmentally oriented and educationally enriching. Thus in many respects, day nurseries can be thought of as an inferior childcare service for a disadvantaged group (Ruggie, 1984: 227).

The principal reason for the inferiority of day nurseries is the selective class character of the facility. While nursery schools are educational institutions for pre-school children in general, being in a welfare situation, that is being in some form of family breakdown requiring the mother to be absent from her normal childrearing duties, is the main determinant of eligibility for day nursery services. The day nurseries are being used by an increasingly narrow range of children and families from very disadvantaged and disturbed backgrounds. In recent years, day nurseries have been altering their focus, changing their names to 'family centres'. However, this family-based care is directed towards families only when they are problematised, thus attaching a stigma to those who are offered places. Day nurseries now rarely offer places for 'normal', healthy children from single parent families (Cohen, 1988a: 28; Moss, 1988: 190).

Thus British childcare policies are designed to assist the welfare family rather than the working mother. Few parents in the UK who are employed, studying or training have access to any form of publicly supported childcare. Most rely on a patchwork of private arrangements, involving relatives, childminders, nursery schools, play groups, nannies or 'au pairs'. Public day-care provision ignores the needs of non-welfare working mothers, and by implication suggests that universal provision of day care is not in the public interest. As Ruggie (1984: 248) argues, this kind of intervention

> is characteristic of a liberal welfare state. A commitment to welfare determines that the state intervenes; a commitment to liberalism determines how and to what extent it intervenes.

Childcare advocacy

As we noted, the British government regards childcare as a private matter for parents themselves to sort out, and as an area in which the government should not intervene. Thus childcare has been edging up on the British political agenda rather slowly. In contrast to developments in Canada and Australia, the British enactment in the 1970s of sex discrimination and maternity leave legislation did not trigger any systematic examination of other related areas of policy. The only exception was the local government level, where the Women's Committee of the Greater London Council provided 'extensive funding (£14 million) for childcare projects in London during its short life. Their funding policy involved not only stimulating the provision of childcare services but also improving the pay and conditions of childcare workers' (Cohen, 1988a: 6).

At the national level, the need for publicly supported childcare has been kept alive by the Equal Opportunities Commission (EOC). In 1978, the EOC commissioned three background papers exploring various forms of day care. Its own policy statement, entitled *'I want to work . . . but what about the kids?' Day care for young children and opportunities for working parents*, was the first offical attempt to stress the central importance of childcare to working parents. In 1985, the EOC organised a scholarly workshop on childcare and equal opportunities, and published its proceedings (Cohen and Clarke, 1986). Another childcare advocacy project undertaken by the EOC was in connection with the European Childcare Network. The EEC Childcare Network is the sixth Network established as part of the European Commission's Equal Opportunity Action Programmes. The Childcare Network consists of an expert from each member state and a co-ordinator. Each of the National Representatives was asked to prepare a report on policies and services for childcare and equal opportunities in their respective countries. The National Representatives were also asked to consult with appropriate organisations which have an interest in childcare and equal opportunities (Moss, 1988: 2).

Bronwen Cohen, an EOC femocrat, used her EEC Childcare Network position to give childcare and equal opportunities much higher profile on the national political agenda. The consultation carried out for the report involved the circulation of a questionnaire to over 200 organisations and experts. In all, a total of 112 organisations and experts took part in the consultation (Cohen, 1988a: 111). Cohen's report was published in a limited edition in June 1988 by the European Commission's London office. It was reissued in July 1989, somewhat surprisingly by the Family Policy Studies Centre rather than by the Equal Opportunities Commission. However, Johanna Foster, the EOC's new chair, was quite enthusiastic about the report, seeing it as 'an exeptionally valuable contribution to the childcare debate in the UK' and as 'a key reference guide to childcare provision' (Family Policy Studies Centre, 1989).

Foster also endorsed the critical conclusions of another study commissioned by the EOC. Mottershead (1988) critically evaluated the three major childcare initiatives launched by the central government in the mid-1980s: the Under-Five Initiative, Information Scheme and Play Policy Initiatives. The six case studies conducted in different local authorities in 1986 revealed wide variation in standards of provision, inequalities in employment conditions for childcare workers, and frequent lack of 'fit' between local provision and what parents require. The major themes of these government initiatives – working through the voluntary sector rather than increasing statutory provision, government's preference for providing parents with information about childcare facilities rather than providing the facilities themselves, a strong belief that the private sector is willing and able to provide funds for childcare projects, and an absence of a national, centrally co-ordinated childcare policy – were all found wanting.

Foster welcomed the study as a 'timely contribution' to the childcare debate, hoping that the government 'will take note of the weaknesses of its previous initiatives while developing any new policy'. Foster was also critical of government's attempts to free holiday care and after-school schemes from all regulations governing standards and quality in order to boost places. In her view, 'as women returners are now recognised as a vital source of labour, they and their children have a right to be assured of legally enforced high standards of childcare' (Hague, 1989).

The EOC's move to make childcare a more political issue had occurred in a new demographic and economic context, the so-called demographic time bomb. As a result of low fertility and the levelling out of the 1970s baby boom, experts are predicting a 23 per cent drop in school leavers during the 1990s and a decline by 1.2 million of 16- to 24-year-old recruits to the labour market. These demographic and labour market trends are expected to result in women taking no fewer than 80 per cent of new jobs from 1995 ownwards (Oakley and Rudd, 1988; ILO, 1988: 265). A high proportion of these labour market recruits will inevitably be mothers, many with pre-school children – hence the sudden interest in childcare.

While in May 1988 the Home Secretary Douglas Hurd urged mothers in a *Weekend World* interview 'to put their children before employment', by the end of that year, Norman Fowler, the Employment Secretary, was declaring that the 1990s will be the decade of the working woman. Labour market changes, namely the projected labour shortage, are the key to this turn-around. This is not unlike the situation in Australia in the early 1970s, when the Child Care Act of 1972 'was not the initative of a social reform government nor a response to feminist pressure, but derived from the demands of the economy' (Franzway *et al.*, 1989: 71).

The decision of the Ministerial Group on Women's Issues in late 1988 to address childcare provision came after the warning from the National Economic Development Council that the country would face a severe recruitment problem over the next seven years unless the 'mum's army' of up to 900 000 women keen to return to work are able to do so (Oakley and Rudd, 1988). However, like the earlier childcare initiatives, the proposal which emerged from the ministerial meeting was strong on encouragement for voluntary schemes and employer-provided childcare, but short on direct provison and increased public expenditure. Moreover, the opening statement on the importance of the family suggests that mothers' employment continues to be seen as something deviant, as something to be tolerated but not positively encouraged.

The ministerial 'blueprint' for expanded childcare came under strong criticism from childcare advocates and the media for its lack of sophistication, continuation of the status quo in terms of expenditures,[5] and for keeping in place the 1985 Inland Revenue decision to treat the amount of subsidy paid by the employer (typically two-thirds of the total cost) towards the child's nursery place as a taxable benefit in kind. The decision of the Inland Revenue to treat workplace nurseries as a perk and a status symbol rather than as an aspect of employment equity advocated by the EOC code of practice politicised the childcare issue. Among other things, it led to the formation of a high-profile workplace nurseries campaign, which lobbied the government to abolish the tax and improve the prospects for work-based childcare. It took five years of intensive publicity and lobbying aided by both trade unions *and* employers before the tax decision was reversed in the 1990 spring Budget, despite the fact that the cost of abandoning the tax was a mere £1 million a year.

Employer-provided childcare

Four major groups of employers provide workplace nurseries in Great Britain: local government authorities, hospitals or health authorities, educational institutions and private companies. While local government authorities developed their workplace nurseries as part of an equal opportunity programme, many of the hospitals, banks and other private companies initiated childcare or career break schemes in order to retain skilled staff. However, such initiatives are few and far between and the impression given by the media that employers all over the country are busily establishing childcare facilities is a myth. In 1988, the United Kingdom had only 100 workplace nurseries, catering for 2000–3000 children. The vast majority of these nurseries were in the public sector (Clement, 1989; Hibbert, 1989). Thus employer-sponsored childcare initiatives remain rather modest.

While childcare policy should not be labour market led (if for no other reason that it leaves little defence against reduction in provision when demand falls or labour expands), employers clearly do have an interest in childcare provision. One way to recognise this interest is through 'partnerships' between employers, various levels of the state and the voluntary sector. Partnership nurseries, currently promoted in Great Britain under the European Commission's programme of childcare action projects, involve 'partnerships' among employers, local authorities, educational establishments and voluntary providers. In Cohen's (1988b: 16) view, the partnership system has advantages for employers, most of whom do not want to become directly involved in setting up or running nurseries and other services but who would be able to directly discuss their requirements and future needs with service providers. At the same time the employers' contributions to the development of services in recognition of their own interest in the availability of provision would assist considerably with its financing and diminish the level of funding required from general taxation revenue.

The costs of not providing public support for childcare

Good-quality childcare is labour intensive and inevitably expensive if adequate pay and work conditions of childcare workers are to be met. However, parental care, when adequately financially compensated, is also not cheap. Yet the costs of *not* providing childcare are rarely recognised by Western governments despite evidence showing that public spending on high-quality children's services can be regarded as a valuable form of social investment. The major potential short- and long-term social benefits accruing from public expenditure on childcare are job creation, increased taxation revenue (from wages of childcare workers and parents being able to join the labour force), reduction in poverty and in the number of parents requiring welfare assistance, facilitation of home ownership (which inreasingly requires two incomes), returns from investment in women's education and skill, early detection of child's developmental problems, reduced expenditure on remedial education, higher likelihood of completing high school and continuing to post-secondary education, greater gender equality, and higher fertility (Brennan and O'Donnell, 1986: 147–8; British Columbia Task Force on Child Care, 1991: 61–4).

CONCLUSION

We have seen that childcare can be conceptualised as an issue of equality of opportunity, influence of feminism inside and outside government, private maternal (parental) responsibility, welfare service for the 'disadvantaged', pre-school education, priority in wage fixing and collective bargaining, employers' problem of recruitment and retention of female labour, pronatalism, or immigration. Since the availability of childcare services and the circumstances under which mothers (parents) themselves provide care are so important in determining the level of income of families with children, childcare provision is also an important issue in child welfare and poverty – a topic addressed in the next chapter.

Childcare in the 1990s is at a strategic crossroads. On the one hand, there is the legacy of post-war childcare policies which had discouraged provision of day-care places except for children with special needs. This legacy has been translated into a residual welfare, 'safety net' type of state intervention, whereby public childcare is provided as a special welfare service for children and families deemed to be in greatest socio-economic need, or, as in Great Britain, at high risk of abuse or neglect. Childcare for children from 'normal' (as opposed to 'dysfunctional') families has been left largely to market forces.

British, Canadian and Australian childcare and educational policies have resulted in four quite different, but overlapping systems: (1) a large unregulated informal sector where care is provided in a domestic setting by an untrained worker (a private childminder or a foreign domestic worker); (2) a considerably smaller (and in Great Britain almost non-existent) licensed sector which serves children whose parents work or study more than 20 hours a week, and are either rich enough to pay the full day-care fee or are able to obtain means-tested subsidies; (3) a pre-school sector offering mostly part-time nursery school, playgroup or kindergarten programmes for four and five year olds; and (4) a sector encompassing unpaid mothers caring full-time for their children in the privacy of their own homes. Locating, assessing, combining and maintaining these various arrangements is a recurring task facing most working parents in the three countries under review. Whatever the setting, the work of childcare is based on an ideology of women's caring.

The formal childcare system, which in Canada and Australia developed as a collection of free-standing individual commercial and non-profit childcare centres, is highly decentralised, fragmented and under-resourced, resembling a cottage industry mode of operation. Many Canadian childcare advocates would like to move childcare out of the jurisdiction of means-tested social services and place it instead under the jurisdiction of education, which is a widely accepted universal programme supported from tax revenue rather than from parental fees or means-tested government subsidies (Colley, 1990). The major danger of this approach is that the effective care component of child rearing may be devalued, and that the distinctions between care and education will increase rather than diminish (Ferguson, 1991).

Economic circumstances (for example high cost of living, career structures based on uninterrupted 'male' work pattern) are now such that a majority of families are locked into the need for two incomes, whatever their preferences for childcare might be. Thus many people increasingly think of childcare in terms of what it can do for adults, as a place to put children while parents work. This 'child parking' concept is asssociated with minimum standards and low quality of care, and with market emphasis on efficiency and the lowest cost per childcare hour. In contrast, a 'child development' model envisages an integrated service for children *and* parents. Parents benefit primarily through increased access to economic resources, while their children receive quality care, education and opportunities for constructive interaction with other children. Accessible quality childcare can also offset the fragmentation and isolation of the small nuclear family which is so characteristic of modern industrial societies (Moller, 1989).

Such an approach would not discriminate against children whose parents (mothers) are *not* in the labour force. Moreover, it would encourage the harmonisation of childcare, employment and education policies. Unfortunately, benefits such as the quality of life of children and parents, better progress later in school, and better social integration are notoriously difficult to measure in cash or to connect directly with the quality of childcare provided. This econometric problem should not stand in the way of state support for the 'child development' rather than the 'child parking' model of childcare.

10 Fiscal Support for Parents and their Children

INTRODUCTION

State subventions to support dependent children and individuals caring for them (primarily mothers) have a long history. The idea of adjusting family income to family size emerged during Roman times, although state income support for families with dependent children is essentially a feature of advanced industrial societies. Such societies are characterised by explicit restrictions on the employment of children, compulsory education, a wage structure that takes no account of family size and the costs of children (thus offering a manifestly unequal standard of living to families of differing sizes), and a political culture that values fairness and distributive justice (Macnicol, 1980; Brown, 1984).

Early debates about policies and programmes providing some measure of income security for families with dependent children focused on basic wage levels necessary to support a family, social recognition of the value of motherhood, and demographic concerns over low fertility. Family assistance programmes were variously conceptualised as an issue of distributive justice (between those with and without dependent children); as a strategy of wage restraint (family income supplementation was seen as a cheaper alternative than across-the-board increase in basic adult male wages); as a mechanism for providing mothers with an independent source of income; as a device to alleviate poverty; or as an explicit pro-natalist incentive to encourage parents to have more children.

In many countries state support for families with dependent children was first provided through the tax system, in recognition of the different capacity to pay tax of taxpayers with and without children. In line with the tax equity principle of 'ability-to-pay', the tax system recognised that a person's tax liability should not only vary with the level of his income, but also with his family responsibilities. The first programmes providing finacial aid to families with children were therefore directed neither to women nor to poor families, but to the few male breadwinners with earnings high enough to pass the tax threshold and pay income tax. Child allowances, paid selectively as cash transfers from employers or

261

through the social security system, developed either just before, during or after World War I. During the inter-war period, several employer-organised child benefit schemes were created in industry, the civil service and the army in many European countries and in Australia, though not in Canada. Such schemes operated along, and were usually of a lower value than, the tax concessions (Oxley, 1987).

The introduction of universal family allowances (child endowment in Australia) payable to all mothers had to wait until the 1940s. The wartime initiation of these programmes has been attributed to similar wartime concerns over inflation and wage restraint, the need for post-war economic, social and demographic reconstruction, and the direct contacts among top civil servants – in all three cases the principal architects of the family allowance programmes (Macnicol, 1980; Watts, 1987). The adoption of family allowances as a universal social programme that did not require a means test was closely related to the original social insurance conception of the modern welfare state. As Banting (1987: 152) has argued, 'universal programs were to redistribute security more than income. In addition, to the extent that redistributive goals were critical in the debates surrounding the creation of the modern welfare state, they focused on horizontal rather than vertical equity. Family allowances . . . were designed to ensure greater equity, at each level of income, between those with and those without family responsibilities.'

Over time, and especially since the rediscovery of poverty in the late 1960s, family allowances became more and more associated with vertical equity. By the mid-1970s, income support measures to combat children's poverty (an issue of vertical equity) were given much higher priority in welfare debates than the earlier feminist and demographic arguments about the need to put money in the hands of all mothers (a horizontal equity issue). The universality of family allowances became a highly contested political issue, revolving around competing definitions of equity, fairness, the value of children and of mothers' work of caring, budgetary constraint, administrative efficiency, priorities in government expenditures, and the internal logic of the tax/welfare system.

The major goals of this chapter are to examine post-war changes in the structure of child income support in the comparative contexts of Canada, Australia and Great Britain. Particular attention will be paid to debates about universalism, selectivity, poverty, the direct and indirect costs of children, the relative merits of cash payments and tax benefits, and the relationship of family support programmes to pronatalism and horizontal and vertical equity.

CANADA

Universality versus selectivity

The Family Allowances Act was passed in 1944, and became effective in July 1945. The programme provided for cash benefits payable to all mothers of children under 16 years of age. The amount of the cash grant varied from $5 to $8 a month depending on the age of the child. Allowances were reduced for the fifth and subsequent children in a family, but this restriction was removed in 1949. The child tax exemption, which was abandoned during 1942–6 in favour of non-refundable tax credit, was reintroduced in 1947. It provided exemptions of $100 for children eligible to receive family allowances and $300 for children who were not eligible, mainly children aged 16 and 17 (Government of Canada, 1985b: 18). During the next two decades, regarded by many as the 'golden age' of social security in Canada,[1] family allowances were not a controversial issue and as such disappeared from the political agenda.

What brought them back were new concerns about social security that had arisen in the late 1960s: the higher levels of unemployment, the rediscovery of poverty, and the recognition of the working poor. The dominant prescription for resolving these problems was a guaranteed annual income.[2] In 1970 and 1971, the Department of Health and Welfare proposed in its White Paper that the universal family allowance plan be replaced with a selective guaranteed annual income for low-income families with children. While Prime Minister Trudeau favoured the measure, the House of Commons was more ambivalent. Many MPs opposed the abandonment of universality, and there was considerable opposition to the fact that 1.5 million mothers, out of 3.5 million, would lose their family allowance payments. In the end, the unanimous consent required to end the debate on the measure before Parliament was prorogued in July 1972 was not granted; one single member dissented, and the bill died on the Order Paper (Johnson, 1987: 56–7).

The subsequent general election brought in a minority Liberal government, with the social democratic New Democratic Party holding the balance of power. One outcome of this left-leaning political alliance was the initiation of a major, three-year review of Canada's social security, which took universalism as a basic premise. The review 'was kicked off, so to speak, by the proposal by the Government of Canada that Family Allowance payments should play a much larger role in supplementing family incomes' (Johnson, 1987: 59). The resulting amendments to the

264   *Women's Equality, Demography and Public Policies*

Family Allowances Act virtually trippled monthly payments (to $20 for each child under age 18), indexed benefits to the consumer price index (as old age security benefits had been a few months before), and made them taxable. In addition, provincial governments were empowered to vary the amount paid for each child according to the child's age and/or birth order. Only two provinces, Alberta and Quebec, have chosen this option (Government of Canada, 1985b: 18; National Council of Welfare, 1985: 34–5; Johnson, 1987: 59–60).

The 1973 amendments to the Family Allowances Act (which became effective in January 1974) led to substantial increase in government expenditures, from $645.3 million in 1973 to over $2 billion in 1977 (National Council of Welfare, 1985: 60). Since family allowances were taxed, some of these expenditures were recovered through the tax system, but this aspect of the child benefit system was not highlighted in public debates on the issue (National Council of Welfare, 1983; Ross, 1984). By the mid-1970s, the top priorities in social security became helping those most in need and constraining government expenditures. The main strategies chosen to meet these objectives were the de-indexation of family allowances, and a closer integration of income transfers with the personal income tax system. As a fiscal restraint measure, Ottawa completely suspended indexation of family allowances in 1976, and partially in 1983 and subsequent years.

The major tax reform was the Child Tax Credit, adopted in 1978. The measure reduced family allowance payments by 23 per cent, from $312 per annum to $240, and introduced a $200 refundable child tax credit payable to families earning less than $18 000 per annum; its value was gradually reduced to those with incomes in excess of $18,000. This was the first time in Canada that a major government benefit was delivered through the tax system in the form of a credit rather than an exemption. It also provided a major building block toward a guaranteed annual income in the income tax system (Johnson, 1985: 107; Bégin, 1987: 212; Ferguson, 1992).

However, the scheme encountered some major administrative problems. In order to claim the benefit, it was necessary to complete an income tax return – a formidable task for all Canadians. Since many welfare recipients had never had to complete a tax return, the tax assessment was a serious impediment to take-up (Mansbridge, 1987: 76). Moreover, several provinces quietly prevented their welfare recipients from receiving the full value of the 1978 changes. In several cases, increases in social assistance payments (which are under provincial jurisdiction) did not match the drop in family allowances. The timing and the size of social assistance are not prescribed by law in most of the provinces, with the result that provinces can, and often do, subvert federal redistributive intensions (Johnson, 1985).

At the time it was adopted, the redirection of expenditures to lower income families via the refundable child tax credit was thought to be virtually self-financing, and seen as a major step towards a more progressive system of child benefits. However, costs continued to rise, because of partial indexation of family allowances, and because more families than initially expected had applied for and received the credit. Foregone revenues were estimated to be approximately $1 billion, slightly less than half of the total disbursements on family allowances. By 1982 overall family allowance payments surpassed 1977 levels by almost $3 million (Johnson, 1985: 107).

The child benefit system was revised again in 1982. Full indexation of family allowances was suspended in 1983 and 1984, but the refundable child tax credit remained fully indexed to the cost of living. A 'one shot' $50 increase was added in 1983 to compensate lower-income families for the capping of their family allowances (Johnson, 1985: 107). Another, more substantial revision occurred after the election of the Mulroney Tory government in 1984. The 1985 federal budget proposed partial deindexation of pensions and family allowances, a substantial increase in the child tax credit (to $524 a year), a reduction in the income level at which the child tax credit begins to phase out, and a reduction in tax exemptions for dependent children.

As Johnson (1987: 65) argues,

> the message was clear: reduce the universal income supplementation payments in favour of more selective ones (income-tested, one assumes). . . . In the absence of a plan for the future, the message became simply one of cutting universality – for the old and for children. The gods of Canada's past had been challenged, and the grey power of Canada's present had been angered. The protests over the partial de-indexation of Old Age Security were so strong, indeed, that the Government quickly backed down. The proposed measure was withdrawn at the end of June 1985. The partial de-indexation of Family Allowances, however, was proceeded with: the protests were not so great, or as well organised, as those in respect of the OAS; nor, of course, was the degree of dependency on Family Allowances as significant as it was in the case of OAS pensions.

By bringing in the Canada Pension Plan, and increasing old age security and the income-conditioned guaranteed income supplement for old age pensioners, the government reduced the rate of poverty among the elderly from 40 to 20 per cent over the past two decades (Spiers, 1991). Canadians over the age of 65 receive governments payments which are almost three times as large as those directed at children. As Bégin (1987: 216–17) has argued, 'politically, it has been relatively easy to mobilize public opinion and resources in favour of programs for the elderly, even in tough economic times. Senior citizens have recognized this political reality through a network of associations and capitalized on it, maximizing their political clout.' Children have not been so fortunate:

> The one powerful voice that used to represent children – women's groups – has shifted towards promoting the many other roles of women, according relatively low priority, or no priority at all, to the role of mother. There is a real vacuum when it comes to defending the interests of children, despite worthwhile individual efforts. The politics of policy making requires a constituency and a voice to mobilize resources in times of scarcity. At present children have neither.

In 1989, a tax reform brought further cuts in benefits for families, although this time the cutbacks also included the elderly. The government introduced a provision for a 'clawback' of family allowances and old age pensions, whereby the 'well off' pay back via the tax system the full value of their family allowances or old age pensions. The clawback provision marked the end of universality of Canadian family allowances. A social programme that delivers benefits to everyone and then collects them all back from some cannot be regarded as a universal programme. The process was completed by the 1992 federal budget, which eliminated universal family allowances, along with the patchwork of child tax credits and refunds. These programmes were replaced by a single tax-free, partially indexed, monthly benefit, which will be paid selectively in amounts to be determined by computerised means tests. The annual value of the child benefit ranges from $3635 for a family with three children and an annual income of $20 000, to zero for a family with two children and an annual family income of $75 000 and up. As of January 1993, the new child benefit provides a monthly cheque of more than $200 to a family with two children and a family income of $25 000, compared with $70 a month provided by the universal family allowance in 1992 (Freeman, 1992).

An estimated 3.1 million families will get monthly cheques from the new social programme, while 'only 600 000 families will not receive any monthly payments. And these families were already losing most or all of their family allowances in a "clawback" when they filed their annual tax return' (York, 1992). However, the payments will be mostly a re-allocation of money the families would have received as income tax refunds. Only $400 million was added to the existing budget of $4.5 billion for family benefits. Moreover, a new system of book-keeping that offsets the new benefit against tax revenue from families, estimates a net gain of $750 million to government accounts (Mollins, 1992). Thus the new integrated child tax benefit is closely related to the Mulroney's government preoccupation with reducing federal outlays and the budget deficit.

The budget also introduced an earned-income supplement of up to $500 per year for poor working families with children. The new system of family assistance therefore favours the working poor at the expense of welfare recipients, who will receive the same amount as they got before. However, another tax provision – the $213 credit for stay-at-home mothers who do not claim a childcare deduction on their income tax returns – encourages single poor mothers with young children to stay at home.

Child poverty

Children now make up more than a quarter of all poor Canadians and constitute the largest single group of poor people in the country. Analysis of poverty trends over the period 1980 to 1986 has revealed that one child in six was growing up in poverty in 1986, an absolute number of 1 016 000. Rates of child poverty increased sharply during the recession in the early 1980s, from 15 per cent in 1980 to 20.6 per cent in 1984. By 1986 the poverty rate had modestly declined to 17.6 per cent. Nevertheless, in 1986 there were 120,000 more children living in poverty than there had been in 1980, while the overall number of children actually fell by 3.7 per cent (Glossop, 1991: 43). At the outset of the most recent recession in 1990, one child in ten in Metropolitan Toronto had to rely on a food bank. Across the country, 40 per cent of those who used food banks were children (Pigott and Freiler, 1990).

Children are poor because their parents are poor. In turn, parental poverty is related to unemployment, low wages, the unfavourable financial situation of families with children relative to childless couples, the high divorce rate and the resulting high numbers of female-headed single-parent families with limited economic resources. Parents run a much greater risk of poverty than adults without children. For example, during the period of 1980–6,

> a family with one or two children was twice as likely to be poor as a childless couple, and families with three or more children were almost three times as likely to be poor. Approximately 60 per cent of poor children live in two-parent families, 35.5 per cent live with sole-support mothers, and the remaining 4.4 per cent live with sole-support fathers. . . . The risk of poverty for a child living in a mother-led, single-parent family is five times greater than for a child in a two-parent family. (Glossop, 1991: 44–5)

The Canadian income security programmes have never provided more than a token compensation for the actual costs of bearing and rearing children. In 1950 and 1984, the value of family allowances to parents represented respectively 2.2 and 0.7 per cent of the average income of parents (National Council of Welfare, 1985: 60). The cost of raising the next generation is paid largely privately, by families and women in foregone income and employment.

The direct and indirect costs of raising children

Direct costs associated with raising children are difficult to assess accurately, because the cost of a child is not an objective fact. Expenditures on children are relative, since they vary by parental income, tastes and preferences, and by the age, birth order, gender and number of children in a family (McDonald, 1990; Gauthier, 1991). Using the expenditure survey equivalent standard of living method of measuring the direct costs of children, Gauthier (1991: 52) defines the direct cost of children 'as the extra income needed by a family in order to maintain its standard of living. The standard of living refers to expenditures on the three basic categories: shelter, food, and clothing, as a percentage of the after-tax income.' Her analysis of how married couples spend their money is based on the 1982 and 1986 Family Expenditures Survey conducted by Statistics Canada. The estimates of the annual average cost of first and subsequent children are calculated for three levels of income, or standard of living – low $15 000, moderate $25 000 and high $40 000.

The estimated annual average costs of a first child for these three income categories are $2800, $4200, and $6000 (in 1986 dollars). Overall, from birth to age 18, the cost of a first child to a family with one wage earner and no childcare expenditures ranges from $50 000 to $121 000, depending on the standard of living of the family. The cost of a second and third child is equal to 80 per cent and 70 per cent, respectively, of the cost of the first. Approximately $3470 per year must be added to these figures if childcare for a pre-school child is required. A one-child family with one spouse working, with an annual income of $25,000 and residing in the province of Quebec, where family benefits are higher than in the rest of the country, received in 1989 $2200 worth of child benefits from the federal and provincial governments. This is $2000 less than the direct cost of a first child, which means that the family will be unable to maintain its standard of living. Gauthier's comparison of disposable income and required income shows that this family would experience a seven per cent decline in its standard of living over the course of the 18 years that the child is considered financially dependent. The decline in the standard of living varies during the child-rearing period, reaching 16 per cent when the child is 17 years old. The magnitude of this decline increases with the number of children (Gauthier, 1991: 54).

There is also a large indirect cost, caused by the interruption of women's paid work to care for children. The estimates of these costs depend on assumptions about the length of the mother's work interruption, and the income foregone during the years of interruption of work and after the mother re-enters the labour market. According to Gauthier's calculations, the indirect cost of one child is $34 000, of two children $59 200 and of three children $84 500, which in each case is approximately 22 per cent of the total cost. However, these estimates are based on conservative assumptions, since they envision a hypothetical low-income mother who is earning $15 000 a year, stops work upon the birth of her first child, and remains out of the labour force until all her children have reached three years of age, assuming an interval of two years between births. If the woman has a higher salary, her time is more costly, and therefore the opportunity cost of childbearing would increase too. For this reason, women with higher education and higher earnings are less likely to interrupt their work. Gauthier (1991: 53) also points out that her estimates do not include the income foregone because of lower earnings when the mother re-enters the labour market.

In Gauthier's view (1991: 55), 'it is the third child which is most problematic financially, and it may be that the cost of child rearing is a more important factor in the decision to have a third child than it is for either the first or second child. If so, family policies desirous of higher fertility should place more emphasis on support for the third child.'

Pronatalist income support policies in Quebec

The Quebec government varies the federal family allowances by both the child's age and his/her birth order; it also pays a supplement above the federal rate which is exempt from income tax. Quebec family-related programmes also include a provincial tax credit for children under six that is not tied to childcare expenses; a $7000 interest-free loan for first-time home buyers who have two or more children under 18 years of age; parental leave; childcare services and subsidies; a student grant and loan programme; and a controversial baby-bonus scheme to increase the birth rate.

In May 1988, Quebec's finance Minister Gerard D. Levesque introduced in the finance budget cash bonuses for children according to their birth order. Parents received $500 for the first child, $1000 for the second and $4500 for the third and subsequent children. The 1990 provincial budget increased baby bonuses for third-born and subsequent children from $4500 to $6000, at an annual cost of $19 million (Macpherson, 1990). The bonuses are spread over four years and disbursed as advances on income tax credits. In September 1989, parents with three or more children were offered an additional 27 weeks of paid parental leave. Parents of first and second children were granted 34 weeks of unpaid leave, five days off for childbirth and five days' annual leave to attend to 'child-related responsibilities'. These leave provisions will cost the Quebec provincial treasury $20 million a year (Baker, 1990: 7–8).

Pronatalism has a long history in Quebec. Prior to the early 1960s, when Quebec had the highest fertility in Canada,[3] the province's procreative ability was widely known as the 'revenge of the cradle'. The phrase referred to the traditional Quebecois belief that an expanding population would ensure Quebec both its leading place in Confederation, and the survival of its French language and culture. Conversely, when Quebec's TFR became the lowest in Canada, bottoming out in 1987 at 1.3 (which was 0.4 below the Canadian average of 1.7), Quebec nationalists began to speak of a 'crisis of depopulation'. Declining fertility is perceived to be a major problem because of Quebec's long struggle for survival in a sea of English-speaking North Americans. Quebec Premier Bourassa told his Liberal party's policy convention in February 1988 that the low birth rate 'is the No. 1 national question of the time, much more than the creation of an independent republic of Quebec' (Rose, 1988).

Thus current pronatalism in Quebec has less to do with demographic change and more to do with nationalist concerns over the potential erosion of French culture and language and the weakening of Quebec's political power within the Canadian federation. However, providing direct pronatalist incentives may not be the best instrument for ensuring cultural survival. Cash bonuses for babies have proved to be more effective among Anglophones and ethnic minorities than among Quebec-born Francophones (Malarek, 1989; Baker, 1990). Other critics have suggested that the pronatalist scheme may encourage fertility among teenagers, or among low-income Quebecers with insufficient resources to provide financial security for their children (Rose, 1988; Anderson, 1990).

The efficacy of the pronatalist scheme is subject to an ongoing debate. While Picard (1991) believes that providing cash bonuses for babies has had the desired effect, Zerbisias (1991) pronounces the 'birth rate a bust despite Quebec baby bonus'. Picard (1991) notes that 'the number of parents having three or more children has jumped more than 20 per cent since 1988', but Zerbisias (1991) argues that 'despite a 17 per cent increase in births since 1987, when the number of babies bottomed out, Quebec still has one of the lowest birth rates in the world, down there with Italy, Spain and West Germany. It stays low, despite a provincial program that gives couples up to $7,500 for having another baby.'

Quebec women's and family organisations have not been strong supporters of the government's pronatalist scheme. For example, the Quebec Advisory Council on the Status of Women views fertility decline and smaller family size as a positive demographic trend, which has improved women's economic equality, financial autonomy and re-tirement benefits. Higher fertility would require women to take more frequent and longer maternity leaves, which may jeopardise recent gains in economic equity. Close to half of Quebec's marriages end in divorce, and sole-support mothers would find it especially difficult to provide for a larger number of children (Baker, 1990). La Confederation des organismes familiaux du Quebec, a federation of family organisations, finds the cash bonuses inconsistent with other policies, which it regards as anti-family. According to Denis Perreault, the Confederation's president,

'Quebec has become a society that does not accept children. Just try to find housing if you have two, three or four kids. We have beautiful parks. But you cannot let your kids wade in the fountains' (quoted in Zerbisias, 1991).

The financial cost of children is not the only factor taken into consideration by women and couples in their decision to have (or not to have) a child. Many of today's young adults come from broken families, and their scepticism and uncertainty about the future might be as strong a variable as their quest for adequate standard of living when it comes to making decisions about having children. With 66 per cent of young mothers in the labour force (compared with 40 per cent ten years earlier), the main considerations in childbearing decisions are housing and employment related. As Bissonette (1988) put it,

> for all its apparent prosperity, Quebec still harbors a high un-employment rate, and newly created jobs are more often than not 'precarious', part-time, short-term, without security, especially for women. Day-care facilities are scarce and costly; non-unionized pregnant women can still get fired over false pretenses; except for organised labor, parental leaves generally amount to little more than four months at unemployment insurance rates. . . . Throwing money at the whole situation and looking the other way on the job market won't do much. . . . Short of a miracle, Quebec is not about to see another revenge of the cradles.

AUSTRALIA

The dual system of child endowment and tax deductions

A universal, non-income-tested child endowment was introduced in 1941. The first child in a family was initially excluded from the scheme 'on economic grounds (because of the costs involved) but also on the ground that the existing basic wage was considered to provide for the needs of two parents and one child' (Cass, 1988a: 77,78). The restriction was lifted in 1950. Like the very limited New South Wales child endowment scheme adopted in 1927, the Commonwealth child endowment programme was enacted primarily as an instrument of wage policy, as a means of channelling money to working-class families in lieu of an inflationary increase in the basic wage.[4] Ever since the 1907 'Harvester Judgment' in the Commonwealth Court of Conciliation and Arbitration, which fixed the 'basic wage' at a level sufficient to meet the needs of an unskilled labourer, his wife and three dependent children, family size and family needs had formed an integral part of the Australian wage determination system. Federal and state wage fixation tribunals formally accepted the principle of a 'family wage' as the basis for fixing a 'living' (later called 'basic') wage for all unskilled male labour (Cass, 1988a).

Wage fixing for women operated on different principles. The female living wage was typically set at 50–4 per cent of the male rate, on the grounds that women were not legally responsible for maintaining a family. While World War II interrupted this sexist pattern of wage determination, it was only in 1974 and 1977 that the Commonwealth Conciliation and Arbitration Commission finally ruled that wage fixation should no longer consider the issue of 'family needs'. The Commission argued that family responsibilities should be recognised through government family support programmes rather than through the wages system (Cass, 1986a: 6).

Child endowment payments for two children reached their peak value in 1950, when they represented 11 per cent of the basic wage and 7 per cent of average earnings. During the subsequent two decades, their value was substantially eroded because of inflation and increases in real incomes. By 1971, child endowment for two children represented 3 per cent of the basic wage and 2 per cent of average earnings (Cass, 1988a: 80). In the original 1941 legislation, tax deductions with respect to endowed children were to be abolished, but in 1942, the Labor government reintroduced income tax rebates. Together with child endowment, this rebate brought the total value of non-income-tested family assistance to much higher levels than have since been achieved. In 1948, total assistance for a family of two children reached over 19 per cent of average earnings (Fogerty and Grecl, 1990).

When tax rebates were replaced in 1950 by tax deductions, the vertical equity of the system was undermined. Although rising incomes throughout the 1950s and 1960s increased the value of child deductions for all tax-paying families, high-income earners paying tax at higher marginal rates benefited the most. By 1959, the total value of family assistance per child in the lowest income group was only 26 per cent of that in the highest. Middle-income families received about a third of the support enjoyed by those earning high incomes. By 1968–9, the real value of child endowment for the first and second child in a family was half of what it had been in 1950–1 (Fogerty and Grecl, 1990).

The dual tax/cash transfer system provided the highest benefits for high-income earners, for most part fathers; mothers were left with non-indexed cash transfers. After the endowment of the first child in 1950, advocacy for the extension and increase in the rate of child endowment was left to the Australian Council of Trade Unions (which in 1955 and 1960 sought substantial increases in the rate of benefits), various women's groups, and the National Catholic Social Welfare Committee which argued in 1962 for increased endowment for third and subsequent children to alleviate poverty. According to Cass (1988a: 80, 81), 'it was the "rediscovery" of poverty at the end of the 1960s, and in particular the work of the Poverty Commission, which brought the issue of child endowment or family allowances back on the political agenda'. The Commission recommended an increase in cash transfers to mothers of dependent children, along with the abolition of regressive tax deduction, 'as an effective strategy for alleviating poverty in large families, for maintaining horizontal equity between families of different sizes in the same income class, and for establishing and maintaining income differentials between low-paid families with a breadwinner in the workforce and low-income pensioner and beneficiary families'. The Asprey's Committee's Report on the Australian Taxation came to a similar conclusion. Both reports contributed to the introduction of the Family Allowance Scheme in 1976.

The single scheme of family allowances

In 1975, the Labor government replaced tax deductions with less regressive tax rebates. However, low-income parents who paid no tax derived no benefit from the rebate. Moreover, as Cass (1988a: 81) argues, 'the tax rebate scheme did not have as its guiding principle redistribution to mothers caring for children, but concessions to taxpayers to recognise their reduced capacity to pay tax in the period of childrearing'. In May 1976, the new coalition government put an end to the system of dual assistance for families, and replaced it by a single scheme of family allowances. Tax rebates were abolished and the resultant additional revenue was disbursed in the form of large increases in the cash grants. When justifying its decision to create the new system of family allowances, the government cited the major inequities associated with the earlier scheme. It pointed out that inflation had seriously eroded the value of child endowment (which had in fact decreased in value by 64% since its last increase at the end of 1971) till 'the cost to the Budget of assistance through the taxation system (was) about three times as great as the direct expenditure on child endowment.' As Treasurer Lynch said at the time 'A system under which low income families are denied the main form of assistance to families is clearly a matter of great inequity'. (Cass *et al.*, 1981: 62)

The new family allowance programme was initially widely acclaimed. It benefited 800 000 children in 300 000 families which had previously derived no benefit from tax rebates, and it redistributed income within the family 'from wallet to purse', from the male taxpayer to the care-providing mother. However, disillusionment soon set in, because the new family benefit was accompanied by substantial cuts in public expenditure in the areas of housing, health, community amenities and Aboriginal services. In addition, the introduction of family allowances was used to justify a decision in the National Wage Case of August 1976 not to implement full wage indexation (Cass, 1988a: 82).

However, the most serious problem was the failure to index the cash payments. Between 1976 and 1980 the real value of family allowances fell by 44 per cent. The decision to move family benefits out of the tax system and to rely solely on unindexed cash transfers, precisely at the time when personal tax indexation was introduced, resulted in substantial savings to government revenue. Cass *et al.* (1981) estimate that during the period 1976–7 and 1980–1, moving from an indexed system of 'fiscal welfare' to an unindexed system of social welfare saved the government between $252 and $458 million. Between 1976 and 1986, the real value of family allowances fell by 30 per cent, despite increases in levels of payments in 1983. In 1976, payments for two children amounted to 4.7 per cent of average weekly earnings, but by 1986, this had fallen to 3.1 per cent (Cass, 1988a: 86).

Benefits which remained in the tax system fared much better during this period. The dependent spouse rebate for those with children declined by 'only' 3 per cent in real terms, while the sole parent rebate increased by about 5 per cent in real terms (Whiteford, 1986: 36). Another consequence of the removal of family asssistance from the tax system to the social welfare system was to make it vulnerable to attacks as a 'middle-class welfare' benefit. As Maas (1988: 2) argues, 'government commentators, in the company of leading members of the conservative opposition, constantly referred to the allowance as a "welfare" measure and conveniently forgot that it was the only universal feature of the tax-transfer system and was introduced as a measure to extend tax justice to families with children.'

Because of their visibility, the cash outlays on family allowances were generally seen as representing a cost to taxpayers. In contrast, similar measures in the tax system (for example the old tax deductions and rebates for dependent children, the dependent spouse rebate, the sole parent rebate) represented foregone revenue rather than direct expenditure, and as such were not regarded as a cost to anyone. Yet, as Whiteford (1986: 17, 19) argues, 'both cash transfers and assistance through reductions in tax liabilities involve calls on revenue and have similar implications for the budget deficit or surplus. . . . The distinction made between the two systems is convenient for analytical purposes, but when considering distributional policies, tax and social security should be seen as two sides of the same coin.'

Ending universality: the means-testing of family allowances

The electoral victory of the Hawke Labor government in 1983 marked a significant shift in the allocation of family assistance.

> In 1976–7 about 15 per cent of all payments for children was income-tested; by 1985–6, 34 per cent of the $2.3 billion spent on family income support was income-tested. In a context of fiscal stringency and of demonstrably increased financial need in families, the debate about the relative weight to be given to universal assistance to all children (and thus to all mothers) or to poverty alleviation shifted inexorably both in the public opinion and in government policy. (Cass, 1988a: 86)

Women's groups across the political spectrum continued to put forward arguments about horizontal equity and about the need to redistribute to all mothers, but found it difficult to get their message across (Sawer, 1990: 98–9).

The mean-testing of family allowances started in October 1987. The income test for the first-born child was set at $50,000 of joint parental income, with steps of $2000 for each additional child. It was estimated that 10 per cent of families with dependent children would lose their entitlement to family allowances as a result of the income test (Cass, 1988a: 86). As we noted in Chapter 4, the decision to means test family allowances was a major symbolic defeat for Australian feminism. A survey commissioned in 1985 by the Office of the Status of Women revealed that 90 per cent of mothers who received family allowances valued them highly, regardless of their income level. For 40 per cent of the respondents, family allowances were their only independent source of income. Yet, at the bureaucratic level, OSW failed to argue the case for universal family allowances (Sawer, 1990: 99).

Moreover, the abolition of universality had not been recommended by the Social Security Review.[5] Bettina Cass (1986a), the Review's Director, favoured the continuation of the universal family allowance programme, with an additional supplement for large families (with four children or more), for families with young children under six and for families with a disabled child, all to be indexed. The Australian Council of Social Service, the leading welfare organisation, organised a national conference in response to Cass's Issue Paper and resolved 'that family allowances should be retained as a basic payment, but be supplemented substantially by an income-tested additional payment for low income families' (Cass, 1988a: 84). Several additional reports written for the Social Security Review suggested that much of the concern about the imbalance in spending on low-income families and families in general is misplaced. Whiteford (1986) found that in 1986 nearly 50 per cent of total spending on family income support (on both universal and income-tested payments) went to the families with the lowest income. Whiteford (1986: 46) also stressed the need to look at the distributional effects of family allowances from a lifecycle perspective rather than cross-sectionally, and in terms of equivalent incomes between childless individuals and parents:

> A cut in family allowances through their income testing or taxing is no different in effect from an increase in tax liabilities of those with children. If it is considered appropriate to increase the tax burdens of middle and higher income groups with children, horizontal equity would suggest that the tax burdens of high income individuals without children should be similarly increased. In fact . . . the decline in the real value of family allowances since their introduction has constituted an effective shift in the tax burden away from individuals on to families with children.

The means testing of family allowances was accompanied by a new poverty alleviation measure, the Family Allowance Supplement. Combating children's poverty by the end of the Labor government's third term in 1990 became an important promise Prime Minister Hawke made in the election campaign that preceded the 1987–8 Budget. In Cass's view (1988a: 88), the

> substantial additional expenditure ($500 million in a full year) and restructuring of the system of children's payments, based explicitly on a poverty alleviation objective, represented a significant departure from the philosophical premise on which the family allowance program was originally based. It was, however, a clear extension of a trend in policy development well under way from 1983. . . . Taken together, the income-testing of family allowances and the introduction of the family allowance supplement signify the demise of universality in current social security debates, and in the context of the story of child endowment and family allowances, the dominance of vertical equity over horizontal equity concerns. Class rather than gender prevailed: some women lost, and a substantial proportion of low income women gained an increase in payments for their children and the promise of a much improved and indexed payment for the future.

However, when briefly turning to the other side of the tax/transfer coin, Cass noted that the dependent spouse rebate (DSR), which provides tax relief for taxpayers with a dependent spouse,[6] 'was much more rarely depicted as "middle class welfare" during these debates, and in the climate of expenditure restraint escaped income-testing. Since men comprise 96 per cent of recipients of the dependent spouse rebate (comprising a cost to revenue of $1.01 billion in 1985/86), it could be said that gender interests prevailed after all.' While the Social Security Review did not recommend the abolition of DSR, many submissions to the 1989 Women's Tax Convention did so, 'seeing as inappropriate its emphasis on dependence, its disincentive effects and its payments to the paid worker, almost always to the male' (Hyman, 1990: 61). Both Canada and the UK have similar rebates, with similar effects, and similar feminist criticisms.

The cost of children

As we noted, an accurate assessment of the direct and indirect costs of children is quite difficult, because spending on children tends to increase as family income increases. The isolation of the proportion of costs due to children rather than to their parents (when allocating electricity bills or rent or mortgage payments) is also quite difficult. The OECD equivalence scales suggest that couples with children require almost 30 per cent more income than couples without children to achieve the same standard of living. However, Harding (1986) found that in 1985–6, family allowances increased the disposable income of a single-income family with one child and average weekly earnings by only 1.6 per cent.

In comparative terms, Australian family assistance is approximately half the OECD average. In 1978, the combined value of cash transfers and tax relief provided for two children amounted to 3.8 per cent of the income of the average Australian production worker, compared to 8.2 per cent in Canada, 7.6 per cent in the United Kingdom and 11.4 per cent in France. Of the twenty OECD countries examined, only the United States (with 3.3 per cent) and Japan (with 3.4 per cent) provided less general family assistance; Denmark provided the same amount (Harding, 1986; Oxley, 1987).

In 1986, family allowance payments ranged from $22.80 per month for the first child to $45.55 per month for fifth and subsequent children. These rates covered between 25 and 50 cents for each meal that a child had in a week. Additional income-tested payments provided a subsidy of 76 cents per meal per week. Moreover, the total payments for a child represented only 13 per cent of the social security payments of an adult couple, whereas comparative research into the costs of children suggests that payments should be around 20 per cent (Whiteford, 1986: 31–3).

As we noted earlier, there are also large indirect costs associated with having children, paid for largely by women in terms of foregone income. Beggs and Chapman (1988: 40–1) have estimated that a woman with average education who upon the birth of a child withdraws from the labour force will lose about $336 000 (Austr.) of the salary she would have otherwise earned. Second and third children bring an additional loss of $50 000 and $35 000, respectively. Women with below-average education lose less ($282 000 for the first child and additional $30 000 and $20 000 for the second and third), but women with above-average education lose more. A woman with 16 years of schooling will lose $439 000 for the first child, an extra $98 000 for the second, and an additional $78 000 for the third. Assuming the lost income were invested at 7 per cent per annum she would lose $2 million for the first child, an additional $400 000 for the second and $250 000 for a third, which amounts to $2 650 000 for a three-child family.

The higher cost of children of more educated women may explain why fertility among highly educated women is lower than among women with lower education (Betts, 1989: 109). Maas (1988: 3) comes to similar conclusions:

> With birth rates falling and the timing of first births getting later in marriage, it seems that young people now place having children in the 'maybe' category. With the price of housing soaring in Australia and the spectre of widespread unemployment only recently receding, research shows that prospective young parents are extremely cautious about the prospect of committing themselves to the expensive business of raising a new generation. Equally important is the reluctance of many young women to risk the returns and security of steady work and career when so many may be thrown into poverty as a result of placing themselves in dependent situations through marriage and parenthood.

Based on research showing relative reluctance among individuals currently without children to commit their dollars to measures that would assist parents, Maas sees little immediate prospect for a return to universal income support programmes for families with children. As there seems to be more acceptance of tax relief measures, Maas (1988: 4) suggests bringing back the old 'messy' mix of tax deductions, rebates and cash payments.

GREAT BRITAIN

The dual system of tax and family allowances

Child tax allowances were first introduced by William Pitt in 1798, but for only eight years. They were reintroduced a century later in 1909 by Lloyd George, then Chancellor of the Exchequer. Set at £10 per child under the age of 16, the amount involved was not large. Moreover, it was of no value to working-class families with incomes below the tax threshold. Out of 18 million income recipients in 1910, only 3.5 million had earnings high enough to pay income tax and benefit from the allowances (Brown, 1984: 26–7).

Family allowances, the British state's second form of support for families with dependent children, were not introduced until 1946, despite the fact that a campaign for family endowment had been under way since 1917. Over the years, the arguments for and against family allowances varied. The Family Endowment Society (FES), led by Eleanor Rathbone, was prepared to make the case for family endowment in any way which made it attractive to decision makers and those who could influence them (Macnicol, 1980; Brown, 1984). Women's organisations in this early period were quite divided in their attitude to the scheme. Socialist feminists were generally suspicious of family cash grants on the grounds that they would undermine male wage bargaining, and instead compaigned for better maternity and child welfare services. Middle-class feminists supported family allowances on the grounds that such a scheme would undermine the concept of the family wage and thus set the stage for equal pay for equal work. Fabian women preferred direct payments to mothers as a means by which mothers can gain economic independence from their husbands, and as a way of freeing mothers from the need to engage in paid work, which was seen as detrimental to mothering. However, once family allowance schemes had been implemented, most women's groups united to defend them whenever they appeared under threat (Ungerson, 1985).

The Beveridge Report, the blueprint for the British post-war welfare state, saw family allowances primarily as an adjunct to the wage and social security system, and as a form of state pronatalist and child health support. In discussing the financing of the scheme, Beveridge made out a case for a non-contributory, tax-supported, universal scheme, without any income test. Beveridge set the allowance at a rate which could cover the subsistence of a child minus the value of free school meals and milk, and other such subsidies in kind. Acting on the assumption that the 'family wage' should be able to fully cover the living costs of two adults and one child, Beveridge excluded the first child from coverage (Brown, 1984: 31–5). However, evidence through the 1960s showed that the 'family wage' system did not provide adequate income to cover a three-person household (Field, 1989: 3).

The Beveridge proposals were accepted in principle in 1942, and in due course the Family Allowance Bill 1945 was passed and implemented. Like its Australian and Canadian conterparts, the British government found family allowances attractive 'only in so far as they were an alternative to, and a way of avoiding, the whole question of minimum wages, and also as a way of insuring the work-incentives and labour mobility essential to the successful working of a free-market economy' (Macnicol, 1980: 217). Since it was decided not to withdraw the child tax allowance, family allowances were made taxable.

In 1948, family allowances stood at 25 pence per week and the child tax allowance at £60 per annum. Between 1948 and 1967, family allowances were increased only twice, in 1951 (to 40 pence per week) and 1956 (to 50 pence for third and subsequent child). While in 1948 family allowances for two, three and four children represented 3.6, 7.3 and 10.9 per cent of average male manual wages, respectively, by 1967 these percentages declined to 1.9, 4.2 and 7.7 (Brown, 1984: 46–8). Child tax allowances were also adjusted infrequently, but still resulted in an increase in real value over time. By 1970, only the tax allowance for the youngest child had failed to maintain its real value, and this shortfall was more than compensated for in the following year (Field, 1989: 19).

From the government's perspective, the cash grant suffered from a number of disadvantages. Since it was a universal benefit, any rate increase was regarded as extremely costly, especially in comparison with the more modest cost of increasing selective welfare benefits. Moreover, Brown (1984: 50) argues,

> in so far as it was regarded as a pro-natalist measure (and this is how it was presented to the public by Churchill in 1943), it seemed to have been made superfluous by the post-war baby boom. For politicians, it was never seen as a political asset. . . . According to policy makers, many voters believed that the allowances were dissipated on bingo, cigarettes and drink, or that they encouraged irresponsibly large families. Both Labour and Conservative politicians regarded Family Allowances as vote losers and promises to increase them found no place in election manifestos.

As in Canada and Australia, what punctured the bubble of complacency was the rediscovery of poverty in the mid-1960s. The catalysts in focusing public attention on the problem of poverty were the publication in 1965 of *The Poor and the Poorest* by two leading academics, Brian Abel-Smith and Peter Townsend, and the founding of the Child Poverty Action Group (CPAG), a welfare pressure group. According to Townsend (1986: iii), one of the founders of CPAG,

> the Child Poverty Action Group was formed in the crucible of outrage – particularly by Quakers and social workers with first-hand acquaintance with poverty and by social scientists whose research demonstrated comprehensively that the phenomenon was as unnecessary as it was widespread. The first step was to publicise the evidence. . . . Despite the initial success in demonstrating the huge scale of poverty and the need to redistribute resources to the young families, these ideas came to be resisted by Departments of State

(especially the Treasury), Government Ministers and many agencies of the media.

Debates soon focused on the disadvantages of the dual system of family assistance. It became clear that in the context of public expenditure restraint adopted in 1967 by the Wilson Labour government as a response to difficult economic circumstances, an improvement in the level and coverage of family allowances could be financed only out of a 'clawback', or complete abolition, of child tax allowances. The first step in this direction was taken in 1968 by the Labour government, which increased family allowances (by 50 pence), but also cut the personal allowance (rather than the child tax allowance) for those in receipt of family allowances by an average £42; childless taxpayers kept their personal allowance intact. The effect of this 'was to maximise the confusion in the public mind and minimise the popularity of the Family Allowance increase' (Brown, 1984: 54).

During the 1970 election campaign, CPAG secured a pledge from the Conservative Party to allocate £30 million to increased family allowances. Once in office, the pledge was abandoned – the rates set in 1968 were still in operation in 1974 when the Heath government was defeated. Instead, the government increased the child tax allowance by £40 across the board at an estimated cost in foregone revenue of £201 million. Keeping the link made in 1945 between the levels of family allowances and benefits in kind, the price of school meals was increased, and welfare milk was withdawn from primary school children over seven years of age. A similar course of action was adopted in 1968 by the previous Labour government, which withdrew free milk from secondary school children and increased the price of school meals by 50 per cent (Brown, 1984: 52–5).

Rather than increasing family allowances, the Heath government introduced the family income supplement (FIS) – a means-tested subsidy to very low wage earning families. FIS was made available to an estimated 190 000 families with 500 000 children, including one-child families. While family allowances achieved an almost 100 per cent take up rate among the eligible 4.2 million families and 11 million children, the FIS take-up rate hovered around the 50 per cent mark. In the meantime, the universal family allowance benefit, while boosted by the 1968 increase, resumed the process of decline (Brown, 1984: 56–7).

The next stage in the drive to integrate family and child tax allowances occurred in 1972 when the Heath government published a Green Paper on tax credits. The paper was subsequently examined by a parliamentary Select Committee, which proposed a new tax credit for children to be paid to the husband through his wages. This aspect of the proposal aroused considerable hostility among women's and family organisations, which mounted a successful nationwide campaign to change this aspect of the proposal. In the end, the Select Committee recommended that the whole child tax credit should be paid in cash, at the Post Office, to the mother (Brown, 1984: 59–61; Field, 1989: 4).

The child benefit scheme

In the two 1974 elections,[7] both political parties promised the introduction of a new benefit for children along the lines suggested by the Green Paper. The Labour Party was committed to merging family and child tax allowances into a single child benefit scheme, and upon assuming office set about quickly to put the scheme onto the statute book. The Child Benefit Act received its second reading in May 1975, and received Royal Assent in August 1975. It provided for a tax-free cash grant for every child in the family (thus ending the exclusion of the first child), payable weekly to the mother or the child's care giver. However, no specific rate was set for the benefit. As with other social security benefits, there was no mechanism tying the benefit to increases in wages or cost of living, although a duty was laid down to review the benefit annually – a provision which had never applied to family allowances.

The implementation process of the child benefit created considerable political furore during the early years of the new Labour administration. Several leading members of the trade union movement and the Cabinet, including James Callaghan, who in April 1976 succeeded Harold Wilson as Prime Minister, attempted to sabotage the implementation of the scheme. However, leaked cabinet papers on the issue, which were published on 17 June 1976 in *New Society*, created a boomerang effect. The leak galvanised considerable grass-roots trade union and Labour backbencher support for the proposed scheme. The leak also gave new lease of life to the 'Child's Benefit Campaign Now' campaign, led by the Child Poverty Action Group (CPAG). As the leading interest group in the field, CPAG provided much of the required evidence and informed opinion for the campaigners, the media and the TUC–Labour Party Liasion Committee's Working Party on Child Benefits. CPAG also established a successful dialogue about the scheme with the Treasury and the Department of Health and Social Security (DHSS). Due to the embarrassment of the leak, and the groundswell of support for the child benefit, the government eventually agreed to a 1977–9 timetable, and the child benefit scheme finally got off the ground (Land, 1978; McCarthy, 1986: 262–81; Field, 1989: 5).

The inclusion of the first child improved the position of all families, as did the relatively generous April 1979 child benefit increase of £4 per child. However, benefits for a two-child family in that year formed a lower proportion of the average male manual earnings than it had in 1945–6 (Brown, 1984: 67). Like the equivalent family allowance scheme in Australia, the child benefit represents a significant intra-family income redistribution from male taxpayers to mothers. Moreover, it is a very easy benefit to administer. The administrative simplicity makes for very low cost – just over 2 per cent of expenditure – which is the lowest of any major social security scheme (Brown, 1984: 109). Because flat-rate payments are of greater value to low-income families than to high-income families, and because the take-up rate is virtually 100 per cent (which cannot be said for any means-tested benefit), the child benefit scheme is also an effective form of vertical redistribution.

When the Conservative Party was in opposition, it favoured 'modernisation' of social security through its closer integration with the tax system. The Tory tax credit proposal of the 1970s, and the Labour introduction of child benefit from 1977, were seen as promising examples of such modernisation (Brown, J. C., 1988: 62–3). However, once the Conservatives were well established in government, they ceased to regard child benefit as a new form of tax relief and instead began to classify it as a social security expenditure. Indeed, as J. C. Brown (1988: 30) points out, one of the Thatcher government's early actions was to refuse to increase child benefit in the November 1979 social security upratings. Another freeze occurred in 1988 and again in 1989.

In line with the government's commitment to move away from universalism to selectivity targeted on the poor, the freezing of the child benefit was accompanied by a substantial increase in means-tested family credit payments. As Field (1989: 10) points out, 'while help was targeted on the poor, it was substantially less than what a universal increase in child benefit in line with tax allowances would have cost. The cost of the additional 50p a week on child premiums came to £70m – a £136m less than what an indexed child benefit increase would have come to.' At the same time, the 1988 Budget allocated over £6 billion pounds to tax cuts through increased personal allowances and reductions in the rate of tax. The cost of reducing the higher rate of tax from 60 to 40 per cent alone was over £2 billion (Brown, J. C., 1988: 67).

The more favourable fiscal treatment of childless individuals and households is a long-standing trend. Between 1960 and 1986, there was an increase of 47 per cent and 39 per cent, respectively, in the real value of tax-free income received by a single person and a childless couple. However, for a couple with two children the increase was only 4 per cent, and for a couple with four children there was actually a decrease of 16 per cent (Taylor, 1988). As Oxley (1987: 7) points out,

> the question of the appropriate level of family allowances has usually been resolved in a political context rather than depending upon carefully reasoned arguments of the costs of children or the desirable degree of sharing costs between State and family or consideration of the level that would allow the achievement of equity between families with and without children. No country has attempted to set its universal payments at a level that would cover basic costs of raising a child. . . . When child benefit was introduced in the United Kingdom in 1977, it was explicitly stated that the rate would be fixed on the basis of available public funds and in the light of economic prospects of the time. Concern was expressed that setting family allowances in relation to subsistence needs could lead to future demands to maintain their value in relation to the cost of living.

The direct and indirect costs of children

The two pioneering studies on measuring the minimum costs of children were conducted by David Piachaud (1979, 1981) for the Child Poverty Action Group. Using the basket-of-goods or budget approach, Pichaud specified a minimum 'basket' of goods that a child of a given age would need. Based on a low-cost diet from a US study on nutrition, prices for minimum quantities of meat, milk, vegetables and so on were collected from a London Safeway supermarket; required items of clothing were priced at Marks & Spencer. Other costs included estimates for basic hygienic supplies, toys, pocket money, school outings, other schooling costs (including transportation and uniforms for older children), sports equipment and entertainment. The costs of wear and tear of collectively consumed articles such as furniture, appliances or housing were excluded, since it was too difficult to attribute a proportion of these costs to a child. The study also ignored (deliberately) the indirect costs incurred by mothers who gave up work to rear children.

Thus the rates suggested by Piachaud were rather austere, and represented neither the total costs incurred by parents nor an ideal level of spending on children. In 1987 figures, the minimum weekly cost of a

child aged 2–11 was between £11.40 and £16.60. Teenagers, that is
children aged 13–15, cost almost twice as much, £30.10 (Brown, J. C.,
1988: 37). It is hard to conceive that any Canadian or Australian family
could spend so little on children. As we noted, Gauthier estimates the
annual cost of a low-income family in Canada to be $15 000 annually.
While the cost of children calculated by the equivalent standard of living
methods allows for higher expenditures than the minimum 'basket' of
goods approach, the gap between the estimated weekly cost of £390 for
a Canadian child living in a low-income family, and just over £30 for a
British teenager is quite staggering, reflecting the considerably lower
living standards in the UK. However, the enormous gap between the
actual costs of bearing and raising children and the value of family
assistance programmes is broadly similar in all three countries.

When the minimum British costs were matched against supplementary
benefits for children, the benefit levels fell well below what was needed,
to 64 per cent of estimated costs for an eight-year-old child. Thus large
numbers of British children are living in poverty, which is also
confirmed by official statistics. For example, DHSS figures reveal that
between 1979 (when Mrs Thatcher's Conservative government took
office) and 1981, the number of children living in families below supplementary benefit (SB) level nearly doubled to over half a million. Of
these, 55 per cent were children of wage earners. If we include children
in families with incomes up to 40 per cent above SB level (defined by
DHSS as low income), the number of children living in poverty or on
its margins increases to a staggering 3.7 million. Of these, 1.75 million
were being raised in families of the working poor. According to the
Central Statistical Office, the proportion of households in the bottom
fifth of incomes that contained children rose from 7 per cent in 1975 to
17 per cent in 1983 (Walsh and Lister, 1985: 4). As we noted, an
alarming increase in child poverty has occurred in recent years also in
Canada and Australia.

In Great Britain indirect costs of children appear considerably higher
than direct costs. Joshi's (1987) pioneering study of the indirect costs of
children focuses on cash opportunity costs of childbearing. Since it is
rare both for British fathers to divert time from paid work to assume
prime responsibility for unpaid childcare or for mothers to resort to paid
childcare, mothers' foregone earnings are a particularly relevant measure
of cash opportunity costs of children. Based on a host of assumptions
about women's earnings and labour force attachment, Joshi concludes
that the foregone earnings are roughly two to three times the direct cost
of having children. The opportunity costs of having the first child are

around three times the direct expenditure on the child, while the opportunity costs of subsequent children are approximately equal to the direct costs. Unlike Canada, where the marginal cost of the third child is particularly high, the British indirect costs do not increase proportionately with the number of children in a family, although they vary with the interval between births. In Canada, the indirect costs are 'only' 22 per cent of the total cost of having children (Gauthier, 1991).

As Joshi (1987: 23) argues, mothers of pre-school children who are not prepared to undertake paid work 'can reduce the opportunity cost of bearing two children to the tune of £9,000 (1.2 full-time equivalent years) by shortening the space between births from three years to two, or raise it by the same amount if the gap between births is stretched to a four year interval'. However, Joshi admits that this relationship does not hold for women with a high degree of labour force attachment, who enter employment between births. Ni Bhrolchain (1986a, b) has suggested that increased labour force attachment of British childbearing women in the 1970s led to a reversal of the employment – birth spacing link, with the propensity to work between births providing an incentive to prolong, rather than shorten birth intervals.

In a similar vein, Ermish (1986) has argued that following the adoption of the Equal Pay Act of 1970, the relative increase in female earnings (from 63 per cent to 74 per cent of men's earnings) encouraged a shift to a later childbearing. Higher earnings raised the opportunity cost of leaving paid employment to start a family. This effect on the timing of childbearing made an important contribution to the relatively large fluctuation in births during the 1970s, but it had little apparent effect on family size.

The foregone earnings of childbearing in the UK are large: a typical British mother with two children has a lifetime earning loss of £122 000. This is broadly similar to what mothers lose in Australia, but almost four times as much as Gauthier (1991) estimates women forego in Canada. The difference is due both to the shorter period Canadian mothers stay out of paid employment (three years compared to eight years in Great Britain), and to the fact that Gauthier did not take into account the lower earnings mothers experience when they re-enter the labour force.

Joshi (1987, 1991) attributes the income foregone by British mothers, in roughly equal proportions, to three factors: staying out of employment for eight years, lower hours of work thereafter (part-time work is often the only form of employment available to mothers with no access to childcare outside school hours), and lower hourly rates of pay in subsequent employment. The three major factors lowering the rates of pay of mothers are loss of seniority, experience or training opportunities; lower rates in part-time jobs than in full-time jobs; and occupational downgrading on labour market re-entry. Like Gautheir, Joshi (1987: i) concludes that 'the income which mothers sacrifice may well be a key element in any economic decision about whether and when to have children'.

CONCLUSION

The two major forms of fiscal support for families with children are child tax allowances and cash transfers. The former were introduced as a measure of horizontal equity, in recognition of different tax capacities of taxpayers with and without dependent children. These first programmes of 'fiscal welfare' were directed neither to women nor to poor families, but to the privileged (in terms of both class and gender) male breadwinners with earnings high enough to pass the tax threshold to pay income tax. Rising real incomes, declining tax thresholds, and the growing labour force participation of women have brought many more people into the personal income tax system. What this means is that most working parents derive some benefit from the tax system. The number of parents to whom the tax system is irrelevant is rather small, especially if we look at families from a lifecycle perspective rather than cross-sectionally. In Canada, the introduction of the child tax credit brought all parents into the personal income tax system, even those on social assistance with no obligation (and no ability) to pay income tax.

From a vertical equity perspective, tax deductions are inequitable because they are worth more to high-income individuals who pay tax at higher marginal tax rates. Another disadvantage of providing child income support through the tax system is the infrequency of payments. While family allowances deliver a regular (weekly or monthly) flow of income to purchase day-to-day necessities, the Canadian Child Tax Credit was provided only twice a year, as an advanced payment in November, and as part of the annual process of assessing and refunding taxes the following spring. Regular child tax allowances deducted at source may not even be recognised as assistance from the government, and as such may be less likely to be specifically used to meet the needs of children. Since men have higher labour force participation rates and higher earnings than women, the tax benefit is usually paid to them. Yet in most cases it is the mother rather than the father who is the main care provider. On the positive side, tax allowances and credits are typically worth more than direct cash grants.

Child cash allowances were introduced during World War II primarily as an adjunct of wage policy, and as an aspect of the social insurance conception of the welfare state. Universal family allowances (child endowment in Australia) were designed as a multipurpose benefit payable to all mothers at each level of income to give the primary care providers some financial resources which are independent of their husbands; to express general community interest in the well-being of children; to reduce poverty; to encourage the birth rate and ensure a healthy population; to resist high wage demands and keep down inflation; to remove the work disincentive created by an overlap between social security benefits and wages; and to redistribute income across the lifecycle from those currently without children to those with children.

With the rediscovery of poverty in the mid-1960s and the subsequent breakdown of consensus on the welfare state, the broad philosophical premise on which the universal family allowance programme was originally based was lost. The rapid increase in child poverty, increasing budget constraints, and the restructuring of the welfare state away from an 'expensive' universal provision towards a leaner, more selective and 'targeted' approach, gradually reduced the child cash transfer programme to its poverty alleviation objective. The emerging vision of social security for the 1990s and into the next century in all three countries under review is a consolidated, highly selective family support (or guaranteed annual income) programme, which is made available only to poor families. Vertical rather than horizontal equity considerations won the day.

Child tax and social security measures can be regarded as integrally related, interchangeable mechanisms for achieving policy objectives, as two sides of the same tax-transfer coin. Failing to pay in money not collected through the personal income tax system on one side of the balance sheet is exactly the same as taking money out on the other side of the sheet in the form of social security outlays, but the tax-transfer system is usually not presented in this way. Tax allowances are typically treated as 'costless' offsets to revenue which reduce the size of the government, while social security outlays are generally presented as costly expenditures out of the general tax revenue, which increase the size of the government. This negative presentation of income security programmes and positive characterisation of tax concessions is misleading and unfortunate. Among other things, it has resulted in tax concessions being subjected to less scrutiny and fewer attacks as 'middle-class welfare' than child cash transfers, irrespective of the actual merits and efficiency of direct expenditures in comparison with taxation instruments.

When Great Britain and Australia merged their two principal forms of state fiscal assistance to working families into a regular single payment, the benefit soon lost the appearance of a tax relief, and quickly came to be regarded solely as a social security expenditure. The decision to move family benefits out of the tax system and to rely solely on unindexed cash transfers contributed to the decline of real value of these benefits, and resulted in substantial savings to government revenue, both in Australia and the UK. In Australia, the family allowance even ceased to be a universal benefit and is now a subject to income test, thus in effect increasing tax liabilities of those with children. Tax relief for mostly male taxpayers with a dependent wife was not subjected to the same pressure to restrict eligibility, and in the climate of expenditure restraint escaped income testing, at considerable cost to government revenue.

Canada has also pursued greater integration of the tax-transfer system, but until quite recently, the terms of the integration have been different. While the 1973 Family Allowances Act represented mainly changes in social expenditure, subsequent revisions have been largely income tax changes. Moreover, when family allowances were substantially increased and indexed to inflation in January 1974, they were also made taxable. Since they were taxed at the taxpayer's marginal tax rate, they had the opposite effect from child tax deductions: they were worth less to high-income earners than to lower income earners, thus creating more progressivity in the tax system. The introduction of the 'clawback provision' in 1989, whereby the 'well off' pay back via the tax system the full value of their family allowances, was the first indication of the end of universality. The process was completed by January 1993, when family allowances and child tax concessions were merged into a new selective monthly child benefit for low- and middle-income families, payable to the mother.

The value of the benefit varies according to family income and number of children, and many parents will have to rely on the tax office to calculate the amount. Most low-income parents will receive more money than they did under the system of universal family allowances and child tax credits. Parents whose combined annual income exceeds $75 000 will receive no child benefit, and like in Australia, will pay the same income tax as childless individuals. Yet a family earning $75 000 with two children in Toronto is not rich. Why should that family, supporting four people, pay the same tax as a couple with no children?

There is a horizontal equity principle here. Even parents who are better off financially should receive some social recognition of their increased financial responsibilities in comparison with childless individuals.

The three countries under review exhibit significant differences in their respective direct and indirect costs of children, reflecting different living standards, variations in the length of mother's work interruption, and in the income foregone during the years of interruption of work and after the mother re-enters the labour market. While the typical British mother interrupts paid employment for eight years upon the birth of each child, her Canadian counterpart leaves the work force for only three years. As a result, the indirect cost of children in Great Britain is around three times the direct expenditure on the child, while in Canada it is just over one-fifth of the direct expenditure.

In all three cases, mothers' foregone income, and the high risk of poverty associated with childbearing, may be the key elements in any decision whether and when to have children. This conclusion strengthens the case for integrated labour market, childcare, tax and social security policies. Provision of reliable, affordable and quality childcare, along with 'family-friendly' policies in the workplace, are likely to do more for pronatalism and women's equality than any form of isolated state income support for families.

11 Conclusion

WOMEN'S EQUALITY AND POSITIVE (AFFIRMATIVE) ACTION

We have seen that women's equality and pronatalism are terms that cover a broad spectrum of ideas and practices. Women's equality can be defined as formal equality of opportunity or as substantive equality of outcome. The egalitarian standard against which persons are to be measured can entail equal, differential or pluralistic treatment. Women's equality can take the form of assimilation (women becoming like men), androgyny (enlargement of the common ground on which women and men share their lives together) or maternal feminism that rests on the complementarity of sex differences and the special moral qualities and needs of women. During the last two decades, women's equality moved from being a radical demand of feminists and socialists to a legitimate issue on the economic and social policy agendas of various levels of the state, major international organisations, private business corporations, and trade unions. The traditional liberal notions of equal rights and treatment, and absolute equality of opportunity, have given way to a much broader definition of relative equality of opportunity, which recognises indirect and systemic discrimination.

This new approach to women's equality has been described as state feminism. It is characterised by broad bans on sex discrimination, positive (affirmative) action, strong emphasis on the need to build up monitoring systems, and a favourable attitude to active state intervention both in the labour market and in the interface between work and family life. State feminism is based on the premise that family and work responsibilities should be shared by both women and men, and that workers with dependents should not be disadvantaged vis-à-vis workers without dependents.

State feminism does not attempt equality in the socialist sense of equality of outcome. It accepts the fact that the promotion of equality of opportunity in a competitive society inevitably produces highly unequal results for both women and men. The main goals of state feminism are to redress past gender inequalities; ensure that women have equal access with men to the competitive spheres of politics and work; reward female-dominated occupations with better working conditions, higher pay and greater upward mobility; encourage the sharing of work and family responsibilities between the sexes; and eliminate or at least reduce violence against women.

Positive (affirmative) action often encompasses not only measures directly related to the removal of discriminatory practices, but also policies and programmes that facilitate women's access to the labour market. These can take the form of pregnancy, maternity and parental leaves; retention of job security and pension coverage during those leaves; flexible hours of work; opportunities for re-entry training programmes and employment after extended parental leaves; childcare services; and social welfare and taxation structures than encourage women's economic self-sufficiency. As a labour market policy, positive action rests upon a concept of work that is centred on *paid* work in the competitive market place, thus devaluing women's traditional unpaid work in the home and its associated values of nurturing, caring and altruism. The evident danger of masculine assimilation, and the desire to preserve at least some of the traditional women's values and lifestyles, have led many anti-feminists to oppose gender equality, and some feminists to question whether the drive for equality in a patriarchal world should be an important strategic goal.

Childbearing (both potential and actual) presents a unique case for positive action, because the case for meeting its special needs cannot rest, like other forms of affirmative action, on giving women a temporary hoist up the ladder to achieve equality with men. It rests on its intrinsic and perpetual relationship to sex equality. In Canada, feminist lawyers have persuaded the Supreme Court to use a broader definition of equality than the one based on a comparison with men. They have argued that in situations such as childbearing there can be no valid comparison between women and men and for that reason equality rights must be conceived separately. In contrast, the tradition of 'equal rights' feminism in the United States has meant that feminist organisations have not campaigned on gender-specific issues such as maternity leave. There has been a general fear in the American context that recognition of the special reproductive needs of women workers would give rise to discrimination against them.

PRONATALISM AND PRONATAL POLICIES

In its most extreme, and most discredited version, pronatalism has been associated with imperialism, racism, eugenism, reinforcement of the

traditional family model of father as breadwinner and mother as economically dependent homemaker, and a severe limitation of reproductive
choice. Since coercive, right wing pronatalist policies infringe upon the
reproductive rights of women and couples to determine the number and
spacing of their children, they cannot be seen in any way as being
compatible with the goals of women's equality. As such, reactionary
pronatalist policies have been excluded from this study.

At the other end of the ideological spectrum is pronatalism in support
of the working mother (or parent). It promotes intervention with policies
supporting women's emancipation and economic independence, and
various forms of state assistance to families with children. The common
rationale for these very different pronatalist policies has been the belief
that below-replacement fertility is socially undesirable, and that the
reversal of the decline in fertility would serve the 'national interest',
however that may be defined. Yet, as we noted, the long-term consequences of below-replacement fertility – population ageing and slow-
down in population growth – are not as serious as is often thought.
While an older age structure and slower population growth rates are
bound to require some social adjustments, many of these adjustments
can also benefit others, and can be justified on universal grounds of
justice, equity and human welfare. Examples include fewer age-based
restrictions and greater flexibility in retirement, labour force participation and pay; better public transportation; and shift of emphasis from
hospital- to community-based health care.

Moreover, the argument that the aged cost more than the young rests
solely on the *public* costs of caring for dependants. Restricting the costs
to what is covered by taxpayers is an incomplete way of considering the
social costs of dependency because it ignores private costs incurred by
families, especially women. The private costs of children (both direct
expenditures and indirect costs borne by women in terms of lost earnings
and career prospects) are enormous, and go a long way towards
explaining why women (and men) are reluctant to have more than one
or two children, if any. Once the *total* costs (i.e. both public and private)
of youth and aged dependency are taken into account, supporting a child
far exceeds the total costs of supporting an elderly person.

Relatively few of the developed countries have explicit pronatalist
policies. However, almost all of the countries in the developed world can
be described as welfare states. They have legislation, social services and
income transfers that provide some form of assistance to mothers (and
increasingly also to fathers), and to families with children, and as such,
can be seen as pronatal. The main thesis of this book has been that

broadly conceived women's equality policies, which encompass not only measures directly related to employment practices, but also policies attempting to facilitate the access of women to the labour market, offer a more compelling rationale for pronatal policies than the traditional demographic and political arguments.

Various support services for young children and their parents, flexible work arrangements, re-entry training programmes, and social security and taxation structures that do not penalise women for motherhood have been promoted as measures of equal opportunities for women, yet they are quite compatible with pronatalism. While it is quite conceivable that broad equal opportunity policies will have no effect on fertility (after all, an increase in fertility is not their explicit objective), it is equally plausible that they may at least prevent further fertility decline. Potential integration of pronatal and women's equality policies has been conceptualised in terms of six sets of specific policies as outlined in the Appendix. These policies involve gender-neutral and gender-specific income transfers for families with children; employment leaves; occupational and reproductive health and safety; state subsidies for, or direct provision of, childcare; and employment and pay equity.

Pronatal health, family, taxation, social security, childcare and labour market policies that do not attempt to reconcile the demands of parenthood with those of participation in the labour force, are unlikely to succeed in stimulating a higher birth rate, especially among the more educated women. Needless to say, making the role of a mother (or a parent) more compatible with that of a wage earner closely corresponds to the goals of women's equality, as viewed both from the traditional socialist perspective and from the liberal state feminist framework.

Broad pronatal and affirmative action policies and programmes are of particular importance to women who have postponed their childbearing. If women have children at a young age, (inegalitarian) traditional sex role behaviour is likely to be reinforced. The longer women postpone childbearing, the more likely they are to be well educated and committed both to long-term continuous participation in the labour force and to sex equality. Thus a woman's age at the time of the birth of her first child has important implications for women's equality. With the postponement of first births from the early to mid-20s and early 30s, women increasingly are in the paid labour force when they are making decisions (often in conjuction with their partners) as to whether and when to have their first or subsequent child. Their decision is likely to be constrained by the opportunity costs of having children, and by the poor availability of dependable, inexpensive childcare.

CHILDCARE

How does the availability of childcare affect fertility? To the extent that childcare availability increases women's entry into paid employment, it may be anti-natalist, but, to the extent that it reduces the burden of child rearing for those who are in the labour force, it may be pronatalist. In industrialised societies with large numbers of mothers with young children already in the workforce, and with fertility desires often exceeding actual behaviour, subsidising childcare for employed mothers (or parents) would seem to be pronatalist, as would a reduction of the caring burden after women (or parents) come home from work. Both aspects of childcare become problematic with the increase of the women's age at first birth, because women are more likely to want to remain in the labour force with minimal interruption after their first child is born. Furthermore, they will be making subsequent childbearing decisions while they are employed and experiencing these difficulties (Presser, 1986).

However, an expanded, properly funded, fully accessible national childcare programme has not become a reality in any of the countries examined in this book. While the Canadian federal government spent most of the 1980s drafting plans for a new national childcare programme, developments in the 1990s suggest that Ottawa is unlikely ever to play a leading role in the field. The era of big-budget social programmes seems to have come to an end also in Australia and Great Britain, where both the central government and the trade unions are encouraging employers to establish workplace nurseries. The shift from a big-budget national childcare programme to a small-scale package of tax incentives and subsidies to employers to encourage workplace day care raises troubling questions about private sector involvement in social policy, and about the disproportionate benefit accruing to a selected (i.e. technically skilled or female-dominated) workforce.

Lack of childcare can be also addressed through immigration. For example, the Foreign Domestic Movement Program, which allows Canadians to sponsor foreign domestic workers on a two-year temporary work permit, was created to help ease Canada's childcare crisis, and to protect domestics from undue exploitation. In recent years, the Program has been plagued by complaints from employers (mainly professional women), domestic workers (for most part women from the Philippines and the Caribbean) and the immigration officials who manage it, thus raising a myriad of questions about immigration management, women's equality, class and racial inequality, domestic work, childcare, and migrant women's experiences of dependency and subordination. Prior to the creation of the Foreign Domestic Worker Program, domestics could enter Canada only on temporary work permits that left them totally at the mercy of their employers. With the Program, at the end of the two-year period, the domestic is eligible to apply for permanent residence in Canada, provided she has taken upgrading courses, done volunteer work and built up some savings. Critics of the Program have pointed out that it places the burden of childcare on the most vulnerable group of workers, and that no other group of immigrants is brought to Canada on a probation of this type, during which they must earn the right to stay permanently. As a policy, the domestic worker programme presupposes not just an employer–employee relationship but a mistress–servant one, which creates and builds on class differences. The cost of having a live-in domestic almost always ensures that employers are in high-income families, whereas the requirements of domestic work tend to draw upon lower-class migrant workers.

Live-in domestic and childcare work also builds upon racial and ethnic divisions. Historically and currently, the immigration of women as domestics has been racially selective. During the early part of the twentieth century, British domestics were preferred to the Irish. During the 1950s and 1960s, the Caribbean Domestic Scheme rested on racial images of a nurturing Aunt Jemina, and backward colonies (Calliste, 1989). With the implementation of the Foreign Domestic Workers Program in the 1980s, workers from the Caribbean area have been replaced by domestics from the Philippines. Cohen (1987) suggests that 'lighter races' are preferred for positions which are solely childcare (as opposed to household and childcare), while other scholars have commented on the higher status accorded to the British nanny (Boyd, 1991).

Thus childcare has emerged as a crucial theme of this study, because it is relevant to women's equality, immigration, class and racial inequality as well as pronatalism. It is no accident that childcare figured as an important electoral issue during the 1984 and 1988 federal elections in Canada and more recently in Australia. Towards the end of the 1980s, childcare even entered the political agenda in Great Britain. While the Thatcher government consistently regarded childcare as a private responsibility of parents, it none the less encouraged employers to set up workplace nurseries. This shift in policy was justified on demographic grounds, by the looming labour shortage, a result of low fertility during the last two decades. Low fertility is now manifested in the relatively small cohorts of school leavers entering the labour market.

Even if equal opportunity has not been the major rationale for promoting workplace nurseries in Great Britain, judging from comparative evidence from elsewhere, it is likely to be an important policy outcome.

INTEGRATION OF WORK AND FAMILY RESPONSIBILITIES

The last decade has been characterised by growing official recognition of the connection between family responsibilities and equality in employment. In fact, reconciling family responsibilities with occupational aspirations has been given a high priority in European Community initiatives regarding women, reflecting a shift in focus from equal pay (Article 119 of the Treaty of Rome and the 1975 Equal Pay Directive) to equal treatment (several Directives and Recommendations on equal treatment in the labour market, occupational and state social security schemes, and for the self-employed, adopted during 1975–86) to equal opportunities in working life in general (the two Community Action Programmes on Equal Opportunities for Women, 1982–5, 1986–90).

Under the category of sharing family and occupational responsibilities, the Community Programme recommends that member states establish a system of parental leave (after a period of maternity leave) and leave for family reasons; promote the continuous and diversified development of pre-school and after-school childcare; provide for career breaks and flexible work conditions; and promote, especially among young people, the acceptance of more equal sharing of family, occupational and social responsibilities. Similar objectives have been announced in Canada, where the federal, provincial and territorial governments formally committed themselves at the 1987 Annual Conference of First Ministers to adopting policies that encourage integration of work and family responsibilities. However, the only concrete step towards the implementation of these objectives has been the transformation (in November 1990) of maternity leave into a parental leave, largely in response to a legal challenge under the constitutional Charter of Rights and Freedoms. Moreover, the abandonment in 1992 of the eight-year-old promise to create a national childcare system gave a clear signal that the Canadian government no longer assigns a high priority to assisting parents in their efforts to integrate work and family responsibilities.

In Australia, anti-discrimination legislation, affirmative action and equal opportunity regulations have acted as an external impetus for public and private employers to implement (or to consider implementing) policies which ensure that working conditions do not discriminate against the ability of women to maintain their jobs or to enhance their career opportunities (Wolcott, 1987:17). Expansion of day care and the ratification of ILO Convention 156 concerning 'Equal Opportunities for Workers with Family Responsibilities' provided the main planks of the Australian Labor government's electoral commitment to women in 1990. Shortly after the election, the Hawke government established a Work and Family Unit within the Department of Industrial Relations. The Unit's initial focus has been on reducing the rigidity of work practices which impede workers' capacity to care for their families. Particular attention has been given to the needs of disadvantaged groups such as sole parents and migrants. The Unit's main contention is that organisational recognition of workers' family responsibilities has the potential to yield significant productivity benefits, generate improved morale and corporate commitment, and contribute to decreased absenteeism, lower staff turnover, greater return on training investment, fewer industrial accidents and better industrial relations (Kidston, 1991:16).

In Canada and Australia, promoting the integration of work and family responsibilities is also aimed at increasing organisational efficiency – by preventing absenteeism, developing under-utilised personnel resources, and legitimating a progressive, socially conscious management. When the mighty Toronto Dominion Bank adopted in 1988 a 'dependent care leave' policy for its 25 000 employees, it did so for pragmatic rather than altruistic reasons. The bank wanted to know how much time employees were taking off on account of their own sickness, and how much time was taken off to care for other people. Rather than telling a lie and saying that they are themselves sick, employees are now encouraged to be honest every time they need time off for family sickness or appointments. All supervisors have been ordered to grant that time off, with pay. There is no set limit on the number of leaves (Brown, L., 1988).

While these policies are a step in the right direction, they will work only if men assume their share of domestic responsibilities. If men do not ask for the leave and continue to act as if women were the only workers who have family responsibilities, women may be reluctant to ask as well, for fear that doing so may reinforce negative attitudes towards women as unstable and unproductive workers. Thus the creation of supportive work structures and family services also requires attitudinal changes, both among employers and employees. The majority of employers *and* employees have yet to be convinced that making special arrangements for workers with family responsibilities is a good management practice. For example, 65 per cent of employees in a Conference Board of Canada survey of 385 companies employing more than one million Canadians felt that family concerns were the primary responsibility of the individual. In turn, employers who must balance employee benefits against profits, prefer to handle work/family linkages on an *ad hoc* basis, rather than having legislation mandating the provision of a minimum number of paid and unpaid leave days for family-related reasons imposed on them (MacBride-King and Paris, 1989). Most employers are quite content to leave working parents with the full responsibility for juggling, rather than harmonising, their work and family roles.

With the increase in the number of dual-earning families and families in which a single parent is responsible for carrying both work and family tasks, the juggling of work and family commitments has become one of the major issues of the 1990s. Work as the key to an income is central both to women's economic independence and to a decent standard of living. The need for more income inevitably leads to a reduction in family time. Time conflicts are particularly problematic for the large numbers of working women who continue to assume the majority of childcare and domestic tasks.

Women with higher education and good career opportunities have tended to adapt to the time strain involved in establishing a career and a family by postponing and limiting the number of children they bear, by rearranging their timetables, by buying domestic labour-saving devices and convenience foods, and by hiring domestic and childcare help. The high opportunity costs of establishing a family at the expense of one's career have then been converted into lower direct costs. As Harel-Giasson *et al.* (1987: 22) found in their study of Quebec women chartered accountants,[1]

> when the moment arrives for making the decision to have a first child, women CAs do not hesitate or worry. They can deal with this just as they manage the other activities that they pursue. As they had rightly anticipated, it's up to them to organise themselves to plan the date of delivery for the least busy period, to ensure a substitute during their maternity leave, and to find a good babysitter willing to work long hours.

However, these private solutions are contingent on the availability of supply of lower class women, frequently migrants from poor countries in the Third World, willing to work long hours in low-paid domestic and childminding labour. Hiring domestic help enables high-income women to avoid a confrontation with their husbands about sharing domestic work. Moreover, the considerable class inequality and social distance between the domestic worker and her employer is likely to act as a barrier to gender solidarity. There are, however, limitations to what invidual women and families can do to manage their time without concomitant changes in employment policies and organisational cultures. The cultural context of most professions places a high value on a total, full-time commitment to one's professional career, requiring women either to have no children or to act as if they did not have any. When the Quebec chartered accountants returned to work after maternity leave, they had to prove that they still shared the dominant values of their profession and that they wanted to pursue their careers as before. To do this they had to show that they were as productive as before.

At the same time the women chartered accountants wanted to be good mothers and spend time with their children. The main strategies they adopted were working at home after the children were asleep, increasing their office efficiency by cutting out their lunch hours and informal chats with their colleagues, and intensifying their work pace. Thanks to the repeated proof of commitment the women chartered accountants gave, their colleagues and superiors gradually lost their misgivings, forgot that the chartered accountants were mothers and progressively reintegrated them back into the professional and corporate fold (Harel-Giasson *et al.*, 1987: 22).

Since individuals with a strong professional identity will reduce excessive work hours only if the dominant professional norms are not synonymous with long hours of work, women (or men) with the desire to establish a career and a family simultaneously have little choice but to become *Supermoms* (or *Superdads*). Negotiating the intertwining pathways among the constraints of professional norms, the number of non-discretionary hours that are required on the job, productivity, and domestic arrangements becomes particularly problematic with the birth of a second child.

Harel-Giasson *et al.* (1987) found that the chartered accountants' decision to have a second child was very different from the one preceding the first pregnancy. In terms of time management, the women accountants could not change much, because they already had increased their productivity, and reduced their hours at the office to the barest minimum possible. Besides, they were now at a higher hierarchical level than during their first pregnancy, with greater responsibility and higher workload. The women chartered accountants also feared losing clients and control over their staff during maternity leave. Worries about neglecting their families, raised already during their first pregnancy, were exacerbated by the idea of having a second child, and by a sceptical or negative attitude on the part of their husbands. Several husbands of the women in the study felt that their wives were giving the maximum possible with one child. They realised only too well that their own participation would have to be increased with the birth of a second child. As a result, they began to focus on the advantages for the whole family of having a mother who stays at home or who only works part-time. The absence of support at work and at home provoked a feeling of conflict among the women chartered accountants. A good number of them began to doubt their ability to manage their different responsibilities. This situation was all the more painful because they loved their work and the idea of leaving public accounting was a great cost to them.

Will women have to continue to choose between having children and enjoying professional success and a decent standard of living? The current structure of most professional, business and civil service careers is too standardised to adapt to the needs of individuals at different stages of their lifecycle. Harel-Giasson *et al.* (1987) recommend multiple career models that would permit individuals to pursue a career at their own pace, alternating between a slower and a more rapid progression. Since most of these 'individuals' are likely to be women, there is a real danger that such a model will be used to support the idea of a 'mommy track'. This type of perspective places mothers on a special low pressure (and presumably lower paid) career track in order that they may attend to family responsibilities. Women without children, perceived as being more dedicated to their jobs, are placed on a fast career track with men. Two categories of women are then created, where bearing children becomes a liability to career advancement. There is no comparable 'daddy track'.

The most common strategy adopted by two-parent families is for the woman to drop her working hours to part-time after the first birth. While detrimental to her career advancement, this strategy enables her to retain most of her technical skills, contribute economically to the household, and at the same time raise her child(ren). Mothers are much more likely than fathers to adjust their working patterns to accommodate family commitments, reflecting their more marginal attachment to the work force while children require care. Older women also tend to reduce their working hours in order to assist with grandchildren or the needs of ageing parents. In Glezer's (1991: 8) view, grandparents are 'the main backstop for families juggling work and child rearing'.

One outcome of the increase of dual-earner families is the growing gap between lone parents and husband–wife families. For example, in Canada in 1986, the total earnings of non-elderly female lone-parent families were barely one-third of dual-earner families at $12 563 per annum. The greatest hardships are faced by young lone mothers (less than 25 years of age), with an average income of only $7879. The financial situation improves with the age of the mother and the children, because as the children grow older, involvement in the labour force for the mother becomes easier (Burch and McQuillan, 1988). The necessity for two incomes means that the situation of female lone-parent families in comparison with multiple-earner families is unlikely to improve, even with employment and pay equity. Increased support services for single mothers, such as childcare and subsidised housing, are therefore crucial.

FEMINIST POLITICS, GOVERNMENT POLICIES AND WOMEN'S POLICY MACHINERY

Australia and Canada have well-established political traditions of using the state to achieve important economic and social goals. Consistent with that tradition, reformist feminist movements in those countries have looked to the state as the main agency capable of redressing a whole range of women's grievances. Since the 1970s, various levels of the state have responded favourably, both by creating distinctively feminist political and bureaucratic structures, and by placing broadly conceived women's equality on their economic and social policy agendas.

In Canada, the political climate in the 1970s encouraged the promotion of equality, justice and 'compensatory' social services for the 'disadvantaged'. There was a lot of interest in citizens' participation in public policy making, and state bureaucracies were willing to hire people with radical views, even some socialist feminists dedicated to extra-parliamentary opposition. The landmark Report of the Royal Commission on the Status of Women (RCSW), tabled in Parliament in December 1970, contained a comprehensive, well-articulated set of recommendations on a wide range of public policy issues.

Over time, the majority of the 167 recommendations were implemented, mainly in areas of economic and social policy that did not involve much expense, that did not threaten the power structure, and on which there was broad social consensus. Canadian policy makers and the general public have become increasingly sympathetic to the feminist claim that women should have equal access with men to the competitive spheres of politics and work. To this end, there has been general support for the granting of maternity and parental leaves, increased women's participation in politics, the reduction of systemic barriers to women's employment opportunities, the elimination of discriminatory legislative provisions, and women's policy machinery. RCSW recommendations on which there was no broad social consensus or which were too costly, such as a national childcare system, equal pay for work of equal value, pensions for homemakers, a guaranteed annual income for single parents and abortion on demand in the first 12 weeks of pregnancy, were implemented only partially, if at all, and are still today on the agenda of the feminist movement.

In Australia, the 1970s optimism about the potential for social change through government polices and bureaucracies sprang from the energy of a burgeoning feminist movement, and from the election in December 1972 of a Labor government after 23 years of uninterrupted conservative rule. The new Prime Minister, Gough Whitlam, appointed Elizabeth Reid as his women's adviser. During the two years of her appointment, Reid was involved in travelling across Australia and listening to women talk about their problems; changing the direction of the pre-school and childcare programme; monitoring of Cabinet submissions for their impact upon women; committing the government to major political and financial support for International Women's Year; and answering the huge volume of correspondence that her appointment had generated. She was seen as a major point of access to government by women in the community, and received more letters than anyone else in the government other than the Prime Minister.

A more permanent feminist machinery of government, based on a centre-periphery model, was endorsed in 1975 both by the outgoing Whitlam government and by the incoming conservative Liberal administration of Malcolm Fraser. In 1983, the Fraser government was replaced by a new Labor administration, which came to power with the most developed women's platform of any Australian government to date. The platform included promises of immediate anti-discrimination legislation, a programme of affirmative action in public and private sector employment, and a relatively high-status, well-resourced Office of Status of Women within the Department of Prime Minister and Cabinet. Labor's swift implementation of several of the major planks of its women's policy were undoubtedly also guided by the recognition that women swing voters had helped to deliver electoral victory.

Australia and Canada have both played major roles in strenghthening international instruments and mechanisms for the advancement of women, and these in turn have provided the basis for several domestic initiatives. The UN-initiated International Women's Year (IWY) made a significant contribution to the widespread acceptance of feminist notions about women's equality, and led to significant empowerment of women. Many Canadian and Australian women's services and bureaucracies have their origin in IWY. Canadian and Australian officials played a major role in drafting the Copenhagen World Plan of Action and the Nairobi Forward-looking Strategies. In turn, the first Canadian government plan of action to improve the status of women, *Towards Equality for Women*, was developed as a response to the UN World Plan of Action. Australia was one of the first countries to translate in 1988 Nairobi FLS into its own National Agenda for Women. The relatively long lead time betweeen the years 1988 and 2000 enabled the government to push planning well beyond the time frame provided by Australia's short electoral cycle of only three years.

Since the Second UN World Conference for Women held in 1980 in Copenhagen, there has been a shift among UN member states from the pattern of non-governmental and advisory machinery on the status of women towards a government machinery. Australia and Canada have been early pioneers in the field of national machinery for the status of women, and their respective women's policy machineries have been regarded by the relevant UN bodies as models for other countries. Great Britain has no central government machinery for day-to-day monitoring and auditing of government policies and programmes for gender impact, although it has a judicial human rights body which administers the application of sex discrimination law and promotes equal opportunities between men and women. Moreover, the British Labour Party is committed to establishing a Ministry of Women.

The role of feminism in government is subject to an ongoing debate in Canada and Australia, as is the extent of femocrats' influence and the quality of their representation of feminist concerns. Over the years, there has been a general shift of machinery activities from a pattern of active lobbying for new women's policies, programmes and approaches towards a pattern focusing on the co-ordination and monitoring of existing departmental programmes and policies. This drift from a 'Missionary' towards a 'Mandarin' model of state feminism has been reinforced by the drop in grass-roots feminist activism, and by its fragmentation into a variety of specific causes concerning the environment, women's health, racism, immigration, poverty, violence against women, and feminist research and publishing. The links among these various groups are quite weak, with the result that the political pressure needed for pro-active lobbying, and for the consolidation of feminist gains in government, is not always available. Status of Women Canada and the Australian Office of Status of Women, along with their respective provincial and state counterparts, are generally perceived to be far removed from the lives of ordinary women. This perception is reinforced by the mandate of women's policy machinery to act as a women's advocacy group within government, to develop and co-ordinate policy, but not to deliver specific services directly to women.

The policy advisory/co-ordinating role is confusing to most people and women's groups, and even the government does not appear to fully understand it. When grass-roots feminists (negatively) evaluate femocrats, they often forget that femocrats are civil servants rather than politicans. Femocrats are generally not free to operate independently of their host agency or government department. They cannot take on the role of autonomous politicians and publicly demand, defend or denounce (as the case may be) specific government policies relating to women. Femocrats, like their counterparts in political parties and the union movement, are confronted by the fact that organisational loyalty is the precondition of political effectiveness, not to mention career prospects.

In contrast to Canada and Australia, the UN Decade for Women was largely 'invisible' in Great Britain. With the exception of the local and metropolitan levels of government in the early 1980s, British feminism has not been accepted as a legitimate political force that can set a political agenda, participate in a dialogue about specific policy initiatives, monitor the implementation of relevant policies and otherwise engage in interest politics on behalf of women. The strong antagonism to feminist viewpoints and issues by a powerful female prime minister, Margaret Thatcher, has also worked against the interests of women, as has the existence of mostly covert procedures governing appointments to 'quangos' (quasi-governmental bodies), which include the Equal Opportunities Commission (EOC). While in Canada and Australia femocrats and women's groups routinely consult each other and often offer mutual support, EOC femocrats have lacked the supportive political constituency that is neccessary for a successful bureaucratic confrontationist stance. There is no powerful national women's lobby to press for specific reforms across a range of women's issues and for greater access to elite institutions.

In the 1970s, Canadian and Australian machineries had many points of similarity. The very existence of these machineries has given women's issues (e.g. employment equity, equal pay for work of equal value, social provision for maternity and childcare, violence against women, integration of work and family) a much greater degree of visibility and legitimacy than has been the case in Great Britain. By the late 1980s, however, the Canadian political environment under the Mulroney Tory government had become less favourable to further progress of feminist intervention in government than that under the Hawke Labor government in Australia.

PROSPECTS FOR THE 1990S AND BEYOND

The major challenges for public policies for the 1990s are how to accomodate to continuing low fertility, population ageing, marital instability, immigration and rising ethnic and cultural diversity. Governments also need to address the growing inequality and polarisation among the unemployed, those caught in the welfare-poverty trap, those who have low paying ghettoised low-skilled jobs, and professionals and business executives who have relatively safe and well-paid work. At the same time, we are witnessing an erosion of confidence in the liberal welfare state's ability, willingness and fiscal capacity to effect social change.

Governments are increasingly accepting below-replacement fertility and ageing population as permanent features of advanced industrial societies. While the announcement by Statistics Canada on 30 March 1992 that the annual birth rate increased in 1990 for the third consecutive year was front page news, the news release was accompanied by a cautionary note that the figures indicate a temporary peak in the birth rate rather than a turning point in the basic downward trend of the last two decades. The temporary increase was attributed to changes in birth timing, i.e. the postponement of the first child and the shortening of the birth interval between the first and the second child, and to the effects of the age structure. Once 'baby-boom' women have passed through their reproductive years and once most women start giving births by their late 20s and early 30s, Statistics Canada expects a further drop in the annual birth rate. Officials are well aware, however, that birth rates can be affected by many factors, and that making accurate long-term demographic predictions is extremely hazardous. The news release also notes, without comment, that the biggest change occurred in Quebec, where the birth rate jumped by 14.2 per cent from 1987 to 1990, with some 14 000 more births in 1990 than in 1987, and that the rise in

Quebec birth rates followed provincial incentives designed to encourage more births (*Peterborough Examiner*, 1992).

While Quebec's population policy is attempting to influence demographic trends directly, most of the other provinces, along with the federal government, are pursuing policies aimed at adjusting to actual demographic trends of population ageing, single-parent families (typically the largest group of welfare recipients) and immigration. In recent years, the federal government has improved tax incentives for registered retirement schemes that encourage everybody, including young people, to save for periods when they no longer derive income from employment. Faced with the growing share of their budgets being taken up by health care expenditures, provincial governments are taking measures to limit the supply of physicians (found to be much more significant in generating higher health care costs than population ageing), curtail the open-ended nature of the national health insurance scheme, and shift resources from hospitals towards community care. The Ontario New Democratic Government is moving away from the punitive model of welfare towards an empowerment model. Transforming the system along empowerment lines will involve welfare officials in establishing a legal contract with clients (many of whom are lone mothers) to specify goals and training, plan for opportunities, and target employment.

In Australia, the three major themes examined by the Social Security Review (1986–8) were income support for families with children, social security and workforce issues, and income support for older people. The Review recommended an increase in the level of social security payments; active labour market policies to improve the access of particularly disadvantaged groups (such as migrants and lone parents) to employment, education and training opportunities; and higher levels and better integration of pension, occupational superannuation and tax measures to achieve more adequate retirement incomes. Many of these recommendations have been implemented. Income support and labour market programmes are therefore seen as dual strategies to alleviate poverty, especially among families with children.

Anglo-American policy makers have been increasingly moving away from a universalist social responsibility approach, replacing it with an emphasis on public/private partnership, or helping individuals, employers and communities to help themselves. Privatisation, economic rationalism, reduction in government spending, client empowerment and the selective targeting of social security programmes on the very poor, have become as important as the equal rights mentality in setting policy limits. The rhetoric of 'shared partnership' with the private sector may indicate a new philosophy for the delivery of social programmes, but it is worth remembering that private sector involvement in social policy is not entirely new.

For example, during the first part of this century many companies showed considerable concern about the welfare of their employees. Company 'welfarism' or paternalism began to decrease in the early 1930s, and was replaced with the view that work and family are separate spheres, and that personal and family matters should be dealt with on employee's own time and in a way that did not hamper work activities. As we noted, a tacit rule in most professions, large corporations and government departments has been that those who expect to climb the corporate ladder should put in long hours, relocate or travel as needed, and ensure that family problems do not interfere with work. As a policy, the doctrine of separation between work and family rests on the assumption of man as the sole breadwinner and the woman as a full-time housewife. As such, it is increasingly obsolete, as is the organisation of much of the infrastructure of modern societies.

We have sprawling dormitory suburbs requiring long travel to and from work, highways facilitating car travel (for men) rather than public transportation (for women), a school system organised on the faulty assumption that there is always an adult (a mother) present at home sending children off in the morning and receiving them back during lunch hour or early in the afternoon, well before the typical work day in factories, offices and health care establishments is over. The transformation of the physical infrastructure, and the organisation of the working life to meet the needs of modern families is another major challenge for the 1990s.

Modern nation states also need to accommodate to the age of refugees (the majority of whom are women and children), immigration and rising ethnic and cultural diversity. As we noted in Chapter 6, immigration is an inefficient instrument with which to address below-replacement fertility. While immigration can increase population size, it has only a marginal effect on the age structure of the population. To the extent that it is viewed as making up for deficit fertility, questions are raised about the meaning of procreative choice. In Australia, immigration as a policy of population growth has been negatively linked to congestion, urban sprawl, encroachment on farming and forest lands, higher housing costs, lower real wages, and delayed childbearing. Migration of 'foreigners' in EEC countries has been associated with growing racial and ethnic tensions.

Whatever concerns there may be, however, the scale of demographic imbalances and economic inequalities between the poor, high-fertility countries of the Third World and the rich, low-fertility Western countries, makes migration virtually inevitable. The collapse of communism in East Central Europe and the resulting economic and social dislocation has created another large pool of individuals who through migration seek better lives in the affluent West. An adaptation to these trends at the national, regional or international level requires a concerted effort to manage pluralism. Based on the successful experiences of the US, Canada and Australia, refugees and immigrants from all over the world need to be welcomed and absorbed so that they begin to feel a part of their new societies within a reasonable period of time. Immigration imbued with positive values can be a viable strategy, provided there are sufficient policies and programmes that facilitate the arrival and integration of individuals from diverse ethnic groups.

With the growing integration of the nation state into a broader web of institutional arrangements, important levels of decison making are emerging below it, at the regional level, and above it, at the supra-national level. The post-national state arises when national sovereignty is transcended through the voluntary pooling of power to create a common state across a vast region. Laxer (1991) regards the European Community as the most important global example of the post-national state.

The United Nations has declared 1994 as the International Year of the Family. As we noted in Chapter 3, the main purpose of United Nations International Years (of women, the child, the disabled, and so on) is to increase awareness about an issue, stimulate research, and identify resources that can be mobilised to improve the situation of the designated subjects. If the International Year of the Family achieves only half of what the International Women's Year and the UN Decade for Women have achieved, then it will be quite a remarkable year or a decade. It may even make the connection between women's equality and pronatal policies.

Appendix
Matrix of Egalitarian Components of Specific Pronatalist Policies

Type of non-coercive pronatalism	Type of sex equality		
	Traditional sex roles	*Sex equality based on sex differences and special needs of women*	*Androgynous gender-neutral sex equality*
	Couples (single parents) where the mother has never been engaged in or does not intend to return to paid employment; can benefit from:	Couples (single parents) where the woman stops working temporarily after childbirth and intends to return to her previous employment; can benefit from:	Measures for all parents or couples:
'Facilitative' measures associated with 'social protection of motherhood'	Full access to birth control information and safe techniques; protective labour laws for women in general and pregnant women in particular; free obstetrical and paediatric care	Full access to birth control information and safe techniques; protective labour laws for women in general and pregnant women in particular; free obstetrical and paediatric care; short-term and long-term, paid and unpaid pregnancy and maternity leaves; day-care facilities at the woman's place of work; reduction of the age at which women are entitled to pension depending on the number of children they have had; flexible working hours and conditions for women workers; pay and employment equity	Full access to birth control information and safe techniques; occupational health legislation applicable to all workers; free obstetrical and paediatric care; paid parental leave; fully or almost fully paid leaves to look after sick children for the individual parent, which cannot be transferred to the other parent; community or gender-neutral workplace day care; flexible working hours and conditions for parents of young children

Type of non-coercive pronatalism	Type of sex equality		
	Traditional sex roles	*Sex equality based on sex differences and special needs of women*	*Androgynous gender-neutral sex equality*
'Positive' fiscal incentives	Maternity grant for women who do not claim paid pregnancy and maternity leave; dependent child grant for which only mothers not in paid employment are eligible – fathers qualify only on the grounds of mother's disability; special awards for women who have a large number of children, coupled with preferential treatment for housing, short-term childcare service, holiday homes and so on; exemption from military service for fathers of at least one child	Childbirth grants/family allowances payable to the mother only; maternity (childcare) grant payable during extended maternity leave; special awards for women who have a large number of children, coupled with preferential treatment for housing, day- care and holiday homes	Low-interest loans to newlyweds that are (partially) written off when children are born; tax and rent deductions according to the number of dependent children; (progressive) family allowance payable to either or both parents; state subsidies for children's goods and services

Notes

1 Women's Equality, Childbearing and the State

1. The term 'pronatalist' refers to cases where the intention to raise the birth rate is quite explicit. The greater range of policies which coincidentally make childbearing/rearing easier without the increase in the birth rate being an explicit objective are described as 'pronatal', 'enabling' or simply 'family' policies. This distinction is further elaborated in Chapter 5.
2. After the union of Parliament of England and Scotland in the eighteenth century, Scotland preserved some of its autonomy. Its distinctive Scottish pound (on par with the English pound), church, legal system, education and a separate Scottish administration remain to this date. Legislation passed by the British parliament does not automatically apply to Scotland, but usually Scotland toes the line and accepts the legislation shortly after it had been passed in England. As Oldman (1991: 12) argues,

> a political undercurrent in favour of devolution of some or all of the government of Scotland to a Scottish Assembly ebbs and flows with the pressure of events. It is formally represented by a political party – the Scottish National Party – and proposals for some form of devolution are on the agenda of all other oppositional parties. In the last year a cross-party initiative has created a Scottish Convention which is meeting regularly to debate the form of the future devolution.

2 Models of Women's Equality

1. However, there are important differences between the Roman Law and the English Common Law in this respect. As Lovenduski (1986: 15) argues,

> Roman Law is essentially private law, a means of the regulation of private relationships between individual citizens. By contrast, English Common Law is a system of public law, with private matters between citizens traditionally only of interest if they affect the Crown, other cases being left to equity or ecclesiastical courts. Accordingly, systems based upon Roman Law are more likely to intervene in family relations than is the case with the English system.

2. The 'pay equity', 'equal pay for work of equal value' or 'comparable worth' principle allows for comparison of dissimilar male and female jobs on the basis of a points system evaluating skill, effort and responsibility. The comparisons which a woman may draw with a man's job are limited to men employed by her employer or associated employer at the same establishment. While the British Equal Pay Act of 1970 (which came into force in

December 1975) does not require the undertaking of job evaluations, the Ontario pay equity legislation requires all public sector organisations and private sector firms with 100 employees or more to develop and implement pay equity plans.

3. However, full incorporation of part-time work into organisational practices and structures runs the risk of part-time work becoming the dominant employment norm rather than a tool to permit flexible working hours. Once part-time work, which is generally more unstable and less secure than full-time work, becomes a 'take-it-or-leave-it' managerial norm rather than an employee's option, it becomes quite discriminatory, and as such ceases to have any connection to positive action.

4. Indirect and systemic discrimination are often used interchangeably. In Canada, Judge Rosalie Abella's (1984) multifaceted use of the term systemic discrimination is virtually indistinguishable from the way in which Byre (1988) describes indirect discrimination within the European Community framework. The OECD Working Party on the Role of Women in the Economy (1989: 13) describes systemic or structural discrimination as

> the combined effect of direct and indirect discrimination and societal behaviour and attitudes which operate to limit or restrict the opportunities of a particular group. For example, the absence of any child care facilities can operate to prevent women with dependent children from entering the labour market.

3 International Women's Policy Machinery

1. The European Court of Justice, based in Luxembourg, is not to be confused with the European Court of Human Rights, based in Strasbourg. The latter deals with breaches of the Council of Europe's Convention for the Protection of Human Rights and Fundamental Freedoms, generally known as the European Convention of Human Rights. Inspired by the 1948 UN Universal Declaration of Human Rights, it codifies fundamental human rights and the basic principles of democracy.

4 National Women's Policy Machinery

1. The Women's Bureau was established in the Department of Labour in 1954, with a mandate to provide research on women workers, make information on women workers available to the general public, advise the Department of Labour on its programmes affecting women workers, and promote inter-departmental co-operation on women's issues. From the outset, the Bureau also served as a vehicle for bringing issues and positions taken by women's groups to the attention of policy makers. Thus for almost two decades prior to the Royal Commission report, the women's policy network

> was dominated by the Women's Bureau which slowly achieved recognition

within government as the authority on 'women's issues', although it never achieved autonomy within the Department of Labour. There was little challenge or support from women's groups which had not yet been drawn into the network of government funding and policy participation. Until the 1970s, the government had no clear policy on status of women's issues, and the Bureau provided the expertise and the pressure to create the conditions for change. (Burt, 1990: 203)

When Status of Women Canada was accorded legitimacy as the state agency most authoritative on status of women questions, the Bureau suffered a loss of power and personnel.

2. However,

NAC has had some difficulty exercising its leadership. Since it brings together a wide variety of women's groups, some of which hold conflicting positions, NAC's strength as a national. lobby group is sometimes weakened by internal dissension. . . . In addition to problems arising within NAC, the group has recently faced a loss of legitimacy with the federal government as the major representative of women's views in Canada. For the first time, in 1989, the Minister responsible for the status of women refused to meet with NAC in a closed session to receive its annual cabinet submission. (Burt, 1990: 195)

3. For example, in 1980, CACSW published one of the first comprehensive, in-depth studies of wife battering, entitled *Wife Battering – the Vicious Circle*. Its recommendations provided the direction for subsequent development of policies and programmes of various levels of government. The feminist perspective and specific recommendations of the CACSW report were themselves a reflection of the insight of various grass-roots women's organisations involved in the provision of front-line services to battered women. Status of Women Canada (1987: 10–13) regards the response to wife battering in Canada as an ideal case study of the way in which a grass-roots feminist concern has been placed on the national political agenda and followed up inside government by a national women's policy machinery, resulting in multifaceted government response to this problem.

Spurred by the impetus provided by women's groups, Canada's national machinery co-ordinated a comprehensive review of widely diverse set of government programs and provided guidelines for concerted action. Consistent with the policy of integration, the reponsibility for policy and program development on wife battering was maintained by those government departments with sectoral responsibility and specific expertise.

5   Pronatalism and Women's Equality Policies

1. The material presented in this chapter is a revised version of Heitlinger (1991).

2. The various tensions between 'working moms' and 'at-home mothers' in the United States and Canada have been described by Darnton (1990) and McCabe (1990) as 'Mommy Wars'. The 'Wars' are evident in battles over notions of selfishness and motherly love, abortion rights, publicly funded quality day care or kindergartens, tax breaks for 'stay-at home mothers', decent part-time jobs, and various affirmative action programmes. The moral controversies over abortion, and whether mothers of small children ought to work for wages, remain much alive in the hearts and minds of women in most countries in the Western world. The fall of communism has reopened these passionate debates also in Central and Eastern Europe.

3. The EPP acronym stands for the European People's Party of the European Parliament. It is a grouping of Christian democratic parties in the member states of the European Community. Unlike the more individualistic liberals or conservatives, Christian democrats have traditionally supported the adoption of explicit family policies.

4. Whether or not having both parents in the paid workforce has an impact on father participation in childcare is a controversial question in family research. The considerable variation in methods and samples used has made it difficult both to compare findings and to reach some reasonable conclusions. Russell's (1984) research on Australian families revealed that sharing the breadwinning and the day-to-day childcare does not necessarily lead to sharing other aspects of parenting. In many families, the mother retained greater responsibility for planning, monitoring, and anticipating the needs of the children, while the father retained greater responsibility for breadwinning, with the mother's employment being considered a short-term option. Conversely, Russell interviewed families in which the father was employed and the mother was at home, but all the decision making for the children was shared, with child management and childcare tasks evenly divided when both parents were at home. These couples commonly considered breadwinning and childcare as jobs which made equal contributions to the family, and as jobs which had equivalent demands and rewards. Caring for two pre-school children all day was accepted as being stressful, and the need for relief from this was recognised.

5. Gustafsson and Meissari-Polska (1990) conclude that the recent rise in the Swedish birth rate was mainly due to changes in the timing of births. They do, however, think that the 'family friendly' policy has been pronatalist in preventing birth rates dropping as low as those in Germany. In a similar vein, Pavlík (1978) concludes that the main effect of the various pronatalist measures adopted in Czechoslovakia during the years 1968–73 has been on the timing and spacing of children rather than on the desired family size (of one or two children) and the ultimate number of births. However, this conclusion is disputed by Frejka (1980) and Srb (1981: 44), who consider the pronatalist policies to have had 'an extraordinarily effective result'. The efficacy of vigorous pronatalist policies is subject to an ongoing debate also in France, where Girard and Roussel (1982) take issue with the prevailing view that couples actually wish to have more children than they do, but are deterred from doing so by financial constraints.

6. The pronatal potential of these policies is much more significant than their often non-existent pronatalist intent. Thus the recent report of the European

Community Childcare Network (1990) headlined the sex equality objective as foremost among a number of objectives of childcare. The report discussed a number of other objectives of the childcare policy, but pronatalist objectives were not paid much attention. They were only explicitly mentioned at a later stage and only in the context of France.

6 Immigration as Substitution for Higher Birth Rates and Pronatalism

1. As McIntosh (1983: 104) argues,

    working and social conditions of immigrants are increasingly mandated by international conventions that exert pressures toward the continual evolution of costly social and education programs to facilitate the integration of foreign workers. . . . Several international organizations in Europe, including the ILO, the OECD, and the Council of Europe, have been active in furthering the social, civic and political rights of immigrant workers and their dependants.

7 Protective Legislation and Equal Employment Opportunity

1. By contrast, an equivalent health and safety legislation in Ontario grew out of the more business-oriented Progressive Conservative government's concerns with the high cost of work-related disease and injury, and the recognition of links between health and productivity. While some aspects of the legislation have been shaped by strongly articulated concerns of organised labour, the Ontario 1981 Occupational Health and Safety Act reflected more the corporate position than that of labour. Although the Act sets specific standards instead of the flexible guidelines demanded by business, the levels of exposure to toxic substances are much higher than those proposed by labour, and they opened the door to discrimination against women. While the August 1980 draft regulations for lead and mercury did not differentiate between men and women, the 1981 legislation allowed special treatment for women of childbearing capacity without providing specific reassignment or income security protection (Labour Canada, 1989: 39–40).

8 Maternal and Parental Leaves and Benefits Programmes

1. Maternity Alliance is an independent, voluntary, national organisation which is concerned with the welfare of parents, parents-to-be, and children in their first year of life. Formed in 1980 to campaign for improvements in the rights of, and services for, Britain's mothers, fathers and babies, it has since forged links with more than 70 other voluntary organisations and consumer groups. Apart from organising national campaigns on major issues affecting parents

and babies, the Alliance monitors and responds to new developments and proposals from government and from statutory and professional bodies. It has sponsored research on a range of issues of concern to parents and professionals. Recent reports and information leaflets have looked at child health services, homeless families with babies, sugar in baby foods, working parents' rights, childcare availability and the above-mentioned study of women's experiences of going on maternity leave and returning to work. The Alliance also publishes five times a year its bulletin, *Maternity Action*. Funded by grants from central and local government, trusts and companies, and by membership affiliations, publication sales and conference fees, Maternity Alliance's major concern is with poverty, economic discrimination and health problems of mothers and babies. Low fertility has been of no interest to the Alliance and no measures have ever been advocated on the grounds that they may increase the birth rate or prevent its decline.

2. Paternity leave refers to paternal leave around childbirth. Most fathers in Britain have no statutory right to take time off work when their baby is born, and negotiated agreements on such leave are rare. A study of 100 collective agreements in the private and public sectors conducted by the Confederation of British Industry (CBI) in 1985 found that only seven contained clauses which gave paid paternity leave. The leave granted ranged from one to four days. A related study of 64 national wage claims during the same year revealed that 15 (23 per cent) of these claims included requests for the introduction of paternity leave. The CBI attributed the growing commitment of trade unions to paternity leave to the impetus stemming from the European Commission's proposed Directive on parental leave (*EOR*, No. 2, July/August 1985). Bell *et al.* (1983: 6) found that 'there is a strong cultural commitment to the idea of men being at home for a short time, around the time of childbirth and especially when the mother and baby come home from hospital'. Their study found that only 13 respondents from a sample of 230 employed fathers took no time off at any stage during their wives' pregnancies or in the postnatal period. The majority of the fathers used their annual holidays or sick leave entitlements or took unpaid leave.

3. The 'disturbing demographic changes in our societies' is a vague term covering a number of distinct demographic trends. It could refer to below-replacement fertility, population ageing, rising rates of childlessness, teenage mothers, divorce or child poverty. Judging by my interviews at the Equal Opportunities Office of the European Commission in Brussels in August 1988, the Commission is not particularly concerned with declining birth rates. Of much greater concern are single-parent families headed by women unable to earn a decent income, and the general economic discrimination against mothers in the labour market.

4. The major change under Bill C-21 was the abandonment of the federal government's $2 billion annual contribution to the UI fund, which has been financed mostly through premiums from employers and employees. Under the new legislation, those premiums increased by approximately 30 cents per person per week. Other changes involved tougher eligibility requirements, redirection of up to $800 million into job-training programmes for laid-off workers, and the extenstion of UI benefits to workers over the age of 65. Like the parental leave benefits, the latter was a response to a Federal Court

ruling, which forced the federal government to make the UI system conform with the Charter of Rights and Freedoms.

9 Childcare Policies and Programmes

1. In recent years, the federal government had abandoned the open-ended 50–50 cost-sharing formula. In 1990, the federal government unilaterally limited the growth of Ottawa's annual contribution to welfare payments in the country's three richest provinces – Ontario, Alberta and British Columbia – to 5 per cent. What this means is that there are no longer any national standards and the poor, a category which includes many parents with small children, are increasingly dependent for social assistance on their provincial treasuries.

2. See Ruggie (1984) for a detailed review of comparable jusrisdictional conflicts between the Department of Health and Social Services (DHSS) and the Department of Education and Science (DES) in Great Britain. DHSS (since 1989 split into two separate ministries of health and social services) and local government are responsible for day nurseries; DES and local education authorities oversee nursery schools.

3. Johnson and Dineen (1981) report similar findings from Canada. However,

   > with the move to licensing agencies and setting standards for private day care homes, with increased reporting and training requirements, and with more progresive labour legislation, private home day care services have become more professionalised and the employment status of providers (employee or independent contractor) has come into question. Because of these changes, the overall costs of private home day care have increased dramatically, so that what was once thought to be inexpensive service is now equal to and in some cases more costly than group care.
   > (Lero and Kyle, 1990: 67)

   Private home day care is becoming more costly also in Australia. In September 1989 the Australian Industrial Relations Commission ruled that family day care caregivers were 'employees of local governing authorities' and as such entitled to appropriate increased wages (Evans *et al.*, 1990).

4. Playgroups are mainly voluntary, self-help middle-class organisations, which had developed as a response by women themselves to the play requirements of children and their own needs as mothers. Most playgroups have a qualified supervisor, but the 'staff' consists mainly of mothers who participate on a rotational basis. Any child whose parents can pay the fee can attend. Playgroups are used by over 40 per cent of three and four year olds in England and Wales, clearly demonstrating that it is not only employed parents who require childcare (Ruggie, 1984: 196–7; Cohen, 1988a: 38–9).

5. In 1985, total public expenditures on childcare services for under-fives amounted to only 0.1 per cent of gross domestic product (GDP), having barely increased at all during the previous decade. Britain spends considerably less than many other OECD countries on childcare provision. In

1985, it spent six times less of its national income on these services than Denmark. Portugal, the EEC member state with the lowest level of GDP per head, has substantially higher levels of publicly funded services for children under 3 and 'outside school hours care' than Great Britain, whose per capita GDP is more than three times higher. Germany has substantially lower levels of publicly funded childcare than Belgium, even though Germany's per capita GDP is more than 40 per cent higher. Thus the link between the level of national income and the level of investment in childcare services is of a political rather than an economic nature (Cohen, 1988b; Moss, 1988: 289–90).

10 Fiscal Support for Parents and their Children

1. The major social programmes introduced during this period were the 1951 Old Age Security Act, the 1956 Unemployment Assistance Act, the 1966 Canada and Quebec Pension Plans, the 1966 Canada Assistance Plan, and Medicare, which was enacted after much delay in 1968.
2. The idea of a guaranteed annual income dates back to the late 1960s when the renowned University of Chicago economist Milton Friedman proposed a negative income tax (or a refundable tax credit) to establish an income floor for the poor. As the poor household's income rises, the negative tax is gradually removed. At a certain income threshold, the benefit disappears completely and the family starts paying positive tax. The main goals of guaranteed annual income are to meet financial need, and to ensure that the working poor are not worse off than those on social assistance. Because of the gradual withdrawal of the tax credit payments, families can take part-time or low-paying jobs and not be penalised by the complete withdrawal of benefits. The Canadian groundwork for such a scheme was laid by a number of federal studies in the 1970s. A move in that direction was also recommended in 1985 by the royal commission on the economy headed by the former Liberal Finance Minister Donald Macdonald. The commission called for all existing income supports and tax exemptions to be rolled into one payment, a universal income security program (UISP), that would gradually decline as a family's income increases. The UISP would have been available to families up to an annual income of $45 000, which would have included well over half the population. The new Conservative government (elected in 1984) dismissed UISP as too grandiose, while the social democratic opposition, the New Democratic Party, saw it as too stingy. Another move toward guaranteed income was made by the 1992 federal budget, which ended universal allowance payments and introduced a $500 earned-income supplement if family earnings reached at least $10 000. The supplement begins to disappear at $21 000 of annual family income, and at $26 000, it is gone completely (Ferguson, 1992). Critics of the scheme have pointed out that it represents a backward slide to the poor laws when one was either deserving or not deserving of government's help; that it is likely to end universality and establish fees for all social services; that using tax breaks to help the working poor will keep them poor because they would not want to lose the

322 Women's Equality, Demography and Public Policies

benefits; that the low cut-off point will lead to a Canadian underclass of working poor similar to the impoverished underclass in the United States; and that the monthly refundable tax credits would be paid to households rather than to individuals. Negative income tax proposals assume that the head of the household passes on a fair share of any payments to dependents within the household. When this does not happen, which is often the case, such payments are obviously not well targeted at the poorest individuals.

3. Between 1956 and 1961, the average French-speaking Quebec woman had more than 4.2 children in her lifetime, while the average English-speaking Quebec woman had 3.3 children. Between 1961 and 1966, the total fertility of Quebecois women fell to 3.5 children; between 1966 and 1971 to 2.3 children; between 1971 and 1976 further still to 1.8 children. Another drop between 1981 and 1986 brought the rate down to 1.5 children per woman, the lowest of all the provinces. The substantial decline in the Quebec birth rate has been attributed by Baker (1990: 2)

> to the cultural changes of the 'Quiet Revolution', when the Catholic Church lost much control over Quebec society, the education system became more secularized, young people placed more emphasis on occupational success, and young women played down their traditional roles as mothers. Another reason for the lower birth rates probably relates to young women's personal reactions against their mothers experience in childbearing and childrearing. After seeing their mothers become emotionally and physically exhausted raising extremely large families, daughters were determined not to repeat their mothers' lives.

4. The child endowment scheme also had a limited demographic rationale. In 1942, the Labor government commissioned the National Health and Medical Research Council to investigate the decline in fertility, which had become an issue as an aftermath of the 1930s depression. The interim report, published in 1944, defined the steadily falling birth rate of the last two decades as a serious social problem. However, its policy prescription placed more emphasis on the provision of social services than on cash transfers. The report's social services orientation reflected the dominant social welfare concerns of the 1942–8 period of federal politics in Australia (Cass, 1988b). When the opposition parties returned to government in 1949, the advocacy of a pronatalist population policy based on a social services package was abandoned. As the post-war baby boom continued, there seemed to be no need to stimulate the birth rate (United Nations, 1982: 263).

5. The Social Security Review was established by the Minister for Social Security, the Honourable Brian Howe MP, in February 1986, initially for two years. The Review examined income support for families with children, social security and workforce issues, and income support for the aged. Its main focus was on coverage, adequacy of payments, targeting, redistribution, opportunities for employment, and the simplicity, access and community awareness of social security programmes (Cass, 1986a, 1986b; Donald, 1986; Harding, 1986).

6. Eligible taxpayers who have no dependent children receive slightly less in tax relief. In 1989, DSR for taxpayers with dependent children stood at

$1300, while those with no children could claim only $1100 (Hyman, 1990: 61).

7. The February election put Labour in office as a minority government, while the October election gave Labour a slim majority.

11 Conclusion

1. The study is based on a random sample of 60 women chartered accountants who were interviewed in 1984–5. Eighty-four per cent of the participants were Francophone, 16 per cent were Anglophone. Their ages ranged from 25 to 35 years.

References

Abbott, Ruth and R. A. Young (1989) 'Cynical and Deliberate Manipulation? Child Care and the Reserve Army of Female Labour in Canada', *Journal of Canadian Studies*, vol. 24, no. 2 (Summer) pp. 22–38.

Abella, Rosalie Silberman (1984) *Equality in Employment. A Royal Commission Report* (Ottawa: Ministry of Supply and Services).

Adams, Carolyn Teich and Kathryn Teich Winston (1980) *Mothers at Work. Public Policies in the United States, Sweden and China* (New York: Longman).

Ainstee, R., R. G. Gregory, S. Dowrick and J. J. Pincus. (1988) *Government Spending on Work-Related Child Care. Some Economic Issues.* Discussion Paper no. 191 (Canberra: Centre for Applied Economic Research, Australian National University).

Alexander, Morag (1985) 'The Contribution of the European Economic Community to Equality between Women and Men', *Equal Opportunities International*, vol. 4, no. 4.

Anderson, Doris (1990) 'Bribery for Babies Won't Work', *Toronto Star*, 11 May.

Andorka, Rudolf (1978) *Determinants of Fertility in Advanced Societies* (London: Methuen).

Arat-Koc, Sedef (1990) 'Importing Housewives: Non-Citizen Domestic Workers and the Crisis of the Domestic Sphere in Canada', in Meg Luxton, Harriet Rosenberg and Sedef Arat-Koc, *Through the Kitchen Window: The Politics of Home and Family*, 2nd and enlarged edn (Toronto: Garamond Press) pp. 81–103.

Armstrong, Pat and Hugh Armstrong (1987) 'Looking Ahead: the Future of Women's Work in Australia and Canada', in Heather Jon Maroney and Meg Luxton (eds), *Feminism and Political Economy. Women's Work, Women's Struggles* (Toronto: Methuen) pp. 213–25.

Ashworth, Georgina and Lucy Bonnerjea (eds) (1986) *The Invisible Decade. UK Women and the UN Decade 1976–1985* (London: Gower).

Atkins, Susan and Brenda Hoggett (1984) *Women and the Law* (Oxford: Basil Blackwell).

Australian Council of Trade Unions (1979) *Maternity Leave – the Award Provision Explained* (Melbourne: ACTU).

Australian Council of Trade Unions (1983) *Working Women's Charter* (Melbourne: ACTU).

Australian Council of Trade Unions (1988a) *Employer Supported Child Care* (Melbourne: ACTU).

Australian Council of Trade Unions (1988b) *Employer-Supported Child Care. A Negotiating Document* (Melbourne: ACTU).

Australian Council of Trade Unions (1989) *Parental Leave Test Case: Background Information* (Melbourne: ACTU).

Bacchi, Carol Lee (1990) *Same Difference. Feminism and Sexual Difference* (Sydney: Allen & Unwin).

Baker, Maureen (1990) *The Politics of Declining Fertility: Family Policy in*

324

Quebec. Paper presented at the Annual Meetings of the Canadian Sociology and Anthropology Association, Victoria, B.C., 26–30 May.

Banting, Keith (1987) 'Visions of the Welfare State', in Shirley B. Seward (ed.), *The Future of Social Welfare Systems in Canada and the United Kingdom*. Proceedings of a Canada/UK Colloquium, 17–18 October 1986, Ottawa/Meech Lake (Ottawa: The Institute for Research on Public Policy) pp. 147–63.

Beaujot, Roderic (ed.) (1990) *Facing the Demographic Future*. Summary of a conference organised by the Royal Society of Canada and the Federation of Canadian Demographers, Laval University, Quebec, 7–9 June (Ottawa: Royal Society of Canada).

Beggs, J. and B. Chapman (1988) *The Foregone Earnings from Child-Rearing in Australia*. Discussion Paper no. 190 (Canberra: Centre for Economic Policy Research, Australian National University).

Bégin, Monique (1987) 'Demographic Change and Social Policy: Implications and Possible Alternatives', in Shirley B. Seward (ed.), *The Future of Social Welfare Systems in Canada and the United Kingdom*. Proceedings of a Canada/UK Colloquium, 17–18 October 1986, Ottawa/Meech Lake (Ottawa: The Institute for Research on Public Policy) pp. 209–30.

Bell, Colin, Lorna McKee and Karen Priestly (1983) *Fathers, Childbirth and Work* (Manchester: Equal Opportunities Commission).

Bennet, James E. and Pierre M. Loewe, with a foreword by Laurent Picard (1975) *Women in Business. A Shocking Waste of Human Resources* (Toronto: Maclean-Hunter).

Bertin, Joan E. and Mary Sue Henifin (1987) 'Legal Issues in Women's Occupational Health', in Ann H. Stromberg, Laurie Larwood and Barbara A. Gutek (eds), *Women and Work. An Annual Review* (London: Sage) pp. 93–115.

Betts, Katharine (1988) *Ideology and Immigration. Australia 1976 to 1987* (Melbourne: Melbourne University Press).

Betts, Katharine (1989) 'Does Australia's Low Fertility Matter?', *Journal of the Australian Population Association*, vol. 6, no. 2 (November), pp. 102–20.

Betts, Katharine (1990) 'Sydney and the Bush: No Growth and Some Hope', *Migration Action*, vol. 12, no. 3 (November) pp. 21–4.

Bissonette, Lise (1988) 'Infantile Approach to Falling Birthrate', *Globe and Mail*, 20 May.

Blake, Judith (1974) 'Coercive Pronatalism and American Population Policy', in Ellen Peck and Judith Senderowitz (eds), *Pronatalism. The Myth of Mom and Apple Pie* (New York: Thomas Y. Crowell).

Bock, Gisela (1984) 'Racism and Sexism in Nazi Germany: Motherhood, Compulsory Sterilization, and the State', in Renate Bridenthal, Atina Grossmann and Marion Kaplan (eds), *When Biology Became Destiny. Women in Weimar and Nazi Germany* (New York: Monthly Review Press) pp. 271–96.

Booth, Anna and Linda Rubenstein (1990) 'Women in Trade Unions in Australia', in Sophie Watson (ed.), *Playing the State. Australian Feminist Interventions* (Sydney: Allen & Unwin) pp. 121–35.

Bouchier, David (1984) *The Feminist Challenge: The Movement for Women's Liberation in Britain and the United States* (New York: Schocken Books).

Boyd, Monica (1991) *Migrating Discrimination: Feminist Issues in Canadian Immigration Policies and Practices*. Paper presented in the Centre for

326   *Women's Equality, Demography and Public Policies*

Women's Studies and Feminist Research Distinguished Series, University of Western Ontario, 12 February. Working Paper no. 6 (London: Centre for Women's Studies and Feminist Research, University of Western Ontario).

Brannen, Julia (1987) *Taking Maternity Leave. The Employment Decisions of Women with Young Children* (London: Thomas Coram Research Unit, University of London Institute of Education).

Brannen, Julia and Peter Moss (1988) *New Mothers at Work. Employment and Childcare* (London: Unwin Hyman).

Brazao, Dale (1989) 'Some Day Cares Called Worse than Dog Kennels', *Toronto Star*, 15 September.

Brennan, Deborah and Carol O'Donnell (1986) *Caring for Australia's Children. Political and Industrial Issues in Child Care* (Sydney: Allen & Unwin).

Breton, Raymond (1988) 'French–English Relations', in James Curtis and Lorne Tepperman (eds), *Understanding Canadian Society* (Toronto: McGraw-Hill Ryerson) pp. 557–85.

British Columbia Task Force on Child Care (1991) *Showing We Care. A Child Care Strategy for the 90's/Complete Report* (Victoria, BC: Ministry of Government Management Services and Minister Responsible for Women's Programs).

Brocas, Anne-Marie, Anne-Marie Cailloux and Virginie Oget (1990) *Women and Social Security. Progress towards Equality of Treatment* (Geneva: International Labour Office).

Brown, Joan C. (1984) *Family Income Support Part 2. Children in Social Security*, Studies of the Social Security System no. 3 (London: Policy Studies Institute).

Brown, Joan C. (1988) *Child Benefit. Investing in the Future* (London: Child Poverty Action Group).

Brown, Louise (1988) 'Smart Bank Gives Staff Family Leave', *Toronto Star*, 20 December.

Brown, Mona G. and Delia J. Power (1986) *Child Care and Taxation in Canada: Who Pays?*, Study for the Task force on Child Care, Series 1, Financing Child Care: Current Arrangements (Ottawa: Minister of Supply and Services Canada).

Brundtland, Gro Harlem (1983) 'Statement by the Chairman of the Conference at the Opening Session', in *Proceedings of the European Population Conference 1982* (Strasbourg: Council of Europe) pp. 13–19.

Buckley, Mary and Malcolm Anderson (1988) 'Introduction: Problems, Policies and Politics', in Mary Buckley and Malcolm Anderson (eds), *Women, Equality and Europe* (London: Macmillan) pp. 1–19.

Burch, Thomas (1986) *Pronatalist Policies: An Appraisal with Special Reference to the Canadian Demographic Situation.* A Report prepared for the Review of Demography and Its Implications for Social and Economic Policies, Health and Welfare Canada.

Burch, Thomas and Kevin McQuillan (1988) 'One-adult and Two-earner Households and Families: Trends, Determinants and Consequences', *The Review of Demography and its Implications for Economic and Social Policy. Update Number Five* (Ottawa: Health and Welfare Canada) pp. 8–10.

Burns, Aisa (1981) 'Advance or Retreat? Early Childhood Services in the

Eighties', *Australian Journal of Early Childhood*, vol. 6, no. 2 (June) pp. 9–14.

Burt, Sandra (1986) 'Voluntary Affirmative Action: Does It Work?', *Relations Industrielles*, vol. 41, no. 3, pp. 541–50.

Burt, Sandra (1988) 'Legislators, Women and Public Policy', in Sandra Burt, Lorraine Code and, Lindsay Dorney (eds), *Changing Patterns. Women in Canada* (Toronto: McClelland & Stewart) pp. 129–56.

Burt, Sandra (1990) 'Organized Women's Groups and the State', in William D. Coleman and Grace Skogstad (eds), *Policy Communities and Public Policy in Canada: A Structural Approach* (Mississagua, Ontario: Copp Clark Pitman) pp. 191–211.

Byre, Angela (1988) 'Applying Community Standards on Equality', in Mary Buckley and Malcolm Anderson (eds), *Women, Equality and Europe* (London: Macmillan) pp. 20–32.

Calliste, Agnes (1989) 'Canada's Immigration Policy and Domestics from the Caribbean: The Second Domestic Scheme', in Jesse Vorst *et al.* (eds), *Race, Class, Gender: Bonds and Barriers* (Toronto: Between the Lines) pp. 133–65.

Cameron, David M. (1981) 'Introduction and Summary', in David M. Cameron (ed.), *Regionalism and Supranationalism. Challenges and Alternatives to the Nation-State in Canada and Europe* (Montreal: The Institute for Research on Public Policy) pp. xiii–xviii.

Canada Employment and Immigration Advisory Council (1987) *Workers with Family Responsibilities in a Changing Society* (Ottawa: Canada Employment and Immigration Advisory Council).

Canadian Advisory Council on the Status of Women (1986) *Brief to the Legislative Committee on Bill C-144, the Proposed Canada Child Care Act* (Ottawa: CACSW).

Canadian Advisory Council on the Status of Women (1988) *Becoming a Parent: A Guide to Maternity/Parental Leave and Benefits in Canada* (Ottawa: CACSW).

Canadian Press (1989) 'Report Urges Crackdown on Day-Care', *Globe and Mail*, 29 November.

Carter, April (1988) *The Politics of Women's Rights* (London: Longman).

Cass, Betina (1986a) *Income Support for Families with Children*, Isssues Paper no. 1, The Social Security Review (Canberra: Australian Government Publishing Service).

Cass, Betina (1986b) *The Case for Review of Aspects of the Australian Social Security System*, Background/Discussion Paper no. 1, The Social Security Review (Woden ACT: Social Security Review).

Cass, Betina (1988a) 'Redistribution to Children and to Mothers; a History of Child Endowment and Family Allowances', in Cora Baldock and Bettina Cass (eds), *Women, Social Welfare and the State in Australia*, 2nd ed (Sydney: Allen & Unwin) pp. 54–88.

Cass, Betina (1988b) 'Population Policies and Family Policies: State Construction of Domestic Life', in Baldock and Cass (eds), *Women, Social Welfare and the State in Australia*, pp. 168–89.

Cass, Betina and Heather Radi (1981) 'Family, Fertility and the Labour Market',

328   *Women's Equality, Demography and Public Policies*

in Norma Grieve and Patricia Grimshaw (eds), *Australian Women. Feminist Perspectives* (Melbourne: Oxford University Press), pp. 190–212.

Cass, Betina, Carol Keens and Jerry Moller (1981) 'Family Policy Halloween; Family Allowances: Trick or Treat?' *Australian Quarterly*, vol. 53, no. 1, pp. 56–73.

Castleman, Tanya, Julie Mulvany and Maryann Wulff (1989) *After Maternity: How Australian Women Make Decisions About Work and Family* (Hawthorn: Swinburne Institute of Technology, Centre for Women's Studies).

Castles, Francis (1985) *The Working Class and Welfare. Reflections on the Political Development of the Welfare State in Australia and New Zealand, 1890–1980* (Sydney: Allen & Unwin).

Central Office of Information (1987) *Policies for the Advancement of Women in Britain*, no. 295/87, Classification 1(b), May, 10 pp.

Chavkin, Wendy (ed.) (1984) *Double Exposure: Women's Health Hazards on the Job and at Home* (New York: Monthly Review Press).

Chesnais, Jean-Claude (1983) 'Fertility and the State', in *Proceedings of the European Population Conference 1982* (Strasbourg: Council of Europe) pp. 367–87.

Chenier, Nancy Miller (1982) *Reproductive Hazards. Men, Women and the Fertility Gamble* (Ottawa: Canadian Advisory Council on the Status of Women).

Clark, Pilita (1990) 'Up to $86 a Week Child-Care Relief', *Sydney Morning Herald*, 9 March.

Clement, Barrie (1989) 'Employers Failing to Provide Nurseries', *Independent*, 13 March.

Clichet, Pierre (1984) 'Quebec's Family Policy: Social Policy or Demographic Policy', in *XXth International CFR Seminar on Social Change and Family Policies*, Melbourne, Australia, 19–24 August, Final Papers, Part 5 (Melbourne: The Australian Institute of Family Studies) pp. 58–85.

Coale, Ansley (1986) 'Demographic Effects of Below-Replacement Fertility and their Social Implications', *Population and Development Review*, vol. 12 (Supplement) pp. 203–16.

Cockburn, Milton (1990) 'Labor To Up the Ante on Child Care', *Sydney Morning Herald*, 3 March.

COFACE (1985) *Women's Rights and Family Policy* (Brussels: COFACE)

COFACE (1986) *Families and Demographic Facts* (Brussels: COFACE).

Cohen, Bronwen (1988a) *Caring for Children. Services and Policies for Childcare and Equal Opportunities in the United Kingdom*. Report for the European Commission's Childcare Network (London: Commission of the European Communities).

Cohen, Bronwen (1988b) *Childcare Provision: Meeting the Needs of Families*. Paper presented at a National Conference on 'Child Support: Policies for the Future', Family Policy Studies Centre, London, 1 December.

Cohen, Bronwen and Karen Clarke (eds) (1986) *Childcare and Equal Opportunities: Some Policy Perspectives* (London: HMSO).

Cohen, Rita (1987) 'The Work Conditions of Immigrant Women Live-In Domestics: Racism, Sexual Abuse and Invisibility', *Resources for Feminist Research*, vol. 16 (March) pp. 36–8.

Colley, Sue (1990) *Childcare in the 1990's: Education or Social Service?* Paper presented at a Conference entitled 'Moving Forward: Creating a Feminist Agenda for the 1990's'. Organised by the Peterborough–Trent Women's Coalition, and held at Trent University, Peterborough, Ontario, 15–17 June.

Collins, Doreen (1983) 'Social Policy', in Juliet Lodge (ed.), *Institutions and Policies of the European Community* (London: Frances Pinter) pp. 97–109.

Collins, Mary (1991) 'Interview', *Status of Women Canada Perspectives*, vol. 4, no. 2 (Spring) pp. 1–4.

Commission of the European Communities (1986) 'Equal Opportunities for Women. Medium-term Community Programme 1986–90', *Bulletin of the European Communities,* Supplement 3.

Commission of the European Communities (1987) *Protective Legislation for Women in the Member States of the European Community* (Brussels: Commission of the European Communities).

Commonwealth of Australia (1989) *Implementation of the Nairobi Forward Looking Strategies. Report of Australia.*

Coote, Anna (1975) *Women Factory Workers. The Case Against Repealing the Protective Laws* (London: National Council for Civil Liberties).

Coote, Anna and Beatrix Campbell (1987) *Sweet Freedom. The Struggle for Women's Liberation,* 2nd edn (Oxford: Basil Blackwell).

Corcoran, Jennifer (1981) 'UK Sex Discrimination and the European Court', *Equal Opportunities International,* vol. 1, no. 1, pp. 18–21.

Coussins, Jean, Lyn Durward and Ruth Evans (1987) *Maternity Rights at Work,* revised edn (London: National Council for Civil Liberties).

Cox, Eva (1988) 'Pater-patria: Child-rearing and the State', in Cora V. Baldock and Bettina Cass (eds), *Women, Social Welfare and the State,* 2nd edn (Sydney: Allen & Unwin) pp. 190–204.

Cox, Eva (1989) 'Response to the Background Paper', in Child Accident Prevention Foundation of Australia and Australian Early Childhood Association, *A Research Conference. Funding Options for Child Care and their Relation to Social Justice and Quality Issues,* Melbourne, 11–12 December.

Cox, Eva (1990) 'Childcare', *Refactory Girl. A Feminist Journal,* Issue no. 34, January.

Daniel, W. W. (1980) *Maternity Rights. The Experience of Women* (London: Policy Studies Institute).

Daniel, W. W. (1981) *Maternity Rights. The Experience of Employers* (London: Policy Studies Institute).

Darnton, Nina (1990) 'Mommy Vs. Mommy', *Newsweek,* 4 June.

Davies, Patricia Wynn (1989) 'The Battle Against Bias', *The Sunday Times,* 29 January.

Davis, Lynne (1983) 'Now You See It, Now You Don't: The Restructuring of Commonwealth Government Child Care Policy, 1972–1982', *The Australian and New Zealand Journal of Sociology,* vol. 19, no. 1 (March) pp. 79–95.

Day, Lincoln H. (1988a) 'Limits and Possibilities Relating to Family Structure and Care of the Aged in Populations with Unprecedently Low Fertility', *Journal of the Australian Population Association,* vol. 5, no. 2, pp. 178–86.

Day, Lincoln H. (1988b) 'Numerical Declines and Older Age Structures in European Populations: An Alternative Perspective', *Family Planning Perspectives,* vol. 20, no. 3 (May/June) pp. 139–43.

de Lepervanche, Marie (1989a) 'Women, Nation and the State in Australia', in Nira Yuval-Davis and Floya Anthias (eds), *Woman-Nation-State* (London: Macmillan) pp. 36–57.

de Lepervanche, Marie (1989b) 'Breeders for Australia: A National Identity for Women?', *Australian Journal of Social Issues*, vol. 24, no. 3 (August) pp. 163–82.

Demeny, Paul (1986a) 'Population and the Invisible Hand', *Demography*, vol. 23, no. 4, pp. 473–87

Demeny, Paul (1986b) 'Pronatalist Policies in Low-Fertility Countries: Patterns, Performance, and Prospects', *Population and Development Review*, vol. 12 (Supplement) pp. 335–58.

de Sandre, Paolo (1978) 'Critical Study of Population Policies in Europe', in the Council of Europe (ed.) *Population Decline in Europe* (New York: St. Martin's Press), pp. 145–70.

Devine, Marion (1989) 'New Welcome for Women', *The Sunday Times*, 29 January.

Docksey, Christopher (1987) *Sharing of Occupational, Family and Social Responsibilities – the Case for Parental Leave*. Paper presented at an expert Seminar on Independence between Women and Men, Salzburg, 9–13 July.

Donald, Owen (1986) *Social Security Reform*, Backgound/Discussion Paper no. 2 (Woden ACT: Social Security Review).

Dowse, Sara (1988) 'The Women's Movement's Fandango with the State: the Movement's Role in Public Policy since 1972', in Cora Baldock and Bettina Cass (eds), *Women, Social Welfare and the State in Australia*, 2nd edn (Sydney: Allen & Unwin), pp. 205–26.

Edwards, Meredith (1981) *Financial Arrangements within Families* (Canberra: National Women's Advisory Council).

Eichler, Margrit (1988) *Families in Canada Today. Recent Changes and Their Policy Consequences*, 2nd edn (Toronto: Gage Publishing).

Eisenstein, Hester (1985) 'The Gender of Bureaucracy: Reflections on Feminism and the State', in Jacqueline Goodnow and Carole Pateman (eds), *Women, Social Science and Public Policy* (Sydney: George Allen & Unwin) pp. 104–15.

Eisenstein, Hester (1990) 'Femocrats, Official Feminism and the Uses of Power', in Sophie Watson (ed.), *Playing the State. Australian Feminist Interventions* (Sydney: Allen & Unwin) pp. 87–103.

Eistenstein, Zillah (1981) *The Radical Future of Liberal Feminism* (New York: Longman).

Employment and Immigration Canada 1979–92 *Annual Reports to Parliament on Future Immigration Levels* (Ottawa: Minister of Supply and Services).

Employment and Immigration Canada (1985) *Report to Parliament on the Review of Future Directions for Immigration Levels* (Ottawa: Minister of Supply and Services).

Employment and Immigration Canada. Unemployment Insurance (1988) *Maternity and Adoption Benefits. . . . We've Made Some Changes* (Ottawa: Employment and Immigration Canada).

Employment and Immigration Canada (1989) *Immigration to Canada: Issues for Discussion* (Ottawa: Employment and Immigration Canada, Public Affairs and the Immigration Policy Branch).

Equal Opportunities Commision (1978) '*I Want to Work . . . but What About the Kids?*' *Day Care for Young Children and Opportunities for Working Parents* (Manchester: EOC).

Equal Opportunities Commission (1979) *Health & Safety Legislation: Should We Distinguish Between Men & Women?*, Report & Recommendations of the Equal Opportunities Commission, submitted to the Secretary of State for Employment, March.

Equal Opportunities Commission (1987) *Equality arid Europe. EC Legislation and Non-Binding Acts* (Manchester: EOC).

Equal Opportunities for Women in the United Kingdom and Australia (1984) Occasional Seminar Papers, no. 3, June (London: University of London, Australian Studies Centre).

Ergas, Yasmine (1987) *Child Care Policies in Comparative Perspective: An Introductory Discussion*. Paper prepared for the OECD Conference of National Experts on 'Lone Parents. The Economic Challenge of Changing Family Structures', 15–17 December (Paris: OECD).

Ermish, John (1986) *Impacts of Policy Actions on the Family and the Household*, Discussion Paper no. 116 (London: Centre for Economic Policy Research).

Erwin, Lorna (1988) 'REAL Women, Anti-feminism, and the Welfare State, *Resources for Feminist Research*, vol. 17, no. 3, pp. 147-9.

Esping-Andersen, Gosta (1989) 'The Three Political Economies of the Welfare State', *The Canadian Review of Sociology and Anthropology*, Special Issue: Comparative Political Economy, vol. 26, no. 1 (February) pp. 10–36.

European Commission Childcare Network (1990) *Childcare in the European Community, Women of Europe Supplements* (August) (Brussels: Commission of the European Communities).

European People's Party (CD) of the European Parliament (1988) 'Towards a European Family Policy. Text Adopted by the Steering Committee of the EPP Women's Organization on 1 February 1988 in Brussel', *European Digest*, no. 56, May, pp. 147–56.

Evans, Darma, Bryan Patterson and Jane Phillips (1990) 'Child Care a Growing Frustration', *Sunday Age*, 4 March.

Family Policy Studies Centre (1989) *News Release. Caring for Children and Equal Opportunities in the UK*, 17 July.

Federation of Canadian Demographers (1990) *Comments on 'Charting Canada's Future'* (London, Ontario: Population Studies Centre, University of Western Ontario).

Felker, Marcia (1982) 'The Political Economy of Sexism in Industrial Health', *Social Science and Medicine*, vol. 16, pp. 3–13.

Ferguson, Evelyn (1991) 'The Child-Care Crisis: Realities of Women's Caring', in Carol Baines, Patricia Evans and Sheila Neysmith (eds), *Women's Caring. Feminist Perspectives on Social Welfare* (Toronto: McClelland & Stewart) pp. 73–105.

Ferguson, Jonathan (1992) 'Can Tory Plan Help the Poor?', *Toronto Star*, 8 March.

Field, Frank (1989) *The Challenges to Child Benefit* (London: Family Policy Studies Centre).

Fillion, Kate (1989) 'The Daycare Decision', *Saturday Night*, January, pp. 23–30.

Findlay, Sue (1987) 'Facing the State: The Politics of the Women's Movement Reconsidered', in Heather Jon Maroney and Meg Luxton (eds), *Feminism and Political Economy. Women's Work, Women's Struggles* (Toronto: Methuen) pp. 31–50.

Findlay, Sue (1988a) 'Feminist Struggles with the Canadian State, 1966–1988', *Resources for Feminist Research*, vol. 17, no. 3, pp. 5–9.

Findlay, Sue (1988b) 'Canadian Advisory Council on the Status of Women: Contradicitons and Conflicts', *Resources for Feminist Research*, vol. 17, no. 3, p. 90.

Findlay, Sue (1991) 'Making Sense of Pay Equity: Issues for a Feminist Political Practice', in Judy Fudge and Patricia McDermott (eds), *Just Wages. A Feminist Assessment of Pay Equity* (Toronto: University of Toronto Press) pp. 81–109.

Fine, Sean (1990) 'Yuppies Pose Day-Care Problem, Beatty Says', *Globe and Mail*, 24 October.

Finley, Lucinda (1986) 'Transcending Equality Theory: A Way Out of the Maternity and Workplace Debate', *Columbia Law Review*, vol. 86, no. 6, October, pp. 1118–83.

Fisher, Douglas (1989) 'Charting the Changes', *Toronto Sun*, 27 December.

Flannery, Kate and Sara Roeloffs (1984) 'Local Governments' Women's Committees', in Joy Holland (ed.), *Feminist Action* (London: Battle Axe Books) pp. 69–90.

Flavell, Dana (1990) 'The Dilemma over Domestic Workers', *Toronto Star*, 1 February.

Fletcher, A. C. (1981) *Reproductive Hazards of Work* (Manchester: Equal Opportunities Commission).

Fogerty, Jacky and Ervin Grecl (1990) 'W(h)ither Horizontal Equity?: The Distributional Effects of Family Assistance in Australia, 1968–69 to 1989–90', in Peter Whiteford (ed.), *Social Policy in Australia: What Future for the Welfare State?* Proceedings of National Social Policy Conference, Sydney, 5–7 July 1989, Vol 5: Concurrent Sessions, Income Maintenance and Income Security (Kensington: Social Policy Research Centre, The University of New South Wales), pp. 37–60.

Franzway, Suzanne, Dianne Court and R. W. Connell (1989) *Staking a Claim. Feminism, Bureaucracy and the State* (Sydney: Allen & Unwin).

Freeman, Allan (1992) 'Budget Gives Taxpayer "A Break". Income Surtax Cut; Improved Child-Benefit Package Replaces Universal Baby Bonus', *Globe and Mail*, 26 February.

Freestone, David (1983) 'The European Court of Justice', in Juliet Lodge (ed.), *Institutions and Policies of the European Community* (London: Frances Pinter) pp. 43–53.

Frejka, Tomas (1974) 'Which Road Will Population Take on the Way to the 21st Century?', *People*, vol. 1, no. 4, pp. 5–9.

Frejka, Tomas (1980) 'Fertility Trends and Policies: Czechoslovakia in the 1970s', *Population and Development Review*, vol. 6, no. 1 (March) pp. 65–93.

Friendly, Martha and Laurel Rothman (1988) 'No Way to Bring Up Baby.

Ottawa's Child-Care Strategy Misses a Golden Opportunity To Do Things the Proper Way', *Globe and Mail*, 19 January.

Fruman, Leslie (1988) 'Fighting for Fathers' Rights', *Toronto Star*, 8 February.

Gauthier, Anne H. (1991) 'The Economics of Childhood', in Alan R. Pence (ed.), *Childhood as a Social Phenomenon. National Report Canada*, Eurosocial Report 36/6: Childhood as a Social Phenomenon (Vienna: European Centre for Social Welfare Policy and Research) pp. 49–55.

Gelb, Joyce (1989) *Feminism and Politics. A Comparative Perspective* (Berkeley and Los Angeles: University of California Press).

Gerson, Kathleen (1985) *Hard Choice. How Women Decide About Work, Career and Motherhood* (Los Angeles: University of California Press).

Gifford, Jean (1989) 'What Is Child Care For? A Necessary First Question in the Funding Debate', in Child Accident Prevention Foundation of Australia and Australian Early Childhood Association, *Funding Options for Child Care and Their Relation to Social Justice and Quality Issues. A Research Conference*, Melbourne, 11–12 December.

Gimenez, Martha E. (1983) 'Feminism, Pronatalism, and Motherhood', in Joyce Trebilcot (ed.), *Mothering. Essays in Feminist Theory* (Totowa, New Jersey: Rowman and Allanheld) pp. 287–314.

Girard, Alain and Louis Roussel (1982) 'Ideal Family Size, Fertility, and Population Policy in Western Europe', *Population and Development Review*, vol. 8, no. 2, pp. 323–44.

Glezer, Helen (1988) *Maternity Leave in Australia. Employee and Employer Experiences. Report of a Survey*, Australian Institute of Family Studies Monograph no. 7 (Melbourne: Commonwealth of Australia – Australian Institute of Family Studies.

Glezer, Helen (1990) 'Fathers Are Parents too. Parental Leave in Australia', *Family Matters*, no. 27 (November) pp. 23–6.

Glezer, Helen (1991) 'Juggling Work and Family Commitments', *Family Matters*, no. 28, pp. 6–10.

Glossop, Robert (1991) 'Distributive Justice', in Alan R. Pence (ed.) *Childhood as a Social Phenomenon. National Report Canada*, Eurosocial Report 36/6: Childhood as a Social Phenomenon (Vienna: European Centre for Social Welfare Policy and Research) pp. 41–7.

Goar, Carol (1992) 'Nation Deserves Better than Death of Day Care', *Toronto Star*, 9 February.

Goss, Sue (1984) 'Women's Initatives in Local Government', in Martin Body and Colin Fudge (eds), *Local Socialism? Labour Councils and New Left Alternatives* (London: Macmillan) pp. 109–32.

Gotell, Lise (1990) *The Canadian Women's Movement, Equality Rights and the Charter*, Feminist Perspectives no. 16 (Ottawa: Canadian Research Institute for the Advacement of Women).

Government of Canada (1985a) *A Framework for Economic Equality for Canadian Women*, submitted by Ministers Responsible for the Status of Women to the Annual Conference of Ministers, Halifax, November.

Government of Canada (1985b) *Child and Elderly Benefits. Consultation Paper* (Ottawa: Government of Canada).

Government of Canada (1986) *Towards a Labour Force Strategy: A Framework for Training for Women*, submitted by Ministers Responsible for the Status of

Women to the Annual Conference of First Ministers, Vancouver, 21–1 November.

Government of Canada (1987) *Toward a Labour Force Strategfy: A Framework for Training for Women – Progress Reports*, submitted by Ministers Responsible for the Status of Women to the Annual Conference of First Ministers, Toronto, 26–27 November.

Government of Canada (1989) *Integration of Work and Family Responsibilities: Report on Strategies*, submitted by Ministers Responsible for the Status of Women to the Annual Conference of First Ministers, Ottawa, 9–10 November.

Gunningham, Neil (1986) 'Equal Employment Opportunity and Protective Legislation: Directions for Reform', *Federal Law Review*, vol. 16 (September) pp. 240–68.

Gustafsson, S. and T. Meisaari-Polsa (1990) *Why Does Fertility Increase in Sweden?* Report prepared for PA Cambridge Economic Consultants, Department of Economics, University of Amsterdam and Statistics Sweden, Stockholm.

Haddow, Rodney (1990) 'The Poverty Policy Community in Canada's Liberal Welfare State', in William D. Coleman and Grace Skogstad (eds), *Policy Communities and Public Policy in Canada: A Structural Approach* (Mississagua, Ontario: Copp Clark Pitman) pp. 212–37.

Hague, Helen (1989) 'Commission's Campaign for Equality Threatened by Cuts', *Independent*, 18 April.

Harding, Ann (1986) *Assistance for Families with Children and the Social Security Review*, Background/Discussion Paper no. 4 (Woden ACT: Social Security Review).

Harel-Giasson, Francine, Marie-Francoise Marchis-Mouren and Louise Martel (1987) 'The Challenge of Becoming a Professional Chartered Accountant and a Mother in Early Adulthood', *Equal Opportunities International*, Vol. 6, no. 4, pp. 21–4.

Hawkins, Freda (1987) 'Non-European Receiving Countries', in OECD, Working Party on Migration, *The Future of Migration*. Proceedings of a Conference of National Experts on the Future of Migration, 13–15 May, 1986 (Paris: Organisation for Economic Co-operation and Development) pp. 86–109.

Hawkins, Freda (1991) *Critical Years in Immigration. Canada and Australia Compared*, 2nd edn (Kingston and Montreal: McGill-Queen's University Press).

Hay, John (1982) 'Canada's Leaking Immigration Lifeboat', *Maclean's*, vol. 95, no. 45, 8 November.

Hay, John (1990) 'Charting Canada's Future', *Ottawa Citizen*, 21 January.

Health and Welfare Canada (1989) *Charting Canada's Future. A Report of the Demographic Review* (Ottawa: Minister of Supply and Services Canada).

Heitlinger, Alena (1979) *Women and State Socialism. Sex Inequality in the Soviet Union and Czechoslovakia* (London/Montreal: Macmillan/McGill-Queen's University Press).

Heitlinger, Alena (1985) 'Women in Eastern Europe: Survey of Literature', *Women's Studies International Forum*, vol. 8, no. 2, pp. 147–52.

Heitlinger, Alena (1987a) *Reproduction, Medicine and the Socialist State* (London/New York: Macmillan/St Martin's Press).

Heitlinger, Alena (1987b) 'Maternity Leaves, Protective Legislation, and Sex
  Equality: Eastern European and Canadian Perspectives', in Heather Jon
  Maroney and Meg Luxton (eds), *Feminism and Political Economy. Women's
  Work, Women's Struggles* (Toronto: Methuen) pp. 247–61.
Heitlinger, Alena (1991) 'Pronatalism and Women's Equality Policies',
  European Journal of Population, vol. 7, no. 4, pp. 341–75.
Hernes, Helga Maria (1987) *Welfare State and Woman Power. Essays in State
  Feminism* (Oslo: Norwegian University Press).
Hevener, Natalie Kaufman (1982) *International Law and the Status of Women*
  (a Westview Replica edition).
Hewlett, Sylvia Ann (1986) *Lesser Life. The Myth of Women's Liberation in
  America* (New York: William Morrow).
Hibbert, Vicky (1989) 'Childcare. Bringing Women Back into Employment',
  Equal Opportunities Review, no. 23 (January/February) pp. 14–21.
Hochschild, Arlie with Anne Machung (1989) *The Second Shift: Working
  Parents and the Revolution at Home* (New York: Viking Penguin).
Höhn, Charlotte (1988) 'Population Policies in Advanced Societies: Pronatalist
  and Migration Strategies', *European Journal of Population*, vol. 3, no. 3/4
  (July) pp. 459–81.
Höhn, Charlotte (1989) 'Policies Affecting Families and the Population', in
  Jacques Légaré, T.R. Balakrishnan, Roderic P. Beaujot (eds), *The Family in
  Crisis: A Population Crisis?* Proceedings of a Colloquium organised by the
  Federation of Canadian Demographers and sponsored by the Royal Society of
  Canada (Ottawa: The Royal Society of Canada) pp. 385–94.
Holterman, Sally (1986) *The Costs of Implementing Parental Leave in Great
  Britain* (Manchester: Equal Opportunities Commission).
Home Office (1989) *News Release. Ministerial Group on Women's Issues –
  Choice and High Standards Are the Key to the Provision of Childcare*, 11
  April.
Hoskyns, Catherine (1985) 'Women's Equality and the European Community',
  Feminist Review (Summer) pp. 71–88.
Hoskyns, Catherine (1988) '"Give Us Equal Pay and We'll Open Our Own
  Doors" – A Study of the Impact in the Federal Republic of Germany and the
  Republic of Ireland of the European Community's Policy on Women's
  Rights', in Mary Buckley and Malcolm Anderson (eds), *Women, Equality and
  Europe* (London: Macmillan) pp. 33–55.
House of Commons Standing Committee on Labour, Employment and Im-
  migration (1985) 'Second Report to the House', *Minutes of Proceedings and
  Evidence*, First Session, 33rd Parliament, 20 (1984–5), 3–6.
House of Lords. Select Committee on the European Communities (1985)
  Parental Leave and Leave for Family Reasons. With Minutes of Evidence
  (London: HMSO)
Hurford, Chris (1986) 'Address to the Third National Conference of the
  Australian Population Association, Adelaide, 3 December', in *Proceedings of
  the Third Australian Population Conference*, vol. 1, pp. 1–9.
Hyman, Prue (1990) 'The Royal Commission on Social Policy (New Zealand)
  and the Social Security Review (Australia) – A Comparison of Their Reports
  and Recommendations, Particularly in Terms of Their Implications for
  Women', in Russell Ross (ed.), *Social Policy in Australia: What Future for*

336 *Women's Equality, Demography and Public Policies*

the Welfare State? Proceedings of National Social Policy Conference, Sydney, 5–7 July, vol. 4: Concurrent Sessions, Social Policies in Australia and New Zealand (Kensington: Social Policy Research Centre, The University of New South Wales) pp. 51–64.

ILO (1985) *Maternity Benefits in the Eighties. An ILO Global Surevey (1964–84)* (Geneva: International Labour Office).

ILO (1987) 'Women Workers: Protection or Equality?', *Conditions of Work Digest*, vol. 6, no. 2.

ILO (1988) 'Work and Family: The Child Care Challenge', *Conditions of Work Digest*, vol. 7, no. 2.

Institute of Intergovernmental Relations (1991) *Approaches to National Standards in Federal Systems*. A research report prepared for the Government of Ontario (Kingston, Ontario: Institute of Intergovernmental Relations, Queen's University).

Jaggar, Alison M. (1983) *Feminist Politics and Human Nature* (Totowa, New Jersey: Rowman & Allanheld).

Johnson, Andrew F. (1985) 'Restructuring Family Allowances: "Good Politics at No Cost"?', in Jacqueline S. Ismael (ed.), *Canadian Social Welfare Policy. Federal and Provincial Dimensions* (Kingston and Montreal: The Institute of Public Administration of Canada and McGill-Queen's University Press) pp. 105–19.

Johnson, A. W. (1987) 'Social Policy in Canada: The Past as it Conditions the Present', in Shirley B. Seward (ed.), *The Future of Social Welfare Systems in Canada and the United Kingdom*. Proceedings of a Canada/UK Colloquium, 17–18 October 1986, Ottawa/Meech Lake (Ottawa: The Institute for Research on Public Policy) pp. 29–70.

Johnson, Laura and Janice Dineen (1981) *The Kin Trade. The Day Care Crisis in Canada* (Toronto: McGraw-Hill Ryerson).

Jones, Frank (1990) 'Why Dads Don't Want To Stay Home', *Toronto Star*, 6 August.

Jones, Judy (1989) 'Patten's Balancing Act on Childcare Policy', *Independent*, 12 January.

Jones, Charles, Lorna Marsden and Lorne Tepperman (1990) *Lives of Their Own. The Individualization of Women's Lives* (Toronto: Oxford University Press).

Jones, Laura and Maxine Nunn (1986) 'Reproductive Hazards in the Workplace', *Women and Environments* (Spring) pp. 14–16.

Jonkheere, Christine and Florence Gerard (1984) 'Women at Work in the European Community: 50 Questions, 50 Answers', *Equal Opportunities International*, vol. 3, no. 3, pp. 1–16.

Joshi, Heather (1987) *The Cash Oportunity Costs of Childbeaqring: An Approach to Estimation Using British Data*, Discussion Paper no. 208 (London: Centre for Economic Policy Research).

Joshi, Heather (1989) *Changes in Family Structure and their Linkages with the Labour Market*. Paper presented at the 21st IUSSP International Population Conference, New Delhi, September.

Joshi, Heather (1991) 'Sex and Motherhood as Handicaps in the Labour Market', in Mavis Maclean and Dulcie Groves (eds), *Women's Issues in Social Policy* (London: Routledge) pp. 179–93.

Joske, Stephen (1989) *The Economics of Immigration: Who Benefits?* A background paper from the Legislative Research Service, Department of the Parliamentary Library (Canberra: The Parliament of the Commonwealth of Australia).

Kaloyanova, Fina (1976) 'Women at Work', *World Health* (August–September) pp. 32–5.

Kamerman, Sheila (1980a) 'Managing Work and Family Life: A Comparative Policy Overview', in Peter Moss and Nickie Fonda (eds), *Work and the Family* (London: Temple Smith) pp. 87–109.

Kamerman, Sheila B., Alfred J. Kahn and Paul Kingston (1983) *Maternity Policies and Working Women* (New York: Columbia University Press).

Kendig, Hal L. and John McCallum (1986) *Greying Australia. Future Impacts of Population Ageing* (Canberra: The Migration Committee, National Population Council, Commonwealth of Australia).

Kernaghan, Kenneth (1982) 'Politics, Public Administration and Canada's Aging Population', *Canadian Public Policy*, vol. 8, no. 1 (Winter) pp. 69–79.

Kidston, Robert (1991) 'New Work and Family Unit Established', *Family Matters*, no. 28 (April) p. 16.

Kitchen, Brigitte (1987) 'The Introduction of Family Allowances in Canada', in Allan Moscovitch and Jim Albert (eds), *The Benevolent State. The Growth of Welfare in Canada* (Toronto: Garamond Press) pp. 222–41.

Klinger, Andras (1987) 'Policy Response and Effects', in *Proceedings of the European Population Conference 1987: Issues and Prospects*, Jyvaskyle, Findland, 11–16 June.

Klug, Francesca (1989) '"Oh to be in England": the British Case Study', in Nira Yuval-Davis and Floya Anthias (eds), *Woman-Nation-State* (London: Macmillan) pp. 16–35.

Kome, Penny (1983) *The Taking of Twenty-Eight* (Toronto: Women's Press).

Kramar, Robin (1988) 'Progress Towards Equal Employment Opportunity in 1987: Two Steps Forward, One Step Back', *Human Resource Management Australia*, vol. 26, no. 1, pp. 33–45.

Labour Canada (1981) *Canadian Women and Job Related Laws* (Ottawa: Women's Bureau, Labour Canada).

Labour Canada (1984) *Maternity and Child Care Leave in Canada* (Ottawa: Minister of Supply and Services).

Labour Canada (1989) *The Selective Protection of Canadian Working Women* (Ottawa: Women's Bureau, Labour Canada).

Lalonde, Marc (1975) *Status of Women in Canada* (Ottawa: Information Canada).

Land, Hilary (1975) 'The Introduction of Family Allowances: An Act of Historic Justice', in Phoebe Hall *et al.* (eds), *Change, Choice and Conflict in Social Policy* (London: Heinemann) pp. 157–230.

Land, Hilary (1978) 'The Child Benefit Fiasco', in Kathleen Jones (ed.), *The Yearbook of Social Policy in Britain 1977* (London: Routledge and Kegan Paul) pp. 116–31.

Landau, Eve C. (1985) *The Rights of Working Women in the European Community*, The European Perspectives Series (Luxembourg: Office for Offical Publications of the European Communities).

Landsberg, Michele (1991) 'It's Nannies vs. Employers in this Ploy', *Toronto Star*, 23 February.

Law, Sylvia A. (1984) 'Rethinking Sex and the Constitution', *University of Pennsylvania Law Review*, vol. 132, no. 5, June, pp. 955–1040.

Laxer, James (1991) *Inventing Europe. The Rise of a New World Power* (Toronto: Lester Publishing).

Leeuw, Frans L. (1985) 'Population Policy in Industrialized Countries: Evaluating Policy Theories to Assess the Demographic Impact of Population Policy', *Genus* (Rome), vol. 41, no. 1, pp. 1–19.

Lero, Donna S. (1991) 'Child Care Needs and Child Care Use Patterns', in Statistics Canada, Family and Community Supports Division (ed.), *Caring Communities. Proceedings of the Symposium on Social Supports*, (Ottawa: Minister of Supply and Services Canada) pp. 111–24.

Lero, Donna S. and Irene Kyle (1990) 'Work, Family and Child Care in Ontario', in Laura C. Johnson and Dick Barnhorst (eds), *Children, Families and Public Policy in the 90s* (Toronto: Thompson Educational Publishing) pp. 25–72.

Lesthaeghe, Ron (1988) *Are Immigrants Substitutes for Births?* Paper presented at 'Symposium on Population Change and European Society', sponsored by the Commission of the European Economic Community and the European University Institute, European University Institute, Florence, 7–10 December.

Levi, Margaret and Sara Singleton (1991) 'Women in "the Working Man's Paradise": Sole Parents, the Women's Movement and the Social Policy Bargain in Australia', *Social Research*, vol. 58, no. 3 (Fall) pp. 627–51.

Lewis, Jane (1983) 'Dealing with Dependency. State Practices and Social Realities, 1870–1945', in Jane Lewis (ed.), *Women's Welfare Women's Rights* (London: Croom Helm) pp. 17–38.

List, Wilfred (1982) 'Bell to Pay for 15-week Maternity', *Globe and Mail*, 16 February.

Livi-Bacci, M. (1974) 'Population Policy in Western Europe', *Population Studies*, vol. 28, no. 2 (July) pp. 191–204.

Lodge, Juliet (1983) 'Introduction', in Juliet Lodge (ed.), *Institutions and Policies of the European Community* (London: Frances Pinter) pp. xii–xv.

Lodh, Francoise (1987) *Explaining Fertility Decline in the West (With Special Reference to Canada): A Critique of Research Results from the Social Science* (Ottawa: The Vanier Institute of the Family).

Lovenduski, Joni (1986) *Women and European Politics. Contemporary Feminism and Public Policy* (London: Wheatsheaf Books).

Lucie, Patricia (1988) 'Discrimination Against Males in the USA', in Sheila McLean and Noreen Burrows (eds), *The Legal Relevance of Gender. Some Aspects of Sex-Based Discrimination* (London: Macmillan) pp. 216–43.

Maas, Frank (1988) *A Fair Go for Aussie Kids? Recent Developments in Australian Social Policy Affecting Children and their Families.* Paper presented at the Family Policy Studies Centre National Conference on 'Child Support: Policies for the Future', London, 1 December.

Maas, Frank and Peter McDonald (1989) 'Income Splitting. No Answer to the Needs of Women, Families or the Economy', *Family Matters*, no. 24 (August) pp. 34–7.

MacBride-King, Judith and Hélène Paris (1989) 'Balancing Work and Family

Responsibilities', *Canadian Business Review*, vol. 16, no. 2 (Autumn) pp. 1–5.

MacIntyre, Sally (1976) 'Who Wants Babies: The Social Construction of "Instincts"', in Diana Leonard Barker and Sheila Allen (eds), *Sexual Divisions and Society. Process and Change* (London: Tavistock) pp. 150–74.

Macnicol, John (1980) *The Movement for Family Allowances, 1918–45: A Study in Social Policy Development* (London: Heinemann).

Macpherson, Don (1990) 'More Babies Won't Boost Population', *Montreal Gazette*, 28 April.

MacQueen, Ken (1988) 'Cabinet OK on Paternity Leave Would Be Worth $5,000 to Parents', *Montreal Gazette*, 24 September.

Malarek, Victor (1989) 'Quebec Grapples with how to Maintain French-speaking Majority', *Globe and Mail*, 30 October.

Mansbridge, Stanley H. (1987) 'Social Policy in Canada: Past, Present, Future', in Shirley B. Seward (ed.), *The Future of Social Welfare Systems in Canada and the United Kingdom*. Proceedings of a Canada/UK Colloquium, 17–18 October 1986, Ottawa/Meech Lake (Ottawa: The Institute for Research on Public Policy) pp. 71–9.

Marsden, Lorna (1972) *Population Probe: Canada* (Canada: Copp Clark Publishing).

Marsden, Lorna (1980) 'The Role of the National Action Committee on the Status of Women in Facilitating Equal Pay Policy in Canada', in Ronnie Steinberg Ratner (ed.), *Equal Employment Policy for Women. Strategies for Implementation in the United States, Canada and Western Europe* (Philadelphia: Temple University) pp. 242–60.

Marston, Paul (1988) 'Seven-year Breaks for Teachers', *Daily Telegraph*, 11 March.

Martin, Jean and Ceridwen Roberts (1984) *Women and Employment. A Lifetime Perspective*, the report of the 1980 DE/OPSC Women and Employment Survey (London: HMSO).

Maternity Alliance (1988) *Pregnant at Work* (London: Maternity Alliance).

Mayfield, Margie (1985) *Employer-Supported Child Care in Canada* (Ottawa: Health and Welfare Canada).

McCabe, Nora (1990) 'Mommy Wars. Who Mothers Best: Careerists or Stay-At-Homes?', *Chateleine*, March.

McCarthy, Michael (1986) *Campaigning for the Poor. CPAG & the Politics of Welfare* (London: Croom Helm).

McDonald, Peter (1990) 'The Costs of Children. A Review of Methods and Results', *Family Matters*, no. 27 (November), pp. 18–22.

McInnes, Craig (1990) 'Ontario to Increase Parental Leave', *Globe and Mail*, 14 November.

McIntosh, Alison C. (1983) *Population Policy in Western Europe. Responses to Low Fertility in France, Sweden, and West Germany* (New York: M. E. Sharpe).

McIntosh, Alison (1986) 'Recent Pronatalist Policies in Western Europe', *Population and Development Review* (Supplement), vol. 12, pp. 318–34.

McIntosh, Alison and Jason Finkle (1985) 'Demographic Rationalism and Political Systems', in International Union for the Scientific Study of

340   *Women's Equality, Demography and Public Policies*

Population, *International Population Conference*, Florence, 5–12 June, vol. 3, pp. 319–28.

Meehan, Elizabeth (1983) 'Equal Opportunity Policies: Some Implications for Women of Contrasts Between Enforcement Bodies in Britain and the USA', in Jane Lewis (ed.), *Women's Welfare Women's Rights* (London: Croom Helm) pp. 170–192.

Michel, Andrée (1986) *Positive Action for the Benefit of Women. Preliminary Study* (Strasbourg: Council of Europe).

Minister of Supply and Services Canada (1990) *1990–91 Estimates. Part III. Status of Women Canada. Expenditure Plan* (Ottawa: Minister of Supply and Services).

Mishra, Ramesh (1990) *The Welfare State in Capitalist Society. Policies of Retrenchment and Maintenance in Europe, North America and Australia* (Toronto: University of Toronto Press).

Moller, J. (1989) 'A Response to Funding Options for Child Care and their Relation to Social Justice and Quality Issues' in Child Accident Prevention Foundation of Australia and Australian Early Childhood Association, *Funding Options for Child Care and Their Relation to Social Justice and Quality Issues. A Research Conference*, Melbourne, 11–12 December.

Mollins, Carl (1992) 'The Baby Bonus: R. I. P. New Child Benefits Depend on Means Test', *Maclean's*, 9 March.

Moloney, Joanne (1989) 'Maternity', *Canadian Social Trends* (Autumn) pp. 9–12.

Morton, Mary (1988) 'Dividing the Wealth, Sharing the Poverty: the (Re)-formation of "Family" in Law in Ontario', *The Canadian Review of Sociology and Anthropology*, vol. 25, no. 2, pp. 254–75.

Moss, Peter, Childcare Network Co-ordinator (1988) *Childcare and Equality of Opportunity*. Consolidated Report to the European Commmission (Brussel: Commission of the European Communities).

Mottershead, Peter (1988) *Recent Developments in Childcare: A Review* (London: Equal Opportunities Commission, HMSO).

Mullen, Tom (1988) 'Affirmative Action', in Sheila McLean and Noreen Burrows (eds), *The Legal Relevance of Gender. Some Aspects of Sex-Based Discrimination* (London: Macmillan Press) pp. 244–66.

Munter, Alex (1990) '1970 Royal Commission Report Still Debated by Feminists', *Ottawa Citizen*, 1 November.

National Council of Welfare (1983) *Family Allowances for All?* (Ottawa: Government of Canada).

National Council of Welfare (1985) *Opportunity for Reform. A Response to the Consultation Paper on Child and Elderly Benefits* (Ottawa: Government of Canada).

National Council of Welfare (1988) *Child Care: A Better Alternative* (Ottawa: Ministry of Supply and Services).

National Council of Welfare (1990) *Women and Poverty Revisited* (Ottawa: Minister of Supply and Services).

National Population Inquiry, W.D. Borrie, Chairman (1975) *Population and Australia: A Demographic Analysis and Projection*, 2 vols (Canberra: The Parliament of the Commonwealth of Australia).

National Population Inquiry, (1978) Supplementary Report. *Population and*

Australia, Recent Demographic Trends and Their Implications (Canberra: The Parliament of the Commonwealth of Australia).

Nevitte, Neil and Roger Gibbins (1990) *New Elites in Old States. Ideologies in the Anglo-American Democracies* (Don Mills, Ontario: Oxford University Press).

New, Caroline and Miriam David (1985) *For the Children's Sake: Making Child Care More than Women's Business* (Harmondsworth: Penguin Books).

Ni Bhrolchain, M. (1986a) 'Women's Paid Work and the Timing of Births: Longitudinal Evidence', *European Journal of Population*, vol. 2, pp. 43–70.

Ni Bhrolchain, M. (1986b) 'The Interpretation and Role of Work-associated Accelerated Childbearing in Post-war Britain', *European Journal of Population*, vol. 2, pp. 135–54.

Nielsen, Ruth (1983) *Equality Legislation in A Comparative Perspective – Towards State Feminism?* (Copenhagen: Kvindevidenskabelight Forlag).

Niemann, Lindsay (1984) *Wage Discrimination and Women Workers: The Move Towards Equal Pay for Work of Equal Value in Canada*. Women's Bureau, Labour Canada, Series A: Equality in the Workplace (Ottawa: Ministry of Supply and Services).

Niphuis-Nell, Mary (1987) *The Emancipation of the Sexes and a Pronatalist Population Policy in the Netherlands*. Paper presented at the Third Interdisciplinary Congress on Women, Trinity College, Dublin, 6–10 July.

Novarra, Virginia (1980) *Women's Work, Men's Work. The Ambivalence of Equality* (London: Marion Boyars).

Oakley, Robin and Roland Rudd (1988) 'Drive to Help Mothers at Work in 1990s', *The Times*, 14 November.

O'Donovan, Katherine and Erika Szyszczak (1988) *Equality and Sex Discrimination in Law* (Oxford: Basil Blackwell).

OECD (1979) *Equal Opportunities for Women* (Paris: OECD).

OECD (1985) *The Integration of Women into the Economy* (Paris: OECD).

OECD (1988) *Ageing Populations. The Social Policy Implications* (Paris: OECD).

OECD, Working Party on the Role of Women in the Economy (1989) *Equal Employment Opportunity Policies and Programs: Evaluation Panel's Report*, MAS/WP6 (89) 3, 1st revision.

O'Grady, Frances and Wakefield, Heather (1989) *Women Work and Maternity. The Inside Story* (London: Maternity Alliance).

Oldman, David (1991) *Childhood as a Social Phenomenon. National Report Scotland*, Eurosocial Reports vol. 36 (Vienna: European Centre for Social Welfare Policy and Research).

O'Neil, Maureen (1990) *Institutional Structures*. Paper presented at an interdisciplinary conference entitled 'Women and the Canadian State' to mark the 20th anniversary of the Report of the Royal Commission on the Status of Women in Canada and to evaluate the successes, the failures and the limits of State response to the needs of Canadian women, Faculty of Law, Ottawa University, 1–2 November.

Ontario Women's Directorate (undated) *Managing Employment Equity. Introduction to a Series* (Toronto: Ontario Women's Directorate, Minister Responsible for Women's Issues).

OSW, Department of Prime Minister and Cabinet (1989a) *The Office of the*

342   *Women's Equality, Demography and Public Policies*

Status of Women. An Introduction (Canberra: Australian Government Publishing Service).

OSW, Department of Prime Minister and Cabinet (1989b) *Women's Budget Statement 1989–90*, Budget Related Paper no. 6 (Canberra: AGPS).

OSW, Department of Prime Minister and Cabinet (1989c) *A Say, a Choice, a Fair Go. The Government's National Agenda for Women* (Canberra: AGPS).

OSW, Department of Prime Minister and Cabinet (1989d) *National Agenda for Women Implementation Report* (Canberra: AGPS).

OSW, Department of the Prime Minister and Cabinet (1990) *Realising the Potential. Women and Award Restructuring*, Discussion Paper of the Award Restructuring Workshop sponsored by the Office of the Status of Women (Canberra: Commonwealth of Australia).

Oxley, Carol (1987) *The Structure of General Family Provision in Australia and Overseas: A Comparative Study*, Background/Discussion Paper no. 17 (Woden ACT: Social Security Review).

Pahl, Jan (1980) 'Patterns of Money Management within Marriage', *Journal of Social Policy*, vol. 9, no. 3, pp. 313–35.

Palmer, John (1991) 'EC Rules on Pay During Pregnancy', *Manchester Guardian Weekly*, 17 November.

Paltiel, Freda (1972) *Status of Women in Canada. Report of the Co-ordinator Status of Women* (Ottawa: Information Canada).

Pascall, Gillian (1986) *Social Policy: A Feminist Analysis* (London: Tavistock).

Pavlík, Zdenek (1978) 'Baby Boom in Czechoslovakia', *Intercom*, vol. 6, no. 6, pp. 8–9.

Peterborough Examiner (1992) Birth Rate Rises among Older Women', 31 March.

Phillips, Anne (1987) 'Introduction', in Anne Phillips (ed.), *Feminism and Equality* (Oxford: Basil Blackwell) pp. 1–21.

Phillips, Angela and Ruth Evans (1987) *Working Parents' Rights. A Maternity Alliance Charter* (London: Maternity Alliance).

Piachaud, David (1979) *The Cost of a Child* (London: Child Poverty Action Group).

Piachaud, David (1981) *Children and Poverty* (London: Child Poverty Action Group).

Picard, Andre (1991) 'Quebec Birth Rate Multiplies', *Globe and Mail*, 5 January.

Pietila, Hilka and Jeanne Vickers (1990) *Making Women Matter. The Role of the United Nations* (London: Zed Books).

Pigg, Sue (1991) 'Day Care in Metro Nearing Collapse', *Sunday Star*, 27 January.

Pigott, Susan and Christa Freiler (1990) 'What Can We Do to Put Food on their Tables', *Globe and Mail*, 12 October.

Prentice, Susan (1988) 'The "Mainstreaming" of Day Care', *Resources for Feminist Research*, special issue on 'Feminist Perspectives on the Canadian State', vol. 17, no. 3, pp. 59–63.

Presser, Harriet B. (1986) 'Comment on Samuel H. Preston's "Changing Values and Falling Birth Rates"', *Population and Development Review*, vol. 12 (Supplement) pp. 196–200.

Preston, Samuel H. (1984) 'Children and the Elderly: Divergent Paths for America's Dependents', *Demography*, vol. 21, no. 4, pp. 435–455.

Public Service Commission of Canada (1984) *Family Responsibility Leave in the Federal Public Service* (Ottawa: Minister of Supply and Services Canada).

Quintin, Odile (1988) 'The Policies of the European Communities with Special Reference to the Labour Market', in Mary Buckley and Malcolm Anderson (eds), *Women, Equality and Europe* (London: Macmillan Press) pp. 71–77.

Rauhala, Ann (1988) 'Canada Lags in Parental Benefits, Expert Says', *Globe and Mail*, 13 May.

Rauhala, Ann and Susan Delacourt (1988) 'Ottawa Urged to Expand Benefits to "Give Men a Chance to Nurture"', *Globe and Mail*, 10 June.

Richmond, Anthony (1987) 'Demographic Research and Public Policy: The Case of Immigration', in *Contributions to Demography: Methodological and Substantive*, vol. 2, pp. 597–622 (Edmonton: Department of Sociology, University of Alberta).

Richmond, Anthony (1991) 'Immigration and Multiculturalism in Canada and Australia: The Contradictions and Crises of the 1980s', *International Journal of Canadian Studies*, vol. 3 (Spring) pp. 87–110.

Riley, Denise (1983) *War in the Nursery. Theories of the Child and Mother* (London: Virago).

Romaniuc, Anatole (1984) *Current Demographic Analysis. Fertility in Canada: from Baby-boom to Baby-bust* (Ottawa: Statistics Canada, Minister of Supply and Services).

Romaniuc, Anatole (1989) 'Fertility in Canada: A Long View – A Contribution to the Debates on Population', in Jacques Légaré, T. R. Balakrishnan, Roderic P. Beaujot (eds), *The Family in Crisis: A Population Crisis?* Proceedings of a Colloquium organised by the Federation of Canadian Demographers and sponsored by the Royal Society of Canada (Ottawa: The Royal Society of Canada) pp. 251–70.

Rose, Michael (1988) 'Revenge of the Cradle', *Maclean's*, 30 May.

Ross, David (1984) 'The Great Universality Debate: What Was It All About?', *Perception*, vol. 8, no. 3, pp. 5–8.

Rowbotham, Sheila (1989) *The Past Before Us. Feminism in Action Since the 1960s* (London: Pandora Press).

Rowland, D.T. (1986) 'Immigration and Ageing', *Journal of the Australian Population Association*, vol. 3, no. 1 (May) pp. 18–25.

Rudd, Roland (1988) 'Give Career Women 7-year Baby Break, CBI tells Employers', *The Times*, 12 March.

Ruggie, Mary (1984) *The State and Working Women. A Comparative Study of Britain and Sweden* (Princeton: Princeton University Press).

Russell, Graeme (1984) 'Changing Patterns of Divisions of Labour for Paid Work and Child Care', in *XXth International CFR Seminar on Social Change and Family Policies*, Melbourne, Australia, 19–24 August, Free Papers, Part 4 (Melbourne: The Australian Institute of Family Studies) pp. 1069–96.

Russo, Nancy Felipe (1979) 'Overview: Sex Roles, Fertility and the Motherhood Mandate', *Psychology of Women Quarterly*, vol. 4, no. 1 (Fall) pp. 7–15.

Ryan, Lyndall (1990) 'Feminism and the Federal Bureaucracy, 1972-1983', in

Sophie Watson (ed.), *Playing the State. Australian Feminist Interventions* (Sydney: Allen & Unwin) pp. 71–84.

Sawer, Marian (1989) *The Battle for the Family: Family Policy in Australian Electoral Politics in the 1980s,* Urban Research Unit Paper no. 15 (Canberra: Research School of Social Sciences, Australian National University).

Sawer, Marian (1990) *Sisters in Suits. Women and Public Policy in Australia* (Sydney: Allen & Unwin).

Sawer, Marian (1991) 'Why Has the Women's Movement Had More Influence on Government in Australia than Elsewhere?' in Francis G. Castles (ed.), *Australia Compared: People, Politics, Policies* (Allen & Unwin) pp. 258–77.

Scott, Joan W. (1988) 'Deconstructing Equality-Versus-Difference: or, the Uses of Poststructuralist Theory for Feminism', *Feminist Studies,* vol. 14, no. 1 (Spring) pp. 33–50.

Séguin, Rhéal (1990) 'Parental Leave Extended', *Globe and Mail,* 15 November.

Sharir, Shmuel (1990) 'On Population and Well-Being: An Economist's View', in Federation of Canadian Demographers, *Comments on 'Charting Canada's Future'* (London, Ontario: Population Studies Centre, University of Western Ontario) pp. 18–26.

Shifrin, Leonard (1988) 'Quebec's Message to Women: Make Babies', *Toronto Star,* 23 May.

Smart, Carol (1989) *Feminism and the Power of the Law* (London: Routledge).

Smith, Dan (1988) 'Paternity Leave Fight Abandoned', *Toronto Star,* 25 January.

Spakes, Patricia (1989) 'Reshaping the Goals of Family Policy: Sexual Equality, Not Protection', *Affilia. Journal of Women and Social Work,* vol. 4, no. 3 (Fall) pp. 7–24.

Special Parliamentary Committee on Child Care (1987) *Sharing the Responsibility* (Ottawa: Minister of Supply and Services).

Spiers, Rosemary (1991) 'Do We Care About Poor Kids?' *The Toronto Star,* 14 April.

Srb, Vladimír (1981) 'Woman's Fertility in Czechoslovakia during 1970–1979', *Demosta,* vol. 14, no. 2, pp. 44–9.

Status of Women Canada (1985) *The Nairobi World Conference on Women* (Ottawa: Status of Women Canada).

Status of Women Canada (1987) *National Case Studies: Canada.* Background Paper for the United Nations Seminar on National Machinery for Monitoring and Improving the Status of Women, Vienna, 29 September–2 October.

Status of Women Canada (1988) *Status of Women Canada: Working for Equality* (Ottawa: Status of Women Canada).

Status of Women Canada (1989a) *Dimensions of Equality: An Update of the Federal Government Work Plan for Women* (Ottawa: Status of Women Canada).

Status of Women Canada (1989b) *Directory of Federal Government Programs and Services for Women* (Ottawa: Status of Women Canada).

Status of Women Canada (1990) *Fact Sheets – 1990 Update. Nairobi Forward-looking Strategies for the Advancement of Women. Issues and the Canadian Situation* (Ottawa: Status of Women Canada).

Steiner, Gilbert (1984) 'Family Policy as Latter-Day Children's Policy', in *XXth*

International CFR Seminar on Social Change and Family Policies, Melbourne, Australia, 19–24 August, Key Papers, Part 1 (Melbourne: The Australian Institute of Family Studies) pp. 209–29.

Stellman, Jean Mager (1977) *Women's Work, Women's Health. Myths and Realities* (New York: Pantheon).

Stienstra, Deborah (1988) 'A Feminist Perspective on the Canadian State at the International Level', *Resources for Feminist Research*, special issue on 'Feminist Perspectives on the Canadian State', vol. 17, no. 3 (September) pp. 83–86.

Summers, Ann (1986) 'Mandarins or Missionaries: Women in the Federal Bureaucracy', in Norma Grieve and Ailsa Burns (eds), *Australian Women: New Feminist Perspectives* (Melbourne: Oxford University Press) pp. 59–67.

Sweet, Lois (1987) 'Is Women's Advisory Group Pandering to Petty Politics?' *Toronto Star*, 18 December. Reprinted in *Resources for Feminist Research*, vol. 17, no. 3, 1988, pp. 90–1.

Sweet, Lois (1990) 'Day Care in Schools. Will Ontario Act on Major Changes Urged in MPP's Report?', *Toronto Star*, 15 July.

Task Force on Child Care (1986) *Report of the Task Force on Child Care* (Ottawa: Minister of Supply and Services).

Taylor, Chris (1987) *Demography and Immigration in Canada: Challenge and Opportunity.* Paper presented to the Fall Conference of the Association for Canadian Studies in the Netherlands, 'The Canadian Society: A Mosaic', De Eenhoorn, Amersfoort (Ottawa: Employment and Immigration Canada).

Taylor, Marilyn (1988) 'Move that Penalises the Family', *Independent*, 29 October.

Teitelbaum, Michael (1990) 'Population Policies in Other Countries', in Roderic Beaujot (ed.), *Facing the Demographic Future.* Summary of a conference oranised by the Royal Society of Canada and the Federation of Canadian Demographers, Laval University, Quebec, 7–9 June (Ottawa: Royal Society of Canada) pp. 19–21.

Teitelbaum, Michael S. and Jay Winter (1985) *The Fear of Population Decline* (San Diego: Academic Press).

Tomlinson, Richard (1984) 'The French Population Debate', *The Public Interest*, no. 76 (Summer) pp. 111–20.

Tongue, Carol and Eva Eberhardt (1987) *Women and Social Policies of the European Community.* Unpublished manuscript.

Townsend, Peter (1986) 'Foreword: Democracy for the Poor', in Michael McCarthy (ed.), *Campaigning for the Poor. CPAG & the Politicis of Welfare* (London: Croom Helm).

Townson, Monica (1983) *A National System of Fully-Paid Parental Leave for Canada: Policy Choices, Costs and Funding Mechanisms* (Ottawa: Women's Bureau, Labour Canada).

Townson, Monica (1987) *Women's Labour Force Participation, Fertility Rates, and the Implications for Economic Development and Government Policy*, Studies in Social Policy (Ottawa: The Institute for Research on Public Policy).

Townson, Monica (1988) *Leave for Employees with Family Responsibilities* (Ottawa: Women's Bureau, Labour Canada).

Tuohy, Carolyn (1990) 'Institutions and Interests in the Occupational Health

Arena', in William D. Coleman and Grace Skogstad (eds), *Policy Communities and Public Policy in Canada: A Structural Approach* (Toronto: Copp Clark Pittman) pp. 238–65.

Turner, Bryan S. (1986) *Equality* (Chichester and London: Ellis Horwood and Tavistock).

Ungerson, Clare (1985) 'Motherhood. Introduction', in Clare Ungerson (ed.), *Women and Social Policy. A Reader* (Basingstoke: Macmillan Press) pp. 1–8.

United Nations, Economic and Social Commission for Asia and the Pacific (1982) *Population of Australia*, Country Monograph Series no. 9, 2 vols (New York: United Nations).

United Nations (1985) *The Nairobi Forward-Looking Strategies for the Advancement of Women*, adopted at the World Conference to Review and Appraise the Achievements of the United Nations Decade for Women: Equality, Development and Peace (New York: United Nations).

Vallance, Elizabeth (1988) 'Do Women Make a Difference? The Impact of Women MEPs on Community Equality Policy', in Mary Buckley and Malcolm Anderson (eds), *Women, Equality and Europe* (London: Macmillan).

Vallance, Elizabeth and Elizabeth Davies (1986) *Women of Europe. Women MEPs and Equality Policy* (Cambridge: Cambridge University Press).

van den Brekel, J. C. (1983) 'Population Policy in the Council of Europe Region: Policy Responses to Low Fertility Conditions', in *Proceedings of the European Population Conference 1982* (Strasbourg: Council of Europe) pp. 389–417.

Vienneau, David (1991) 'Most Want Preschoolers at Home, Tory Poll Finds', *Toronto Star*, 6 June.

Vlassoff, Carol (1987) *Fertility and the Labour Force in Canada: Critical Issues*, Studies in Social Policies (Ottawa: Institute for Research on Public Policy).

Vogel, Lise (1987) *The Pregnancy Discrimination Act and the Debate over Special Treatment*. Paper presented at the Annual Meeting of the Americal Sociological Association, Chicago, 17–21 August.

Vogel-Polsky, Eliane (1988) *Positive Action and the Constitutional and Legislative Hindrances to Its Implementation in the Member States of the Council of Europe. Summary of the Study* (Strasbourg: Council of Europe).

Vogel-Polsky, Eliane (1989) *Positive Action and the Constitutional and Legislative Hindrances to Its Implementation in the Member States of the Council of Europe* (Strasbourg: Council of Europe).

Walsh, Alison and Ruth Lister (1985) *Mother's Life-Line. A Survey of How Women Use and Value Child Benefit* (London: Child Poverty Action Group).

Walsh, Diana Chapman and Susan E. Kelleher (1987) 'The "Corporate Perspective" on the Health of Women at Work', in Ann H. Stromberg, Laurie Larwood and Barbara A. Gutek (eds), *Women at Work. An Annual Review* (London: Sage Publications) pp. 117–42.

Wasserstrom, Richard (1977) 'Racism, Sexism and Preferential Treatment: an Approach to the Topics', *University of California Los Angeles Law Review*, vol. 24.

Watson, Sophie (1990) 'The State of Play: An Introduction', in Sophie Watson (ed.) *Playing the State. Australian Feminist Interventions* (Sydney: Allen & Unwin) pp. 3–20.

Watts, Rob (1987) 'Family Allowances in Canada and Australia 1940–1945. A Comparative Critical Case Study', *Journal of Social Policy*, vol. 16, part I (January) pp. 19–48.

White, Julie (1980) *Women and Unions* (Ottawa: The Canadian Advisory Council on the Status of Women).

White, Julie (1990) *Mail and Female: Women and the Canadian Union of Postal Workers* (Toronto: Thompson Educational Publishing).

White, Robert (1989) 'Changing Needs of Work and Family: A Union Response', *Canadian Business Review*, vol. 16, no. 3 (Autumn) pp. 15–17.

Whiteford, Peter (1986) *Issues in Assistance for Families — Horizontal and Vertical Equity Considerations*, Background/Discussion Paper no. 5 (Woden ACT: Social Security Review).

Whitworth, Sandra (1990) *Gender, International Relations and the Case of the ILO*. Paper presented at the Annual Meetings of the Canadian Political Science Association, Victoria, British Columbia, May.

Williams, Louise (1988) 'Toxic Exposure in the Workplace: Balancing Job Opportunity with Reproductive Health', in Ellen Boneparth and Emily Stoper (eds), *Women, Power and Policy. Toward the Year 2000*, 2nd edn (New York: Pergamon Press) pp. 113–30.

Wilson, Elizabeth with Angela Weir (1986) *Hidden Agendas. Theory, Politics, and Experience in the Women's Movement* (London: Tavistock Publications).

Winsor, Hugh (1990) 'McDougall Wins Battle to Increase Immigration', *Globe and Mail*, 24 October.

Wolcott, Irene (1987) *Workers with Family Responsibilities: Implications for Employers*, Discussion Paper no. 14 (Melbourne: Australian Institute of Family Studies – Commonwealth of Australia).

Wolgast, Elizabeth (1980) *Equality and the Rights of Women* (Ithaca: Cornell University Press).

Women 2000, no. 3 (1987). Published by the UN Branch for the Advancement of Women to promote the goals of the Nairobi Forward-looking Strategies for the Advancement of Women (Vienna: Branch for the Advancement of Women, Centre for Social Development and Humanitarian Affairs, Vienna International Centre).

World Health Organization (1983) *Women and Occupational Risks*. Report on a WHO meeting, Budapest, 16–18 February, 1982, Euroreports and Studies 76 (Copenhagen: WHO, Regional Office for Europe).

World Health Organization (1985a) *Women, Health and Development*, a report by the Director-General, WHO Offset Publication no. 90 (Geneva: WHO).

World Health Organization (1985b) *Having a Baby in Europe*. Report on a study, Public Health in Europe, 26 (Copenhagen: WHO, Regional Office for Europe).

Wulf, Deidre (1982) 'Low Fertility in Europe: A Report from the 1981 IUSSP Meeting', *International Family Planning Perspectives*, vol. 8, no. 2 (June) pp. 63–9.

Wulff, Maryann (1987) 'Full-time, Part-time, or Not Right Now?', *Family Matters*, no. 19 (October) pp. 14–17.

York, Geoffrey (1992) 'Ottawa Scraps Baby Bonus System. Restructured Program Drops Universality, Targets Low-Income Families', *Globe and Mail*, 26 February.

Young, Christabel (1988) 'Towards a Population Policy: Myths and Misconceptions Concerning the Demographic Effects of Immigration', *The Australian Quarterly*, vol. 60, no. 2 (Winter) pp. 220–230.

Young, Christabel (1989a) 'Population Policies in Developed Countries: How Do Australia's Policies Compare?' *Journal of the Australian Population Association*, vol. 6, no. 1, pp. 38–56.

Young, Christabel (1989b) 'Australia's Population. A Long-term View', *Current Affairs Bulletin* (May) pp. 4–11.

Young, Christabel (1990a) *Balancing Families and Work. A Demographic Study of Women's Labour Force Participation*, Women's Research and Employment Initiatives Program, Department of Employment, Education and Training (Canberra: Commonwealth of Australia).

Young, Christabel (1990b) *Australia's Ageing Population – Policy Options* (Canberra: The Bureau of Immigration Research, Australian Government Publishing Service, Commonwealth of Australia).

Zerbisias, Antonia (1991) 'Birth Rate a Bust Despite Quebec Baby Bonus', *Toronto Star*, 10 November.

Author Index

Subject Index

abortion 1, 6, 27, 57, 82–3, 94, 95,
  107, 128, 129, 130, 305, 317n
accidents *see* industrial accidents
Accord of prices and income in
  Australia 19, 246
Action Program for Women Workers
  in Australia 40–1, 207
adoption leave benefits 207, 208,
  212, 213, 215–8
advancement of the status of
  women 52, 58, 76, 77, 78, 81,
  83, 84, 208, 306
  see also advocacy, equality of
    women, feminism,
    international instruments,
    women's policy machinery,
    women's groups
advisory non-governmental
  machinery on women's issues
  78, 80, 87–8, 106–8, 114, 306
  see also bureaucracy, feminist;
    policy-making and
    implementation, consultation
    on; women's policy
    machinery
advocacy 4, 20, 55, 91
  in Australia 20, 94–5, 102, 103,
    157, 162, 165, 240–4, 251–2,
    274, 306–7
  in Canada 17, 20, 82, 91, 151,
    165, 219, 222, 231–9, 306–7,
    316n
  in Great Britain 14, 80, 110,
    111, 114, 254–7, 282–3, 307,
    318–19n
  on childcare and pre-school
    education 105, 222,
    231–44, 251–2, 254–7, 259
  on immigration 150–1, 157, 162,
    165
  see also advancement of the status
    of women; equality,
    promotion of; women's
    policy machinery

affirmative action *see* positive action
Affirmative Action Agency
  (Australia) 36
age structure 126, 143–4, 149–50,
  158, 159, 166, 310
  see also population ageing
aged, the *see* the elderly, population
  ageing
ageing *see* population ageing
agriculture, women in 69
Alberta 264, 320n
America *see* North America, United
  States
Anderson, Doris 88
androgyny 1, 25, 44, 294, 313
  see also gender neutrality
Anglo-American democracies
  13–14, 309–10
Anglophones in Canada 16, 17,
  162, 271, 322n, 323n
antenatal and birthing care 60, 61,
  81, 138, 186–7, 190, 191–3,
  205, 313
  see also health, reproductive and
    foetal; maternity leaves and
    benefits; pregnancy
anti-discrimination legislation 8, 14,
  18, 33–8, 41, 51, 55, 59–60, 99,
  104, 105, 111–13, 136, 169,
  171, 172, 181–2, 185, 254, 293,
  300, 305
  see also discrimination;
    non-discrimination; Sex
    Discrimination Act; United
    Nations, CEDAW
anti-feminism 25, 45, 90, 94, 107,
  109, 110, 294
anti-immigration groups 162, 165
anti-natalism 122, 123, 124, 140,
  141, 224, 297
Article 119, Treaty of Rome *see*
  European Community
assimilation *see* equality
Australia 1, 2, 4, 6, 7, 8, 9, 11, 12,

human rights *see* rights, human
Human Rights Commission
(Australia) 104
see also Canadian Human Rights
Commission
humanitarianism 154, 164, 174,
Hungary 128, 129, 171
Hurford, Chris 154–5
husbands 7, 135, 231, 281, 303
see also fathers, sharing of domestic work and parental roles

ILO Conventions and
Recommendations 52–5, 61,
63, 68, 139, 172–3, 175, 177,
190, 300
see also international instruments,
International Labour
Organisation
ILO Convention 156 concerning
"Equal Opportunities for
Workers with Family
Responsibilities" 54–5, 139,
175, 300
illegitimacy 27, 124
immigrant women *see* migrant
women
immigrants, classes of 146, 151,
230–2
immigration
and foreign domestic workers
143, 170, 221, 223, 230–2,
297–8
as a substitute for higher birth
rates and pronatalism 12,
125, 126, 143– 66, 310
immigration levels and intake 11,
144, 147–8, 150–62, 165
immigration planning and
management 146–58, 162,
163–4, 230–1, 297–8, 311
immigration policies and measures
2, 11, 12, 21, 85, 95, 117, 122,
125, 143–66, 310–11, 308, 309,
310–11, 318n
incentives, pronatalist 128–31, 141,
142, 160, 225, 261, 270–1, 290,
309, 313, 322n

income equivalence between
childless individuals and
parents 261, 268–9, 277, 279,
286, 291–2
see also parents, tax liabilities of
parents with dependent
children, increase in
income splitting 136–7
income support programmes 9, 13,
17, 19, 57, 142, 309
during pregnancy/maternity/
parental leave 9, 53, 190–3,
203, 209–20
for parents with dependent
children 2, 9, 82, 95,
128–30, 132–5, 261–92,
270–72, 295, 309, 322n
pronatalist 128–30, 270–72
see also child benefit, child
endowment, family
allowances, guaranteed
income, social security,
tax/cash transfer system
income testing *see* means-testing
indexation of social security
benefits 264, 265, 274, 275,
277, 278, 284, 285, 291
individualism 6, 26, 27, 34–5, 48,
54, 182
industrial accidents and injuries 43,
176, 300
see also occupational health and
safety, reproductive hazards
industrial tribunals
in Australia 18, 53–4, 202–3, 273
in Great Britain 35, 110, 112, 136
inequality, social 31, 32, 240,
273–4, 297–8, 308
infants and toddlers *see* children,
very young
infertility 123, 178,
see also childlessness
integration of women into national
and international policy
making *see* women's policy
machinery
integration of cash transfers and
personal income tax system
see tax/cash transfer system

trade unions – *continued*
  see also Australian Council of
    Trade Unions, Canadian
    Labour Congress, collective
    bargaining and agreements,
    Trade Union Congress (Great
    Britain); wages, bargaining
    for
training *see* education
Treaty of Rome *see* European
  Community
tribunals *see* industrial tribunals
tripartism 19–20, 101, 176
Trudeau, Pierre E. 263
Turkey 62

unemployment 40, 171, 319–20n
  in Australia 19, 154, 244
  in Canada 147, 263, 268
  in Great Britain 40, 136, 201
  and maternal salary 138
  and parental leave 199, 201–2,
    209–220
  of women 57, 136, 180
Unemployment Insurance (UI)
    (Canada) 209–20, 222, 272,
    319–20n
unions *see* trade unions
United Nations (UN) 5, 51, 52,
    55–60, 61, 64, 73, 76–7, 100,
    104, 116, 158, 170
  Branch for the Advancement of
    Women 78
  Commission on the Status of
    Women 55, 78
  Convention on the Elimination of
    All Forms of Discrimination
    Against Women (CEDAW)
    55, 59–60
  Copenhagen World Conference for
    Women 57, 78, 306
  Decade for Women 55, 57–8, 60,
    61, 76, 78, 92, 107, 172,
    306, 307, 311
  International Year of the Child
    56, 61, 311
  International Year of the Family
    311

International Women's Year
    (IWY) 55–7, 62, 76, 84, 90,
    96, 107, 172, 243–4, 305–6,
    311
  Mexico City World Conference for
    Women 57, 234
  Nairobi Forward-looking
    Strategies for the
    Advancement of Women
    55, 57–60, 78, 105, 306
  Nairobi World Conference for
    Women 57, 61
  Unified Long-term Programme for
    the Advancement of
    Women 78
  Universal Declaration of Human
    Rights 315n
  World Plan of Action 57, 234,
    306
United Kingdom *see* Great Britain
United States 1, 9, 13–14, 17, 38,
    42, 49–50, 53, 63, 94, 95, 110,
    112, 126, 131–2, 158, 159, 163,
    170–1, 175, 177, 178–80, 182,
    184, 185, 190–1, 216, 240, 253,
    279, 286, 294, 317n, 322n
Universal Income Security Program
    (UISP) (Canada) 321–2n
universality in social programmes
    13, 19, 262–7, 272–8, 280–5,
    290, 291, 309, 321n
  see also childcare as a universal
    service and a right
unmarried women 27, 136
urban areas 310
  and children 129–30, 158, 272
  and immigration 149, 159, 161–2
user fees for childcare and social
    services 226–230, 232–3, 239,
    241, 246, 248, 253, 259, 321n

Victoria (Australia) 203
violence
  domestic/family 85, 91, 101,
    102, 105
  against women 4, 20, 57, 89,
    102, 115, 117, 294, 307
  see also wife battering